LANGUAGE AND LANGUAGE LEARNING

The Edinburgh Course in Applied Linguistics

Volume 2

LANGUAGE AND LANGUAGE LEARNING

General Editors: RONALD MACKIN *and* PETER STREVENS

Henry Sweet *The Practical Study of Languages*

J. R. Firth *The Tongues of Men and Speech*

Randolph Quirk and A. H. Smith *The Teaching of English*

Neile Osman *Modern English*

H. E. Palmer *The Principles of Language-Study*

N. E. Enkvist, J. Spencer and M. Gregory *Linguistics and Style*

H. E. Palmer *Curso Internacional de Inglés*

J. C. Catford *A Linguistic Theory of Translation*

David Abercrombie *Studies on Phonetics and Linguistics*

Five Inaugural Lectures edited by Peter Strevens

Axel Wijk *Rules of Pronunciation for the English Language*

L. A. Hill *Selected Articles on the Teaching of English as a Foreign Language*

H. H. Stern *Foreign Languages in Primary Education*

Peter Ladefoged *Three Areas of Experimental Phonetics*

A. S. Hayes *Language Laboratory Facilities*

H. E. Palmer *The Scientific Study and Teaching of Languages*

Language Testing Symposium edited by Alan Davies

H. E. Palmer and Sir Vere Redman *This Language-Learning Business*

An Annotated Bibliography of Modern Language Teaching: Books and Articles 1945–1967 Compiled by Janet Robinson

Languages and the Young School Child edited by H. H. Stern

Prosodic Analysis edited by F. R. Palmer

Edward M. Stack *The Language Laboratory and Modern Language Teaching* Third Edition

The Prague School of Linguistics and Language Teaching edited by V. Fried

The Indispensable Foundation: a selection from the writings of Henry Sweet edited by E. J. A. Henderson

J. B. Pride *The Social Meaning of Language*

W. H. Mittins et al. *Attitudes to English Usage*

Chomsky: Selected Readings edited by J. P. B. Allen and P. van Buren

Active Methods and Modern Aids in the Teaching of Foreign Languages: Papers from the 10th FIPLV Congress edited by R. Filipovic

Peter MacCarthy *Talking of Speaking: Papers in Applied Phonetics*

Randolph Quirk *The English Language and Images of Matter*

The Edinburgh Course in Applied Linguistics. Vols. 1–3 edited by J. P. B. Allen and S. Pit Corder. *Vol. 4* edited by J. P. B. Allen and Alan Davies

The Edinburgh Course in Applied Linguistics

Edited by J. P. B. ALLEN *and* S. PIT CORDER

VOLUME TWO

Papers in Applied Linguistics

LONDON

OXFORD UNIVERSITY PRESS

Oxford University Press, Ely House, London W.1
LONDON OXFORD GLASGOW NEW YORK
TORONTO MELBOURNE WELLINGTON CAPE TOWN
IBADAN NAIROBI DAR ES SALAAM LUSAKA ADDIS ABABA
KUALA LUMPUR SINGAPORE JAKARTA HONG KONG TOKYO
DELHI BOMBAY CALCUTTA MADRAS KARACHI

Library Edition ISBN 0 19 437123 9

Paperbound Edition ISBN 0 19 437058 5

First published 1975
Second impression 1976

Printed in Great Britain at
The Pitman Press, Bath, England

Contents

Editors' Preface

Our aim in applied linguistics is to make use of the knowledge and insights gained from scientific investigations into the nature of language, in the hope that we may solve some of the problems which arise in the planning and implementation of language teaching programmes. There are two ways in which the relationship between linguistics and language teaching can be approached. One approach is from the end of language teaching, that is, the practical end, when we identify and analyse the problems that arise in teaching and then see what sort of linguistic knowledge is relevant for their solution. This is the approach which has been adopted in Volume 3. The other way is to start from the theoretical end, giving an account of the goals, scope and findings of the various enquiries into the nature of language, in order to identify what aspects of the knowledge yielded by them may, in the light of a practical experience of language teaching, be relevant to the solution of problems in that field. This is the approach which we have taken in the present volume.

The plan of this book is the following: Chapter 1 consists of a short general conspectus of applied linguistics in language teaching. In this respect it aims to combine both approaches mentioned above and to provide a general picture of all those activities and procedures which go to make up applied linguistics. In this sense it forms an introduction to both Volumes 2 and 3. Chapters 2–5 give an account of the main concepts in what is now often called theoretical linguistics to differentiate it from the sociological and psychological approaches to language. These latter approaches and their relevance to language teaching are discussed in the last three chapters of the book.

Although the papers in this volume give an outline of the main theoretical approaches to language, they are necessarily introductory and selective and in no sense claim to give a comprehensive and detailed account of the present state of linguistic theory. It is assumed that the reader is already familiar with the general aims and methods of linguistic research or is concurrently studying linguistics. For this reason the bibliographical sections include not only references to articles and papers concerned with specific points raised in the texts but also suggestions for further reading.

In a field as rapidly developing and changing as that of linguistic enquiry at the present time, the body of established and generally accepted knowledge is not easy to determine. The points of view adopted in the papers in this volume are necessarily those of the authors but in every case their contributions have been submitted to a detailed and searching criticism by colleagues in order that alternative views shall not have been neglected and differing evaluations of the relevance of linguistics to language teaching shall not have been overlooked. In all cases the views presented and evaluations put forward have been based on several years of teaching these topics and of discussing them with the experienced language teachers who form the main body of students following courses in applied linguistics in the Department in Edinburgh. In this sense the contributors to this volume owe a considerable debt not only to their immediate colleagues but also to several generations of students who have helped to develop and clarify their understanding of the relevance of linguistic studies to language teaching.

We wish to acknowledge the generous help given by David Abercrombie, Keith Brown, Tony Howatt, Sandy Hutcheson, Roger Lass, John Laver, John Lyons and Jim Miller, who have kindly read parts of the book and offered their comments and criticisms. While various improvements suggested by these colleagues have been incorporated into the book, they are, of course, in no way responsible for the opinions expressed or for the many imperfections which no doubt remain.

Finally, we must express our thanks to Ethel Bacon, Anne MacDonald and Anna Rossi, who have borne without complaint a heavy burden of typing. We are also grateful to Mary Bratt for her invaluable help in checking reference material, and performing with great efficiency a variety of editorial tasks.

Department of Linguistics, Edinburgh
July 1974

J. P. B. Allen
S. Pit Corder

1 S. PIT CORDER
Applied Linguistics and Language Teaching

Practical tasks such as language teaching—or baking—can be performed either by following a very detailed and precise set of instructions about how to proceed, or by applying some set of general principles to the particular situation. When someone sets about carrying out some unfamiliar task for the first time, for instance baking a rich fruit cake, he would have no alternative but to follow the instructions in the recipe meticulously and in every detail. Even then the cake might not turn out a success because the beginner might be working under conditions which were not exactly those presupposed in the instructions. In such a case he would not have the experience or knowledge of the relevant general principles to allow him to adjust or vary his approach appropriately.

Good language teachers do not work by rule of thumb or recipe. They possess, like good cooks, a set of principles which guide their work, in other words, some general notions about what is going on when people learn languages, an informal 'theory' about how languages are taught and learned. I call it an informal theory because, while experienced teachers certainly do possess such general principles, they may not be able, or may not have tried, to formulate them explicitly and clearly in words. This is understandable since most teachers see their task to be that of teaching rather than 'theorizing'.

But it is only when principles are explicitly formulated that one can evaluate them or test them in order to see whether they might, in parts, be mutually contradictory and whether they are sufficiently comprehensive and detailed to provide a basis for solving the many different kinds of problems that arise in the course of the teacher's professional work.

To say all this is to say no more than that language teaching is an art rather than a scientific process and proceeds to some extent by trial and error. Nevertheless to have some general principles is clearly better than having none, and to formulate these principles is more useful than leaving them implicit because then at least one can set about examining them systematically in order to evaluate them. When people talk about language teaching they tend to think of it as something which goes on in a classroom, where the teacher meets face to face with his pupils. Teachers know, however, that this is only part of their job, the end-point of a time-consuming and exacting activity much of which takes place outside the classroom: planning lessons, correcting, assessing progress, discussing with colleagues, selecting and perhaps producing textbooks and teaching materials. All these activities involve making decisions. But there are other decisions which are not necessarily, or indeed ever, made by classroom teachers, concerned with the organization of the educational system in general, the relative place of language teaching in the curriculum, the nature of the syllabus and examining systems, all of which influence and to some extent determine what goes on in the classroom. We must, I think, consider all of these activities as part of the total 'language teaching operation'. If teaching is to be described as creating the conditions in which learning is facilitated then all the decisions which bear on that objective are part of the process of planning the total language teaching operation.

In making many of these decisions a wider set of principles will be appealed to than the teacher as a specialist in his own field will possess. Some of these decisions are of a political, economic or social nature and imply a different training and experience in the persons who take them. They will be taken at different levels in the educational system. Wherever they are taken we expect that the appropriate knowledge is available for making the correct decision. For instance, decisions about what languages are to be taught in the school system are political and social, about how much money is to be made available for language teaching, political and economic. Decisions about how to present and practise in the classroom certain aspects of the language chosen are, however, pedagogic and methodological. In the planning and implementation of the total language teaching operation many different branches of knowledge and expertise are called into play. Some of these have to do with educational policy, educational economics or educational sociology, and some with general pedagogy, but some decisions depend upon a knowledge of the nature of language, how it is learned and its function in society; in other words, upon knowledge derived from the scientific study of language in all its aspects. Just which aspects of the knowledge derived from these studies are relevant to making decisions in language teaching is the subject of the other chapters in this volume, and a detailed study of how this knowledge is used in making these decisions is the subject of the papers in the third volume in this series.

Applied linguistics is concerned with the identification and analysis of a certain class of problems which arise in the setting up and carrying out of language teaching programmes, and with the provision of the answers or part of the answers to them. It does not claim, of course, to be able to provide all the answers to all the questions. Nor obviously can it claim to provide the final answer to any of the problems with which it deals. Some of the decisions, as we have seen, will be based on principles which do not derive from the knowledge gained by the scientific study of language; those, for example, which are based on political, economic or educational policy and those which are matters of general pedagogy and teaching methodology. And even to those whose solution does depend upon an understanding of the nature of human language we can only give partial answers because of our still inadequate knowledge in this field. I have used interchangeably up till now the terms 'question' and 'problem' and 'decision' and 'answer' in discussing the planning of a language teaching programme. I have said that applied linguists are engaged in solving certain classes of problems or answering certain sorts of questions that arise in the course of such planning. When I use the term 'problem' in this way I do not refer only to specially difficult or intractable questions, but to any questions that may arise in the course of planning. Nor do I wish to suggest that the applied linguist is some sort of outside expert or consultant who is called in when some particularly knotty problem turns up. All I mean is that there is an area of decision making in the planning and execution of a language teaching programme in which the application of linguistic principles and knowledge is relevant, namely that in which the questions have linguistic answers. Anyone who deals with these problems in the light of linguistic knowledge is applying linguistics.

A great many courses and programmes are constructed without any conscious attempt on the part of the designers to apply the knowledge provided by the linguistic sciences to what are basically linguistic problems. When language courses and programmes are constructed without a conscious attempt to apply such knowledge it means that decisions on linguistic matters have been taken without an explicit consideration of the nature of the problems. If we wish to get the right answer to a problem then we must apply to it the appropriate theoretical analysis. Identifying and analysing problems is thus part of the application of theory to a practical task. Getting the right answers to a question means having the right language to ask the questions in the first place. This is why the application of linguistic knowledge is necessary right from the start of the planning process and not just when particular difficulties arise.

It is a common experience for a person who possesses special knowledge in some field to be asked to give his advice on some practical problem to which this knowledge is thought to be relevant. The difficulty he often faces in this situation is that he cannot always understand the nature of the problem as explained by the person seeking advice because the latter cannot analyse and describe it in the specialist's terms. To describe adequately the structure of language, how it is learned and how it functions in society, involves inventing new terms or redefining old ones. This is not just a case of using an alternative jargon but rather of having a more developed conceptual framework and a more differentiated and precise set of terms for talking about the problem.

I have suggested that there is a specific set of questions which arise in planning a total language teaching programme to which linguistic theories might help to provide answers. Some of these questions have to do with the problem of the content of the teaching programme. If an educated layman without any special training were required to teach, say, French, the problem of the content of the course would be the first he would have to face and he might express it in the form of the question: *What am I to teach?* A non-technical answer would be: 'a knowledge of French'. But this would not be of much help to him. In fact the educated layman does possess, as a result of his general education, some notions of how 'a knowledge of a language' can be analysed. He will be aware of the levels of analysis of grammar, vocabulary and pronunciation. And within the level of grammar he will have available such descriptive categories as 'parts of speech' and of such syntactic relations as subject and object, though at the other levels his descriptive powers may be more limited. An analysis of what to teach in these terms derives from theoretical or structural linguistics. But it is not the only possible analysis of 'a knowledge of a language'. Another analysis would be in terms of such activities as speaking, reading or writing French, and still another in terms of the communicative uses to which the language could be put: discussing the weather, asking the way or going shopping. There are as many ways of answering the question: *What am I to teach?* as there are to the question: *What is language?* Although we can describe what is to be taught in linguistic, behavioural or functional terms, we are still talking about the same thing, a knowledge of French. All we are doing is adopting a different theoretical framework for talking about it.

The problems facing an untrained teacher are, however, not solved when we have listed for him the content of a syllabus, in any of these terms. A syllabus is more than a list of items, it is a plan for teaching. The material selected must be organized in a systematic fashion. This is no longer a problem of what to teach but part of the problem of when and how to teach. Finally, the material selected and organized into a syllabus must be presented in such a way that any particular group of learners can best learn from it. This is now clearly a problem of how to teach. Any teaching operation is faced with these three basic problems, whatever the subject. The techniques of applied linguistics have to do with the *selection* of language data and their *organization* and *presentation* in the form of teaching materials.

These techniques are not independent of each other. Possessing a solution to one problem is a necessary condition for solving another. We cannot, for example, set about organizing the teaching material until we have decided what to teach, nor can we prepare the material for presentation to the learner until we have decided how it shall be organized in the syllabus. These fundamental problems and the techniques connected with their solution are logically related; to the extent that the solution of them is dependent upon the application of linguistic knowledge, then these applications are logically related. Applied linguistics is a set of related activities or techniques mediating between the various theoretical accounts of human language on the one hand and the practical activities of language teaching on the other. The relation between linguistic theory and classroom activities is thus an indirect one. It is made up of a number of processes or procedures, each one necessary for the solution of one of the component parts of the problems of what, when and how to teach—selection, organization and presentation. It is because of the indirectness of the relation between the insights that theoretical studies of language yield and the practical preoccupations of the classroom that many teachers have failed to see the relevance of linguistic studies to language teaching.

Language teaching is not, of course, the only practical activity in the planning and implementation of which linguistic knowledge has a part to play. Other practical tasks such as data retrieval, mechanical translation and interpreting also make appeal to linguistic knowledge. The diagnosis and treatment of speech defects and of certain psychiatric disorders also call upon such knowledge. There are applications in literary studies and in the design of communication systems. Indeed, people are slowly coming to realize that wherever language plays a central part in some practical every day task there is a potential application of linguistic knowledge. It will be clear, therefore, that on the one hand applied linguistics in its broadest sense is concerned with many activities apart from language teaching, and that on the other, as has been made plain, language teaching involves the application of knowledge derived from many theoretical studies apart from linguistics.

The starting point of every application of linguistics to any of the practical tasks is a description of the language or languages involved in the task. The possession of an adequate description of natural languages is a prerequisite for the most efficient carrying out of these tasks and is common to all uses of linguistic knowledge in practical affairs. In the case of language teaching it is true to say that we cannot teach systematically what we cannot describe. This is not, of course, to say that people do not learn what is not specifically taught. Our ability at the present time to describe a language from any of the various theoretical points of view is still severely limited and yet learners do succeed to a large extent in learning languages.

All linguistic studies have as their object the investigation of the nature of human language. But human language manifests itself in a myriad of differing forms and serves a multiplicity of different functions. The linguist must make descriptions of different languages in order to test the validity of his theories, to see if his theoretical predictions about human language are borne out in fact. Describing languages is part of the methodology of constructing theories about language. But to test his theories it is not necessary for the linguist to produce descriptions which aim at comprehensiveness. It is usually sufficient to make an intensive and detailed description of some restricted aspect of the language. For this reason in recent years we find linguists concentrating, in the area of syntax for example, on such features as negation, pronominalization, adverbs or the passive in English, or on the functions of language in some restricted context or situation. It is by pressing theory to its limits in description that the adequacy of the theory is assessed. Descriptions which aim at comprehensiveness cannot readily at the same time pay detailed attention to every aspect of the language. We find consequently that the great comprehensive and scholarly grammars of languages have been compiled with prescriptive or didactic purposes in mind, that is, they have the aim of teaching, informing, correcting or otherwise helping the student or the layman to learn the language, correct his own speech or simply provide him with information about his language in a form which is easily accessible to him.

Descriptions of languages or parts of languages may be made, therefore, for reasons both internal and external to linguistics. The making of a description involves the use of the categories and relations recognized by the theory in the analysis of the data of the language being described. The theory is said to be applied to the data. The making of descriptions is in this sense an application of linguistic theory, but it is not necessarily part of applied linguistics in the sense outlined in the previous pages. If the description is being made for reasons internal to linguistics then it is not an application of linguistics; if, on the other hand, it is being made for purposes external to linguistics as I have suggested is often the case with descriptions which aim at comprehensiveness, then the making of such descriptions can be regarded as an application of linguistics. This point will be taken up later in the discussion of pedagogic grammars.

The making of a description, then, involves the application of theory to data. An adequate theory is one which can provide a complete and logically coherent analysis of any data to which it is applied. But descriptions are of languages, dialects or varieties of a language. This means that the data to be analysed must be in the form of samples drawn from that language, dialect or variety, and this in turn means that we must have some criterion for deciding whether a particular bit of data does or does not belong to a particular language, dialect or variety. It is perhaps not commonly realized that purely structural linguistic criteria will not serve to make such distinctions. The criteria for distinguishing between languages, dialects and varieties are sociological and psychological and involve such notions as 'speech community', 'attitude to language', 'language loyalty' and 'linguistic norm'. These are matters which concern the sociologist and the psychologist. We can see therefore that when it is a question of making a description of what is called a language or a dialect, criteria other than purely structural linguistic ones are involved.

It is a characteristic of applied linguistics that the practical problems with which it attempts to deal can rarely if ever be solved by reference to one theoretical approach to language alone.

The acquisition of adequate descriptions of the languages, dialects and varieties of language involved in the practical activity with which the applied linguist is concerned is his first task. From the language teaching point of view the result is as comprehensive and detailed an account of the structural properties—phonological, semantic and syntactic—of the language involved in the teaching situation as current linguistic theories permit. This means at least descriptions of the mother tongue of the learner, the target language and perhaps any other languages that the learner already possesses. The learner may be bilingual, or he may be learning another closely related form of the same language, say its written code, or if he is a speaker of a non-standard dialect, he may be learning the standard dialect.

The descriptions which result from this activity are the raw material for the next process in applied linguistics. This is one in which use is made of linguistic descriptions to solve some problem in the planning of a practical task. In the case of language teaching these procedures are all concerned with establishing the *content* of the teaching syllabus, with the techniques for selecting out of the most comprehensive descriptions of the target language those items which are to be taught. These procedures are all comparative. The reasons for this are clear. Selection involves weighing up one thing against another. To do this they have to be seen together, their similarities and differences have to be discovered and analysed and their relative importance evaluated in relation to the needs and objectives of the teaching task.

Comparing language descriptions is, and for long has been, part of linguistics. Linguists may be interested in the properties of particular languages for their own sake, but they are also centrally interested in the nature of human language as such. Languages are very various in their structural properties, and by comparing them the linguist seeks to classify them, discover what is common to all languages and finally delimit the boundaries of human language. He is also interested in discovering the genetic relations between languages and how one and the same language changes over time; all these aims involve comparative procedures.

However, under the name of *contrastive linguistic studies*, the comparison of pairs of languages has a different and practical objective, that of showing up in what respect two languages differ from, or resemble each other. The practical problem which such studies seek to solve is essentially: *What is it we have to teach the speaker of language A who is learning language B?* The result of such comparison aims at yielding insights which are relevant to the compilation of a syllabus for a particular language teaching programme. Comparing two different languages with this aim may be called inter-linguistic comparison.

The learning of a second language is different from acquiring a mother tongue, since the learner already possesses language as a means of communication; he knows what communicative functions language performs, at least in his own community, and may to some degree be aware of the variability of language in different situations of language use. This knowledge can have a facilitating effect in the learning of a second language, since it is plausible to assume that language in different communities fulfils a similar though not necessarily identical range of functions. While differences in the function of language in different cultures may present a learning task, it is certain that differences between the structural properties of the mother tongue and that of the target language do so, just as where similarities exist learning may be facilitated. Contrastive linguistic studies have as their object the revealing of these structural differences and similarities. To the extent that they are successful in doing so they provide us with information which is of value in determining where the main emphases in teaching should fall, in explaining difficulties when they arise and suggesting ways in which some of the material may be presented, described and practised in the classroom.

A closely related descriptive and comparative technique in applied linguistics is *error analysis*. In the course of learning a second language the learner produces many forms which are not those which would be produced by a native speaker of the standard form of the target language. For a certain period in his learning career many of the incorrect forms will be sufficiently well-established for us to regard the learner as speaking a language of his own, similar in many respects to the target language but nevertheless describable as a distinct form of that language. This language of his will demonstrate certain idiosyncratic characteristics some of which may resemble his mother tongue or some other language which he already knows. A comparison of the learner's form of the target language at any particular point in his learning career with the target language yields information about what part of the target language as prescribed in the syllabus he has already learned, and what still remains for him to learn. This comparison provides part of the answer to the question: *What does the learner know or not know of the target language*? In this respect error analysis is an activity in applied linguistics similar to the use of language tests, chiefly of the diagnostic type. As in the case of contrastive comparisons, it will yield insights into the learner's problems which will suggest ways of presenting and practising the language in the classroom.

Error analysis is also part of the methodology of psycholinguistic research into the learning of second languages. It is a first and necessary step towards explaining why learners make errors. Ultimately it may yield information about the best sequence which learners of one particular mother tongue should follow in the learning of some particular second language. Information of this sort would be of the greatest value in the task of organizing the material in a syllabus for particular language teaching programmes and for making decisions about the best manner to present the material of that language.

Error analysis as an application of linguistics is relevant not only to the study of second language learning. As a technique it also has a place in the study of language disorders where it offers answers to the question: *What does A still know of his mother tongue?* Used for this purpose it provides information which, when analysed appropriately, can yield differential diagnoses of the disorders and suggest appropriate treatments. In the study of child language acquisition a description of the child's non-adult forms—although these are not normally called 'errors' of course—offers an answer to the question: *What does the child know so far of the adult target language?* And in literary stylistic studies, a description of the poet's deviant grammatical forms provides an answer to the question: *What is the relation between the idiosyncratic language of the poet and the standard language?* In all these cases, the aphasic, the infant and the poet are regarded as speaking an 'idiosyncratic dialect' which bears some sort of regular relation to the standard adult language. Thus, although these techniques are not normally called 'error analysis' they are fundamentally the same process of comparing two 'languages'.

Language is used in many different social situations, for many different purposes and is expressed in different media—writing, speech or some combination of these, such as dictation or reading aloud. When we teach a language we are preparing the learner to behave appropriately and purposefully in a variety of social situations. In the case of some learners the range of situations may be very restricted, but for others it will be wide. The content of the syllabus must reflect the needs and intentions of the learners as far as these can be established. To prepare an appropriate syllabus and suitable teaching materials for him we need some account of the nature of the language used in the situation and for the purposes for which he is being prepared. Where the aims of the learner are not known or diffuse, as may be the case in most situations where languages are taught in school, we must attempt to establish what are the basic elements of a knowledge of the language which anyone must possess in order to use it for any purpose. This central body of knowledge is sometimes known as 'the common core'.

The discovery of the nature of this central body of knowledge does not involve making comparisons between the target language and any other language but is a process of making a selection from within the target language itself. As a selection procedure it is a question of weighing up the relative importance of one form against another. In this sense it is an *intra-linguistic* comparison. A speaker or writer of what is regarded as one and the same language makes a differential use of the repertoire he possesses in different social situations and for different communication purposes. Language demonstrates in this sense great formal variability in use. One of the tasks of the sociological approach to language is to discover the dimensions of this variability and to relate the use of certain forms of the language to certain social characteristics of the situation of language use. It is upon the information derived from this descriptive work that decisions about the selection of material for the syllabus must be made. It may be that there are certain linguistic forms which occur uniquely in certain situations of language use, for example in scientific, legal or religious discourse, or—and this is the case with the great majority of forms—it may be that they occur more or less frequently according to the social nature of the interaction. The problem of selection is then one of determining the relative utility to the particular group of learners of particular linguistic forms in the light of the situation in which they will use the language and the communicative purposes they will have for the language.

Although I have classified comparative studies into three sorts: inter-linguistic, intra-linguistic and error analysis, it must not be thought that there is any fundamental difference between them. Broadly speaking, inter-linguistic comparisons and error analysis are concerned with differences of kind, whilst intra-linguistic differences are matters of degree, but when we remember that, linguistically speaking, distinctions drawn between varieties of a language, or between dialects, and even between languages themselves are ultimately arbitrary, the essential unity of comparative studies becomes apparent.

I have spoken so far about the processes of linguistic description and comparison as if they were clearly distinct or distinguishable activities. In fact, of course, they may well in many cases be a combined operation. In describing a language one sets up whatever categories appear necessary to account for the data. It cannot be assumed that the same set of categories will prove adequate for the description of another set of language data. The making of comparisons, on the other hand, presupposes the existence of descriptive categories which are equally applicable to two sets of language data. In the making of comparisons, therefore, a common set of descriptive categories must be established, and this may and usually does involve re-describing both languages in terms of a new set of common categories. Comparison, therefore, usually involves redescription. Similarly, from the applied point of view, I have spoken about selection, organization and presentation as if they were distinct and separate techniques. But as I have also suggested the activities of contrastive comparison and error analysis yield information and insights relevant both to the selection of material for the syllabus, its organization into a structure and its presentation in teaching materials. There is thus no neat one-to-one relationship between description and comparison on the one hand, and the processes of selection, organization and presentation on the other. It remains true, however, that in a general sense description identifies the range of what is there for learning, while comparison serves to select out of that range what has to be learned in the case of any particular set of learners. Both processes—description and comparison—call into use theoretical and sociolinguistic approaches to language, consequently the answer to the problems of what has to be taught can be couched both in terms of a set of linguistic items drawn from the vocabulary, grammar and phonological features of the language, as well as in terms of a set of sociolinguistic items, i.e., speech acts and communicative functions.

The problem of organizing the material to be taught, however it is described and classified, introduces psycholinguistic and pedagogic considerations. Indeed the task of organizing the syllabus material into some sort of a structure appears to owe little to theoretical linguistic knowledge. Whatever logic there may be in the grouping, sequencing or staging of a teaching syllabus does not derive exclusively or to any great extent from structural linguistic theory. For example, there are no theoretical linguistic reasons why one tense should be taught before another, nor why the singular/plural contrast should be introduced before the definite/indefinite contrast or why *this/that* should be taught first as pronouns and later in their adjectival function. The fact that some tense forms are morphologically simpler than others and might for that reason be taught earlier is a psycholinguistic reason not a theoretical linguistic one. The fact that a knowledge of the various forms of the verb *to be* is necessary for the forming of the progressive aspect forms of the verb in English does not logically require that *to be* must be introduced first in its function as a copula. Decisions of this sort are based on pedagogic or psychological principles. Linguistic descriptions tell us what forms are related to each other, e.g., simple to complex sentences, finite to non-finite clauses. It does not follow from this that the 'simpler' sentence, linguistically speaking, must be presented before the more complex. Simplicity and complexity, difficulty and ease of learning are psychological or psycholinguistic problems, related perhaps, but not in any simple way, to theoretical linguistic descriptions.

Ease or difficulty of learning is itself only one of a number of criteria in the organization of a syllabus. Criteria of usefulness to the learner may also play a role, and such criteria would be based on sociolinguistic considerations of the functions of language in communication. So may some general classification of the material into areas of socialization: the home, the school, the work place. The analysis of language behaviour into different types of verbal activity such as speaking, writing, reading and listening also provides a rough psycholinguistic categorization relevant to the structuring of the syllabus. There is at the moment no compelling reason to prefer one kind of classification to another, nor any evidence that one provides some sort of superior logic to another. But that some sort of classification and structuring of the material in the syllabus is necessary on pedagogic grounds is clear. Good learning depends on the material being taught having some internal structure or set of associative links; that is, on its being coherent and meaningful to the learner. The different types of associative links within the material are numerous, psychological, sociological and linguistic. In practice all these principles of classification are used in syllabus organization; which one is dominant in any particular language teaching operation depends very largely on the nature and needs of the learner.

Whatever criteria or set of criteria one adopts, and it is likely to be a mixed set, the detailed syllabus will eventually be expressed in terms of an ordered list of formal linguistic entities: sounds, intonation and rhythmical patterns, lexical words, grammatical items, structural rules, sentence patterns and so on. It is most important not to fall into the error of assuming that because a syllabus is expressed in terms of an ordered list of linguistic items the principles of syllabus structuring must derive from theoretical linguistics.

If one goes back into the history of language teaching no more than half a century, one finds that the form of the descriptions of the language being taught was not significantly different from that used in the works of linguistic scholarship or for the enlightenment of an educated general public. Where differences existed, they were matters of degree, such as the amount of detail, e.g. listing of exceptions to rules or the range of coverage or comprehensiveness, rather than of kind. Thus we might find beside 'A Grammar of Latin' a 'Shorter Grammar of Latin' by the same author intended for students of Latin rather than classical scholars. In more recent years, however, both the form and the content of the descriptions of a language intended for language learners has become increasingly distinct from the descriptions used by linguists for linguistic research and exemplification. That this divergence should have taken place is a result of the increasing realization that the materials of teaching should be adapted to the needs, abilities and strategies of learning of the pupil. The descriptions of the target language intended for teaching purposes are often called pedagogic grammars. The term 'grammar' is here used, of course, in its traditional sense of the 'description of a language' including statements about its phonology and semantics as well as its syntax and morphology. A similar development has taken place in lexicology. We now have monolingual dictionaries specially written for language learners.

This change has taken place because notions about how languages are learned have changed. Whereas forty years ago each learner of French had in his hands a textbook entitled, for example, 'A Grammar of French', few students will now possess such a work. This is because it is no longer so widely accepted that the only, or indeed the best, way in all cases to help a learner internalize the rules of a language is to make statements about them. We have moved from a predominantly deductive view of language learning to a more inductive one. What then is a 'pedagogic grammar' in present day language teaching? No one doubts that the learner must internalize the rules of the target language and discover the rules for its appropriate use; the argument is about how he does this and consequently about the best way of presenting the 'facts of the language'. The problem of writing pedagogic grammars is that of finding the most efficient way of presenting the facts of language to the learner.

If we rarely nowadays put a book entitled 'A Grammar of French' into the hands of the learner, where does he find out about the language? In the most extreme case, as in someone learning a language by living among the people who speak it, he learns it by induction from the 'unorganized' data of everyday speech. The most important difference between learning a language in this way and learning it in the classroom is that in the classroom the data has been controlled and structured in some way to facilitate the process of discovery, and that practice in the use of the language is directed to one or at most a limited number of features of the language at any moment. This data is most usually accompanied by descriptions and explanations of the systems and use of the language. At the other extreme we find the so-called grammar-translation method in which teaching consists of the enunciation of the rules of the language and their exemplification, followed by practice in applying them. This is the most deductive approach. In between these two extremes there is a range of intermediate methods in which stress falls more heavily on exemplification and practice on the one hand, or on description and explanation on the other. Any attempt to draw a line at some point within this range and say that everything on one side makes use of pedagogic grammar and everything on the other side does not is bound to be an arbitrary procedure. For this reason some people prefer to restrict the use of the term to those statements about, and exemplifications of, the language which are for the use of teachers rather than learners, the object of which is then to guide the teacher in the way he is to present the language material to his pupils.

The classroom teacher has a domain of decision making which is peculiarly his own because of his training and his particular knowledge of the characteristics of his pupils—this is the area of classroom methodology. It will have become clear, however, that no hard and fast line can be drawn between the techniques of producing teaching materials and the techniques of classroom practice. This is because the same set of psycholinguistic principles guides both activities; a particular form of presentation implies a particular classroom methodology and, vice versa, a particular set of classroom procedures requires teaching materials of a particular sort. Until recent times most teaching materials were produced by practising classroom teachers. It is only recently that some degree of specialization has occurred and that the production of teaching materials has been a matter for cooperative work by teams of writers.

We can see then that textbooks, language laboratory tapes, programmed instructional materials, reading texts, work books and visual materials are all individually or collectively devices for the presentation of the material selected for the syllabus. They are all realizations, in concrete form, of the particular grammatical pedagogy adopted for the course. They will differ from each other, either because they are intended for different sorts of learners, varying in age, intelligence, maturity or motivation or because they have been based upon different psycholinguistic interpretations of the process of language learning, or to put it another way, because they derive from different pedagogic grammars.

In order to achieve reliable and consistent results in any practical task, whether baking or language teaching, it is not sufficient simply that one's decisions should be based upon the best available knowledge; one has also to be able to check that this knowledge has been properly applied, that the decisions made were the right ones, that the knowledge appealed to was in fact relevant and appropriate to the task in hand. We need therefore a means of checking our results. In the case of cooking 'the proof of the pudding is in the eating' quite literally; in the case of language teaching the validation of the techniques of applied linguistics lies in the classroom, measured by the learner's progress in learning and ultimately in his ability to make purposeful use of his knowledge. These are measured by language tests. Traditionally these have taken the form of examinations. However, the latter have not always proved to be entirely reliable instruments for measurement, nor was it always clear that what was measured was exclusively the learner's knowledge of the language. We need instruments which will be not only reliable in their measurement but also specific in what they measure.

Measuring individuals in a number of psychological dimensions, such as intelligence, personality, motivation and perception is the field of psychometry, a branch of applied psychology. If linguistic knowledge and skills are something we wish to measure then the making of tests presupposes a description of the structure and use of the language being learned. If a test is to be used to evaluate the adequacy of syllabuses, pedagogic grammars and teaching materials, then it presupposes their existence. Thus, language testing is an integral part of applied linguistics and the making of tests is logically the last in a series of applied linguistic procedures, since the object is to evaluate all or any one of these previous activities.

Language testing is, of course, used for other purposes than the evaluation of the techniques of applied linguistics. Tests may be used for prediction. We may wish to measure the aptitude of a learner for learning a language or for continuing further study of a language. Tests may be used for assessing the present knowledge of a learner without reference to the course or courses, if any, he may have followed. These are tests of proficiency in language. Tests may attempt to discover the problems a learner is facing in learning a language. Such tests are diagnostic. Whatever function the test may be designed for, the construction of tests is an applied linguistic procedure, inasmuch as it draws upon knowledge of the structure of language, how it is learned and its functions in society.

The remaining contributions to this volume take as their starting point a particular approach to the study of language—its structural properties, its function in society or as an aspect of human behaviour or development. They outline these approaches, their scope, aims and methods in order to show what insights into language they yield which have relevance to language teaching. In this chapter the approach has been in a sense the reverse. I have started out with an informal account of the sort of questions which must be answered in the planning and implementation of a language teaching programme, identified those to which an understanding of the nature of human language may contribute to a solution, particularly the problems of what to teach and how to teach, and then discussed in general terms the various procedures/techniques whereby this understanding is used to provide a solution. The relevance of linguistics to what goes on in the classroom is seen as indirect. There are a number of broadly-defined procedures—description, selection, organization, presentation and assessment—which go to make up the field of applied linguistics; these and the relationship between them provide a framework for discussing applied linguistics in language teaching as a coherent activity. The thesis presented here is that the relationship between the various fields of linguistic enquiry and the procedures of applied linguistics is a complex one. For example, the process of selection makes appeal to knowledge derived from several different approaches to language. The relative importance of one approach may nevertheless be greater in one case then another; for example, the particular relevance of psycholinguistic studies is felt in the problem of presentation.

Human language is such a complex phenomenon that scientific enquiries into it have necessarily had to restrict their approaches to one aspect of the problem at a time. There is no one comprehensive theory about human language. Knowledge of a language cannot be adequately explained simply in terms of the possession of a set of grammatical and phonological rules or simply as a matter of knowing the appropriate use of a set of utterances or indeed as the ability to speak, read and write. It is all these things and more. Applied linguistics is an integrative activity; the insights acquired from the different approaches to the study of language have to be drawn together, reconciled and used to make the acquisition of a knowledge of a language a more efficient, useful and pleasant task.

2 J. P. B. ALLEN
Some Basic Concepts in Linguistics

1 The scientific study of language

Although linguists can trace the origins of their subject back to the fourth or fifth centuries B.C., it is only in comparatively recent years that linguistics has begun to be studied and taught on a really wide scale. Because linguistics is a comparative newcomer to the academic scene, there is a tendency to regard it as a difficult and esoteric subject. Most people think they have a clear idea of what the more traditional subjects of the school or University curriculum are about. At social gatherings one does not often hear the question 'What is chemistry?' or 'What is engineering?' A linguist who goes to a party, however, is quite likely to be called upon to expound the basic principles of linguistics several times during the course of an evening. How, then, might a linguist attempt to state, in a few words, the basic characteristics of his subject? He might begin by saying that a linguist is not necessarily someone who is a fluent speaker of foreign languages. Undoubtedly, it is an advantage if a linguist has a practical mastery of one or more languages apart from his own, but this is not essential to his main business, which is the study of language in general. In linguistics, we do not give priority to the language of any particular society; we study the languages of any or all human societies. We study how each language is constructed, how it is used by its speakers, and how it is related to other languages. In addition, we study how it varies from dialect to dialect, and how it changes from one historical period to the next.

Linguistics may be defined as the scientific study of language. This apparently straightforward definition conceals a wide divergence of views about what is meant by 'scientific'. A number of papers representing various views about the nature of scientific knowledge and methods, and the ultimate goals of linguistics, can be found in Volume 1, section 6. For our present purposes let us say simply that a 'scientific' study is one which is based on the systematic investigation of data, conducted with reference to some general theory of language structure. The linguist studies data in order to discover the nature of the underlying language system, but he is not likely to make sense of the data unless he has some prior concept of the way in which language is structured. On the other hand, any theory of language structure that the linguist may formulate must be checked against the data to make sure that the theory is consistent with the observed facts of language use. If we study the history of linguistics we notice periodic shifts of emphasis in the type of question that linguists attempt to answer. Sometimes interest appears to be focused on the organization of data and the methodological problems involved in describing it, while at other times the pendulum swings in the opposite direction and it becomes fashionable to seek an explanation of how speakers are able to handle data and achieve meaningful communication. In the working methods of all linguists, however, theory formation and the study of data have always proceeded side by side. We may say that in linguistics, as in other areas of science, data and theory 'stand in a dialectical complementation' and that neither can be profitably studied without the other.

All types of linguistic analysis are based on the assumption that language is structured; i.e., each utterance, far from being a random series of words, is put together according to some principle, or set of principles, which determines the words that occur and the form and order of the words. In his analysis a linguist is guided by the three major canons of exhaustiveness (adequate treatment of all the revelant material); consistency (the absence of contradiction between different parts of the total statement); and economy, whereby, other things being equal, a shorter statement or analysis employing fewer terms is to be preferred to one that is longer or more involved. Exhaustiveness and economy are interdependent, in that there is no point in setting up a description which is economical but which does not cover all the data. On the other hand, an exhaustive description may not be aesthetically pleasing because of the inevitable exceptions. As a result of applying these criteria, the linguist expects to achieve the greatest possible degree of objectivity in his descriptions. The aim is to present an analysis in such a way that every part of it can be tested and verified, not only by the author himself, but by anyone else who chooses to refer to it or to make a description of his own based on the same principles. It is partly the insistence on objectivity which gives linguistics the status of a science, and leads us to expect that modern linguistic studies will provide particularly accurate information about language structure.

It is generally useful to distinguish between a broader and a narrower aspect of linguistic study; the terms 'macrolinguistics' and 'microlinguistics' have been used to describe these two aspects. Macrolinguistics refers to the whole study of language, including such widely diverse fields as psycholinguistics, sociolinguistics, historical linguistics, speech pathology, lexicography, computational linguistics and communication theory. Microlinguistics refers to what may be called the 'central core' of language study, the areas of phonology, grammar and semantics. Phonology is the study of the sound patterns of language; grammar is concerned with the form of the words and the manner of their combination in phrases, clauses and sentences; while semantics is concerned with the meaning, or content, of the words and of the larger units into which they combine. In the next three chapters we will confine ourselves in the main to a 'micro' interpretation of linguistics. Our concern will be with phonology, grammar and semantics, and their relation to problems of language teaching. First of all, however, it may be useful to look more generally at language in comparison with other aspects of behaviour, and then to examine some concepts which are fundamental to the scientific study of language.

2 Some characteristics of human language

I have defined linguistics as the scientific study of language. It would be more accurate to say that linguists are concerned with the study of human language. This does not mean that other living beings do not have forms of language in which they can communicate with members of their own species. Bees and dolphins, for example, are two species which are known to have quite elaborate forms of communication. However, none of the systems of animal communication which have been studied so far possess anything like the flexibility and complexity of human language. What is it, then, that makes human language unique? In an attempt to answer this question, the American linguist C. F. Hockett has proposed a set of 'design features' which all human language displays. Some of these features are found in the communication systems of other animals, and also in certain human systems (e.g., instrumental music and gesture) which do not constitute language in the usual sense of the word. Human language, however, is the only form of communication in which all the design features are combined. Let us take a brief look at some of the more important characteristics of human language, so that we can understand the nature of the phenomenon with which the linguist has to deal.

If we were to observe the everyday life of a human community with a view to determining the general characteristics of language, we would quickly come to a number of important conclusions. We would realize, for example, that among human beings the typical way of transmitting messages is via the speaker's mouth and the listener's ear; in other words, language utilizes the *vocal-auditory channel*, unlike gestures, the dancing of bees or the courtship ritual of the stickleback. We would also notice that language differs from the ritual of the stickleback with respect to the feature of *interchangeability*: a speaker of a language can reproduce any linguistic message he can understand, whereas the characteristic courtship motions of the male and female stickleback are different, and neither can act out the motions appropriate to the other.

Continuing our observations, we might conclude that a linguistic message brings about a particular result because there are relatively fixed associations between words and recurrent features of situations in the world around us. For example, when we say 'Pass the salt' we generally get what we want because the English word 'salt' means salt, not sugar or pepper. Hockett gives the name *semanticity* to this feature of language. Furthermore, we would realize that in language the ties between meaningful elements and their meanings are *arbitrary* and a matter of convention. There is nothing inherently 'dog-like' about the word *dog;* the same animal is called *Hund* in German, *chien* in French, *perro* in Spanish, and so on. Apart from a few 'imitative' words which occur in every language (neigh, bleat, crash, etc) there is no connection between the physical form of a word and what it signifies. A child learning his first language or an adult a foreign language might feel that the feature of arbitrariness is a disadvantage. Since most words in the vocabulary are not 'natural', or onomatopoeic, in origin, an effort has to be made to learn each one. But because of the arbitrary nature of the link between message elements and their meanings there is no limit to the number of words in a language, and therefore no limit to what can be talked about.

One of the most important features of language is *productivity*, the capacity of man to say things that have never been said or heard before, and yet to be understood by other speakers. As far as we know only man has the means to coin new utterances by selecting familiar words and phrases, and assembling them into new combinations according to rules which are known to all the speakers of a language. In this respect the 'open' system of human language differs fundamentally from the gibbon call system, which is 'closed', in that each vocal sound is one of a small finite repertoire of fixed, unitary calls. *Displacement*, another of Hockett's terms, refers to the ability of man to talk about things that are remote in time and space. This feature occurs in bee-dancing but seems to be lacking in the vocal signalling of man's closest living relatives, the gibbons and great apes. It is the faculty of displaced speech that enables man to recount events that happened in the past, to talk about future plans and to create the imaginative events of myth and fiction. Displaced speech too has made possible the development of science, since it enables man to accumulate records of his experiences, and to work out problems at leisure without being distracted by the needs of a particular set of circumstances.

In our role as observers of human society, we could not help noticing the importance of *cultural transmission* in the life of a community. Human genes transmit the capacity to acquire language, but the detailed conventions of a particular language—the vocabulary and grammatical rules—are transmitted by teaching and learning. Children are not born with the ability to speak, say, French or English; they have to acquire this ability in the first few years of life, first by hearing and imitating what adults say and later by inferring the processes by which the basic elements of language are built into complete utterances. It is not known to what extent teaching and learning, rather than genetic inheritance, plays a part in gibbon calls or other mammalian systems of vocal signals.

Another important feature of language is *discreteness*. There is virtually no limit to the variety of sound which can be produced by the human vocal organs, but in any one language only a relatively small number of sound-ranges are used, and the difference between these ranges is absolute. For example, the sounds *t* and *d* in the English words *seating* and *seeding* are distinguished from one another only with respect to one phonological feature, that of voicing or voicelessness. Both sounds are alveolar stops, but *t* is a member of the class of voiceless stops, while *d* is a member of the class of voiced stops. No speaker will pronounce *seating* and *seeding* exactly alike on all occasions, and it is usual to find considerable variation between speakers in the way these words are pronounced. It is quite likely, for example, that a speaker might produce syllables that deviated from the normal pronunciation of *seating* in the direction of that of *seeding*, or vice versa, and that on some occasions his pronunciation of *seating* is indistinguishable from that of *seeding*. However, in every case he will be understood as saying either *seating* or *seeding;* the principle of discreteness operating in the sound system of English rules out the possibility of a third word containing an alveolar stop with a pronunciation mid-way between *seating* and *seeding*.

Linguists studying human speech have established a number of important principles for the description of language structure. For example, it is generally acknowledged that any utterance in any language can be represented as a sequence of distinctive sounds, or phonemes. Thus, the word *give* consists of a sequence of three phonemes /g/ /ɪ/ /v/, *him* consists of three phonemes /h/ /ɪ/ /m/, *a* consists of one phoneme /ə/, and *pen* consists of three phonemes /p/ /e/ /n/. Phonemes have no descriptive meaning in themselves; they serve only to keep meaningful utterances apart, as when *Lend him a pen* is distinguished from *Lend him a pin* by the difference between the second phonemes of /pen/ and /pin/. Compare also *Send him a pen* with *Lend him a pen*, and *Lend Jim a pin* with *Lend him a pin*. Language also has a structure in terms of minimum meaningful elements, or morphemes. The utterance *He works at night* can be analysed as containing the morphemes *he*, *work*, *-s*, *at*, *night*. It is distinguished from *He worked at night* by the fact that the morpheme *-s* marking the present tense appears in the first utterance, whereas the morpheme *-ed* marking the past tense appears in the second utterance.

This feature of language, whereby morphemes are represented by varying arrangements of contrasting sounds which are in themselves meaningless, is called *duality of patterning*. It is duality of patterning that makes it possible for a language to possess thousands of morphemes and to represent them economically by different permutations of a relatively small stock of phonemes, of which there are rarely more than fifty in any one language. The flexibility of language structure is illustrated by the English words *tack*, *cat* and *act*—phonemically /tak/ /kat/ /akt/—which are quite distinct in meaning and composed of three phonemes combined in different ways. It is possible that none of the animal communication systems share this feature of language, certainly none among the other hominids. In a typical animal call system each call differs as a whole from the rest, both in total sound effect and in meaning. There must therefore be a practical limit to the number of distinct messages that can be discriminated, especially when transmission takes place under less than perfect conditions. As a result of duality of patterning, there is no such limit where human language is concerned.

3 Form and meaning

It is a basic principle of linguistics that we should make a clear distinction between a formal analysis of language, and one which is based on meaning. A formal analysis is concerned with the observable, actually occurring forms of language and the relationships between them, while a meaning-based analysis is concerned with the ways in which the forms are used as a vehicle for communication. The views of linguists have differed with respect to the necessity or otherwise of a formal basis for language study. Thus, if we take for granted universal concepts such as 'subject', 'predicate', 'dative', 'locative', we might feel justified in categorizing the forms of different languages in terms of these concepts, without having to define their meaning afresh each time we embarked on the analysis of a language. On the other hand, we might feel that it is more appropriate to an objective scientific study if we approach each language with a minimum of preconceptions and attempt to explain its regularities only on the basis of observable evidence. The two approaches result in two different types of descriptive framework, neither of which we can afford to neglect, since each has contributed significantly to our understanding of language.

Linguists who adopt a strictly formal approach to the analysis of language aim to establish a set of units which are describable 'in physical terms of form, correlations of these forms, and arrangements of order' (Fries 1952). This type of analysis is based on the fact that every linguistic unit below the level of sentence has a characteristic distribution; that is, it is restricted to a greater or lesser degree with respect to the environments in which it can occur. Two or more units occurring in the same range of contexts are said to be distributionally equivalent; if they never occur in the same context they are in complementary distribution. There are certain intermediate cases where the distribution of one unit may include the distribution of another without being totally equivalent to it, or where the distribution of two units overlap but without either of the two occurring in all the contexts where the other occurs, but these need not concern us here. The important point is that in the majority of cases the distribution of units is sufficiently clear-cut to enable the principal grammatical categories to be established without difficulty. It should be noted that distributional equivalence implies grammatical identity only insofar as the contexts are specified by the grammatical regularities of the language. For example, *ate* and *bought* are regarded as distributionally equivalent because they both occur in the context *John—a cake*, and on these grounds we are able to identify them as members of the same class of lexical items (those usually called 'verbs'). Since co-occurrence is established between classes not items, the classification remains valid even though there are some contexts where *bought* occurs and *ate* does not, for example we have *John bought a car* but not *John ate a car*. The classification of *ate* and *bought* is not affected since the non-occurrence of the second sentence can only be explained in terms of the meaning of the particular words in the sentence, which many structural linguists would regard as being outside the scope of a systematic grammatical statement.

A language has a highly complex structure, and it is impossible for the linguist to describe it all at once. The usual procedure is to divide up the subject-matter into a number of different but interrelated aspects, and to attend to these one at a time. By this means linguists have come to recognize various levels of analysis in the study of language, three of the most commonly discussed levels being those of phonology, syntax and semantics. In addition to various levels the analysis of which may involve different kinds of criteria, we distinguish different ranks at any one level where the same criteria are used to establish units of greater or lesser extent. The sentence is traditionally regarded as the longest structural unit of which a full grammatical analysis is possible, since it is only within a sentence that the interrelation of the elements are completely describable in terms of grammatical rules. It is convenient, therefore, to assume that the domain of grammar is circumscribed by the upper limit of the sentence and the lower limit of the morpheme or minimal grammatical unit. Between these two limits units are abstracted at various ranks and given such names as clause, phrase and word. This arrangement of contrasting categories at successive ranks, the categories at any one rank being included in a category at the next higher rank, is known as a taxonomic hierarchy—a method of classification used in many of the natural sciences. Thus, we may say that sentences consist of one or more clauses, clauses consist of one or more phrases, phrases consist of one or more words, and words consist of one or more morphemes.

Linguistic elements enter into two main types of relation with one another, syntagmatic and paradigmatic. A linguistic element enters into syntagmatic relations with other elements at the same rank with which it forms a serial structure related to linear stretches of writing or the temporal flow of speech. At the same time it enters into paradigmatic relations with other elements which may appear in a given context and which are mutually exclusive in that context. Syntagmatic relations are relations of co-occurrence; paradigmatic relations are relations of substitutability. The first are 'overt' relations, realized in the word order of sentences. By contrast, paradigmatic relations are not revealed directly by the observation of any particular sentence, but by comparing a number of similar sentences and ascertaining which elements substitute for one another in a given grammatical context. An illustration should serve to make the distinction clear. In the following diagram the elements in each column are in a paradigmatic relationship to one another. An example of a syntagmatic relationship is that which holds between each of the elements *John*, *met* and *the vicar* in the sentence *John met the vicar*, or which links the vowel-sound /e/ with the /m/ that precedes it and the /t/ that follows it in /met/:

1	2	3
John	met	the vicar
My brother	invited	Mary
He	liked	the Wilsons
Everyone	criticized	our new secretary

Figure 1

The linguist's identification of levels, ranks and form classes is widely exploited in language teaching material. Perhaps the most common type of pedagogic presentation is one in which each 'pattern' or grammatical sequence is considered as a row of vacant pigeon-holes into which the grammatical units are sorted in their correct order. Suitable labels may then be given to the contents of each pigeon-hole, e.g. 'determiner', 'numeral', 'adjective', 'noun attribute', 'noun head'. In many textbooks the arrangement of data is governed by a desire to facilitate a process of substitution. According to H. E. Palmer, an 'ideal' substitution table is one in which all the elements are mutually intercombinable, as in Figure 1. In other types of table students must use their own semantic judgement in deciding which elements may be combined. A comparatively simple substitution table can yield a very large number of sentences, all of which belong to a single sentence-type. For example, it is not difficult to construct a table with five columns and five items in each column which will yield thousands of perfectly acceptable sentences (Palmer 1916). It is often said that substitution tables encourage an over-mechanical activity with insufficient scope for the creative intelligence of the student. If there is a fault, however, it would seem to lie not in the concept of substitution tables but in the way such tables are commonly used. There is nothing facile or 'meaningless' in the procedure recommended by Palmer, whereby each sentence produced by the substitution table should be 'examined, recited, translated, retranslated, acted, thought and concretized'.

Turning again to Figure 1 we see that the elements in column 1 are not interchangeable with those in column 2. Nor are the elements in column 2 interchangeable with those in column 3. However, the elements in columns 1 and 3 are interchangeable. Thus we do not normally find *Met John the vicar* or *My brother Mary invited* but we do find *The vicar met John*, *Mary invited everyone*, etc. The fact that nothing in the first column can be substituted for anything in the second column and vice versa shows that the grammatical functions of the elements in the first two columns are quite distinct, and this enables us to set up the two form classes which are traditionally labelled 'nouns' and 'verbs', but which Fries, in the interests of objectivity, prefers to call Class I words and Class II words respectively. The fact that all the elements in the third column can substitute in the first column and vice versa enables us to identify all the elements in columns 1 and 3 as members of the same form class. Consequently all the sentences in Figure 1 are examples of a sentence-type in which form classes are arranged in the order Class I + Class II + Class I. This pattern is often referred to as a Subject + Verb + Object, or S + V + O sentence type.

We know that *John loves Mary* does not mean the same thing as *Mary loves John*. This suggests that the elements in column 1 have a different function from the elements in column 3, even though both columns are made up of members of the same form class. The nouns in column 1 function as subjects, while those in column 3 function as objects and have a different relationship with the verb. The notions 'subject of', 'predicate of', 'object of', etc. differ from class names such as 'noun' or 'verb' in that the former are essentially relational (e.g., subject and object are differentiated according to the way in which they relate to the verb, while 'predicate' is traditionally defined as that part of the sentence which 'says something' about the subject). Relational terms such as 'subject' and 'object' must be handled with care since these expressions can mean different things to different people. For example, in traditional logic the term 'subject' refers to a component of a proposition distinguished according to the part it plays in certain rules of inference. Many linguists, on the other hand, define 'subject' as the noun, or equivalent word or word group, found in the minimal sentence-type represented by *John works* ('predicate' may then be used to describe the rest of the sentence after the subject has been defined). Others prefer to say that the subject is that part of a sentence which refers to an actor, one who does something, and the object is the part referring to the goal, that which undergoes the action. In many teaching grammars a number of different criteria are used for establishing the identity of subject, predicate and object in different types of sentences. A flexible approach of this type often gives quite good results in the classroom but to avoid confusion it is important that teachers should realize the difference between the various types of definition, and know exactly what criteria are being used at any particular time.

During the past twenty-five years it is the formal aspect of the form-meaning dichotomy that has tended to be dominant in second language teaching. Language teachers have seen it as their main task to give their students a knowledge of the formal, structural patterns of the language being taught. As a result, a typical modern textbook contains plenty of practice in the composition of sentences, but gives little systematic attention to the ways in which the sentences are used for purposes of communication. The assumption is that once the grammatical system has been learned the student will know how to put the system to use in producing sentences of his own, without the need for any further instruction. Even when attempts are made to make the lesson material more meaningful to students, as when the introduction of new structures is associated with explanatory actions and pictures, the highest priority is still given to grammatical criteria, and the artificially-created 'situations' bear little resemblance to natural language use.

The so-called audiolingual method of language teaching depends heavily on the use of intensive oral drills, or 'pattern practice', designed to give maximum opportunity for practising the structures being taught. Such drills are associated with a high degree of control by the teacher. In a typical syllabus the grammatical patterns are presented one by one, and care is taken to allow the learner plenty of time to absorb each new pattern before he goes on to the next. The aim of this type of teaching is the establishment of automatic speech habits. The exercises are repeated until the student can produce the correct grammatical forms promptly, accurately and with minimum conscious thought. There is no doubt that some aspects of language, especially those involving automatic patterns of concord or 'agreement', can be taught very effectively by means of intensive oral drills. Critics of the audiolingual method, however, have pointed out that students tend to become bored by the incessant repetition of formal patterns, especially if no meaningful purpose is apparent in the exercises. Many drills are designed in such a way that the student is able to produce strings of sounds quite mechanically without a thought for the meaning of what is being said. Whatever the intention of such drills may be, their effect is to encourage students to practise the forms of the language, and to neglect the meanings which ought to be associated with the forms.

As an alternative to the pattern-based, habit-formation method, a number of writers have recently proposed a notional or semantic approach to language teaching in which the traditional structural syllabus would be replaced by one based on meaning rather than form. Instead of bringing together sets of grammatically identical sentences, the writer of a notional syllabus would attempt to teach language appropriate to the kind of situation in which the learner is likely to want to use the foreign language. Learning units would have functional rather than grammatical labels; the resulting materials would be functionally unified but grammatically heterogeneous, reflecting how things are in real life where situations do not contain grammatically uniform language. The proposal that text-book writers should pay attention to the context in which language is used is of course not new. Generations of tourists visiting foreign countries have equipped themselves with handbooks in which 'useful phrases' are collected under headings referring to physical situations—'at the bank', 'at the station', 'at the theatre'—or to types of functional communication—'ordering a meal', 'buying a suit', 'asking the way'. In order to develop a genuine creative use of language, however, the learner must not confine himself to learning forms solely for their value in a single situation. He needs to study not complete situations but the component parts of situations, not complete sentences but the underlying speech acts—denial, disagreement, affirmation, approval—by means of which we give expression to our views, and attempt to influence the behaviour of others. The aim of the learner should be, not to learn a series of 'model conversations' off by heart, but to acquire a set of variable strategies which he can employ for himself as the need arises.

4 Speech and writing

Another general principle of linguistic analysis is the primacy of speech over writing. Some linguists go so far as to say that speech is language, and that writing is simply a reflection of speech in a different medium. Others prefer a less extreme point of view, but most linguists are agreed that speech is the primary medium in that it is older and more widespread than writing, and children always learn to speak before they learn to write. More important for linguistic analysis is the fact that all systems of writing can be shown to be based upon units of the spoken language, rather than the reverse. On the other hand, it must be acknowledged that in a literate society the written and the spoken language may show a substantial divergence in both vocabulary and grammar. At the moment considerable interest is being shown in the analysis of written forms of English, especially in the important area of written scientific English. As improved methods of analysis are found for handling the description of written varieties of language we may expect some modification of the principle that the spoken language always has priority in linguistic studies. It is not likely that the principle will be abandoned entirely, however, since it is only exceptionally that a written language becomes completely independent of the spoken language from which it originally derived.

In the field of foreign language teaching there has been a tendency to advocate the primacy of speech over writing as a general educational goal. Generally speaking, it is sound practice, particularly in the early stages of learning a language, to give first priority to the development of automatic speech habits. The aim of oral drill is to develop the student's capacity for immediate and spontaneous assimilation of complete speech units. Students must be prevented from developing what Palmer (1921) calls the 'isolating habit'; he must be made to 'think the whole sentence integrally' instead of piecing it together bit by bit while he is saying it. However, a number of the arguments that have been advanced in support of teaching the oral skills first appear to be based on questionable assumptions. Typical arguments in favour of speech before writing are: it reflects the way children learn their native language; writing is only an imperfect representation of speech, and involves extra problems of orthography; the transfer in learning from the spoken to the written form is greater than the reverse. On closer examination it appears that all these arguments are open to question. Because speaking before writing is the natural order in first language learning, it is not necessarily the only, or the most advantageous, order in second language learning. The spelling system of English, which is often characterized as highly arbitrary and confusing, in fact contains a variety of useful morphological information which is not present in the acoustic signal. Finally, there has never been any convincing demonstration that students transfer more easily from speech to writing than the other way round. In fact, most adult students find it easier to understand and retain what is orally presented if they are able to refer to written notes. As far as we can tell, this does not prevent them from achieving oral fluency so long as they do not become overdependent on the written symbol.

The view that the spoken language has priority and that writing is a secondary reflection of speech, to be practised only when the speech patterns have been well established, is particularly prejudicial to the teaching of writing in a foreign language. The principle of speech before writing may be justified at the beginning of a syllabus, when the aim is to establish a basic vocabulary and the essential sentence patterns as quickly as possible, but as soon as students have progressed beyond the elementary stage it becomes obvious that writing is a skill in its own right which owes little to the inculcation of patterns of speech behaviour. It is virtually impossible by means of oral drill alone to elicit the complex patterns which are a commonplace in writing and which have to be mastered if a student wishes to write effectively. If we want to teach advanced students how to write in a foreign language we must find some way of promoting composition as an end in itself and not simply as an adjunct to speech.

Linguists who have made a close study of current speech habits are in a position to refute some of the popular misconceptions about language use. There is an idea, for example, that 'educated speech' is clearer and more precise than that heard in the community at large. People who pride themselves on their careful speech habits are often considerably dismayed when it is pointed out to them that in all forms of English, naturally spoken, there is a strong tendency towards the reduction and obscuring of unaccented words. Linguists have identified about 50 monosyllabic words in English which have two or more phonemically different pronunciations according to whether they occur in stressed or unstressed positions in discourse (see Gimson 1962). Compared with the accented realizations of these words, the unaccented ('weak') forms show reduction of vowels towards /ə, ɪ, ʊ/, and the elision of vowels and consonants:

	Unaccented	*Accented*
a	/ə/	/eɪ/
and	/ənd, nd, ən, n/	/and/
can	/kən, kn/	/kan/
does	/dəz, z, s/	/dʌz/
has	/həz, əz, z, s/	/haz/
of	/əv, v, /	/ov/
will	/l/	/wɪl/
would	/wəd, əd, d/	/wʊd/

It is not always appreciated by native speakers that the above words are accented only in special positions or when said in isolation, and that the normal pronunciation in each case is the 'weak' form. In the field of English as a second language, it is particularly important for teachers to be aware of how the language is really spoken. If students are unacquainted with the weak forms and fail to practise them in appropriate contexts, they will almost certainly come to speak English with a stilted and unnatural accent, and they will be unable to understand English as it is normally spoken.

Since modern linguists have devoted a great deal of time to the study of speech, most of the grammars produced in recent years have been influenced by the spoken language. On the other hand, many of the teaching materials in use today derive from descriptions which were based on the written language. On occasions a description of speech rather than writing leads to a simplification of the grammar which may have implications for language teaching. For example, a traditional statement of French adjective gender runs somewhat as follows. Feminine adjectives are formed from the masculine by the addition of an *-e*: *laid* → *laide*. Masculine adjectives which already end in *-e* do not change: *rouge* → *rouge*. In addition, some adjectives double the final consonant before adding the *-e*: *bas* → *basse*. Others undergo certain consonant changes (*frais* → *fraîche*), insert a further vowel before the *-e* (*long* → *longue*) or place an accent on the preceding vowel (*léger* → *légère*). The above statement is based on the written forms. If we examine the sounds which actually occur in speech, we get a different type of statement. Some adjectives do not change for the feminine, but others add a consonant with or without a change in vowel quality, e.g.: /lɛ/ → /lɛd/, /ba/ → /ba:s/, /frɛ/ → /frɛ:ʃ/, /lɔ̃/ → /lɔ̃g/, /leʒe/ → /leʒɛ:r/. In our new statement we are still following the practice of taking the masculine forms to be basic and deriving the feminine forms from them. However, we now come up against a difficulty. There is no way of predicting which consonant is to be added in a particular instance, so that the student must learn separately all those cases in which /d/ is added, all those in which /s/ is added, all those in which /ʃ/ is added, and so on. Fortunately there is an easier way of handling such forms. If we take the feminine forms as basic, instead of the masculine, we find that a single general rule will cover all the above cases and many others like them: 'The masculine is formed from the feminine by subtraction of the final consonant'. All the other differences between the two forms, for example differences in vowel quality and nasalization, reappear in other areas of French morphology and can be described in terms of the over-all phonological structure of the language (see Bloomfield 1933, p. 217).

5 Language as system

Language, according to de Saussure, is 'un système dont tous les termes sont solidaires'. This view of language as a system in which all the terms are interrelated and where the value of one depends solely upon the simultaneous presence of all the others is a basic postulate of modern linguistics. Not everyone would agree that a language is describable as a single total system, but there is no doubt that parts of a language can be described in terms of systems. It is characteristic of a language system that the functioning parts hang together and condition one another, so that each part acquires a contrastive value which it derives from its membership in the system. For example, when we use a particular tense-form in any language, we convey a meaning because that form contrasts with all the other forms in the tense system which we might have used if we had chosen to do so. The importance of the structural system from the point of view of language teaching has been strongly emphasized during the last thirty years. Thus it is important, according to Fries, that we should not teach 'habits concerning items as items', but 'habits concerning an ordered system of structural patterns' (Fries 1955). Awareness of the over-all structure of a language is important in constructing a pedagogic grammar, since it is one of the first requirements of such a grammar that it should provide a systematic frame of reference by means of which the multitude of details can be related to one another and fitted together into some sort of meaningful whole.

When we hear an unfamiliar language being spoken it is impossible to identify individual words or phrases; all we are aware of is an undifferentiated stream of meaningless sound. The first task in learning a language is to master the sound system. This involves identifying the distinctive sounds and learning to approximate their production. The fact that language is a system and not a mere collection of separate parts can be illustrated on the phonological level with reference to the pattern of English stop consonants. The sounds in the following table are distinguished from one another according to their place of articulation (bilabial, alveolar, velar) and their manner of articulation (voiceless, voiced):

	bilabial	*alveolar*	*velar*
voiceless	p	t	k
voiced	b	d	g

Each of the six sounds has a contrastive value which makes it possible to distinguish words from one another, e.g., *pin—bin*, *pen—ten*, *bed—beg*. The 'value' of /p/ as distinct from /b/ and of /b/ as distinct from /d/ derives from the membership of the sounds in a system. Each significant sound, or phoneme, has an identity which is unlike that of any other in the system; each is delimited by its neighbours and all are interdependent.

The same systematic quality can be observed in the organization of grammar. For example, the eight basic tense-forms in English can be thought of as a three-dimensional system of binary contrasts: each tense unit is either 'present' or 'past'; either 'continuous' or 'non-continuous'; and either 'perfective' or 'non-perfective' as indicated in the following diagram:

	present	past
non-continuous	—perf talk +perf have talked	—perf talked +perf had talked
continuous	—perf talking +perf have been talking	—perf was talking +perf had been talking

The prepositions in a language are also related to one another systematically. Catford (1959) shows how the English preposition system distinguishes between 'static contiguity' (*on*, *at*, *in*), 'arrival or approach' (*onto*, *to*, *into*) and 'departure or separation' (*off*, *away* or *away from*, *out of*). On another dimension, intersecting with the first, English distinguishes between 'exteriority' (*on*, *onto*, *off*), 'interiority' (*in*, *into*, *out of*) and an intermediate set of relations which are neutral with regard to exteriority or interiority (*at*, *to*, *away* or *away from*):

	static contiguity	approach	separation
exteriority	on	onto	off
neutral	at	to	(away) from
interiority	in	into	out of

French, on the other hand, lacks a formal contrast between relations of static contiguity and approach; thus, French *sur* is equivalent to English *on* and *onto*; *à* is equivalent to *at* and *to*; *dans* is equivalent to *in* and *into*. In the separation relation, English *off*, *away from*, *out of* are all translated by French *de*. In Finnish, the system of 'local' cases provides distinctions which are roughly equivalent to those expressed by the English prepositions, except that Finnish distinguishes precisely between exteriority and interiority, with no intermediate 'neutral' series corresponding to *at*, *to*, *away from* in English. Because of the non-correspondence between different systems, prepositions are notoriously difficult for a language student to master. The task is made easier, however, if the prepositions are presented not as isolated, independent items but as items in a unified contrastive system.

In the area of vocabulary the functional range of words is delimited by the co-presence of other words in the same language. Thus the range of German *essen* ('eat', used only for human beings) is limited by the existence in the language of *fressen* ('eat' used, except pejoratively, only for animals) as contrasted with the single word *eat* in English. In a series such as *baby*, *infant*, *child*, *youth*, *man* the denotational range of each term is limited by the other terms in the system; the pattern of contrasts would be different in a language which had words equivalent to *baby*, *child* and *man* but no words to express the idea of 'infant' and 'youth'. French has two words, *fleuve* and *rivière*, corresponding to the one word *river* in English. Welsh has a single word *glas* covering the functional range of the English words *blue* and *green*. In Spanish there are two verbs, *ser* and *estar*, equivalent to the English verb 'to be'. *Ser* is used with reference to permanent states (except location) or inherent qualities, and *estar* is used when speaking of temporary states or conditions, and location. Thus, a Spanish speaker will say *Esto es un libro* 'This is a book' (permanent state) and *El libro está abierto* 'The book is open' (temporary state). This creates a learning difficulty for English speakers, who are accustomed to use the one verb 'to be' in both situations.

Typically, a word is associated not with a single meaning, but with a wide range of meanings. In many cases words in different languages which are commonly regarded as equivalent (e.g. French *prendre*, German *nehmen*, English *take*) do not cover exactly the same areas of meaning, hence one of the dangers of learning lists of 'translation equivalents' out of context. In much the same way, it is the non-correspondence between different grammatical systems that underlies many of the difficulties of learning a foreign language. Again, if we want to know why a student has difficulties with pronunciation, we must look beyond the phonetic character of the sound segments as such and consider the over-all structure of the sound system of the second language, which will almost certainly differ from that of the learner's native language. In teaching it is essential to make allowances for the systematic nature of language. It we are teaching English, we must familiarize our students with those contrastive values which are set up in the system of English. As Catford points out, if we want our students to progress beyond the stage of superficial pattern practice and begin to 'think in English', we must train them to categorize directly in the terms laid down by the systems of the English language.

6 Descriptive or prescriptive?

A linguistic study is said to be descriptive if it is as objective as possible and based solely on observed facts. It is said to be prescriptive if it attempts to formulate a set of directions for behaviour. Linguists have made a special point of guarding against prescriptivism because in the study of language, as in other forms of human activity, there is a great temptation to allow aesthetic judgements to supplant the role of impartial observation. Hence the tradition of prescriptive grammar, still entrenched in many schools, according to which teachers and textbook writers are not content to describe what is said by the speakers of a language but frequently go on to make pronouncements, often on a quite arbitrary basis, about what ought to be said. Most of us can quote examples which are familiar from our schooldays. We remember being told to say 'It's I' rather than 'It's me', to avoid 'split infinitives', never to end sentences with a preposition, and always to use 'whom' for the objective form of 'who' in relative clauses. These 'rules of correct usage', first met with in school, pursue many people into adult life and make them permanently ill at ease both in speech and in writing.

It is perhaps worth remembering that many controversial details of traditional grammatical lore originated in the work of a group of eighteenth-century prescriptive grammarians who made it their aim to establish areas of accepted usage, often on no better grounds than those of personal prejudice. A typical representative of the so-called 'normative' or 'prescriptive' school of grammarians was Robert Lowth, a bishop of the Church of England, whose *Short Introduction to English Grammar* (1762) went through at least 22 editions, and was one of the most influential grammars of the eighteenth century. It was Lowth who set up the restriction for *shall* and *will* according to which *shall* is used for the first person singular and plural in 'simple future' time reference, and *will* for the second and third persons (the other way round if we wish to express commitment or obligation). This 'rule' is still taught to foreign students in spite of the fact that the distinction is obscured in spoken English by the almost universal use of the short forms *I'll*, *he'll*, *they'll*, etc., and increasingly ignored in writing.

Bishop Lowth also condemned the expressions *He is taller than me*, *I had rather* and *I don't like his doing that*, the preferred forms being *He is taller than I*, *I would rather*, *I don't like him doing that*. An echo of Lowth in our own time is found in Fowler's recommendation that *which* should be reserved for use in non-defining relative clauses, and *that* used in all clauses of the defining type, thus allowing *The book, which I bought, was disappointing* and *The book that I bought was disappointing* but not *The book which I bought was disappointing*. As a further example of prescriptivism we may cite the tendency of some British writers to be highly critical of alleged Americanisms. Thus Nesfield and Wood (1964) advise against the use of *aim to do*, *stay home*, *so* instead of *so that* to express purpose, *will* instead of *shall* for first person 'simple future', *stem from*, *human* (as a noun), *get about* and *I wouldn't know*. The authors feel obliged to admit that usage is changing and that some of the expressions may become acceptable in time, but meanwhile they recommend that they should be avoided by those who 'do not like to transgress the laws of propriety and purity of diction'. This type of judgement has been strongly criticized by linguists, who rightly point out that the proper concern of a grammarian is to report the facts of language use rather than to lay down the law in matters of vocabulary and syntax.

A linguist aims to be as objective as possible in his attitude to the data he describes. It is not for him to pass judgement on the language or to lay down norms based on personal criteria of correctness or logicality. The principle of objectivity requires that the whole of the relevant data should be studied, and that none of it should be excluded on the grounds that someone may consider it 'inelegant' or 'substandard'. It is possible, however, that not all the data is relevant to the linguist's needs. We have seen that language is enormously complex, and that in order to describe it we have to divide it into a number of distinct levels and ranks. In much the same way, we find that it is not possible to describe the whole of a language at any one time. Instead of writing a single comprehensive grammar covering every aspect of a language, the usual procedure is to write a number of different grammars, each dealing with a different aspect of the language. Thus, we have grammars of Early Modern English, and of contemporary English; grammars of colloquial spoken English, and of formal written English; one grammar of American English and another of British English, and so on. Some grammarians set out to describe a relatively small number of 'basic sentence patterns', and wish to exclude long and complex sentences, or those which involve special problems of description; others, more comprehensive in their aims, draw upon a far wider range of data. Many linguists take as their object of study sets of abstract idealized sentences considered 'out of context'; others prefer to study the patterns of actual language behaviour, and to examine the means whereby sentences are fitted together to form texts or connected passages of discourse. There is, then, a point in the linguist's work where an element of selection is unavoidable. But it is important to recognize that for a linguist selection is based on a definite methodological decision, and not on some vague aesthetic criteria which cannot be clearly defined.

A descriptive linguist is as objective as possible in his observation of data, but he has to decide which data are relevant to his enquiry. A language teacher, on the other hand, is necessarily prescriptive. Since it is impossible to teach the whole of a language, it is part of the teacher's responsibility to decide which parts of it should be included in the syllabus. Most teachers would probably regard it as their job to teach a type of neutral, 'standard' English which carries no obvious marks of social or geographical origin. Thus, such forms as *He didn't ought to do it*, *Who belongs this book* or *She's a well-like lass*, which are perfectly normal and acceptable in certain areas of Britain but which deviate from the standard forms, are not likely to find a place in a school English syllabus. The difficulty that faces the teacher is to maintain a reasonable and informed attitude to the notion of 'standard English'. It is as well to avoid rigidly prescriptive attitudes, which are likely to encourage an unnatural and stilted style in both speech and writing. Teachers should also scrutinize their textbooks to make sure that they do not advocate 'rules of correct usage' which reflect the norms of fifty years ago, but which may have little or no justification in terms of contemporary English. For example, *It's I* said in reply to the question *Who's there* sounds so odd that one doubts whether it is really English. In fact, it appears to be based on a Latin rule which states the 'nominative case' and not the 'accusative case' is used for complements following the verb 'to be'. This rule is frequently taught as a part of English grammar, and forms like *It's I* are widely used, and sternly advocated, by people who are strongly under the influence of the old-fashioned prescriptivism of their schooldays.

On behalf of the prescriptive grammarians it should be remembered that they did a great deal to codify the principles of the language, to settle disputed points and decide cases of divided usage. There are numerous indeterminate areas of grammar where no clear rules exist, and where many people feel themselves in need of guidance. Such modern works as H. W. Fowler *A Dictionary of Modern English Usage* and Eric Partridge *Usage and Abusage* are rightly esteemed for the thoughtful guidance they provide in many difficult areas of grammar, vocabulary and style. Every society acknowledges certain canons of taste in speech and writing and it is appropriate that school grammars should have a prescriptive element, since it is part of their function to warn students against expressions that would be regarded as inappropriate in certain types of situation. Ultimately each teacher must make up his own mind about such expressions as *It said in the paper that . . .*, *None of the boys were here*, *You are older than me*, *A book whose contents are inaccurate*. The matter is complicated by the fact that many expressions are acceptable in informal styles, but may be frowned on in more formal styles. A keen sense of what kind of language is appropriate on what occasions is indispensable in daily life. Since questions concerning the appropriate use of language are of great interest to the majority of people, it is to be regretted that this topic receives so little attention in the average language class.

7 Synchronic and diachronic studies

One of the most important terminological distinctions introduced into linguistics by de Saussure was the line he drew between the synchronic and the diachronic aspects of language study. A synchronic study is the description of a language at some point in time; a diachronic study treats of the historical development of a language 'through time'. De Saussure's famous analogy of the game of chess is often cited to illustrate the principle that historical considerations are irrelevant to the investigation of particular temporal states of a language. All languages, said de Saussure, are constantly changing: but just as the state of the chessboard at some particular time can be described without reference to the past history of the game, so can the successive states of a language be described independently of one another. The principle of the priority of synchronic description is generally taken to carry the further implication that studies of language change presuppose an analysis of the various states through which languages have passed during the course of their historical development. Synchronic descriptions are often thought of as being descriptions of the language as it exists at the present day, and probably most linguistic studies are of this type. One obvious advantage of writing a description of the contemporary language is the fact that we can check the validity of our statements by studying the utterances of living speakers. However, it is possible to make a synchronic description of a language as it existed at any point in the past, so long as a sufficient quantity of written records survive.

It might appear at first sight that a clear distinction can be made between synchronic and diachronic studies. We know that as children we learn our native tongue and as adults we speak it fluently without, in most cases, knowing anything about the historical development of the language. It seems natural, then, to assume that a linguist should be able to describe each temporal state of a language in its own terms without reference to what has gone before or what is likely to develop in the future. If we look more closely at this question, however, we find that it is not possible to draw a sharp line between the synchronic and the diachronic aspects of language study. Languages are in a constant state of change, and the idea that there is a moment in time when a language can be frozen into a static state and examined as a whole should be regarded as a convenient methodological fiction. Because the successive states of a language overlap instead of being neatly segmented, the notion of language change is most usefully applied in the comparison of different states of a language which are relatively far removed from one another in time. It would be a mistake, moreover, to assume that the language of any speech community is completely uniform, or to think of language change as the replacement of one homogeneous system of communication by another. A speech community is always made up of many different groups, reflecting differences due to age, place of origin, professional interests and educational background, and it is quite possible that many of the features which distinguish two successive states of the language may be present in different dialects or varieties existing at the same point in time. This being so, it is evident that there must be a close connection between the study of diachronic change on the one hand and synchronic variation on the other, and that the methods employed in these two areas must have a great deal in common with one another.

The changes that are constantly going on in a living language can be most easily seen in the vocabulary. We are all familiar with the process whereby new words are coined to meet new requirements, old words die out, and existing words acquire a new meaning. Words that have changed their meaning can be found on every page of Shakespeare, while an estimated 85 per cent of the vocabulary of Old English is unfamiliar to the modern reader. The changes that take place in pronunciation are less familiar but equally important. When we read Pope's verse and come across imperfect rhymes such as *full-role*, *join-divine*, *obey-tea*, it is evident that since the eighteenth century the pronunciation of one word at least in each of these pairs has changed. Many sound changes are so regular as to be capable of classification under what are known as 'sound laws'. A thorough knowledge of articulatory phonetics, and familiarity with the types of modification that sounds have undergone, is essential for understanding the processes which bring about sound changes in a language.

Changes also occur in grammatical forms. Old English was an inflexional language like Greek and Latin, and made extensive use of 'word endings' to denote number, gender, case, tense and voice. By the time of Chaucer (1340 ?–1400) the structure of English had undergone considerable simplification. Inflexion in the noun paradigm had been reduced to a sign to mark the plural and a special form for the possessive case; the elaborate inflexion of the adjective had been completely eliminated except for a simple indication of the comparative and superlative; and the verb had been simplified by the loss of practically all 'personal' endings, the almost complete loss of any distinction between singular and plural forms, and the gradual disappearance of the special forms that marked the subjunctive mood. Whereas Old English was a *synthetic* language, indicating the relations between words in a sentence by means of inflexions, by the end of the fourteenth century English had developed into an *analytic* language. Modern English is typically analytic in that inflexional endings have almost completely disappeared. Instead English speakers depend on a fixed order of words, and make extensive use of prepositions and auxiliary verbs to indicate the relations between words in a sentence.

Few would dispute that language history has considerable importance as a cultural subject, or that it should be one of the aims of general education to ensure that everyone knows something of the nature and development of his mother tongue. It is widely believed that a general knowledge of linguistic science, including the methods of historical and comparative linguistics, is a necessary adjunct to the study of literature and a useful preliminary to the learning of modern languages. When we consider the techniques that are used to teach a foreign language, however, we seem to have moved rather a long way from the sort of consideration that interests a student of historical linguistics. It should go without saying that the aim of a modern language syllabus is to teach the forms that are spoken at the present day, rather than outline the historical development of the language. Nevertheless there are occasions on which it is difficult from the teaching point of view to draw a clear line between the contemporary language and its historical development. Some of the issues on which a teacher must exercise his judgement are the use of citations from the classics (many still remain in the 1964 edition of Nesfield and Wood), reference to the historical development of the language in order to explain points of grammar, and the use of etymological information in order to arouse an interest in vocabulary.

Many textbook writers recommend forms that reflect an earlier period in the development of English, or the rules of Latin, or the invented rules of eighteenth-century prescriptive grammarians. Such terms as 'gerund', 'gerundive' and 'subjunctive mood' are often used in a manner appropriate to Latin rather than modern English. Rowe and Webb (1928) illustrate the expression of a wish by means of the following sentences: *Mine be a cot*, *May a cot be mine*, *Oh would that a cot might be mine*, *If only a cot could be mine*. Nesfield and Wood (1964) give the following paradigm to illustrate the use of the present tense with 'do': *I do love*, *thou dost love*, *he does love*, *we do love*, *ye or you do love*, *they do love*, and attempt to explain the distinction between *will* and *shall* with reference to Old English usage. Quirk (1959) quotes a grammar of English published in Paris in 1949 which has a long chapter on exclamations in which disgust is said to be expressed by *fie*, *fudge*, *harrow* and *whew*; impatience by *buzz*, *whip* and *pop*; joy by *he*, *hey-day*, *indeed* and *aha*; sorrow by *alack*, *alas*, *heigho*, *well-away* and *just my luck*. Other textbooks still in use today ask for a correction of 'improprieties' in Shakespeare, Milton and the Authorized Version of the Bible, thus combining the worst effects of prescriptivism and failure to observe the distinction between the synchronic and diachronic aspects of language study.

8 Langue and parole

In his writing de Saussure maintained a useful terminological distinction between two aspects of language to which he gave the names *langue* and *parole*. The first of these terms refers to the abstract linguistic system which is shared by all the members of a speech community and which underlies the actual utterances of individuals. *Langue* is not actually spoken by anyone, and can be thought of as the generalized rules of the language. By contrast, *parole* is actualized language, the realization of *langue* in speech which is idiosyncratic and specific to the situation in which it occurs. Compared with *langue*, which is stable and systematic, each parole-act is a unique event, subject to a wide range of personal and situational constraints. A similar kind of distinction is made by the American linguist Noam Chomsky and his followers. In

Chomsky's terminology, competence is the ideal language user's knowledge of the rules of grammar, while performance is the actual realization of this knowledge in utterances, and involves a variety of psychological, physical and social factors. Chomsky's terms and de Saussure's terms are not exact equivalents, since de Saussure describes *langue* as a 'social product . . . a collection of necessary conventions that have been adopted by a social body', while Chomsky regards competence as a property of the mind of the individual which is developed as part of his general maturation. Both Chomsky and de Saussure, however, would agree that the proper objective of the linguistic study of language is the characterization of the regular rules of grammar, and not a description of the idiosyncratic utterances produced by speakers of a language.

What most linguists do when they describe a language is to construct a model, not of actual language-behaviour, but of the system of regularities which underlie that behaviour. In most models of linguistic description the main unit of description is the sentence, which is an abstract theoretical unit of the language system. Sentences are related to stretches of actual language behaviour, or 'utterances', by a process of idealization. First, the linguist discounts all 'slips of the tongue', mispronunciations, hesitation pauses, stammering, etc. The first stage of idealization, which consists of the elimination of performance errors in the primary data, is called regularization by Lyons (1972). At the second stage of idealization, which Lyons refers to as standardization, we discount a certain amount of the systematic variation between utterances that can be attributed to personal and sociocultural factors such as geographical and social origin, professional occupation, education and special interests. The third stage of idealization is decontextualization. Utterances are typically context-dependent, with respect both to their meaning and their grammatical structure. An example of a context-dependent utterance might be *John's, if he gets here in time* which might occur after *Whose car are you going in?* but not after *When are you going there?* By 'decontextualizing' an utterance we mean the 'filling out' of the utterance by adding to it various elements 'understood' in the particular linguistic and situational context in which it has occurred: converting *John's, if he gets here in time*, for example, into *We are going in John's car if he gets here in time.* This sequence has the properties normally thought of as being characteristic of 'complete' sentences (a familiar term in traditional grammar, and in traditional grammar lessons). It is such 'complete sentences', and not utterances, that linguists generally describe in their models of the language system.

It is, then, a fundamental principle of modern linguists that all sentences and their constituents are abstract constructs which belong to linguistic theory rather than to the realm of objectively-perceived data. The term 'sentence' refers not to an actual physical speech-event (utterance-token) but to a theoretical unit (sentence-type) which is abstracted by the linguist from a set of similar speech-events by a process of analysis whereby some utterance-tokens are identified as the same and the differences that exist between them in terms of objectively-perceived data are disregarded.

For de Saussure speech, or language-as-a-whole, was a heterogeneous mass of confused facts, and therefore not suitable for systematic enquiry. The solution proposed by de Saussure was to abstract *langue* from instances of *parole*; since there was no perceivable over-all regularity in the latter, he took from it what did have regularity and pronounced it the subject of linguistics. Not all scholars, however, have agreed with this narrow interpretation of linguistics. The British linguist J. R. Firth, for example, influenced by Malinowski's study of the relationship between language and social context, rejected the 'static structural formalism' which he believed resulted from de Saussure's strict *langue/parole* distinction. According to Firth, linguists should include statements about the way in which language is used in social interaction, and how it varies in accordance with its social function. In much the same way, a number of writers have recently reacted against Chomsky's almost exclusive concern with those aspects of language structure which can be abstracted from the context in which speech events take place and described in purely formal terms. It has been pointed out that Chomsky's notion of 'linguistic competence' needs to be supplemented with a notion of 'communicative competence'. Thus it is a matter of communicative competence to be able to produce coherent discourse which is situationally relevant, and to use language appropriately for the performance of a variety of 'semiotic acts' such as asking questions, making promises and predictions, giving orders, making statements and so on. After several decades of preoccupation with purely formal studies, there are signs that linguists are beginning to turn their attention once more to the communicative properties of language and the functioning of language in social contexts. This development is of particular interest to language teachers, many of whom have long felt the need to give more attention in the classroom to communicative function as well as, and in relation to, linguistic form.

In teaching, a problem may arise when 'model sentences' intended for imitation are used as illustrations for abstract grammatical statements. Generally speaking, the exemplificatory material in language textbooks is intended to serve two purposes. On the one hand the author has to find some way of teaching the underlying rules, and on the other he wishes to present useful material which the students can use in their own utterances. These aims may often seem to be in conflict. As Saporta points out, an ability to verbalize the rules may interfere with the student's ability to acquire fluent speech habits (Saporta 1966). This is a paradoxical situation which each teacher will attempt to resolve in his own way. Some teachers may be led to make grammatical statements which are oversimplified, others may fall into the error of spending more time talking about grammar than helping the students acquire fluency by means of oral and written practice. Keeping the balance between formal statements about the underlying rules and the presentation of realistic language data is one of the main challenges in designing effective language teaching material. Usually there is no ready-made solution, and a great deal must be left to the judgement of the individual teacher or textbook writer.

The majority of language teaching texts contain comparatively few examples of completely abstract sentence formulas on the one hand or of 'authentic' utterance-tokens on the other. Most classroom material consists of sentences which fall somewhere between the two extremes. A writer who presents pairs of systematically contrasting sentences selected on the basis of grammatical criteria is teaching *langue* rather than *parole.* Many teachers find it hard to accept that examples like *I am walking to the door*, *You are walking to the door* are unusual utterance-tokens, but if we try to contextualize these sentences it is difficult to suggest circumstances in which they might plausibly be used. How, then, are we to impart a knowledge of the rules? A good textbook writer tries to ensure that each of the examples usefully exemplifies a sentence type and is at the same time an acceptable utterance-token. In other words, what we would like in our textbooks are model sentences which draw attention to features of the underlying rules, and at the same time look like the sort of thing that people are likely to want to say. Clearly, the creation of such material requires considerable ingenuity and skill on the part of the textbook writer. The writer's task is made all the more difficult by the need for frequent shifts of emphasis in the text. Sometimes a set of grammatical examples will be the main point of emphasis, sometimes the student's attention will be focused on a more natural-sounding reading-passage or conversation. It is important that the textbook writer should know exactly what function the text is intended to fulfil at any particular point. It is equally important that the teacher should understand the strategies behind different parts of the text, and vary his teaching method accordingly.

9 Chomsky's theory of language

So far our discussion has been consistent with the 'structuralist' view of language which was dominant during the first half of the present century, and which is associated with the names of many great linguists, including Ferdinand de Saussure and Nikolas Trubetzkoy in Europe, and Leonard Bloomfield in the United States. Our review of basic principles would not be complete, however, without a reference to the profound change in linguistic studies which has taken place as a result of the work of Noam Chomsky. In a number of important publications (see bibliography), Chomsky has proposed an approach to language description which is known as transformational-generative grammar. According to Chomsky, in any syntactic description the observable syntactic structure of sentences, the surface structure, should be related to a more abstract deep structure.

The difference between deep structure and surface structure is illustrated by the fact, easily perceived by speakers of a language, that some sentences 'contain' other sentences as part of their internal structure. Thus *I was surprised by John's refusal to come* exhibits a set of internal relations which is identical to those found in the sentence *John refused to come*, although there is nothing in the data itself to show that the relation between *John's* and *refusal* is the same as that between *John* and *refused*. Moreover a fluent speaker knows whether sentences are grammatical or ungrammatical, a fact which emerges from introspection but which cannot be directly perceived as a feature of a text, and he is able to perceive the ambiguity in sentences like *Visiting aunts can be a bore*, where there is only one surface structure but at least two deep structures according to whether the speaker means that he visits the aunts or the aunts visit him.

We can say, then, by and large that surface structure is the aspect of description that determines the phonetic form of sentences, while deep structure determines semantic interpretation. The distinction between deep and surface structure is held to be generally valid although recent work has shown that in some cases surface structure may contribute to semantic interpretation. The rules that express the relation of deep and surface structure in sentences are called grammatical transformations. Various examples of transformational rules are given in the chapter on pedagogic grammer (see Volume 3). Chomsky also makes it a requirement that the rules of the grammar should be absolutely explicit. This means that the rules automatically generate sentences (i.e. the rules 'characterize' sentences, or define them as grammatical) without having to utilize a native speaker's intuitive knowledge of language in the process. These two characteristics—the use of transformational rules linking deep and surface structure, and the explicit, generative nature of the rules—are what we specifically refer to when we talk about 'transformational-generative grammar'.

The pre-transformational school of linguists chose, as a matter of deliberate methodological decision, to restrict their terms of reference to a process of segmentation and classification based on a given corpus, or selection of texts. This process is similar to the traditional technique of parsing and results in a description of the observable syntactic structure of sentences. However, many linguists are not content merely to provide a structural description of the sentences of a corpus, but aim to provide a principled account of the linguistic knowledge of human beings. In pursuit of this aim transformational linguists attempt to specify the nature of language competence, seen as a highly abstract set of organizing principles which underlie the facts of language performance, or the actual use of language in specific situations. Although the abstract system of rules which constitute language competence is the foundation on which overt language behaviour is based, the rules do not stand in any direct or simple relationship to the observable fact of behaviour. For this reason a knowledge of underlying competence cannot be built up through a study of texts or audible speech events by the methods of classificatory, data-based linguistics.

We are accustomed to say that human language is creative. By this we mean that human language behaviour is not restricted to an imitation of those utterances that a speaker happens to have heard before. Rather, speakers have the ability to utilize an unlimited number of combinations of words and phrases to form sentences which are entirely new, not based on any previously existing utterance but produced uniquely for the occasion on which they need to be used. Since a speaker is a finite organism, we assume that the linguistic knowledge he possesses is also finite. On the other hand, a language user is capable of producing or interpreting sentences without limit. It would seem, therefore, that an appropriate model for a speaker's language competence is a set of rules which is finite in itself, but capable of generating the infinite set of sentences that a speaker is potentially able to produce and understand. In principle, according to Chomsky, the aim of a linguistic description should be to specify the nature of language competence by defining the properties of the unbounded series of well-formed sentences of a given language. A grammar should be 'predictive' in that it includes all those sentences which cannot be inferred from direct observation of data but whose existence—or potential existence—is implied by the rules of the grammar.

It is important to realize that the idea of a predictive grammar did not originate with Chomsky. The notion that linguists should aim at a predictive grammar is stated explicitly by Harris (1946) and Hockett (1954). Moreover, the 'traditional' grammars of Jespersen, Poutsma and others do, in a sense, attempt to provide an account of what the native speaker knows intuitively about his language. However, these 'traditional' grammars are not sufficiently explicit in their formulation of rules, with the result that a great deal is left to the reader in deciding how the information in the grammar is to be used in the construction of grammatically well-formed sentences. It is clearly unsatisfactory if a grammar which sets out to explain the nature of linguistic knowledge should have to depend upon that very knowledge existing in the mind of the reader in order to be fully understood. The only way to avoid this type of circularity is to require that a grammar should be able to follow out its own rules and generate sentences automatically, thus becoming a self-sufficient predictive mechanism in its own right.

A transformational-generative grammar of a language is one which, in principle, provides a procedure for testing any combination of words and deciding whether it is a sentence in the language. The grammar 'decides' that an utterance is grammatical if a precise relation can be established between the utterance in question and some combination of symbols which is generated by the rules of the grammar. In theory a transformational grammar should generate all the sentences of a language, and no non-sentences. Obviously this statement represents an ideal, since no existing grammar comes anywhere near meeting this requirement. Furthermore it is possible that the ideal is incapable of fulfilment, in the sense of actually producing a complete generative grammar of a natural language. Even if this turns out to be the case, however, Chomsky's definition of an 'ideal' grammar is useful since it constitutes a goal towards which linguists can look and against which they can measure the value of their efforts. Moreover, the principle that every step in the derivation of sentences must be fully and accurately described, together with a requirement that transformational grammar should achieve the maximum degree of economy in the use of rules, has led to the discovery of many underlying regularities which would not have been apparent from an examination of surface structure alone.

Transformational linguists claim to provide a formal representation of a speaker's idealized linguistic knowledge, or competence. Since this knowledge is the end product of teaching, it is natural to ask whether transformational grammar can provide useful ideas about how a language should be taught. Some linguists have made quite strong statements in support of the view that a knowledge of transformational grammar implies specific decisions about the selection and arrangement of teaching material. However, there is no reason to suppose that the organization of teaching material should necessarily reflect the organization of any particular linguistic description. In the first place, the rules of transformational grammar are highly abstract, which means that they cannot easily enter into language teaching. Teachers can make use of the insights provided by the rules, but not always of the rules themselves. Secondly, those rules and statements which derive from the most highly valued linguistic grammar are not necessarily the same rules and statements which make sense to a student and help him to learn. Thirdly, the presentation of teaching material cannot be dictated by the rules in a linguistic grammar, since in practical classroom teaching we have to take into account a wide range of factors which have nothing to do with linguistics.

It seems likely, then, that the most useful contribution that linguistics, including transformational grammar, can make to language teaching lies not in the provision of specific rules and procedures but in extending the teacher's understanding of the nature of language and his awareness of the complexity of language learning. Much current work in linguistics will find no direct application in the classroom, but this does not mean that it is irrelevant to language teaching. A teacher who is linguistically knowledgeable will be in a better position to exercise his critical judgement in the choice and creation of materials, and more likely to make sound pedagogic decisions.

10 Further reading

General introductions to the scientific study of language

Bolinger, Dwight 1968. *Aspects of Language*. New York: Harcourt Brace.
Crystal, David 1971. *Linguistics*. Harmondsworth: Penguin.

Dineen, Francis P. 1967. *An Introduction to General Linguistics*. New York: Holt, Rinehart, Winston.

Gleason, H. A. Jr. 1961. *An Introduction to Descriptive Linguistics*. 2nd revised edition (First edition 1955). New York: Holt, Rinehart, Winston.

Lehmann, Winfred P. 1962. *Historical Linguistics: An Introduction*. New York: Holt, Rinehart, Winston.

Lyons, John 1968. *An Introduction to Theoretical Linguistics*. Cambridge: Cambridge University Press.

Robins, R. H. 1964. *General Linguistics: An Introductory Survey*. London: Longman and Bloomington, Indiana: Indiana University Press.

Waterman, John T. 1963. *Perspectives in Linguistics*. Chicago: University of Chicago Press.

Collections of papers dealing with more recent developments

Hill, A. A. (ed.) 1969. *Linguistics Today*. New York: Basic Books, Inc.

Lyons, John (ed.) 1970. *New Horizons in Linguistics*. Harmondsworth: Penguin.

Chomsky's theory of language

Allen, J. P. B. and van Buren, Paul (eds.) 1971. *Chomsky: Selected Readings*. London: Oxford University Press.

Lyons, John 1970. *Chomsky*. London: Fontana Modern Masters. (See also books by Chomsky in further reading section of Chapter 3.)

Linguistics in relation to language teaching

Bennett, W. A. 1967. *Aspects of Language and Language Teaching*. London: Cambridge University Press.

Halliday, M. A. K., McIntosh, Angus and Strevens, P. D. 1964. *The Linguistic Sciences and Language Teaching*. London: Longman and Bloomington, Indiana: Indiana University Press.

Politzer, R. L. 1965. *Foreign Language Learning*. Englewood Cliffs: Prentice-Hall.

Wilkins, D. A. 1972. *Linguistics and Language Teaching*. London: Arnold.

Collections of papers on language teaching topics

Perren, G. E. and Trim, J. L. M. (eds.) 1971. *Applications of Linguistics*. London: Cambridge University Press.

Valdman, Albert (ed.) 1966. *Trends in Language Teaching*. New York: McGraw-Hill.

3 J. P. B. ALLEN AND H. G. WIDDOWSON
Grammar and Language Teaching

1 Introduction

Let school masters puzzle their brain
  With grammar and nonsense and learning;
Good liquor, I stoutly maintain,
  Gives genius a better discerning.

Thus sings Tony Lumpkin in *She Stoops to Conquer*, reflecting the popular view that grammar is one of the most boring and obscure subjects in the school curriculum. It is perhaps not surprising that grammar should have acquired a reputation for dullness, since very often the way it is taught in the schools seems deliberately designed to kill all interest in the subject. Many of us retain from our schooldays memories of the repetitious, mechanical parsing of sentences, the rote-learning of paradigms, word-lists and artificial 'rules of diction', and old-fashioned handbooks which quoted abundantly from the classics of English literature but almost entirely ignored the living colloquial language that we hear around us every day.

For a time, in the late fifties and early sixties, it seemed possible that grammar-teaching in the schools would be reinvigorated under the influence of important work being done in the field of linguistics. Unfortunately, however, the idea gained ground among teachers that there was a fundamental conflict between the traditional grammar they were accustomed to using in the classroom, and the 'new linguistics' which was being urged upon them. Soon many teachers found themselves in a serious dilemma. On the one hand, traditional grammar was supposed to be 'unscientific' and therefore unworthy of serious consideration, while linguistics seemed to be a highly esoteric subject beyond the comprehension of any but the most dedicated of University scholars. The situation was made more difficult by the fact that linguists were apparently unable to make up their minds about the nature of language and how it should be studied. Those teachers who attempted to inform themselves about recent developments in the subject found that a number of distinct schools of linguistics had emerged, each with its band of enthusiastic followers who strenuously urged the merits of their own particular approach to the study of language. Many language teachers were further confused by the increasing tendency of linguists to use a highly technical terminology, and a rapid increase in the number of books and articles which assumed a considerable amount of background knowledge and made little or no concession to the general reader. As a result many teachers became disillusioned, not only about modern linguistics, but about linguistics in general, including traditional grammar, and there was a widespread reaction against grammar-teaching in the schools.

Grammar has also been neglected in the field of second language teaching, but for a different reason. Since the end of the Second World War language teaching theory has tended to emphasize the rapid development of automatic speech habits, and the need to discourage students from thinking consciously about the underlying grammatical rules. Advocates of the 'oral method', the 'audiolingual method' and the 'multi-skill method' in their more extreme forms have assumed that language learning is an inductive rather than a deductive process, and that the most effective method of teaching is to provide plenty of oral and written practice, so that students learn to use the language spontaneously without the need for overt grammatical analysis. Recently, however, a change of attitude has been apparent among writers on second language teaching methods. The experience of a large number of teachers over many years suggests that a combination of inductive and deductive methods produces the best results. It is now generally acknowledged that language learning is not simply a mechanical process of habit-formation, but a process which involves the active co-operation of the learner as a rational individual. Far from being the passive recipients of stimuli in the form of exercises and drills, students learn in a selective manner, searching for the information they need to discover the systems of the language being learned.

Most teachers will continue to see language learning as fundamentally an inductive process based on the presentation of data, but one which can be controlled by explanations of a suitable type. An important question concerns the nature of the grammatical explanations given to the students, and the type of linguistic grammar from which these explanations should be drawn. The question of the relationship between formal linguistic grammars and practical teaching grammars based on them is discussed in detail in Volume 3, and we will not repeat the arguments here. Clearly, however, if language teachers are to be called upon to make judgements about what constitutes an appropriate treatment of grammar for classroom use, it will be an advantage if they are conversant with the main developments in modern grammatical theory. We believe that a knowledge of grammatical theory is an indispensable part of every language teacher's training, even if in many cases this knowledge will reveal itself in the teacher's general attitude and approach to problems, rather than directly in the construction of specific diagrams and exercises.

What we are advocating, then, is the reinstatement of some explicit description of the grammar as an essential element in both first language and second language teaching. This does not mean that we are suggesting a return to the so-called 'grammar-translation' method of language teaching, under which students did not easily achieve a fluent use of the spoken language, because they spent much of their time studying abstract grammatical rules, memorizing word-lists and translating from the native to the target language, and vice versa. We do believe, however, that in any given classroom situation just so much attention should be given to grammar as may be necessary in order to promote quick and efficient language learning. Thus we see the teaching of grammar not as an end in itself, but as a useful aid in helping students to achieve the practical mastery of a language.

We believe that there is basically no conflict between traditional grammar and modern linguistics. Some writers have referred to a 'revolution in grammar', thus implying a sharp break between the old and the new. The fact is, however, that the traditional parts of speech approach to grammar is still one of the most widely taught and studied systems of linguistic methodology. Modern grammarians have developed methods that are more concise and more theoretically consistent than the older methods. However, whereas the traditional handbooks provided descriptions of wide areas of surface structure, a typical paper or book written by a contemporary linguist discusses theoretical issues and presents only as much of the data as is necessary to support the hypotheses advanced. In filling out the details, we find ourselves drawing more and more upon the work of the scholarly traditional grammarians. It is particularly important for language teachers to maintain a balanced point of view and to avoid setting the new types of grammar too sharply in opposition to the old.

We saw in the previous chapter that contemporary linguistic theory is very far from being a single monolithic system; rather, it is a combination of different approaches, all of which are subject to constant development and change. We have also emphasized, elsewhere in this course, that a teacher must make his own choice from among the various models of grammar available in linguistics, and decide for himself what kind of grammatical statement is most likely to be suitable for the particular group of students he has in mind. At first sight it may appear that the teacher is faced with a formidable task of selection. Let us suppose that we are setting out to write a textbook for students of English as a second language. What facts should we select from among the vast amount of information available in books and journals, to use as a basis for our classroom presentation of English grammar? Fortunately we will find that, despite the volume of current work in English grammar, and the variety of views expressed, there is a remarkable consensus of opinion about what constitutes the fundamentals of the subject. Over the years linguists have succeeded in identifying a body of basic facts about the structure of English which have been tested and verified, and which can now be stated with a high degree of confidence. Where shortcomings exist in a particular grammar of English, these can be identified and the student advised to proceed with care. If we find failures of coverage in one linguist's description we can often supplement it by drawing upon the work of other linguists, but in order to do this with confidence we must know exactly the terms of reference of each grammar we use, and its characteristic strengths and limitations. In this chapter we hope to make the task of selection easier by outlining the various approaches to grammatical analysis which have been developed during the past fifty years, at the same time attempting to discover what each of these models of grammar can contribute to the practical study of languages.

2 Traditional grammar

Modern structural linguistics can be said to begin with the posthumous publication of Ferdinand de Saussure's lectures under the title of *Cours de Linguistique Générale* in 1916. Behind de Saussure, stretching back over 2,000 years, lies the era of traditional grammar. To write an account of pre-Saussurean grammar with any hope of doing justice to this long, rich and varied tradition would be an immense task. Assuming that we limited our aim to tracing the development of linguistic studies in the West, we would have to go back to the Greek scholars of the fourth and fifth century B.C. to find the origins of the grammar that most of us learned at school.

The linguistic analysis carried out by the Greeks between the fourth century B.C. and the second century A.D. included most of the basic concepts which still constitute the layman's conception of 'grammar'. The classification of words according to gender (masculine, feminine and neuter) was carried out by Protagoras and the fifth century Sophists. The Stoics classified the patterns of inflexion, established the distinction between the active and passive voices and between transitive and intransitive verbs, and defined the function of the nominative and the 'oblique' cases. The Alexandrians classified all Greek words in terms of case, gender, number, tense, voice and mood. Dionysius Thrax classified the words of the Greek language into eight parts of speech—noun, verb, participle, article, pronoun, preposition, adverb and conjunction. The Greek model was largely followed by the later Roman grammarians. The grammars of Donatus (*c.* A.D. 400) and Priscian (*c.* A.D. 500) were used as teaching grammars through the Middle Ages and as late as the seventeenth century. The traditional categories were then taken over by prescriptive grammarians like John Wallis, Robert Lowth and Lindley Murray, thus helping to preserve an unbroken tradition of grammatical analysis which has lasted from the time of Aristotle to the present day.

A study of traditional grammar would not be complete without an account of the work of the medieval scholars who brought about many advances in the analysis of Latin. The scholastic philosophers, or modistae, were interested in grammar as a tool for analysing the structure of reality, and they deliberately attempted to relate the categories of grammar to those of logic, epistemology and metaphysics. The ideals of medieval 'speculative' grammar—'speculative' in the sense of providing a mirror of of the world—were revived in seventeenth century France by the teachers of Port Royal, who believed that the structure of language is a product of reason, and that all the languages of the world are varieties of the same underlying logical and rational system. These philosophical presuppositions, expressed in the famous Port Royal *Grammaire Générale et Raisonnée* of 1660, bear some resemblance to the theory of language currently being developed by Noam Chomsky.

Coming closer to our own time, a writer on the history of linguistics would have to devote many pages to an account of nineteenth-century comparative philology. Towards the end of the eighteenth century a number of scholars including the British civil servant Sir William Jones drew attention to the similarities between many words in Sanskrit and their equivalents in Latin, Greek, Celtic, Germanic and certain other European and Middle Eastern languages, and suggested that all these languages derived from a single source. As a result of this observation linguists became deeply interested in the Indo-European family of languages, and many attempts were made to reconstruct the forms of Proto-Indo-European, believed to be the common ancestor. Throughout the nineteenth century a long line of distinguished scholars studied the systematic correspondences between the sounds of equivalent words and patterns of inflexion in different languages, and as a result they succeeded in establishing a general theory of linguistic relationship and language change.

It will be apparent, then, that 'traditional grammar' although it can be criticized from the point of view of modern ideas of what constitutes scientific precision and objectivity, is far richer and far more diversified than one would suppose on the basis of the rather disparaging references which have been made to it by many modern linguists. Two types of traditional grammar, not always clearly distinguished in the literature, are usually taken as the point of departure for a discussion of modern theories: (a) the 'scholarly' or 'compendious' reference grammars of the late nineteenth and early twentieth centuries, for example those of Kruisinga, Poutsma, Sweet, Curme and Jespersen, and (b) the school grammars, by such writers as Nesfield and Lindley Murray, which were essentially a simplification of the work of the scholarly grammarians. The widespread criticism of traditional grammar voiced in recent years relates in part to the methods employed by the scholarly grammarians, but is mainly concerned with the shortcomings of the simplified versions of scholarly grammar intended for use in schools. A great deal of this criticism fails to take into account the special circumstances for which the simplified grammars were designed.

Both the scholarly and the pedagogic grammarians have been blamed for their too-ready acceptance of 'notional' and 'imprecise' definitions for the parts of speech and other grammatical categories. It should be realized that there is often more than one way of defining a category in linguistics; for example, the definition of a noun may be morphological, functional or notional. By a morphological definition we mean one which is based on the classification of the physical forms of a language. A functional definition is one based on the relation of words to other words in a sentence with reference to such concepts as 'subject', 'object', 'complement', etc., and a notional definition is one based on our understanding of the relationship of words to the actual, real-world phenomena which they denote. Thus, a noun may be defined morphologically as a word that fits into an inflexional series built on the contrast between singular and plural numbers (*boy*, *boys*) and between common and possessive cases (*boy*, *boy's*, *boys*, *boys'*), and on no other contrasts (Sledd 1959). It may be defined functionally as a word that can serve as subject of a verb, and notionally as the name of a person, place or thing. None of these definitions are complete as they stand, but they all draw attention to different characteristics of nouns that are relevant at different points in the description of a language.

In many classroom grammars, nouns and verbs are defined notionally and the other parts of speech are defined functionally, on the basis of the definition of noun and verb: thus, we may say that an adjective is a word that modifies a noun; an adverb is a word that modifies a verb; a pronoun is a word that replaces a noun; a preposition is a word relating other parts of speech; an interjection stands alone with no relationship to other parts of speech. Formal definitions may then be added to the notional and functional definitions; for example, it might be stated that a large subclass of adjectives fit into an inflexional series like *tall*, *taller*, *tallest*, and that most verbs fit into a pattern *sing*, *sings*, *sang*, *sung*, *singing* or *play*, *plays*, *played*, *playing*. The triple basis of definition may appear complicated, but in the classroom it seems to work quite well. Most linguists now acknowledge that it is not possible to formulate simple water-tight definitions of basic categories like noun and verb, sentence, clause and word. It is perfectly feasible, however, to impart a knowledge of word classes by listing typical examples, and this in practice is how many students learn to identify nouns and verbs and other grammatical categories. For example, the teacher or textbook writer might give a partial definition followed by a list of examples. The learner studies the examples, discovers for himself what they have in common, and arrives inductively at an understanding of what a noun is, or a verb. He is not dependent for this knowledge on the 'definition', which in most cases simply serves as a useful reminder.

A more serious criticism concerns the excessively diffuse, 'atomistic' nature of many traditional reference grammars. Much of the work of the traditional scholarly grammarians suffered from the lack of a coherent theoretical framework, or model, which ideally should underlie the analysis and give unity and shape to the way in which the results are presented. Because in writing a grammar we normally progress from more general to more detailed statements—a process which involves an increasingly detailed subdivision of the word classes—there is a tendency for the broad patterns of the language to be obscured as the grammarian accumulates more and more facts. It is therefore important that the grammarian should work within a clearly-defined framework of analysis which will bind all the details together into a unified whole. Without such a framework continually examined in the light of a general theory of language it is difficult to assess what degree of importance should be attached to each of the data being studied. Often on referring to a traditional reference grammar we find that the author devotes lengthy explanations to points of detail, but fails to outline the main constructions clearly. Moreover, when the arrangement of chapters follows the traditional division into parts of speech, much important grammatical information—for example, the facts concerning interrogative, negative or passive sentences—tends to be given in a diffuse, compartmentalized manner.

The aims and methods of traditional grammar have been widely criticized in recent years, mainly by linguists wishing to promote one or other of the currently more fashionable theories. It is possible, however, that this criticism has been overdone. Much has been made of comparatively trivial shortcomings, and the considerable achievements of the traditional grammarians have been belittled or ignored. Teachers who wish to maintain a balanced view of linguistics should not overlook the fact that traditional grammar has many useful virtues. The traditional handbooks provided the array of terms and distinctions which most of us used in learning to talk about our own language, and which many educated people continue to find serviceable throughout their lives. The scholarly reference books, moreover, contain a great deal of material which can be expected to appear, with only slight modifications, in any description of English. The current trend in linguistic studies, involving an attempt to describe the abstract system of rules that underlies the surface forms of utterances, has led to a marked revival of interest in the methods of traditional grammar.

3 Taxonomic grammar

We have seen that a fundamental difficulty in traditional grammar is an over-emphasis on the details of a language and a tendency to obscure the larger patterns. The view that language elements are related to one another in a system (or network of systems) rather than being mere collections of individual items is characteristic of what has come to be known as the structural approach to linguistic analysis. At the end of the nineteenth century linguistic science was still more or less equated with comparative linguistics, which in turn tended to mean the comparison of Indo-European languages and the reconstruction of Proto-Indo-European. The prevailing philosophical point of view was that of the *Junggrammatiker* or 'neogrammarians', whose work tended to result in the amassing of large amounts of data and the proliferation of rules to account for each individual phenomenon without establishing any very clear picture of the language as a whole. In the first two decades of the present century, however, a fundamental change of direction in linguistic studies took place. This change can be characterized as a shift from an item-centred view of language to one which is structure-centred. According to the structuralists, individual sounds, words or parts of sentences have no linguistic significance in themselves; they have significance only as they contrast and combine with other items in the patterns of a linguistic system.

At this point it should be made clear that the expression 'structuralism' has two distinct senses in current linguistic discussion. In its first and more general sense, structuralism is based on the belief that each language is a unique relational structure, and that the key to linguistic scholarship is to study the elements of a language not in isolation but as parts of a systemic whole. Structuralism in this sense of the term had its formal beginnings in the famous *Thèses* presented collectively by the members of the Prague Linguistic Circle to the First International Congress of Slavic Philologists held in Prague in 1929. The interpretation of structuralism associated with the Prague linguists has continued to be the basis of structural linguistics up to the present day. In its second and narrower sense, structuralism refers to the views and methodology of the dominant school of American linguists in the 1940s and 1950s. During this period an important group of linguists, including Bloch, Wells, Harris and Hockett, published a substantial body of work in the tradition which is known variously as 'structural', 'taxonomic' or 'Bloomfieldian' grammar. The term 'structural' in this context indicates a characteristic preoccupation with form rather than meaning, 'taxonomic' refers to the inductive classificatory procedures on which such grammars were mainly based, and 'Bloomfieldian' (or 'post-Bloomfieldian') refers to the influence of Bloomfield's ideas as embodied in his book *Language* (1933), where many of the basic assumptions of the group were set out in a definitive form. As so often in linguistics, the wealth of terminology associated with post-Bloomfieldian grammar can give rise to serious problems for the non-specialist. In this discussion we will use the term 'taxonomic' to refer to that type of linguistic analysis which is concerned mainly with the segmentation and classification of utterances, without reference to the 'deeper', more abstract levels of linguistic organization. The term 'structural' will be used more generally, with reference to all grammars which emphasize the phonological and grammatical structure of language, in contrast with the semantic.[1]

[1] Because many American linguists in the thirties and forties were busy with the task of analysing unknown American Indian languages, the idea has grown up that pre-1957 American linguistics was mainly concerned with the development of so-called 'discovery

The procedures of taxonomic grammar were developed as a conscious revolt against traditional methods of analysis. The features of traditional grammar which taxonomic linguists took particular exception to were the establishment of grammatical categories on the basis of notional definitions and the assumption that there are universal categories (parts of speech, tense, mood, etc.) which hold for all languages. By contrast, taxonomic linguists based their work on the assumption that grammatical categories should be defined not in terms of meaning but in terms of distribution, and that the structure of each language should be described without reference to the alleged universality of such categories as tense, mood and parts of speech. Unlike the work of traditional grammarians, a taxonomic description is said to be formal, in the sense that the units of the analysis are defined internally in relation to each other, rather than externally in relation to psychological, logical or metaphysical categories which are not part of the language system as such.

When we say that every linguistic unit below the level of sentence has a characteristic distribution we mean that it is restricted in a characteristic way with respect to the contexts in which it can occur. The structural framework of English, as analysed by Fries (1952) is made up of four major 'form classes' and fifteen groups of function words. These constitute the 'structural signals' which convey grammatical meaning in a sentence. The parts of speech, or form classes of words, are defined by Fries as follows:

Class 1 words fit into such frames as

(The)——— was good
(The)———s were good
(The)——— remembered the ———
(The)——— went there

Class 2 words fit the frames:

(The) 1 ——— good
(The) 1 ——— (the) 1
(The) 1 ——— there

Class 3 words fit the frames:

(The) 1 is/was ———

(The) ——— 1 is/was ———

---

procedures', that is, techniques for the elicitation and analysis of data which can be applied even when the investigator has had no previous contact with the language. It should be realized, however, that far from being solely concerned with observables and the segmenting of utterances, the leading theorists of the American 'structuralist' school often postulated abstract structures in their solutions to particular problems of description, and that, in general, their work foreshadowed the development of a more abstract, generative theory of grammar (see Miller 1973).

Class 4 words fit the frames:

(The) 3 1 is/was ———
(The) 1 2 (the) 1 ———
(The) 1 2 there ———

The numerals 1, 2, 3 and 4 refer to Class 1, Class 2, Class 3 and Class 4 words respectively. In addition Fries recognizes fifteen groups of 'function words'. The first three groups are illustrated here.

Group A contains all words for the position in which the word *the* occurs:

A 1 2 3
The concert was good.
e.g., *a*, *an*, *every*, *no*, *my*, *our*, *some*, *any*, *six*, etc.

Group B contains words for the position in which words *may*, *had*, etc. occur in the following sentence frames:

A 1 B 2 3
The concert may be good.
e.g., *might*, *can*, *could*, *will*, *would*, etc.

A 1 B 2
The car had moved.
e.g., *was*, *got*

A 1 B 2
The car was moving.
e.g., *got*, *kept*

A 1 B 2
The car did move.
e.g., *had to*

Group C contains one word only, *not* in the following constructions:

A 1 B C 2 3
The concert may not be good.

A 1 2 C 3
The concert was not good.

Many of the units grouped in Form Class 1 would traditionally be called 'nouns'; many of those in Class 2 would be called 'verbs'; many of those in Class 3 would be called 'adjectives' and many of those in Class 4 would be called 'adverbs'. Similarly there is a considerable degree of correspondence between the classes of function words and such traditional terms as 'article', 'auxiliary', 'preposition', etc. The Fries form classes and the traditional parts of speech do not coincide exactly, however. Following the structural approach to linguistic analysis, Fries starts by establishing a set of units which can be described objectively, and uses these formal structural units as a basis for the concept of grammatical meaning. A traditional grammarian, on the other hand, would be more likely to start with an intuitive concept of grammatical meaning, and then proceed to assign technical names to the words and groups of words with which these meanings were associated. The disadvantage of the traditional method lies in the fact that the analysis is heavily dependent on individual intuition, and in the absence of any objective procedure for making decisions in difficult cases grammars may vary considerably in what they include under each of the traditional terms. By basing his description on distributional criteria rather than on meaning, Fries avoids the need for subjective decisions and tries to ensure that every part of the analysis can be tested and verified, not only by the linguist who made the description, but by anyone who chooses to consult it or to make a description of his own based on the same principles.

The procedures of taxonomic linguistics are typically concerned with a formalization of surface structure. By 'surface structure' we mean a type of analysis which segments each sequence of elements of a sentence into its constituent parts, and further segments the constituents in such a way that all the elements in the analysis are directly related to the linearly arranged sequence of events in the original text or speech-signal. Thus the surface structure of a sentence is a linearly arranged sequence of 'immediate constituents' which can be presented in the form of a hierarchical bracketing:

<table>
<tr><td>Harry</td><td colspan="4">enjoyed his first visit</td></tr>
<tr><td></td><td>enjoyed</td><td colspan="3">his first visit</td></tr>
<tr><td></td><td></td><td>his</td><td colspan="2">first visit</td></tr>
<tr><td></td><td></td><td></td><td>first</td><td>visit</td></tr>
</table>

This type of representation is known as an immediate constituent, or IC analysis. It can be made more useful if the constituents are assigned to categories which are given appropriate names, or labels. Thus, *Harry* might be given the label 'Noun Phrase' and *enjoyed his first visit* the label 'Verb Phrase'; *enjoyed* might be labelled 'Verb' and *his first visit* identified as another occurrence of the category 'Noun Phrase', and so on for all the constituents in the sentence.

A well-known analysis of English surface structure is E. A. Nida *A Synopsis of English Syntax*, originally written in 1943 and published in a revised edition in 1966. Nida indicates the immediate constituents by means of a series of brackets drawn below the sentence. In addition, Nida uses a number of symbols to indicate the basic construction types in English. In the following diagram an arrow is used to indicate a modifier-head construction type, with the arrow pointed towards the head, or modified word, and a cross indicates a non-headed construction type:

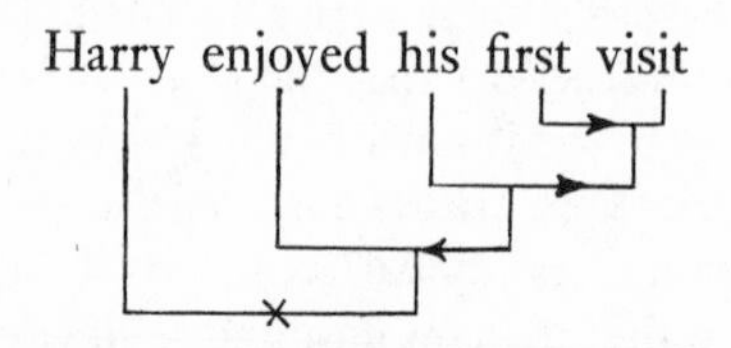

Another way of representing surface structure relations is the 'Chinese box' diagrams used by W. Nelson Francis in *The Structure of American English* (1958). In Francis's presentation, IC structure is indicated by enclosing each ultimate constituent in a box, and drawing larger and larger boxes round each of the structures into which they combine:

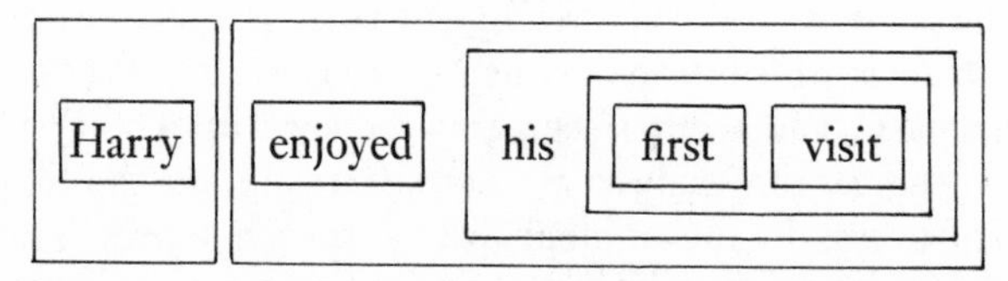

Immediate constituent diagrams like those used by Nida and Francis show the interlocking patterns of relationships in simple sentences in a particularly graphic way, but the diagrams are difficult to draw and quickly become confusing if the method of analysis is extended to longer or more complicated sentences.

In immediate constituent analysis it is usually assumed that constituents should be grouped into binary structures wherever possible. This requirement can give rise to difficulties as, for example, when we attempt to impose a strictly binary analysis on such sequences as *Peter*, *Paul and Mary* and *beautiful big old house*. An alternative approach is to dispense with the requirement that sentences should be analysed in binary terms and to consider them instead as potentially multipartite, i.e., with the constituents arranged like beads on a string. A type of analysis often found in language teaching texts is as follows:

Subject	Predicator	Object		
		determiner	numeral	noun head
Harry	enjoyed	his	first	visit

The analysis of sentences along these lines is similar to tagmemic, or 'slot and filler', grammar and the diagrams are often referred to as slot-and-filler diagrams. As we have seen in Chapter 2 (p. 23), each grammatical sequence may be thought of as a row of vacant pigeon-holes, or 'slots', into which the words are fitted according to their class membership. Labels are provided as a convenient means of referring to the class of forms which appear in a given pigeon-hole.

Tagmemic analysis is primarily associated with the name of the American linguist K. L. Pike, although it has points in common with other models of grammar, including several that have been widely used as a basis for language teaching. According to Pike, the basic units of grammar should neither be expressed in terms of function alone, in such strings as Subject + Predicator + Object, nor in terms of form alone, in such strings as Noun Phrase + Verb Phrase + Noun Phrase. Rather, both function and form should be expressed together, in such strings as S:NP + P:VP + O:NP, which can be read as 'Subject slot filled by a Noun Phrase, followed by Predicator slot filled by a Verb Phrase, followed by Object slot filled by a Noun Phrase'. The basic unit of grammar is a form-class correlation, or *tagmeme* (from the Greek word *tagma* meaning 'arrangement'), which is thought of as corresponding to the contrastive sound units (phonemes) in phonology, and the units of meaningful form (morphemes) in morphology. Each tagmeme is the correlation of a grammatical function or slot with the class of mutually substitutable items occurring in that slot. Tagmemes are strung together into sequences referred to as 'patterns', 'syntagmemes' or 'constructions'. Constructions are found at a number of different ranks (e.g., sentence, clause, phrase, word, morpheme) and a limited number of construction types are identified at each rank. In the analysis of constructions, provision is made for the fact that some tagmemes occur optionally, and that some are relatively fixed while others are movable and occur in more than one position. As with other varieties of structural grammar, the concept is that of a unified, tightly interlocking system, rather than an amorphous mass of unrelated or loosely related details. In a tagmemic analysis the broad outlines are presented first in order to focus attention on the way in which a limited number of structural relationships, occurring again and again in different combinations, build up to form a large number of sentence types.

The grammars of Fries, Pike and Nida have proved popular with language teachers because of their apparent precision and objectivity, their consistent use of one uniform technique of description, and their attempt to show in simple terms how the language system functions as a whole. Of the three types of grammar tagmemics is the most highly developed, and has a number of advantages from a language teaching point of view. One advantage is that the framework of analysis is conceptually simple and requires little explanation. As a result, most of the categories and relationships employed by the tagmemicist in linguistic description can be utilized by the teacher without the need to spend a lot of time discussing the linguistic theory which underlies the pedagogic examples. Another advantage is that language learners readily accept the notion of a set of grammatical patterns that can be identified, remembered and compared with other patterns. A tagmemic analysis containing sets of patterns abstracted at a number of different ranks (e.g., phrase-patterns, clause-patterns, sentence-patterns) appeals to students as a straightforward expression of the concept of linguistic system, and provides a frame of reference in terms of which a multitude of details can be related to one another and fitted together into a meaningful whole. A third advantage is the fact that a grammatical statement of the tagmemic type can easily be converted into simple diagrams, or used as the basis for pedagogically useful exercises.

4 Phrase structure grammar[1]

In the two decades after the Second World War techniques of pattern practice and grading based on a combination of taxonomic linguistics and behavioural psychology were firmly established as a part of foreign language teaching methodology. Methods of mother-tongue instruction, on the other hand, either remained fairly traditional, with much time devoted to précis, the analysis of literary texts, and the parsing of sentences on a largely intuitive, logico-semantic basis, or tended to emphasize creative self-expression with little attempt to provide any systematic instruction in the underlying principles of grammar. More recently, the interest of linguists and language teachers alike has centred on the development of various generative models in linguistics, of which Chomsky's transformational-generative grammar in particular has been very widely discussed. As we have seen (Chapter 2), a generative grammar is one which aims to specify the nature of a speaker's knowledge about his language, but with such accuracy and in such detail that someone who does not know the language will be able to produce its forms simply by following the rules of the grammar, and without having to refer to any source of information outside the grammar. A transformational grammar is one which incorporates two aspects of syntactic description, a surface structure and a more abstract deep structure, together with a set of transformational rules relating deep and surface structure. Transformational-generative grammar as developed by Chomsky is potentially of great interest to language teachers since it provides deep and important insights into language structure, and in recent years a number of writers have attempted to show how these insights can be utilized in the development of teaching materials for first or second language learners.

The transformational grammar outlined by Chomsky in *Syntactic Structures* (1957) contains three components: phrase structure rules, transformational

[1] We would like to acknowledge the help of Keith Brown in this and the following two sections.

rules, and morphophonemic rules. We will not discuss morphophonemic rules here except to say that they operate on the sequences of symbols generated by the phrase structure and transformational rules and assign a phonemic representation to them. Phrase structure and transformational rules must be discussed in some detail, however. As a simple example of phrase structure rules, consider the following:

1 (i) S → NP + VP
(ii) VP → Vb + NP
(iii) NP → Det + N
(iv) Vb → Aux + V
(v) Det → {the, a, this, that, . . .}
(vi) N → {man, boy, letter, car, policeman, thief . . . }
(vii) Aux → {will, can, might, would . . . }
(viii) V → {post, repair, bake, arrest, buy . . . }

Suppose we interpret each rule X → Y of 1 as the instruction 'rewrite X as Y'. In generating a sentence from these rules we start from the initial symbol S which is rewritten as a string of symbols NP + VP. Rules (ii–iv) develop each of these constituents into further structures. In the last four rules each of the symbols Det, N, Aux and V is replaced by one of the words, or lexical items, in the braces on the right of the rule. The rules of 1 will generate such sentences as *This boy will post the letter*, *That man can repair the car*, *A policeman would arrest the thief*, and automatically assign to each sentence a phrase marker as follows:

2

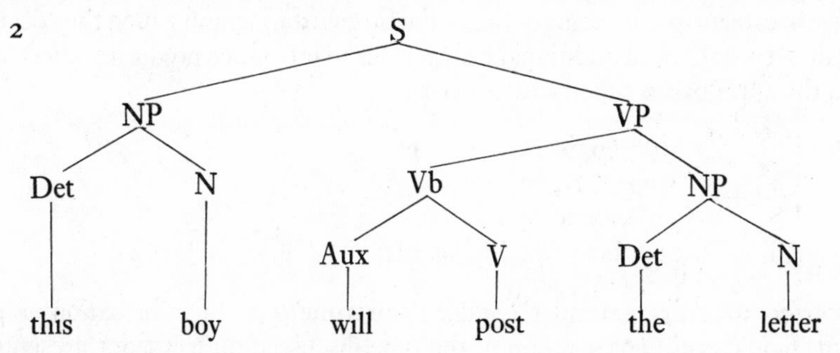

Clearly, we must assume some restriction on the co-occurence of lexical items in order to prevent the grammar from generating such controversial sentences as *The letter will post this boy*, *The policeman can repair that man*. We will return to this question presently; for the time being it is sufficient to see that a problem exists.

So far our rules will generate only a small number of rather simple sentences. We can extend the rules of the grammar and make it capable of generating different types of sentences in various ways. One method is to develop constituents like NP and VP in such a way that we are provided with a set of alternative choices. For example, we might want to include noun phrases consisting of a proper noun, or a pronoun, as well as those which consist of a determiner plus noun as in 1. To allow for such a possibility, rule (iii) would have to be amended as follows (the brackets indicate an alternative choice):

3
$$NP \rightarrow \begin{Bmatrix} \text{Pronoun} \\ \text{Proper Noun} \\ \text{Det} + \text{N} \end{Bmatrix}$$

We would now need additional rules at the end of the grammar:

4 Pronoun → {he, she, you . . .}
Proper Noun → {Robert, Helen, John Brown . . .}

Similarly, we can expand our description of the verb phrase to allow for different types of predicate constructions, for example *The baby should sleep* (intransitive verb); *Helen is happy* (copula verb plus adjective); *He puts the letter in the box* (locational verb + noun phrase + prepositional phrase). Rule (ii) will now look like this:

5
$$VP \rightarrow \begin{Bmatrix} Vb_{intrans} \\ Vb_{trans} + NP \\ Vb_{cop} + Adj \\ Vb_{loc} + NP + \text{Prep Phrase} \end{Bmatrix}$$

In a full grammar of English there would be a very large number of subclasses of verb, categorized in terms of the syntactic environment in which they occur. Again we would need additional lexical rules to introduce predicate adjectives and the appropriate subclasses of verb:

6 $Vb_{intrans}$ → (sleep, work, eat . . .)
Vb_{trans} → (repair, arrest, buy . . .)
Vb_{cop} → (be, become . . .)
Adj → (happy, busy, intelligent . . .)

Phrase structure grammar contains the same type of information as an immediate constituent diagram of the type discussed on p. 55 but presented in the form of rules which are subject to the requirement that every step in the derivation of sentences must be fully and accurately specified. In order to meet this requirement as economically as possible, linguists are constantly searching for new ways of designing the rules of the grammar, and this process may provide pedagogically useful insights into language data. For example, Jacobson (1966) claims that the learning of a number of apparently identical constructions in English can be simplified if the teaching is based on information drawn from a phrase structure grammar. Jacobson discusses three sentences which look alike:

7 (a) He asked me a question.
(b) He made me a suit.
(c) He gave me a book.

When paraphrased, the three sentences still look alike as far as surface structure is concerned:

8 (a) He asked a question of me.
(b) He made a suit for me.
(c) He gave a book to me.

However, a closer examination reveals that 8(a) and 8(b) belong to one sentence type while 8(c) belongs to another type. Thus we can have 9(a) and 9(b) but not 9(c):

9 (a) He asked a question.
(b) He made a suit.
(c) He gave a book.[1]

8(a) and (b) are different from (c) because *of me* and *for me* are independent prepositional phrases while *to me* is an integral part of the sentence. Jacobson calls the first type of sentence a direct object + complement construction and the second type an indirect object construction. The direct object + complement construction is divided into three subtypes as follows:

eliciting: He asked a question of me.
benefactive: He made a suit for me.
directional: He said 'good morning' to me.

The first step is to recognize the grammatical principle involved; the second step is to decide how to teach it. Jacobson suggests that the instructor should teach the indirect object construction independently from the direct object + complement construction, and give extensive practice in the use of the indirect object transformation (*He gave the book to me* ⇒ *He gave me the book*). The direct object + complement construction will be taught at first without the complement expansion, e.g.:

The boy asked a question.
The woman made a dress.
John said 'good morning'.

At this point the instructor will arrange the verb lexicon in three groups: (a) 'eliciting' verbs such as *ask*; (b) 'benefactive' verbs such as *make*, *change*,

[1] *He gave a book* in the sense of 'He gave a book to someone' is questionable. The answer to *What did he give to Mary* is not *He gave a book* but *He gave her a book*. However, *He gave a book* does occur if 'give' has the meaning of 'donate'. Thus, *What did he give to the jumble sale—He gave a book.*

buy; (c) 'directional' verbs such as *say*, *report*, *explain*. Each group of verbs can now be associated with the type of prepositional phrase that follows so that the learner knows he must select *of* + NP in the case of *ask*, *for* + NP in the case of *make*, *change*, *buy*, etc., and *to* + NP in the case of *say*, *report*, *explain*, etc. Finally the instructor presents the optional transformations which turn 8(a) into 7(a) and 8(b) into 7(b), with the warning that they are only acceptable in the case of *ask* and a limited number of benefactive verbs.

5 Transformational grammar

So far, in our discussion of phrase structure grammar, we have only considered rather simple active declarative sentences, but let us suppose we also want to include in our grammar passive sentences like:

10 The letter will be posted by this boy.

Clearly there is a close correspondence in meaning between 10 and the active sentence *This boy will post the letter*, but the two sentences are quite different in terms of the arrangement of their surface structure. It would be possible to write a phrase structure grammar which generated both active and passive forms, but as Chomsky points out, an attempt to extend phrase structure grammar in this way would simply serve to complicate the description without throwing any new light on to language structure. Instead, Chomsky suggests that the notion of phrase structure is adequate for only a small proportion of the sentences of a language, and that the rest should be derived by the application of rules of a different type, called transformational rules, to the structures given by the phrase structure grammar. To illustrate, the passive transformation is given in *Syntactic Structures* as follows:

11 NP_1–Aux–V–NP_2 ⇒ NP_2–Aux+be+en–V–by+NP_1

The sequence of elements to the left of the arrow is called the structural description and the operation indicated by the rule is called the structural change.[1] The passive transformation applies to all strings that can be analysed in terms of the elements referred to in the structural description. For example, the grammar in 1 will generate the phrase marker illustrated in 2. This structure can be analysed in terms of the left-hand side of rule 11, i.e., *this boy* is an NP; *will* is an *Aux*; *post* is a V; *the letter* is an NP. A sentence analysed as *this boy—will—post—the letter* (NP — Aux — V — NP) can be changed by the passive transformation 11 into *the letter—will+be+en—post—by this boy*.[1] This structure becomes *The letter will be posted by this boy* by the operation of further rules. It is necessary to specify the passive transformation in rather an abstract way in order to capture the fact that the rule applies to a wide range

[1] For the purpose of the present discussion the difference between plus-signs and dashes used as concatenation symbols can be disregarded.

of sentences. For example, in the structural description of 11, NP_1 and NP_2 each functions as a variable which may take as its value any noun phrase generated by the phrase structure rules including those which are ultimately realized as *Robert*, *the boy*, *his sister*, *the little old lady with the white cat and the boxer dog who lives across the road*, and others theoretically without limit. In the same way, Aux on the left-hand side of 11 does not refer to any one specific auxiliary, but to a wide range of possible choices, including those which are realized in the sentences *He can deliver the letter*, *He will be delivering the letter*, *He must have been delivering the letter*, and many more.

With respect to their formal properties transformational rules such as 11 are quite different from phrase structure rules like those in 2. Phrase structure rules develop a single symbol at a time. In the fragment of grammar on page 59, for example, the single symbol S is rewritten as NP + VP, the single symbol VP is rewritten as Vb + NP, and so on. Transformational rules are different in that each rule operates on a whole structure, provided it can be analysed in terms of the elements referred to on the left-hand side of the rule. Phrase structure rules are very restricted in terms of the way they can operate, but transformational rules can perform a number of complex operations. For example, rule 11 permutes two NPs and adds a number of elements. Transformational rules can also delete elements, as seen in the rule which changes the underlying structure of *The letter will be posted by NP* into *The letter will be posted*. Rule 11 is fundamentally different from the rules of phrase structure grammar in another important respect. The limitations on phrase structure grammar mean that each phrase structure rule applies or fails to apply to a given sequence of elements according to the symbols actually present in the sequence, without reference to any of the earlier rules in the grammar. In the case of 11, however, we must know not only that *this boy*, *will*, *post*, *the letter* are constituents, but also what kind of constituents they are. Unlike phrase structure grammar, 11 requires us to 'look back' to earlier stages of the derivation in order to determine whether the passive rule will apply.

A study of English reveals many sets of sentences which can be related by transformational rules. For example, Chomsky (1968a) discusses the following interrogative sentences:

12 Who expected Bill to meet Tom?
13 Who(m) did John expect to meet Tom?
14 Who(m) did John expect Bill to meet?
15 What (books) did you order John to ask Bill to persuade his friends to stop reading?

As the above examples show, a noun phrase in any of the three italicized positions in a sentence such as '*John* expected *Bill* to meet *Tom*' can be questioned. The process can be stated informally:

16 (a) Assign the marker *wh*- to a noun phrase.
(b) Place the marked noun phrase at the beginning of the sentence.
(c) Move a part of the verbal auxiliary to the second position in the sentence.
(d) Replace the marked noun phrase by an appropriate interrogative form (*who*, *what*, etc.)

Sentence 13, for example, is formed by assigning the marker *wh*– to the noun phrase 'someone' in 'John expected someone to meet Tom'. The marked noun phrase is then placed at the beginning of the sentence, giving '*wh*-someone John expected to meet Tom'. The process of auxiliary attraction 16(c) gives '*wh*–someone did John expect to meet Tom' and, finally, the process of phonological interpretation 16(d) gives 13.

Sentence 15 shows that these processes can extract any noun phrase, subject to certain restrictions which we need not go into here, and place it at the beginning of the sentence, however complex the sentence structure may be.

Another important series of transformations form what are known traditionally as subordinate clauses and infinitival and gerundial phrases:

17 He said *that John went to the theatre.*
I stayed at home *while John went to the theatre.*
John, *who went to the theatre*, saw 'Hamlet'.
John dined after *going to the theatre.*
John didn't want *to go to the theatre.*
We didn't like *John going to the theatre.*
John's going to the theatre surprised his friends.

In a transformational analysis it can be shown that the italicized portion of each of the above sentences derives from the structure underlying the sentence *John went to the theatre*. In other words, by using transformational rules we are able to state systematic relations between sentences, even though in terms of their superficial structure the sentences may be quite different from one another.

In *Aspects of the Theory of Syntax*, published in 1965, Chomsky suggested a number of important modifications to transformational theory. For example, he proposed an extension of phrase structure grammar to include rules of the following type:

18 (i) $\text{VP} \rightarrow \text{Vb}\begin{Bmatrix} \text{(NP) (Prep Phrase)} \\ \text{S} \end{Bmatrix}$
(ii) $\text{NP} \rightarrow \text{(Det) N (S)}$

In 18(i) the brace brackets indicate that VP may be rewritten either as Verb followed by two optional elements, Noun Phrase and Prepositional Phrase, or as Verb followed by Sentence. In 18(ii) Noun Phrase is rewritten as Noun, preceded optionally by Determiner and followed optionally by Sentence. The new phrase structure rules contain two instances of the symbol S which marks the position where an embedded sentence may be introduced. Rules 18(i) and 18(ii) are recursive in that the symbol S constitutes an instruction to return to the beginning and to run through the rules a second time, thus generating a 'sentence within a sentence'. The process of recursion can apply over and over again so that the phrase structure, or base, rules are capable of generating sentences in which clauses are embedded inside clauses in a series to which there is no definite limit.

We can now return to the question of how to impose restrictions on the co-occurrence of nouns and verbs so that the grammar will generate, for example, *This boy will post the letter* but not *This letter will post the boy*. The approach adopted in *Aspects* is to include rules like those of 19 in the grammar:

19 (i) N → [+N, ±Common]
(ii) [+Common] → [±Count]
(iii) [−Common] → [±Animate]
(iv) [+Animate] → [±Human]
(v) [−Count] → [±Abstract]

The function of rules 19(i–v) is to develop the category Noun into a set of grammatical features. Rule (i) states that every member of the category 'Noun' has the property, or feature, of being a Noun and the property of being either 'Common' (*boy*, *girl*, *table*) or 'non-Common'. Rule (ii) states that all categories with the property 'Common' must be either countable (*boy*, *table*, *chair*) or uncountable (*tea*, *bread*, *sugar*). Rule (iii) states that all categories with the property 'non-Common' must be either animate (*Robert*, *Helen*) or non-animate (*Edinburgh*, *Egypt*), and so on. The grammar will now generate structures which contain complex symbols, e.g.: [+N, +Common, +Count, +Animate, +Human] or [+N, +Common, +Count, —Animate]. If we assume a lexicon, or word list, which has entries in the following form:

20 *boy* [+N, +Common, +Count, +Animate, +Human]
letter [+N, +Common, +Count, −Animate]

we can formulate a rule which allows us to insert a lexical item into a structure generated by the grammar whenever a certain type of symbol in that structure matches a similar symbol in the lexical entry. Since nouns are selected first in the *Aspects* model, verbs have to be specified according to the syntactic environment in which they occur. For example, the deviance of *This letter will post the boy* is accounted for by saying that the verb *post* occurs only with human nouns in the subject position and inanimate nouns in the object position. We can include a rule to this effect which will specify that the verb *post* is selected only in those cases where the subject noun is marked by the feature [+Human] and the object noun is marked by the feature [−Animate].

Given this framework, we can remove rules like those in 5 and 6 from the grammar, and rephrase as in 18(i), where the brackets indicate optional constituents. We can now insert into any of the structures generated by the grammar any verb which is classified in the lexicon as belonging to the appropriate environment.

We saw in the previous chapter that transformational linguists aim to specify the nature of language competence, seen as a highly abstract system of rules which underlie performance. Chomsky makes it quite clear that neither the *Syntactic Structures* nor the *Aspects* model is intended in any sense to be a model of performance, that is, a representation of the way language is used in actual communication. Since the provision of data which can serve as a basis for communication is precisely the purpose of a pedagogic grammar, it might seem that there is little point in looking to transformational grammar for ideas about how to handle language in the classroom. However, we find in practice that the conceptually simpler system of *Syntactic Structures* does suggest many useful ideas for the design of language teaching materials. Many of the rules in *Syntactic Structures* are of a familiar type which differ from traditional presentations mainly in that Chomsky's rules are more carefully formulated and reveal more clearly the importance of deep-level generalizations. The innovations of *Aspects* led to a more comprehensive model, and to a more abstract representation of deep structure. Consequently, although the revised version of transformational grammar has revealed a number of facts about the structure of English which are of great value as background knowledge for teachers, these insights may prove difficult to utilize in the classroom since they cannot be fully understood without reference to a rather complex apparatus of rules.

6 Case grammar

We have seen that a constituent structure analysis of *This boy will post the letter* runs as follows: it is a sentence (S) composed of a noun phrase (NP) and a verb phrase (VP), the noun phrase is composed of a determiner (Det) and a noun (N), and the verb phrase is composed of a verb (Vb) and a noun phrase (NP). In addition, traditional grammar provides information of the following sort: the NP *this boy* functions as the subject of the sentence, whereas the VP *will post the letter* functions as the predicate; the NP *the letter* functions as the object of the Vb, and the Vb *will post* as its main verb. Following Chomsky (1965), we call such terms as 'noun phrase', 'verb phrase' categorial labels, and such terms as 'subject', 'object' functional labels. Chomsky proposes that we define the notion 'Subject of' as [NP, S] and say, with respect to 2, that *this boy* is the subject of the sentence *This boy will post the letter* by virtue of the fact that it is the NP which is directly dominated by S in the phrase marker associated with the sentence. Similarly, the following definitions are proposed:

'Predicate of' [VP, S]
'Direct Object of' [NP, VP]
'Main Verb of' [Vb, VP]

Grammatical relations of the sort that hold between *boy* and *post* and between *post* and *letter* are defined derivatively in terms of the functional relations already established. In principle, then, according to Chomsky, we extract information concerning grammatical functions directly from the rewriting rules of the base, so as to avoid having to elaborate the rules to provide specific mention of grammatical functions.

One reason why sentences with superficially different structures are felt to be related is because the functional relationships between the various noun phrases and the verb remain constant under transformation. For example, the subject noun of an active sentence and the head noun of the by-phrase in its passive transform bear the same functional relationship to the verb—both denote the agent of the action denoted by the verb. Returning to a pair of sentences mentioned earlier:

21 (a) This boy will post the letter.
(b) The letter will be posted by this boy.

we find that *this boy* in both sentences may be referred to as the 'logical subject', whereas it is the 'grammatical subject' of the first sentence only. If we suppose that both sentences derive from a common underlying structure similar to 2, then we can account for this sense of relatedness by saying that the 'logical subject' of a passive sentence is the NP directly dominated by S in the underlying phrase marker, and the 'grammatical subject' is the NP directly dominated by S in the derived phrase marker.

However, not all logical subjects are agents like *this boy* in 21(a). Consider for example the following sentences:

22 The boy received a letter.
The boy fell down the stairs.
The boy had a headache.
The boy owned a boxer dog.

The involvement of *the boy* in the event or situation described appears to be quite different in each case, and in none of the sentences can the subject be regarded as an 'agent' in the sense of 'agent' being the deliberate originator of an action.

It appears from the sentences in 22 and from many other examples that the functional relationships between noun phrases and verbs are a good deal more complex than would seem to be suggested by Chomsky's treatment of function. For this reason, Chomsky's conclusions have been challenged by a number of linguists who argue that the definition of 'subject' and 'object' should take precedence over categorial terms like 'noun phrase' and 'verb phrase'. Others have gone further and have suggested that functions like 'subject' and 'object' are relatively superficial, and that underlying them is a 'deep' syntactic specification in which such items as 'agentive', 'instrumental', 'locative', 'dative' are the determinant elements. In particular, Fillmore has argued that the semantic roles which noun phrases have with respect to their predicate verbs and the position of noun phrases in syntactic configurations are two different aspects of description, and that linguistic theory should provide some way of distinguishing between them.

In an attempt to account for the functional relations between noun phrases and the verb, Fillmore, in an article entitled 'The case for case', suggests that the underlying structure of a sentence contains a verb and one or more noun phrases, each noun phrase being associated with the verb in a particular case relationship. Among the cases he proposes are:

Agentive (A), the case of the typically animate perceived instigator of the action identified by the verb

Instrumental (I), the case of the inanimate force or object causally involved in the action or state identified by the verb

Dative (D), the case of the animate being affected by the state or action identified by the verb

Locative (L), the case which identifies the location or spatial orientation of the state or action identified by the verb

Objective (O) (or *Neutral*), the case of anything representable by a noun whose role in the action or state identified by the verb is identified by the semantic interpretation of the verb itself.

There is no one-to-one relationship between case categories in deep structure, and surface structure categories such as 'subject' or 'object'. Thus, *John* is Agentive in 23(a) and (b):

23 (a) John opened the door.
(b) The door was opened by John.

John is Dative in 24(a) and (b), but also in (c):

24 (a) We persuaded John that he would win.
(b) It was apparent to John that he would win.
(c) John believed that he would win.

In all of the following, *the key* is Instrumental:

25 (a) The key opened the door.
(b) John opened the door with the key.
(c) John used the key to open the door.

In 23, 24 or 25 the function of each noun phrase remains the same despite the different surface realizations of the sentences. If we want to describe the processes whereby a set of case categories in deep structure is realized in different ways in surface structure, we need to know the transformational properties of verbs, which include the selection of prepositions and complementizers (*that*, *-ing*, *to*, etc.) appearing in surface structure, and the choice of one noun phrase to become the surface subject. For example, 'unmarked' active sentences like 23(a) follow the rule suggested by Fillmore: 'if there is an A it becomes the subject; otherwise the subject is the O.' For passive sentences like 23(b) we need a rule which states that if there is an A and an O and the O is selected as subject, then the verb must be in the passive form and the A must be preceded by the preposition *by* and follow the verb.

The emphasis on predicates and role-types in Fillmore's grammar makes it possible to separate purely syntactic phenomena, having to do with the left-to-right positioning of elements in the flow of speech, from semantic interpretation. One advantage of this approach is that two phonologically distinct predicate verbs—*buy/sell*, *teach/learn*, *send/receive*—can be interpreted as being semantically identical in that they have the same number of elements in the same roles, but differ in the processes which arrange their elements into syntactic configurations. Thus, in the pair of sentences *John sold the house to Bill/Bill bought the house from John* the relationship of 'John' to 'sold' is the same as that of 'bought' to 'John', and the relationship of 'sold' to 'Bill' is the same as that of 'Bill' and 'bought'. Using case notions we are able to express the fact that in both sentences *John* is Agentive, *the house* is Objective and *Bill* is the 'receiver' (Benefactive).

The relevance of case grammar to language teaching has not yet been fully explored, but one possible application is suggested by Frederick Bowers (1971). Bowers shows how the notion of optional transformations enables us to distinguish between two kinds of meaning in utterances: 'propositional' meaning which is concerned with the logical relationship of words to each other, and 'situational' meaning, which reflects the speaker's ability to emphasize one part of the proposition rather than another, thus expressing his attitude to the propositional content of the utterance. The relation between propositional and situational meaning may be described in terms of a transformational model of grammar in which the propositional meaning of a sentence is equivalent to its deep structure. The deep structure is then converted into a surface structure by transformations which reorder deep structural items. Fillmore's case grammar has several advantages over Chomsky's transformational model if our aim is to account for the propositional synonymy between sentences, since the deep structures in Fillmore's grammar are further removed from the superficial form of sentences, and more similar to their semantic structure than are the deep structures postulated in *Aspects*. Some of the types of reordering which are possible using Fillmore's model can be seen from the following groups of examples, where noun phrases in deep structure are marked prepositionally to indicate case (of = Objective, to = Dative, by = Agentive, with = Instrumental):

26 *deep structure*:

give (of) that book (to) me (by) John

surface structures:

John gave me that book.
John gave that book to me.
I was given that book by John.
That book was given to me by John.

27 *deep structure*:

please (of) her (to) John

surface structures:

She was pleasing to John.
She pleased John.
John was pleased with her.

28 *deep structure*:

give (of) the money (to) my son (by) me

surface structures:

I gave my son the money.
I gave the money to my son.
What I gave my son was the money.
The person I gave the money to was my son.
What I did was give my son the money.

29 *deep structure*:

break (of) your window (by) us (with) our ball

surface structures:

We broke your window with our ball.
Our ball broke your window.
Your window was broken by our ball.
Your window got broken.
Your window broke.

The effect of these reorderings is to allow the speaker to topicalize or focus attention on any item of the propositional structure of the sentence, either by transferring the topicalized noun phrase to a surface subject position, or by the use of such items as *it* or *what* in subject position. The sentences in 29 are particularly interesting in that they constitute a 'paradigm of increasing irresponsibility'; the speaker increasingly obscures his own role by emphasizing the other noun phrases. Sets of sentences like those illustrated above can clearly play a part in teaching students the use of language. Moreover, the processes described by Bowers have relevance for the study of rhetoric and the interpretation of texts, since one function of rhetoric is to arrange the surface structure of a discourse in such a way that the receiver of the message has as little difficulty as possible in understanding what is being said.

7 Propositional and modal information in a grammar

As we have seen, case grammar represents deep structure in terms of an array of noun phrases in association with a verb. This array constitutes what we might call the propositional content of sentences. A grammar of this type enables us to recognize the cognitive equivalence of sentences which may look very different from each other on the surface. Thus, it enables us to say that the different surface forms in, for example, 29 above are derived from a common proposition in their deep structure representations. This deep structure might be expressed as a simple tree-diagram in the following way:

30

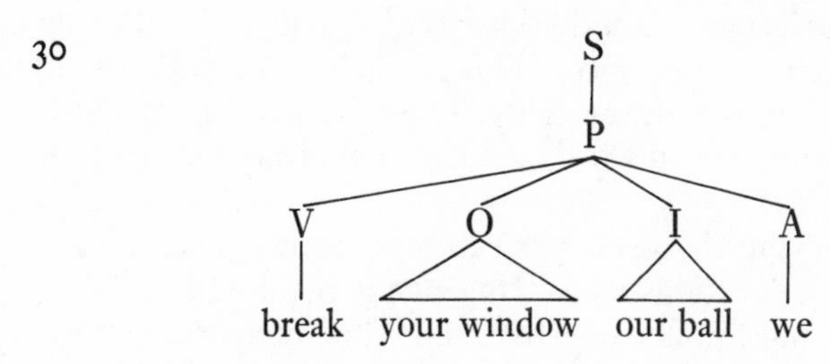

Here, the letters O, I and A stand for the cases Objective, Instrumental and Agentive, and the triangles indicate that other details of the full deep structure formulation have been omitted.

We can say, then, that 30 represents the common propositional content of the first three surface forms in 29. But now suppose we consider sentences which differ from those in 29 in that the tense or aspect of the verb is different, as for example in the following:

31 Our ball has broken your window.
32 Your window has been broken by our ball.

The relationships between the noun phrases and the verb remain the same, and in this respect we might wish to say that these sentences express the same proposition as those in 29. At the same time, it is obvious that they do not express exactly the same cognitive meaning. This is perhaps even more obvious when we compare the following with the sentences in 28 above:

33 I will give my son the money.
34 I may give my son the money.

Again, although these sentences would have exactly the same representation in deep structure as the sentences in 28 in respect of the basic proposition they express, in the sense that the noun phrases and their relationship to the verb remain the same, the use of modal verbs clearly gives them a different meaning.

What these observations indicate is that it is not enough that the deep structure of sentences should only contain information about *propositional meaning*; it must also include information about *modal meaning*. We must therefore postulate two basic elements in the deep structure of sentences: a proposition consisting of noun phrases in association with a verb and a modality constituent consisting of such features as tense, aspect, mood, negation and so on. Such a deep structure would be represented not as in 30 (where the modality element is omitted) but as follows:

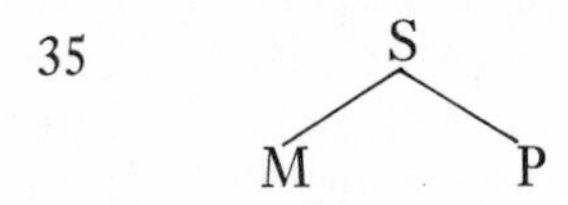

The differences between 31 and 32 and the surface forms given in 29 would be accounted for not in terms of the proposition, which is the same for all of these sentences, but in terms of the modality. The same is true of 33 and 34 in comparison with the sentences in 28; they differ in modality but not in propositional content.

These two basic elements in the deep structure of sentences may be said to reflect two of the basic functions which language is required to fulfil. It is required on the one hand to refer to activities, events, processes and so on, to express the way speakers of a language see the world around them as organized in a certain way. This function is provided for by the propositional constituent of the case grammar. As Fillmore himself puts it:

> The case notions comprise a set of universal, presumably innate, concepts which identify certain types of judgements human beings are capable of making about the events that are going on around them, judgements about such matters as who did it, who it happened to, and what got changed. (Fillmore 1968, p. 24)

The modality constituent of case grammar accounts for a second basic function of language. This has to do with the fact that in referring to events and so on the speaker also expresses his orientation to them. This orientation may be 'physical' in the sense that it involves the speaker placing himself at the moment of speaking in relation to the event he is referring to. This feature of orientation is provided for by tense and aspect. The orientation may also be of a 'psycho-sociological' kind whereby the speaker takes up a certain attitude in relation to what he is referring to, representing it as something which is likely, or possible, or desirable, or questionable, or as requiring to be brought about. This aspect of orientation is provided for by the grammatical categories of mood and modality in the traditional sense.

Speakers of a language, then, use sentences not simply to express propositions which refer to what happens in the world around them but also to express their role as speakers in relation to what they refer to, and therefore, necessarily, in relation to who they are speaking to. The grammar provides the resources for the fulfilling of these functions by means of its propositional component on the one hand and its modality component on the other. In case grammar it is the former which receives detailed attention: the latter is mentioned only so that it may be excluded from consideration. This enables Fillmore to provide a very clear account of the propositional structure of sentences but it must be borne in mind that he does only deal with this aspect of grammar. This is not meant to be a criticism; advances in linguistic description, as in any systematic field of enquiry, are generally made by narrowing the focus of attention to specific areas. Furthermore, such a concentration of interest frequently yields well-defined insights which can be more readily exploited for practical purposes. We have already seen one possible application of case grammar to language teaching and other applications will be considered later in this chapter. Meanwhile we will review certain attempts to widen the scope of grammatical statement to describe those aspects of linguistic structure which reflect the functions which Fillmore does not account for.

8 Halliday's functional grammar

Fillmore does not talk about the basic constituents of his deep structure in terms of functional components of the language. His grammar emerges from a study of the internal working of the linguistic system. Halliday, on the other hand, approaches language not from within, as it were, but from outside. He begins with the question: Why is language structured in the way it is and not in some other way? And his answer is: Because it reflects the functions which language is required to serve as a means of social communication. He distinguishes three major functions. The first is one which we have already recognized as being accounted for by Fillmore's propositional component. Halliday calls it the *experiential* or *ideational* function:

Language serves for the expression of 'content': that is, of the speaker's experience of the real world, including the inner world of his own consciousness. We may call this the *ideational* function . . .. In serving this function, language also gives structure to experience, and helps to determine our way of looking at things, so that it requires some intellectual effort to see them in any other way than that which our language suggests to us. (Halliday 1970a, p. 143.)

It is the ideational function, then, that both expresses and constrains our concept of reality; it is the means by which we impose order on our experience by the recognition of cause and effect relations and so on. Halliday touches here on the question of how far our view of reality is in correspondence with the structure of our language. This question will be taken up in Chapter 6 of this volume. What we are concerned with here is how Halliday sees this ideational function to be reflected in linguistic structure.

Halliday points to the transitivity system of the grammar as being the area which reflects the ideational function of language. Thus he thinks of transitivity as accounting for types of processes in which participant and circumstantial roles are involved. For example, a sentence like:

36 Patrick bought an armchair at the sales.

is said to contain a process, expressed by the verb, two participant roles, an 'actor' (*Patrick*) and a 'goal' (*an armchair*) and a circumstantial role 'place' (*at the sales*). It is the participant roles which enter into the definition of different sentence or clause types, the circumstantial roles being peripheral to the nature of the process itself. Apart from the roles of 'actor' and 'goal', Halliday also distinguishes participant roles like 'resultant', 'beneficiary', 'recipient', 'instrument' and 'force'.

It is easy to see how closely Halliday's transitivity functions correspond to Fillmore's cases. The correspondences might be set out in a simple table:

Fillmore cases	*Halliday roles*
agentive	actor
objective	goal
instrumental	instrument
dative	recipient
factitive	resultant
benefactive	beneficiary
source	force
locative	place

We might notice that Fillmore, working as it were from within the grammatical system, naturally relates these semantic notions to the linguistic category of case, whereas Halliday, working from outside the system, naturally associates them directly with the sociological concept of role. Both, however, are dealing with the same aspect of linguistic structure. The proposition in case grammar corresponds to the transitivity options as described in Halliday's 'systemic' or 'functional' grammar. But Halliday does not confine himself, as Fillmore does, to an account of this area of the grammar. He recognizes as equally important two further functions each of which determines the way language is structured.

The first of these relates to the way the speaker expresses his orientation to the propositional or ideational content of his message—the function which is reflected, as was observed earlier, in Fillmore's undeveloped modality component. This Halliday refers to as the *interpersonal* function and it is manifested by the grammatical category of mood. This category is realized through the system of options exemplified by the 'sentence-types' declarative, interrogative and imperative and through the modality system exemplified by modal verbs like *must*, *will*, *may* and so on and by such adverbs as *possibly*, *perhaps* and *certainly*. Thus, if we consider a sentence like:

37 Did Patrick buy an armchair at the sales?

The proposition which this sentence contains is the same as that contained in 36. It might be represented either by specifying roles operating in a transitivity system as follows: actor-process-goal-place; or by specifying cases after the manner of Fillmore as follows: verb-agentive-objective-locative. But although the two sentences are alike in their exemplification of options in the transitivity system, they differ in that 36 exemplifies the declarative in the mood system, whereas 37 exemplifies the interrogative. An utterance of 37 can be said to have the effect of casting the speaker in the role of enquirer vis-a-vis the hearer and of imposing the role of respondent on the hearer at the same time: in short, it involves interpersonal activity. Similarly, the imperative assigns roles to speaker and hearer in an interaction: the speaker assumes the right to direct the activity of the hearer and thereby assigns, at the moment of speaking at least, a subservient role to the person he addresses.

It is easy to see that certain areas of grammar can be put into correspondence with certain interpersonal functions and can be said to reflect the operation of language as a means of social interaction. Thus the three options in the mood system for English sentences—declarative, imperative, interrogative—can be said to relate to the three principal communicative functions of language: telling someone something, asking someone something, and asking someone to do something. These functions provide for language being, in Abercrombie's phrase, 'a means of social control' (Abercrombie 1956).

We may now look briefly at the modal verbs from this functional point of view. Again, it is clear that these verbs can be fairly closely associated with social activity, and in particular with the rights and obligations which attach to the different roles that people play (see chapter 6 of this volume). Certain modal verbs clearly relate to rights, as for example, *can* and *may* in such sentences as:

38 You can leave at 10 o'clock.
39 You may leave at 10 o'clock.

Other modals just as clearly relate to obligations, as for example *must* and *ought to* in such sentences as:

40 You must leave at 10 o'clock.
41 You ought to leave at 10 o'clock.

As the ambiguity of this last example suggests, however, these modals have to do also with what we might call physical as well as social factors. Corresponding to the social factors of rights and obligations we have physical factors which determine possibility and necessity. Thus, for example, we can have ambiguities as illustrated by the following sentences:

42 Fiona cannot come to the party (her mother won't let her).
43 Fiona cannot come to the party (she's got the 'flu).
44 You ought to leave at 10 o'clock (to catch the train).
45 You ought to leave at 10 o'clock (to avoid compromising me).

Here, 42 refers to what Fiona has the right to do and 43 to what she has the ability to do and relates to possibility. Similarly, 44 refers to necessity and 45 to obligation.

Notice that 44 and 45 introduce another factor affecting modality. Rights/obligations and possibility/necessity do not constrain events in an absolute way. One can recognize an obligation without submitting to it, and one can recognize a general necessity but accept that a particular event may not be bound by it. In other words, the modals also reflect the notions of volition and variation, volition being the individual's scope for freedom of behaviour and variation being the degree to which events are not constrained by what is necessary and possible. Volition and variation are implied in *ought to* but not in *must*, and it is this which distinguishes the two modals. These factors also serve to distinguish the two modals which relate to rights: *can*, we may say, is not marked for volition/variation, whereas *may* is. In other uses of *may*, indeed, it is the volition/variation element which is given prominence, as in sentences like:

46 He may come to the party (but on the other hand he may not).
47 It may rain tomorrow (but on the other hand it may not).

One possible way of thinking of these four modals, then, is to see them as focusing on these different factors. The four modals we have been discussing might then be represented roughly in the following way:

		variation	*volition*
right	You can go.		You may go.
possibility	He can be here by 10 o'clock.	He may be here by 10 o'clock.	

		variation	*volition*
obligation	You must go.		You ought to go.
necessity	He must have arrived by now.	He ought to have arrived by now.	

It is not being claimed, of course, that this is the only way in which the meaning of the modal verbs can be described. Alternative, and more complete, formulations are to be found in Palmer (1965), Boyd and Thorne (1969) and Leech (1971). Our interest here is in considering how modality can be said to reflect the social functioning of language.

It is easy to see that a consideration of what we have called the modal meaning of sentences leads the linguist to investigate how sentences are used to perform different communicative acts. Halliday is not the only linguist who has turned his attention to this aspect of language. In earlier work in transformational-generative grammar it was considered unreasonable to expect the linguist to study anything but the structure of sentences and considerations of use were excluded as being aspects of performance and not of central concern to the linguist, whose purpose was seen to be the description of linguistic competence. Recently, however, there have been attempts to incorporate into a description of sentences information about what sentences count as in the performance of communicative acts. The impetus behind these attempts has come from philosophy, and in particular from Austin (1962) and Searle (1969). Briefly, what they say is that in uttering any sentence one is at the same time performing an action; one is not just saying something. Thus if one says:

48 Close the door.
49 I will give you £10.

one is likely to be performing a command in the first instance and a promise in the second. On this interpretation 48 is said to have the illocutionary force of 'command' and 49 the illocutionary force of 'promise', so that a paraphrase of 48 might be something like:

50 I command you to close the door.

and a paraphrase of 49 might be:

51 I promise you that I will give you £10.

All sentences can be said to have an illocutionary element, so that even a sentence like:

52 The kettle is boiling.

can have its illocutionary force made explicit by a paraphrase like:

53 I inform you that the kettle is boiling.

These observations have led a number of linguists to suggest that in the deep structure of all sentences there is a superordinate sentence which expresses the illocutionary force of the sentence as a whole by means of a performative verb like *inform*, *assert*, *order*, *promise* and so on (see Ross 1970, Boyd and Thorne 1969). The deep structures of 48/50, 49/51, and 52/53 would then take roughly the following form:

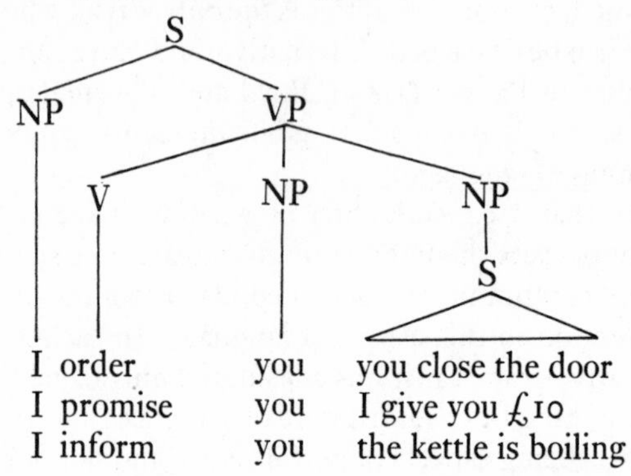

Although syntactic arguments have been proposed in support of the presence of performatives in deep structure (as in Ross 1970), it would appear that by attempting to take into account what sentences mean in terms of the acts they are used to perform, linguists are, in effect, no longer describing competence in the sense in which Chomsky uses that term but aspects of what was previously regarded as performance and so outside the scope of linguistic statement. It can be said that there has been an extension of interest from an exclusive concern with the internal formal properties of language to a consideration of the way in which language connects up with the external world as a means of communication, and this has led to a redefinition of the scope of linguistics. Its aim now is not simply to account for linguistic competence in a narrow sense, the ability to compose and interpret sentences, but to account for communicative competence, the additional ability to use sentences in acts of communication. This widening of scope has important implications for language teaching, as we shall see presently. Meanwhile we have to discuss the third of Halliday's basic functions which is reflected in linguistic structure.

The first of Halliday's functions, the ideational, relates to what he calls transitivity systems, which cover the same grammatical phenomena as the proposition component of the deep structure of case grammar. The second, the interpersonal, relates to mood, including modality, and we have shown how recent developments in generative grammar have attempted to account for this interpersonal function in terms of deep structure, which is essentially an investigation into Fillmore's modality component.

Halliday does not accept the distinction between deep and surface structure, nor indeed between competence and performance, and this leads him to a different formulation of these functional aspects of language. But this formulation is nevertheless based on a distinction between abstract systems and their actual realizations and it is possible to draw parallels between it and the more recent work in generative grammar. We can demonstrate this by considering a sentence cited in Halliday (1970b), and we can then use this sentence as a starting point for discussing the third of Halliday's functions. The sentence is

54 Smith died.

The propositional content of this sentence can be accounted for in terms of transitivity, which expresses the ideational function, and in this respect may be said to contrast with a sentence like:

55 Jones killed Smith.

In Halliday's system 54 might be represented as recipient-process and 55 as actor-process-recipient, and these representations correspond to V–D (verb–dative) and V–A–D (verb–agentive–dative) in Fillmore's case grammar. These two sentences, then, contrast by virtue of their basic propositions, or (equivalently) by virtue of their ideational or experiential functions. But 54 might also be said to contrast with the following sentence:

56 Did Smith die?

This sentence is ideationally identical with 54 in that it contains the same proposition. But it differs in modality. That is to say, it has a different interpersonal function. Thus Halliday would say that in 54 there is a convergence of options from two systems; there is a mapping of an option from the transitivity system on to an option from the mood system.

Transformational grammarians might show the relationship between these sentences in a different way by postulating deep structures in which the basic proposition is contained within an embedded sentence and the interpersonal function accounted for in terms of a superordinate matrix. The deep structures of 54 and 56, for example, might be represented roughly as follows, where the lowest embedded sentence (S_3 in 54 and S_4 in 56) represents the propositional or ideational part of the sentence as a whole and the higher order S nodes account for the modal or interpersonal part:

54

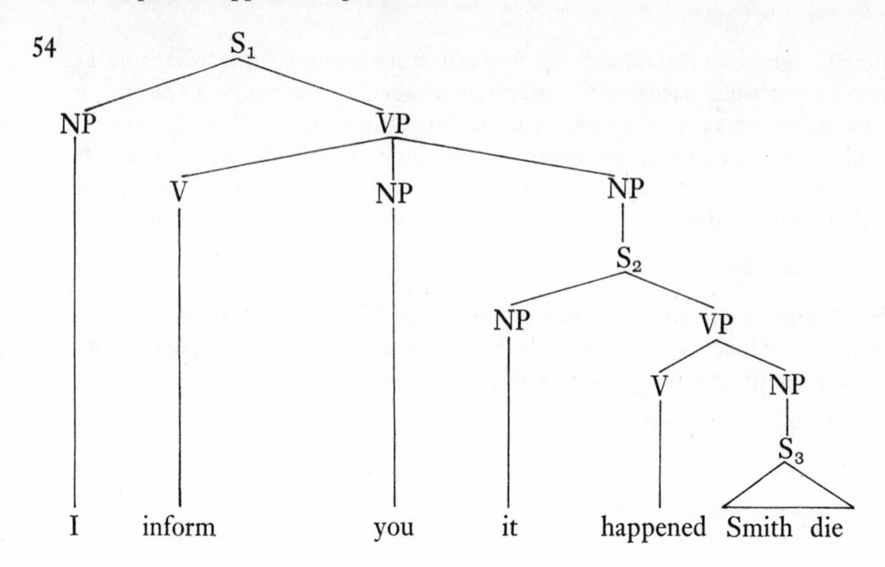
S_1
NP
VP
V
NP
NP
S_2
NP
VP
V
NP
S_3
I
inform
you
it
happened
Smith die

56

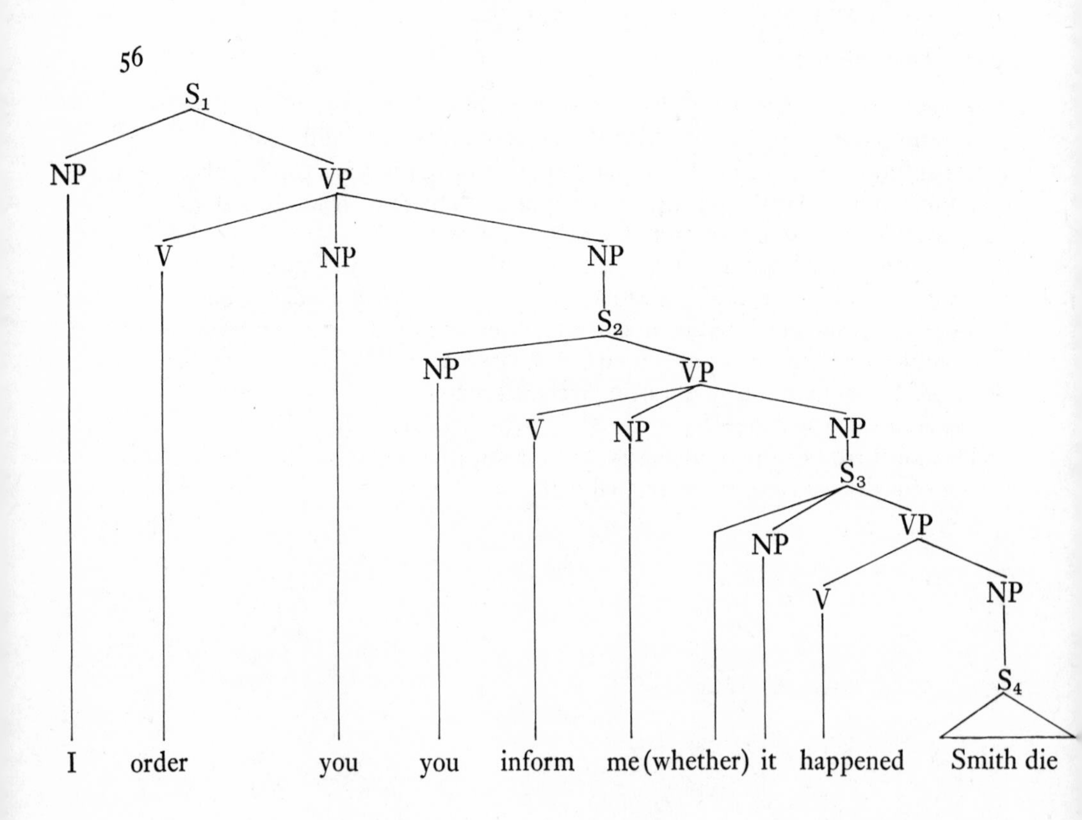
S_1
NP
VP
V
NP
NP
S_2
NP
VP
V
NP
NP
S_3
NP
VP
V
NP
S_4
I
order
you
you
inform
me (whether)
it
happened
Smith die

Actually, it is possible to work out even deeper structures than these. For our purposes, however, there is no need to descend into more detail. All we want to do here is to indicate in a general way how sentences 54 and 56 differ in respect to interpersonal or modal function. Other modal differences can, of course, be indicated in a similar way. Thus the following can be regarded as rough deep structure paraphrases:

57 Smith will die. I predict it happen/Smith die
58 Will Smith die? I order you you predict (whether) it happen/Smith die

Everything in front of the slant line indicates modality or interpersonal function and the proposition after the slant line remains the same.

Sentence 54, then, contrasts with 55 in terms of ideational function, and with 56 in terms of interpersonal function. It also contrasts with the following sentence:

59 The one who died was Smith.

Here we come to the third of Halliday's functions. 59 has the same ideational and interpersonal function as 54, but it differs in respect to what Halliday calls *textual* function. By this he means the way sentences are organized as messages, the way in which the propositional and modal elements are arranged so that they make sense as a piece of communication or a component in discourse. As he puts it:

The basic unit of language in use is not a word or a sentence but a 'text'; and the 'textual' component in language is the set of options by means of which a speaker or writer is enabled to create texts—to use language in a way that is relevant to the context. (Halliday 1970a, pp. 160–1)

Halliday distinguishes six sets of options which constitute the part of language structure which reflects the textual function and to which he gives the general term *theme*. The three most important of these are referred to as *information*, *thematization* and *identification* (Halliday 1967–8). The first of these sets of options, or sub-systems, is realized by phonological means. According to Halliday, any text in spoken English is organized into information units which are marked by tone groups. In 'normal' or 'unmarked' use, the tone group is isomorphic with the sentence so that the sentence represents one information unit. But this is only one option; the sentence can be divided up into a number of information units by means of tone groups. Thus the following sentence is unmarked since the double slant lines indicating tone group boundaries coincide with the sentence boundaries:

60 //John saw the play yesterday//

The following, however, represent marked options:

61 //John// saw the play yesterday//
62 //John// saw the play// yesterday//

Furthermore, according to Halliday, the information can extend beyond clause boundaries, as in the following instance:

//John saw the play yesterday but said nothing about it//

Within each 'message block' or information unit there is a point of 'information focus', an element which is given prominence by being provided with a 'tonic' stress. This element is what is being presented as 'new' within that particular unit of information, the remainder of the unit being 'given', that is to say assumed to be recoverable from previous discourse. In unmarked use, the tonic falls on the accented syllable of the last lexical item in a tone group, but the information focus can be marked by the tonic falling elsewhere. Thus in the following, the elements in italics carry the tonic and are therefore represented as new information:

63 //John gave *Fiona* the tape-recorder// (not Gertrude)
64 //*John* gave Fiona the tape-recorder// (Basil didn't)
65 //John *gave* Fiona the tape-recorder// (He didn't lend it to her)

The information structure of sentences, then, refers to the way sentences are organized phonologically into tone groups each of which represents a unit of information. In each tone group there is a primary stress or tonic and its domain is what is presented as new information, the remainder of the tone group consisting of information which is assumed to be known or given. Information structure, therefore, organizes the sentence as a message, the given and new elements being arranged so that the message form is appropriate in relation to what has preceded it in the discourse. The second set of sub-systems under the general heading of theme, called thematization, organizes a sentence as a message without regard to what has preceded it in the discourse. Thematization has to do with the internal structure of the message as a separate piece of information and not with the external links that relate a particular message with others. As Halliday puts it:

The information systems, in other words, specify a structural unit and structure it in such a way as to relate it to the preceding discourse; whereas thematization takes a unit of sentence structure, the clause, and structures it in a way that is independent of what has gone before. (Halliday 1967–8, p. 212)

Whereas information structure is realized by intonation, thematization is realized by the sequence of elements in the sentence or clause.[1] Thus the

[1] There might be some confusion about the terms *sentence* and *clause* and we have tended to make use of them indiscriminately in this section. Briefly, Halliday uses the term clause in a more traditional sense to refer to a simple or 'kernel' sentence, so that if two of these are conjoined, as in 63 for example, we have a sentence consisting of two clauses. In transformational grammar, all embedded sentences would be clauses and only the superordinate S would be a sentence in Halliday's terms.

first constituent of the clause functions as the *theme* and the remainder of the clause then functions as the *rheme*. Thematization, then, refers to the options available for arranging the elements of a clause into theme and rheme. The unmarked arrangement would be when the theme coincides with the order required by the mood systems. If the mood is declarative, for example, then the first element will be the subject and the following will be unmarked as far as theme-rheme is concerned (a single slant line marks off the theme):

66 John/ saw the play yesterday.

If we have a yes/no, or polar, interrogative then the first element will be that which carries the tense and polarity and the following will be unmarked:

67 Did/ John see the play yesterday?

Similarly, unmarked forms of the *wh*-type interrogatives would be:

68 Who/saw the play yesterday?
69 What/did John see yesterday?

In these two cases, 68 and 69, the theme represents what it is that the speaker wants to know and so marks off what is being talked about, the 'point of departure for the message', as Halliday puts it. Other elements in the clause can be placed in thematic position, however, and then, of course, we get cases of marked theme, as in the following instances:

70 Yesterday/ John saw the play.
71 Yesterday/ did John see the play?
72 Yesterday/ John saw what?
73 Yesterday/ who saw the play?

We now come to the third set of options within the general theme systems of English: that which Halliday refers to as identification. Identification is illustrated by the sentence with which we began our discussion of the textual function:

74 The one who died was Smith.

Here sentence 54 has been 'clefted' to yield an equative form and this, according to Halliday, has the effect of organizing the information in such a way as to give the first part of the sentence the function of 'something or someone to be identified' and the other part—the part after the equating verb—the function of 'identifier'. In the following, however, it is the identifier which serves as theme:

75 Smith was the one who died.

In identifying sentences it is the element which is nominalized which functions as that which is identified, and this may or may not be thematized; it is thematized in 74 but not in 75. The sentences about John seeing the play which we have been considering above can also be converted into equative forms by means of nominalizing certain elements. Thus the following all represent the results of different options in the identification system:

76 The one who saw the play yesterday was John.
77 John was the one who saw the play yesterday.
78 What John saw yesterday was the play.
79 The play was what John saw yesterday.
80 When John saw the play was yesterday.
81 Yesterday was when John saw the play.

Identification, in Halliday's sense, provides for a distribution of information into identified/identifier and so serves to give prominence to different parts of the message or to ensure that the message links up with previous discourse. Halliday points out for example (Halliday 1967–8, p. 210) that the following sentences do not combine to form a text:

82 No one else had known where the entrance to the cave was situated.
83 What John discovered was the cave.

If, however, a different option from the identification system is chosen in the case of 83, then the resulting sentence does form cohesive links with 82. The following, for example, does constitute a text:

84 No one else had known where the entrance to the cave was situated. The one who discovered the cave was John.

9 Transformational and systemic models of grammar

We have pointed out that features of grammar which reflect what Halliday calls the experiential or ideational function and the interpersonal function of language in use are also accounted for in the deep structure of transformational grammars. The theme systems which we have just discussed, and which provide for textual function, however, deal with aspects of linguistic structure which do not appear in the deep structure of sentences. In current transformational analysis the different arrangements of constituents are the consequence of the application of different transformational rules, so that sentences varying with respect to thematization and identification would be represented as stylistically variant surface forms deriving from the same deep structure. This treatment carries with it the implication that two sentences that differ in transitivity or mood, which are accounted for in the deep structure, are more 'different' than two which differ in theme, which has to do with surface structure only. Thus, of the three sentences with which we started our discussion of theme, 54, 56 and 59, 56 would differ more radically from 54 than would 59, which would be thought of as a surface variant. The transformational view of the relationship between sentence 54 and sentences like 59 might be indicated as follows:

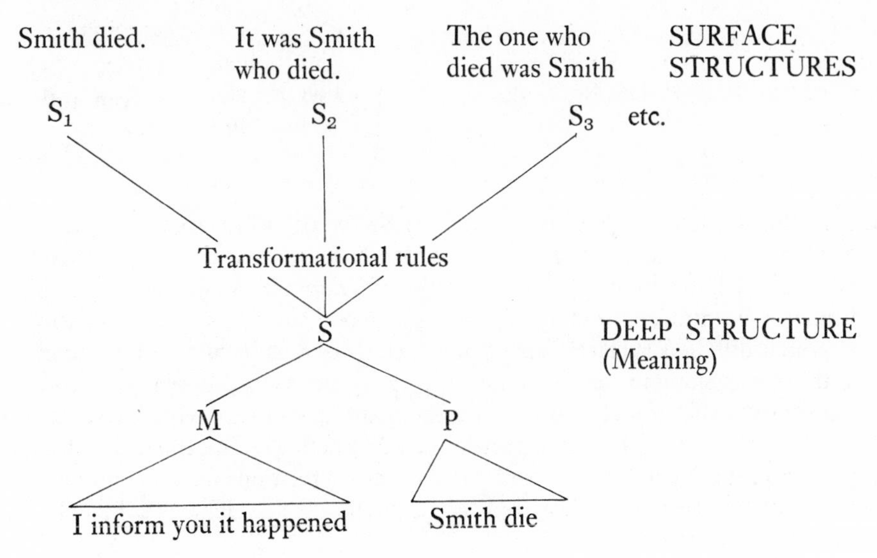

As has already been pointed out, Halliday does not accept the deep structure/surface structure distinction and sees no reason for saying that the meaning residing in those aspects of grammar which reflect ideational and interpersonal functions is more central or basic than that which is associated with the textual function. Since the textual function refers to the way language is used meaningfully to communicate then the part of the grammar which accounts for this function should, in Halliday's view, be given equal prominence and be recognized as having just as much to do with meaning as the other parts of the grammar. As he puts it:

> It is not necessary to argue that one function is more abstract, or 'deeper', than another; all are semantically relevant. (Halliday 1970a, p. 165)

For Halliday, the structure of a sentence exemplifies a number of systems simultaneously: its composition involves the language user in selecting options from the transitivity, mood and theme systems at the same time and mapping them on to each other. The structure of a sentence (or, in Halliday's terms, a clause) is the realization of options from these different systems. Halliday's concept of the relationship between 54, 56 and 59 might be indicated by the following:

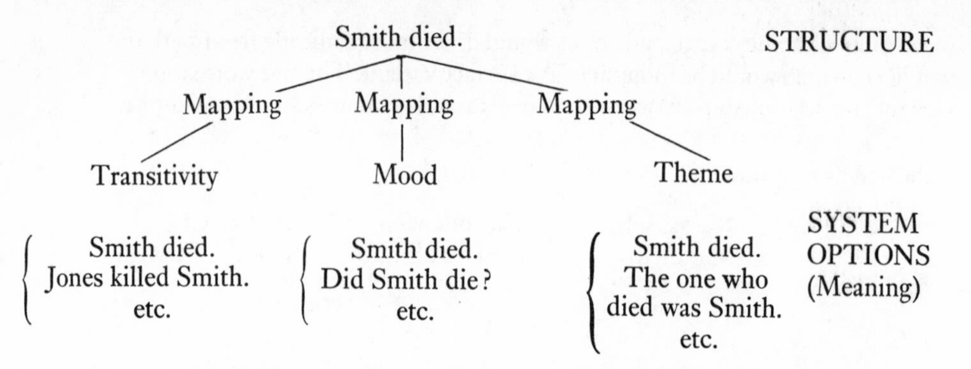

In this section we have tried to clarify the relationship between a transformational-generative approach to linguistic description and the approach taken by Halliday in his systemic 'functional' grammar. As we have seen, the former concentrates attention on aspects of mood and transitivity in relation to which different surface forms can be recognized as having an underlying 'cognitive' synonymy, even though they may function differently in communicative use. Halliday, on the other hand, attempts to give equal weighting to all aspects of linguistic structure and all distinctions of meaning. For him, therefore, there is no set of more basic syntactic relations in terms of which two sentences can be recognized as synonymous. In Halliday's model of description, for example,

54 Smith died.

is neither more nor less synonymous with

59 The one who died was Smith.

than with

85 Smith was dying.

It should be stressed that the generative grammarian's concentration on what Halliday calls transitivity and mood does not necessarily preclude a concern for thematic problems and recent work has shown an increasing interest in the meanings associated with different surface forms of sentences which, with reference to their common deep structure, may still be regarded as 'cognitively' synonymous.

10 Communicative competence

As we have seen, Halliday approaches the description of language structure by asking himself what functions language is required to fulfil. His concern is not simply to describe the system of the language in its own terms but to link this system with the manner in which it is used in communication.

Halliday is not, of course, alone among linguists in recognizing the importance of accounting for the communicative properties of language. His work, as he himself acknowledges, is greatly influenced by the linguists of the Prague School who have for many years been studying what they call 'communicative dynamism' and 'functional sentence perspective', exploring how discourse develops and how the use of different surface forms alters the relative prominence of the items of information which are conveyed. (See Fried 1972, Vachek 1964.)

The interest of the generative grammarians in such notions as illocutionary force also bears witness to a change of emphasis in their work from one which concentrated almost exclusively on the internal formal properties of sentences to one which includes a consideration of what communicative acts sentences may be used to perform. It has also been suggested by some linguists that different surface forms which might otherwise be shown as deriving from a common deep structure may after all be distinguished semantically on the grounds that the use of one rather than another presupposes a different kind of previous knowledge and gives different prominence or focus to the information it contains. It has been proposed, therefore, that presupposition and focus—the latter term being used in a more general sense than in Halliday's 'information focus'—should find a place in deep structure. Others, including Chomsky himself (Chomsky 1968b), feel that this would result in confusion and propose instead that these aspects of meaning should be associated only with surface structures.

It is not clear at present how features like illocutionary force, presupposition and focus in the more general sense can be satisfactorily accounted for in a grammar. What is clear, however, is that the trend in linguistic description is towards what might be called communicative functionalism. A number of writers have expressed the view that Chomsky's delimitation of the scope of linguistic description as having to do with the language user's grammatical competence is too narrow. They point out that 'knowing' a language involves not only the ability to compose correct sentences but also the ability to use them appropriately in acts of communication. (See, for example, Campbell and Wales 1970.) Thus, someone producing sentences 82 and 83, for example, could be said to have grammatical competence in that each of the sentences is correct, but since they do not make sense in combination the second of them is not appropriate in relation to the first. A person knowing English would know this. He would, in other words, have a communicative competence in the language.

To describe communicative competence the linguist has to idealize his data in a different way to allow for considerations of context. How far it is possible to do this without compromising the capacity of a grammar to deal explicitly with underlying syntactic regularities is a matter which is being much debated at the moment. It should be noted that it is far from clear what the term 'communicative competence' itself is intended to cover. Campbell and Wales, for example, speak of it as the linguistic ability 'to produce or understand utterances which are not so much *grammatical* but, more important, *appropriate to the context in which they are made*' (Campbell and Wales 1970, p. 247, our emphasis). The obvious difficulty here is that utterances can take on an enormously wide range of meanings in different contexts. As is pointed out in Bolinger (1971), in the context of, say, a hungry husband returning home from the office, the uttering of the sentence

86 I'm starved.

might well serve the same communicative function as

87 Serve me dinner.

But it is scarcely possible to conceive of a grammar which would represent 86 and 87 as having the same meaning as *sentences*. It is, then, difficult to say how far the scope of grammatical statement can be sensibly extended to account for context. To do so would appear to involve some conflation of the notions of sentence and utterance which linguists have (in theory at least) generally tried to keep distinct.

Not only is there a difficulty in establishing how *many* contexts to consider when specifying the range of appropriateness of an utterance, but there is the problem of knowing how *much* of the context is relevant. We can illustrate this by looking again at sentences 82 and 83. If we assume that the appropriateness of a sentence is dependent only on the sentence that precedes, then it is true, of course, that 83 is not appropriate and the two sentences do not together constitute a text. But if we think of these sentences as part of a larger text, it is possible for them to be linked cohesively together. Let us, for example, assume a context in which two people are discussing what John discovered and let us suppose that one of them insists that what he discovered was not the entrance to the cave but a druidical rocking stone situated nearby. In this context, the second person might utter the following:

88 Everybody had known where the rocking stone was situated. No one else had known where the entrance to the cave was situated. What John discovered was the cave.

Here, sentences 82 and 83 do combine to form part of a text, and in the context provided by the first sentence of 88 the alternative to 83 which appears in 84 is inappropriate. That is to say, the following is *not* a text:

89 Everybody had known where the rocking stone was situated. No one else had known where the entrance to the cave was situated. The one who discovered the cave was John.

What Halliday provides is a systematic account of the options which are available to the users of a language for the creation of texts. He does not provide the conditions whereby the selection of one option is appropriate while the selection of another is not, and in this respect, although his grammar is based on functional notions it cannot be said to be a complete account of communicative competence.

The grammarian can describe the formal resources which are at the disposal of a language user for the performance of communicative acts. Whether he can also describe how these resources are actually used to produce appropriate utterances in context, or whether indeed it is his business to do so, is a controversial question. It is a question which touches on the difference between a linguistic and a sociolinguistic orientation to language study, between a grammatical and an ethnographic description of communicative functions. With the notion of communicative competence we make contact with the area of enquiry which is surveyed in Chapter 6 of this volume.

11 Functional grammar and functional language teaching

Before the learner of a language can be regarded as proficient, he must know not only the basic structural principles of the language (the code) but also how to use sentences in performing acts of communication, and how to combine them to create coherent passages of discourse (use of the code). In other words, in teaching grammar we must set ourselves two goals: we must (a) impart a knowledge of the basic structural principles and (b) ensure that our students know how to put their knowledge of these principles to practical use. In sections 2–6 of this paper we have discussed a number of models of grammar which are concerned with the formal properties of sentences, and which suggest ways in which we might set about imparting a knowledge of the code. In sections 7–10 we have discussed various approaches to grammatical description which take into account the ways in which sentences are related to communicative activity.

For many years, writers on language teaching methodology have tended to stress techniques for teaching the code, but have had relatively little to say about how students can be taught to use the code. In the two previous sections we have seen that grammarians have become increasingly concerned with the characterization of language as an instrument of social communication and that, as a result, the scope of grammatical statement has been extended to cover not only the internal patterns of language as a self-contained system but also the manner in which these patterns relate to the communicative operation of language in use. This change of theoretical perspective coincides with a certain shift of emphasis in language teaching pedagogy. A number of language teachers and applied linguists have suggested that the 'structural' approach to foreign language teaching, which focuses attention on the formal properties of the language being learned and lays stress on the importance of manipulating sentence patterns, does not satisfactorily provide for the learning of communicative competence (see Allen and Widdowson 1974, Allen 1973, Widdowson 1972). This has led to proposals that the 'content' of foreign language courses should be primarily of a communicative rather than of a narrowly conceived linguistic character, and syllabuses have been outlined which consist not of a selection of linguistic structures and lexical items but of communicative, or notional, categories of one kind or another. A syllabus of this sort starts out from the assumption that what the learner needs to know is not so much how to recognize and produce sentences as linguistic objects, but how to make and understand utterances which express certain concepts, perform certain communicative acts, and in general enable the learner to participate in the interactional processes of normal language use.

Recent work in grammar, part of which has been reviewed in previous sections, yields certain notional categories which might be used as teaching units in syllabuses of this communicative kind. In proposals offered by Wilkins (1972), for example, it is suggested that Fillmore's case categories might be included as components of a syllabus. This would mean that instead of having the following sentences introduced in different parts of the syllabus and graded according to their surface structure complexity, they could be introduced together as exemplifying the same basic proposition (i.e. V A O):

90 John broke the window.
91 The window was broken by John.
92 It was John who broke the window.

The first two of these sentences are, of course, often associated by language teachers, but generally the association is made to provide practice in the manipulation of the two sentences as surface structures or 'sentence patterns'. The advantage of the notional approach is that it makes the semantic relationship between the sentences explicit and provides a way of associating them with other forms which are not so obviously related on the surface. This kind of association is also illustrated in Bowers (1971), which was discussed above in section 6.

There are several reasons why we might wish to relate diverse surface forms to a common deep structure proposition in this way, and in general why we might wish to reorganize the content of a language teaching course along notional lines. Consider, for example, the problem of remedial language teaching. It is common to find that remedial courses simply repeat the same kind of practice in handling structures that has already been given before in the initial teaching course. Not surprisingly, many learners find this repetition tedious and unrewarding. A notional approach allows us to regroup the structures in a different way from that in which they were originally introduced.

This not only adds a desirable element of novelty to the learner's activity but enables him to reorganize his knowledge of the language in a meaningful way by reference to semantic principles. He is still given structural practice; however, he is not making sentence patterns in isolation but in relation to the more basic patterns of meaning in the language.

Another application of the notional approach is in the teaching of receptive skills and in particular in the teaching of reading comprehension at the intermediate and advanced levels. One possible consequence of a 'sentence-pattern' approach to teaching is that it might lead the learner to equate different meanings with different surface structures. One effect of this might be that in reading the learner looks for meanings only in so far as they adhere, as it were, to the surface forms of sentences. A grouping of sentences with reference to their basic deep structure can provide the learner with practice in looking beyond the superficial differences and in focusing on the essential propositional content of a sentence and the way it contributes to the main theme of the passage of which it forms a part. The practised reader's skill in extracting the gist of a piece of written communication depends on his ability to focus 'through' the surface and on what lies beneath. One of the principle failings of the 'summary' or 'précis' exercise as practised by many teachers is that it requires the learner to discover deep structure whereas his instruction in the language has led him to a concentration on sentence patterns which discourages such a discovery.

A third reason for considering the notional approach to language teaching is that it opens up the possibility of a reintroduction of translation as a teaching technique. The basic objection to the use of translation in foreign language teaching is that it encourages the learner to think that structurally and lexically similar sentences in two languages mean the same and that it therefore discourages the learner from looking for meanings in the relationship between the sentences and the situations in which they are presented. If, however, one can establish deep structures which represent common propositions expressed differently in the learner's language and the language he is learning, then this objection ceases to be a valid one. The point about deep structure representations is that they reveal underlying meaning and detach it from any particular surface structure manifestation. They enable us therefore to relate two sentences, both within one language and across languages, by reference to the basic proposition that is common to both. The chapter on contrastive analysis in Volume 3 is a detailed discussion of what is involved in setting up such a relationship.

We have discussed the possible pedagogic utility of recent 'semantically-based' models of linguistic description with reference to the 'ideational' or 'propositional' part of underlying structure, but it is easy to see that the 'interpersonal' or 'modal' part has a similar range of potential applications. The essential contribution that recent work in grammar makes to language teaching is that it provides a characterization of what it is that language expresses, and of the kinds of messages which people communicate *by means of* sentences. In short, it has provided a (partial) description of 'communicative competence'. The idea of communicative competence is, of course, not a new one in language teaching. Teachers have generally been aware of the need to teach communicative skills and have recognized that the learner's terminal behaviour should be the ability to use the language he is learning as a means of communication. But language teachers have usually relied on the grammarian to provide the descriptions of language from which the content of language teaching courses can be drawn. Since until quite recently grammarians have been primarily concerned with exploring the nature of the language code as a separate and self-contained system, their descriptions have not yielded the kind of communicative content which is required. The grammarian's present concern with the description of communicative competence goes some way to redress the balance and constitutes a valuable extension to our knowledge of the formal properties of sentences. Taken together, these two approaches—the study of the language system *per se*, and of the communicative properties of this system—promise to provide a more satisfactory guide as to how language teachers might achieve their ends.

12 Further reading

Section 1: Introduction

Palmer, Frank R. 1971. *Grammar*. Harmondsworth: Penguin. A general introduction to the subject, covering traditional, taxonomic and transformational-generative grammar.

Section 2: Traditional grammar

Dinneen, Francis P. 1967. *An Introduction to General Linguistics*. New York: Holt, Rinehart, Winston. Chapters 4–6.

Lyons, John 1968. *Introduction to Theoretical Linguistics*. Cambridge: Cambridge University Press. Chapter 1.

Roberts, Paul 1954. *Understanding Grammar*. New York: Harper & Row. Sets out to explain the traditional grammatical terminology and to give some notion of the assumptions underlying the structure of traditional grammar.

Robins, R. H. 1967. *A Short History of Linguistics*. London: Longman.

Scholarly traditional grammars

The major works should be consulted for any serious research, e.g.: Poutsma's *A Grammar of late Modern English*, Sweet's *A New English Grammar*, Jespersen's *A Modern English Grammar* (see References at the end of the book for details). For ready reference there are four useful one-volume works:

Long, Ralph B. 1961. *The Sentence and Its Parts: A Grammar of Contemporary English.* Chicago: University of Chicago Press.

Jespersen, J. O. H. 1933. *Essentials of English Grammar.* London: Allen & Unwin and New York: Henry Holt. Reprinted, University of Alabama Press, 1964.

Quirk, R., Greenbaum, S., Leech, G. and Svartvik, J. 1972. *A Grammar of Contemporary English.* London: Longman. This is the most comprehensive synchronic description to appear in recent years. Although the grammatical framework is traditional, the book incorporates many insights from contemporary linguistic studies.

Zandvoort, R. H. 1957. *A Handbook of English Grammar.* London: Longman.

Section 3: Taxonomic grammar

(a) *American taxonomic approaches*

Fries, C. C. 1952. *The Structure of English: An Introduction to the Construction of English Sentences.* New York: Harcourt Brace and London: Longman, 1957. A book which has had a profound influence, especially in the language teaching field.

Roberts, Paul 1956. *Patterns of English.* New York: Harcourt Brace. A book written in a clear and simple style and heavily influenced by Fries' *The Structure of English.*

Nida, Eugene A. 1968. *A Synopsis of English Syntax.* 2nd revised edition. The Hague: Mouton. An example of the pure IC approach to the description of English.

Francis, W. Nelson 1958. *The Structure of American English.* New York: Ronald. A good example of the American taxonomic approach. The chapters on syntax illustrate the 'Chinese box' method of presentation.

(b) *Tagmemics*

Cook, Walter A. 1969. *Introduction to Tagmemic Analysis.* New York: Holt, Rinehart, Winston. The most convenient introduction to Pike's theory of grammar.

Pike, K. L. 1967. *Language in Relation to a Unified Theory of Human Behaviour.* 2nd revised edition. The Hague: Mouton. The basic theoretical document of tagmemics.

(c) *Scale-and-category grammar*

Halliday, M. A. K. 1961. Categories of the theory of grammar. *Word* 17, 241–92. The main statement of Halliday's 'scale and category' theory. The paper is far from easy to read, but there is no satisfactory alternative.

Sinclair, J. M. 1972. *A Course in Spoken English: Grammar.* London: Oxford University Press. A grammar of English intended for advanced learners and foreign teachers, broadly based on Halliday's 1961 theory. The book contains copious examples and many exercises.

(d) *General*

Householder, Fred W. (ed.) 1972. *Syntactic Theory 1: Structuralist*. Harmondsworth: Penguin. A representative selection of articles on syntactic topics covering the period 1940 to 1957.

Miller, Jim 1973. A note on so-called 'discovery procedures'. *Foundations of Language* **10**, 123–39. An interesting and well-balanced survey of pre-1957 American linguistics.

Sections 4–5: Transformational-generative grammar

(a) *Easier introductory books*

Lyons, John 1970. *Chomsky*. London: Fontana Modern Masters. A lively and readable introduction to the subject.

Allen, J. P. B. and van Buren, Paul (eds.) 1971. *Chomsky: Selected Readings*. London: Oxford University Press. Presents the main outlines of the 1957 and 1965 models, using as far as possible Chomsky's own words, but arranged so as to make things easier for the non-specialist.

Grinder, John T. and Elgin, S. H. 1973. *Guide to Transformational Grammar*. New York: Holt, Rinehart, Winston.

Roberts, Paul 1964. *English Syntax*. New York: Harcourt Brace. A grammar of English based on Chomsky's *Syntactic Structures*. The text is programmed, which some readers may regard as a disadvantage.

Jacobs, R. A. and Rosenbaum, P. S. 1970. *Grammar 1*, *Grammar 2*, *Grammar 3*, *Grammar 4* (four volumes). *An Introduction to Transformational Grammar*, with teachers' guide. Boston, Mass: Ginn & Co. An easy introduction to the 1965 model, designed to be used by teachers who are unfamiliar with transformational grammar.

Jacobs, R. A. and Rosenbaum, P. S. 1968. *English Transformational Grammar*. Waltham, Mass: Blaisdell. A slightly more technical introduction to the 1965 model, designed for University students.

Liles, Bruce L. 1971. *An Introductory Transformational Grammar*. Englewood Cliffs: Prentice Hall.

Thomas, Owen 1965. *Transformational Grammar and the Teacher of English*. New York: Holt, Rinehart, Winston. An introduction to English grammar based on the 1957 model, considered from the pedagogic point of view.

(b) *Three of the main sources*

Chomsky, Noam 1957. *Syntactic Structures*. The Hague: Mouton. The classic formulation of Chomsky's 1957 model of grammar. Difficult for a beginner.

Chomsky, Noam 1965. *Aspects of the Theory of Syntax*. Cambridge, Mass: M.I.T. Press. The main statement of Chomsky's position in 1965, after several important changes had been incorporated into the grammar. Difficult to read without considerable background knowledge.

Chomsky, Noam 1968. *Language and Mind.* New York: Harcourt Brace. Three lectures, presented in a simple, straightforward style, discussing the linguistic contribution to the study of mind.

Section 6: Case grammar

Fillmore, C. J. 1968. The case for case. In E. Bach and R. T. Harms (eds.) *Universals in Linguistic Theory*. New York: Holt, Rinehart, Winston. A paper written for the professional linguist, but so far the most accessible introduction to case grammar.

Sections 7–9: Propositional and modal information in a grammar

(a) *Halliday's 'functional' grammar*

Halliday, M. A. K. 1967–68. Notes on transitivity and theme in English. *Journal of Linguistics* 3, pp. 37–81, 199–244 and 4, pp. 179–215. A very detailed, and sometimes confusing, description of the operation of the grammatical systems in the three functional components of Halliday's grammar.

Halliday, M. A. K. 1970a. Language structure and language function. In John Lyons (ed.) *New Horizons in Linguistics*. Harmondsworth: Penguin. The simplest statement of the approach to language description adopted by Halliday. It is mainly concerned with transitivity systems, however, and mood and theme are mentioned only briefly. A fuller (and more technical) account of mood can be found in:

Halliday, M. A. K. 1970b. Functional diversity in language as seen from a consideration of modality and mood in English. *Foundations of Language* 6, 322–61.

Halliday, M. A. K. 1973. *Explorations in the Functions of Language*. London: Edward Arnold. A collection of papers which explore the wider implications of Halliday's functional theory of language, with reference to sociology, education and literary criticism. Some papers are relatively simple and some quite technical; the general level of difficulty of the collection is between that of Halliday (1970a) and Halliday (1967–68).

(b) *Modal auxiliaries*

Leech, G. N. 1971. *Meaning and the English Verb*. London: Longman. Chapter 5 deals with the meanings of the modal auxiliaries in English. The meanings are not simply listed; relations between them are explored and demonstrated by diagrams. The book is addressed to teachers and advanced learners of English as a second language.

Palmer, Frank R. 1965. *A Linguistic Study of the English Verb*. London: Longman. Chapter 6 discusses the modal auxiliaries. Each is dealt with in turn and the different meanings associated with each are singled out and illustrated. There is no attempt (as there is in Leech's book) to establish more general principles whereby the different meanings can be related.

(c) *Speech acts*

Austin, J. L. 1962. *How to do things with Words*. Oxford: Clarendon Press.

Searle, J. R. 1969. *Speech Acts*. Cambridge: Cambridge University Press.

These are the two books most often quoted as the standard works on speech acts, illocutionary force, performative verbs and so on. Searle's book is a more technical working out of ideas originally, and more discursively, discussed in Austin. Briefer statements by these philosophers, and others, on these matters and on more general problems of meaning and use are to be found in the following books in the series 'Oxford Readings in Philosophy':

Parkinson, G. H. R. (ed.) 1968. *The Theory of Meaning*. Oxford: Clarendon Press.

Searle, J. R. (ed.) 1971. *The Philosophy of Language*. Oxford: Clarendon Press.

(d) *Other sources*

Fried, V. (ed.) 1972. *The Prague School of Linguistics and Language Teaching*. London: Oxford University Press. A collection of papers by Prague School linguists which illustrates the scope of their activities in the study of language and language teaching. Chapter 1, by Vachek, is a useful survey of Prague School linguistic theory. Chapter 5, by Firbas, discusses the notions of 'functional sentence perspective' and 'communicative dynamism'. Both papers give references which serve as a guide to further reading.

Section 10: Communicative competence

Campbell, R. and Wales, R. 1970. The study of language acquisition. In John Lyons (ed.) *New Horizons in Linguistics*. Harmondsworth: Penguin.

Hymes, D. H. 1972. On communicative competence. In J. B. Pride and J. Holmes (eds.) *Sociolinguistics*. Harmondsworth: Penguin.

The first of these papers discusses the notion of communicative competence from a psycholinguistic and the second from a sociolinguistic point of view. The notion is also considered in Chapter 6 of this volume.

Section 11: Functional grammar and functional language teaching

Wilkins, D. A. 1973. The linguistic and situational content of the common core in a unit credit system. In *Systems Development in Adult Language Learning*.

Strasbourg: Council of Europe. This paper gives an outline of the contents of a syllabus designed along national lines.

Allen, J. P. B. and Widdowson, H. G., Mackin, Ronald (eds.) 1974. *English in Focus* Series. London: Oxford University Press. A series of textbooks of English for special purposes which adopts a functional approach to the development of reading comprehension skills in foreign learners. The first titles are:

Allen, J. P. B. and Widdowson, H. G. 1974. *English in Physical Science.*

Glendinning, Eric H. 1974. *English in Mechanical Engineering.*

Mountford, Alan. 1975. *English in Workshop Practice.*

Maclean, Joan. 1975. *English in Basic Medical Science.*

4 GILLIAN BROWN
Phonological Theory and Language Teaching

I Phonology and phonetics

By the time a child goes to school and begins to learn a foreign language the articulatory movements and perceptual strategies that he needs for communicating in his own language are well established. He has learned to produce a very wide range of phonetically different sounds in speaking his own language in different situations and at different speeds. He has learned to interpret a very wide range of phonetically different sounds spoken by adults and children of varying social and dialectal backgrounds. If he hears a foreign word he will recognize the sounds of the word in terms of the categories of his native language, unless the word contains a sound which is so exotic that he has not encountered it as a speech sound before. For instance if he hears one of the 'clicks' which occur in the 'click languages' of South Africa used as a speech sound, he will perceive this as something exotic, something which will not fit into any of the linguistic categories of his native language. Most sounds in most foreign languages will occur as phonetic sounds either in his own speech or in the speech of those he hears around him. The child is so accustomed to unravelling an obscure acoustic signal, to making sense out of a very unclear message, that he finds little difficulty in dealing with a foreign word. He deals with it in the familiar way. He assigns each sound to the most reasonable of his established phonological categories. Then, when he is asked to reproduce the word, he pronounces it in terms of good clear members of each category. He hears the foreign word in terms of his own categories and he pronounces the foreign word in terms of these same categories.

We need to consider carefully what is meant by 'phonetically different sound' and what is meant by 'phonological category' and what is the relationship between them. Let us begin by deciding what is meant by 'phonetically different sound'. One sound, one actual physical acoustic event may be said to be phonetically different from another sound if it can be shown to be *measurably* different on some scale—if it is louder, or longer, or higher in pitch, or if the structure of the acoustic waveform is different in some other measurable way. If I say the word 'oh' carefully, three times in succession, it will be possible to show, by measuring the acoustic record, that in each case the waveform is slightly different. The physical sound is different. If three different native speakers say 'oh' the word may be shown to have strikingly different acoustic characteristics in each event. The sounds are phonetically different. If each of the speakers is x-rayed while he pronounces the *n* in 'no' we will see that each speaker makes slightly different movements—a slightly different area and amount of the tip and/or blade of the tongue is placed against a slightly different area of the ridge behind the upper teeth for a longer or shorter time. Moreover, to begin with, there will be physiological differences between the speakers' tongues and the configurations of the ridges behind their upper teeth. It would be possible to measure the differences between these speakers' gestures, this time in articulatory terms. The sounds produced by these gestures are, again, phonetically different. The infinitely wide range of phonetically different sounds produced by the members of a speech community will be identified as identical, similar or different to each other in terms of the phonological categories which characterize the speech habits of the community.

Phonetics provides us with a tool, a set of descriptive terms, by which we can describe, as minutely as is necessary for the task in hand, a particular physical sound and the gestures which produced it. It is a tool which is particularly useful for the pronunciation teacher. It enables a teacher to diagnose what is the matter with the pronunciation of a given sound and to teach the student to correct his pronunciation in a controlled and explicit way. It enables him to say 'that's better' when a student is moving his articulators in the right direction but has not yet achieved the right sound. The difficulty for the teacher who knows no phonetics is that there is no intermediate point between the 'right' sound and the 'wrong' sound. He has no way of detecting or of encouraging progress. He has no way of deciding, when a student changes one 'wrong' pronunciation for another, whether the change constitutes a step in the right direction, which should be consolidated, or whether the student has quite arbitrarily shifted a position which was in fact reasonably correct to begin with. A speech sound is produced by a number of articulatory variables—lip position, tongue tip position, tongue back position, soft palate position, state of the glottis, to mention only a few. If the student produces a 'wrong' sound only one of these variables may be at fault but a teacher ignorant of phonetics will insist that the sound is the 'wrong' sound. Suppose he is trying to teach a student to produce an English /v/ and the student produces instead a very creditable /f/. The student has everything correct except for the 'voicing' variable—the state of the glottis. If the teacher now says 'No, that's still the wrong sound', without indicating that the student should hold on to the lower lip upper teeth position, the student may shift this variable in his attempt to find the 'right' sound and move even further away from the sound the teacher is trying to elicit. Phonetics offers the teacher a tool with which, in a controlled and systematic way, he can diagnose errors in pronunciation and devise strategies of correction.

We have seen that phonetically different sounds are physical sounds which are measurably different either in acoustic or articulatory characteristics. We turn now to consider what is meant by 'phonological category'. I suggested that the child hears infinitely many phonetically different sounds but interprets them in terms of the phonological categories of his mother tongue. He hears the phonetically different vowel sounds in 'oh' spoken by our three native speakers and perceives them all as belonging to one phonological category /ou/. He hears 'oh' pronounced by an Englishman, a Scotsman and an Irishman and, despite the wide variety of phonetic sounds, he recognizes all these utterances as pronunciations of 'oh'. His phonological category /ou/ embraces not only the many possible phonetic variants of /ou/ in his own speech—as in 'whole', 'roam' and 'coat'—but also those of different speakers of different accents. He will certainly be aware that they speak with different accents but this will very rarely affect his ability to understand what they say. It is important to note, however, that although his phonological category /ou/ embraces such a wide variety of phonetically dissimilar sounds he will have a very distinct idea of how he himself ought to pronounce this vowel in a word spoken slowly and clearly in citation form. If he is asked to pronounce a foreign word which he regards as like an English word he will produce the clear explicit form which he associates with the English citation form. An English child may produce from time to time in his own language a vowel very like the front rounded vowel in French 'tu'. In a form like 'happy New Year' /hapɪnjujɪə/ the back rounded /u/ vowel may be pulled forward by the surrounding /j/s in a fairly rapid style of utterance. The child is used to classifying a stimulus like this fronted vowel as a member of the category /u/ and he is not consciously aware that this phonetic sound is different from any other realization of the category /u/. When he is asked to interpret the French signal 'tu' /ty/ he perceives it to be like his own 'too' /tu/. When he is asked to repeat the French word he repeats it as the English word 'too'. His ability to produce a front, rounded vowel in the sequence 'happy New Year', where the phonetic context provokes the frontness, is just not available to him independently of the context. The phonetically different sounds are members, or realizations, of one phonological category.

What the foreign language teacher has to do is teach the child to adapt and change his phonological categories in the foreign language situation. The English child learning French has to learn to divide up the perceptual space which is uniquely allocated to the category 'close round' vowel /u/ in English and share it between the categories 'close front round' vowel /y/ and 'close back round' vowel /u/ in French. The French child learning English has to learn to divide the perceptual space allocated to 'close front unrounded' vowel /i/ and share it between 'close front' vowel as in English 'beat' and 'half close front' vowel as in English 'bit'. Similarly the Japanese speaker learning

English has to learn to divide his category 'liquid', which can be realized by a whole range of phonetically different sounds including sounds which the English speaker hears as unambiguous *l*s and *r*s, and divide the *l*s into one phonological category /l/ and the *r*s into another phonological category /r/. This presents considerable difficulty for the Japanese speaker for whom this whole range of sounds is assigned to one phonological category, to one perceptual space. For the English speaker who assigns them to two phonological categories the difference is sharp and clear. For the Japanese speaker they may be no more perceptible than the differences in the vowel of my 'oh', as I utter it on three separate occasions, are to me. As far as he is concerned they are merely phonetically different sounds, not members of different phonological categories.

The foreign language teacher needs the concepts that phonological theory can provide in order to understand that in teaching the pronunciation of a foreign language he is not simply teaching 'new sounds' to his students. No single physical new sound can be taught, because each example of a phonological category will be phonetically different, however minutely, from every other example. The teacher must appreciate that in teaching a new sound he is very likely to be teaching a range of phonetic sounds that the student has heard before, either in his own speech or in that of speakers of different dialects of his own language. What he is teaching is not a new sound but a new phonological category. A new phonological category, however, cannot be taught in isolation as though it were in some way self-contained. It has to be part of a *system* of phonological categories. Consider a language which has six vocalic categories, where the perceptual space available to vowels is divided between these six categories. If a speaker of this language is asked to introduce even just one more category this will have a profound effect on the partition of the perceptual space available to vowels. The newcomer has to squeeze in, and appropriate, part of the share of at least one existing category and possibly part of two or three. The effect then is not simply the addition of a category that did not exist before, but the creation of a new system of categories. The perceptual space available to vowels is divided up in a new and different way.

It has sometimes been assumed that a comparison of the phonological categories of the mother tongue and the target language will be sufficient to allow the teacher to predict the difficulties that his students will encounter in learning the foreign language. Certainly some major difficulties may be predicted where mismatches occur in the categories of the two languages. There are, however, many difficulties which a simple comparison will not reveal. I discuss some of these problems in detail in the chapter on practical phonetics and phonology (see Volume 3). In some cases, for example, categories which are distinguished in one environment, say at the beginning of a word, are not distinguished in another, say at the end of a word. So a Slavic speaker who has no difficulty with a /t/-/d/ contrast at the beginning of a word may find it difficult to hear and to produce at the end of a word. Another problem is that phonological categories which are symbolized with the same symbol in two different languages may in fact be realized phonetically in the two languages in quite different ways. A well-known example of this is the /t/-/d/ distinction in English and French. In English initial /t/ is uttered without voice (without vibration of the vocal cords) and there is a slight pause after its release before the vocal cords begin to vibrate (aspiration). Initial /d/ is also uttered without voice but with immediate vibration of the vocal cords as it is released. In French initial /t/ is uttered without voice and with immediate vibration of the vocal cords on its release and /d/ is uttered with voice (with vibration of the vocal cords during the period of closure). There are other differences as well but these two will suffice to illustrate areas which will provide many difficulties for the pronunciation teacher.

The attentive reader will have noticed that I have avoided giving a definition of the term 'phonological category'. I have used this neutral term because it can apply equally well to basic notions in different phonological theories whose various protagonists have different ideas about the nature and scope of the categories of any given theory. In the next section I consider what are the basic phonological categories in two different theoretical frameworks, phonemic phonology and generative phonology. There are other theories of phonology which I do not discuss here because it is not clear to me that they are relevant to the problems confronting the language teacher. One of these is the theory of prosodic phonology expounded by Firth (see Firth 1957a). Unfortunately many of the valuable insights into phonological structure which can readily be stated within this theory are not easily accessible to the general reader partly because the methodological framework has never been explicitly expounded and partly because the symbolic conventions used in descriptions of different languages vary from one language to another and have never been standardized (see Palmer 1970).

2 Which theory?

It is generally agreed nowadays that it is the language teacher's task to teach the spoken form of the language as well as the written form. Just as the written form divides into two main teaching areas—production and comprehension—so does the spoken form. The teacher must teach production of the spoken form, pronunciation, as well as the ability to understand what a native speaker of the target language is saying. It has sometimes been assumed that it is unnecessary to teach comprehension of the spoken language because the student will inevitably pick it up in the classroom situation. However, the ability to understand the slow formal speech of the classroom where a foreign language is being taught does not entail an ability to understand the language as spoken to and by native speakers. If the foreign student is to understand the English used in speeches, public lectures, and radio and television broadcasts, he must be exposed to the spoken language used in these situations and he must be systematically taught how to extract the message from the indistinct acoustic signal.

In order to teach the *pronunciation* of the spoken language the teacher needs a description of slow, clear pronunciation which his students may use as a model for their own pronunciation. This is the familiar 'slow colloquial' style of speech used in most materials for foreign language learning. In order to teach the *comprehension* of the spoken language the teacher needs a description of the language as normally spoken by native speakers to each other. There are of course a wide number of styles of speech available to the native speaker and there is no clear principle by which one style of speech rather than another should be selected for students to be taught to understand. It seems likely that rapid conversational speech whose intelligibility depends heavily on a shared background of experience will not prove a reasonable model. The style of speech used by newsreaders on radio and television provides a model which should be attainable by any advanced student. We would naturally require that this second description of pronunciation should be expressed in terms of the same theoretical framework as the first. Then the teacher can explicitly relate the 'simplified' forms used in the speech listened to in comprehension teaching to the slow, maximally clear style of the pronunciation model. He can make it quite clear that it is the same system of communication that is being described.

2.1 Segmental phonology

2.1.1 GENERATIVE PHONOLOGY

Which of the available theories is most relevant to the needs of the language teacher who wants to teach a slow clear style of pronunciation together with the ability to comprehend a rapid, reduced style of speech? We shall consider first what the theory of transformational generative phonology developed by Noam Chomsky and Morris Halle has to offer. This theory is most clearly expounded in the first two chapters of their major work *The Sound Pattern of English* (1968). One immediately attractive feature of the theory is that it is based on a distinction drawn between the linguistic competence which is shared by members of a speech community and the variable nature of the performance of a given utterance by a particular speaker in a particular situation.

The competence-performance distinction as drawn by Chomsky distinguishes between the knowledge that a speaker-hearer has about his language and the use he makes of it in a particular situation (1965, p. 4). This intuitively attractive distinction is not however a simple one to operate. Chomsky points out that a speaker's performance cannot directly reflect his competence since the performance will be affected by 'memory limitations, distractions, shifts of attention and interest' (1965, p. 3). Within his theory no special status is assigned to the performance of an utterance which exhibits none of the performance limitations listed above, which consists of a complete sentence and which is spoken slowly and clearly. I would like to suggest that such an utterance is in a special relationship with the speaker's competence. This maximally full, maximally clear citation form most clearly reflects his knowledge of his language.

Throughout this chapter I shall assign special status to the phonological citation form. All other related but simplified forms I shall regard as performance variables of this citation form. Thus I shall regard the simplified English forms [hanbag] and [hambag] as performance variables of the citation form /handbag/. This does not suggest that the simplified forms are simplified in a quite random and unpredictable way; on the contrary, they are simplified by quite general rules. Since these rules of simplification are common to all members of a given speech community they must be regarded as part of the knowledge that a speaker-hearer has about his language—as competence-governed performance.

In the field of syntax teaching this notion is a familiar one. Consider the following utterances:

1 When does Mrs Smith hang out her washing?
2 Mrs Smith hangs out her washing on Thursday mornings.
3 She hangs it out on Thursday mornings.
4 On Thursday mornings.
5 Thursday mornings.

Once upon a time students were always required to answer questions with 'complete' sentences. So 1 would be answered by 2. But it is quite obvious that no native English speaker would normally produce 2 in reply to 1. Within a conversation, 1 could properly be followed by any of the utterances 3–5. Despite the fact that none of these utterances explicitly contains all the information present in 2 the listener will understand from any of these 'reduced' utterances all the information contained in 2. In a simple sense 2 may be said to represent the 'ideal' sentence which 'underlies' the performance of the contextualized utterances 3–5. The notion is also familiar where orthographic conventions represent different phonetic realizations of the 'same' words. The contracted forms 'she's', 'I'll' and 'isn't' are readily related to the 'ideal' full forms 'she is', 'I shall' (or 'I will') and 'is not'. We shall need to extend the notion to cover the many possible phonetic realizations of the 'same' word which are not recognized by orthographic convention. We need to be able to relate, for instance, the many possible phonetic realizations of 'going to', as in [gouɪŋtʊ], [gowɪŋtə], [gɜŋtə], [gənə], to an 'ideal' citation form /gouɪŋtu/. The competence-performance distinction will offer us a framework within which we may discuss the relationship which holds between the 'ideal' citation forms of the pronunciation model and the reduced forms which will be encountered in the style used for comprehension teaching.

The level of phonological competence as I represent it here looks remarkably like what the native speaker considers to be the 'ideal' pronunciation of the citation form of a word, the sort of form that is transcribed in a pronouncing dictionary, and its relation to other, reduced, forms. However, the native speaker knows more than this about the phonological structure of his language. He knows, for example, how to control processes of morphological inflexion in his language. A native English speaker knows the regularities governing the production of regular plural forms in English. He 'knows' this in the sense that if he encounters a new word he will be able to construct a correct plural form. If we want to state the rule governing the formation of regular English plurals in terms of phonemes we must imply that several different phonemes are involved in this rule: two phonemes /ɪ/ and /z/ follow word final /s, z, ʃ, ʒ, tʃ, dʒ/ as in 'kisses', 'roses', 'bushes', 'garages', 'clutches' and 'charges', one phoneme /s/ follows /p, t, k, f, θ/ as in 'taps', 'cats', 'locks', 'muffs' and 'moths' and another phoneme /z/ follows all other segments, for example /b, ɡ, v, m, l, i/ as in 'cubs', 'dogs', 'caves', 'rams', 'mills', and 'seas'. This means that different phonological categories, two different phonemes and one phoneme sequence, form the regular plural in English. Proponents of generative phonology believe that a statement in this form fails to make explicit some important facts about English phonological structure. This statement fails, for example, to make it clear that there are structural reasons why it is /s/ and not /z/ that follows /p, t, k, f, θ/, why it is that the consonants /s, z, ʃ, ʒ, tʃ, dʒ/ are followed by /ɪz/ rather than by /z/ or /s/, and what there is in common between the forms /iz/, /s/ and /z/. In order to make the structural constraints explicit we must appeal to some phonological property which is shared by classes of items which behave in a similar way. We must extract *features* which will characterize such classes. If we characterize the class /s, z, ʃ, ʒ, tʃ,dʒ/ as sharing the features *sibilant* and *consonant* and the class /p, t, k, f, θ, s/ as sharing the features *voiceless* and *consonant* and the class /b, ɡ, v, m, l, z, i/ as sharing the features *voiced* and *segment* (notice that this class includes a vowel /i/ which represents the whole class of vowels in this context) we can state the rules for the formation of regular English plurals in the following way:

(a) plural is vowel/i/ +voiced alveolar sibilant following sibilants
(b) plural is voiceless alveolar sibilant following voiceless consonants
(c) plural is voiced alveolar sibilant following voiced segments

These rules will need to be ordered with respect to each other so that (a) operates before (b) and (c) in order to prevent a word final sibilant being immediately followed by the plural sibilant with no intervening vowel. These rules state explicitly the relevant facts of English phonological structure:

(i) the plural is formed by sibilance, (ii) the voicing value of the sibilant is determined by the voicing value of the word final segment which it follows, (iii) no sequence of two sibilants is allowed in English (within the same syllable). This explicit formulation is highly valued in generative phonology because it states important and general facts about English phonological structure. Since in order to formulate these facts it is necessary to use the phonological category *feature*, the feature is taken as a basic phonological category in this theory.

So far we have discussed two areas of the knowledge that a native speaker has about the sound system of his language—the citation form of words and their relation to reduced forms, and the processes of morphological inflexion. This kind of knowledge can be formally represented by fairly simple rules of the sort we have informally stated for the formation of regular English plurals. Most of the descriptions that have appeared in the framework of generative phonology have made the assumption that the native speaker's knowledge of how his language works also includes rules for deriving words of one grammatical class from words of another grammatical class, that is, rules of derivational morphology. In Chomsky and Halle (1968) rules are given for deriving 'electricity' and 'electrician' from 'electric'. These account for the variation in the form of the stem consonant which is /k/ in /ɪlektrɪk/, /s/ in /ilektrisɪtɪ/ and /ʃ/ in /ɪlektrɪʃən/. Similarly rules are given which derive the correct stress and vowel quality for 'photographer' from the form 'photograph'. The statement of such rules involves a much more complicated formalism than that needed for the statement of the other processes that we have considered. It is open to question whether all such rules form part of the synchronic competence of speakers of English.

It may be objected of generative phonological theory that its protagonists are too ready to attribute knowledge of past processes in their language to present day native speakers. There is a danger that some arbitrary early period of the language may be deemed to be the starting point from which all later stages increasingly depart, so that each succeeding generation is burdened with a knowledge of more historical processes than preceding generations. It would clearly be more rational to suggest that with the passage of time what were related forms to earlier generations do not necessarily become related forms to later generations. The complicated formalism of generative phonology has been developed in the main to express processes which relate some logically prior form to another form derived from that prior form. The development of the formalism has gone hand in hand with development of interest in stating relationships between different pronunciations of the 'same' item at different historical periods, different pronunciations of the 'same' item in different dialects of the same language, and different pronunciations of the 'same' item at different periods of the child's acquisition of his native language. It is not clear how this formalism which expresses processes of change within the grammar of a particular language can be applied to problems raised when the grammars of two different languages come into contact. I see no way at the moment of utilizing the formalism in the teaching of foreign languages.

If we abandon the formalism of generative phonology, what is there left? Most important, I think, is the competence-performance distinction and the adoption of features as basic phonological categories. It is clear that in language teaching we do not need to appeal to a very abstract notion of competence. It may not be possible to try to produce in the language learner much of the knowledge that a native speaker has about the derivational processes available in the language. Certainly this cannot be presented in terms of the complex generative formalism. An attempt to state some of the relevant generalizations in a more accessible manner is made in McArthur (1972). Having mastered the citation forms, the most direct reflection of the competence forms, the language learner should then learn to relate these to the performance forms that he will meet in the 'reduced' style of speech of his exercises in aural comprehension. The student will also need to master the rules for common inflexional processes in the language. These will certainly be more economically and generally stated in terms of features than in terms of a segmental phonological category like the phoneme. For language teaching purposes it may be simpler to state them in terms of the phoneme but the teacher himself should certainly be made aware of the nature of the generalizations that are captured by rules formulated in terms of features.

2.1.2 PHONEME THEORY

There are many versions of phoneme theory and many important differences between them. I shall concentrate here on two versions—the first, that of the American structuralists (represented by Hockett 1942) and the second, that of the British phonetics school (represented by Jones 1962 and Jones 1967). I shall begin by discussing what these theories have in common. They share the belief that it is possible to construct an inventory of phonemes, of vowels and consonants, for any language and that these phonemes represent the basic phonological category. However, even though the phonemes represent the basic phonological category they are classified in terms of phonetic features which they have in common with other phonemes. Notice that the features are specifically stated to be *phonetic* features. It may well appear to the reader that the distinction between phonological features and phonetic features is merely a matter of terminology, and in a certain sense this is true. Consider for a moment, however, what this difference implies in a theory of perception. If a subject correctly identifies the words 'tie' and 'die' the phonemicist claims that what he has perceived is two words each beginning with a different phoneme, the first with the phoneme /t/, the second with the phoneme /d/. The phoneme is conceived of as a unique entity, an indissoluble perceptual unit. It is convenient for the linguist to identify /t/ as a voiceless consonant and /d/

as a voiced sound but to the native speaker these are simply different sounds, each occupying a different perceptual space. The generative phonologist claims that what the subject has heard is two words, each beginning with a closure formed by the tongue tip pressing against the ridge behind the upper teeth (a dental or alveolar stop). In the first word, however, the stop is voiceless and in the second it is voiced. It is the difference in the voicing feature which is perceived as crucial. Each segment is not an indissoluble unit, a 'different sound', but a bundle of features, and it is the presence or absence of a given feature which enables the subject to distinguish between the words.

The phonemicist identifies phonemes by phonetic features. Each consonant and vowel is characterized by a distinguishing set of features which have no theoretical status within the theory but which enable the linguist to refer to them. Thus the set of English consonants /p, t, k/ is separated off from all the other consonants by being characterized as a set of 'voiceless stops'. They are then separated off from each other by the fact that /p/ is articulated at the lips, /t/ against the teeth ridge and /k/ against the soft palate. Similarly the vowels of English are each identified by a set of defining characteristics. The suggestion is, then, that any English utterance can be transcribed in terms of the members of the inventory of vowels and consonants.

A basic difference between the structuralist phoneme and the Jones phoneme appears as soon as we turn to the question of what constitutes an utterance which may be phonetically transcribed. The structuralists believed that they should not accept any pre-theoretical notions, like the notions of word or sentence, which were derived from some other, higher, level of grammatical description. They believed that it should be possible to construct a grammar of a language, beginning with the phonetic transcription of utterances and building up a phonemic transcription, with no information other than that provided by a native informant saying whether he considered two utterances to be 'the same' or 'different'. Having constructed a statement of the phonology of the language on strictly distributional principles they would then proceed to construct a statement of the morphology and eventually of the syntax, always using the same distributional principles and the stern injunction that no category of any higher level might be assumed in formulating a statement at a lower level. These methodological principles, if strictly applied, lead to many insoluble problems. We shall discuss only two specific problems here.

Since, in principle, it is possible to transcribe in its entirety any meaningful utterance, and to ascribe the whole of the acoustic signal to a sequence of phonemes, it should be possible to segment in an unambiguous way any phonetic signal that may turn up in performance in terms of a phoneme sequence. In many accents of English, speakers pronounce 'language' as [lãɡwɪdʒ] rather than as [laŋɡwɪdʒ]. The simple explanation of this must surely be that in the performance of this word the nasalization of the nasal consonant is realized on the vowel rather than on a separate consonant. This simple answer is not available to the phonemicist working within a strict methodological framework. If the vowel is simply nasalized before a nasal consonant, as in [lãŋgwɪdʒ], he can state that [ã] is an allophone, a variant of /a/ which is nasalized before a nasal consonant. But in our example the nasal consonant is not there. Since the phonemicist may only analyse what he perceives to be present in the particular signal that he is transcribing, he must, strictly, introduce a nasal phoneme /ã/ which can contrast with a non-nasal phoneme /a/ in the frame /l–g/ as in the first syllable of the particular performance of 'language' that we are discussing and the word 'lag'. Following the same principle he may have to introduce a complete new set of nasalized vowel phonemes in his description of English in order to account for variation in the performance of the pronunciation of the sequence vowel before nasal + consonant, which is sometimes realized as vowel + nasal + consonant, as in [laŋgwɪdʒ] and sometimes as nasalized vowel + consonant as in [lãgwɪdʒ]. Chomsky (1964) discussed in detail the complexity of statement which a strict application of structuralist principles constantly involves in examples such as these.

The second problem arises for the same reason as the first problem, and is due to the failure to make a distinction between the stable citation form of the native speaker and his variable performance. A necessary part of the description of the phonology of a language is a statement of the constraints on the permitted sequences of vowels and consonants in the language. If you examine the initial sequences of consonants in English words transcribed in a pronouncing dictionary you will find many words beginning with the sequences /sp/, /st/ and /sk/ as in 'spot', 'stop' and 'skirt' but no words beginning with the reverse sequences /ps/, /ts/ and /ks/. Since utterances are composed of words this implies that no utterance will begin with the sequence [ps], [ts], [ks]. And indeed if you listen to utterances spoken slowly and clearly you will find that this is true. However, if you listen to utterances which occur in normal informal interchange you may well hear utterance initial sequences like the following:

[psaɪdz] 'besides'
[tsounlɪ] 'it's only'
[ksɔbɪtənt] 'exorbitant'

A phonemicist working within a strict methodological framework would be forced to list these sequences as possible initial sequences—and indeed if he listened carefully to a great deal of phonetic data he might well find that there were *no* two term sequences of consonants which are excluded from appearing in utterance initial position. But while such a description, if it were possible to make one, might tell us something about the vast range of performance possibilities in a language, it would tell us nothing about the native speaker's knowledge of how his language works. It would not tell us why, when English speakers are confronted with words that are pronounced in the languages they derive from with initial sequences /ps, /ts/ and /ks/, like 'psychology', 'tsetse' and 'xylophone', these sequences are simplified in English to /s/, /t/ and /z/ respectively.

The phoneme theory developed by Daniel Jones avoids many of the problems confronted in a strict methodological framework. Daniel Jones' theory is essentially pragmatic, and is largely geared to the teaching of pronunciation. Jones accepts the pre-theoretical notion of 'the word'. He believes that it is only possible to make a phonemic description of the speech of 'one individual pronouncing in a definite and consistent style' (Jones 1967, p. 9) who is pronouncing citation forms of words in isolation:

> The restriction 'in a word' is important. To extend the definition to cover word-groups or sentences would greatly complicate matters. At the best it would increase the number of phonemes in some languages; it might even be found to render the elaboration of any consistent theory of phonemes impossible, since variations of sound at word junctions may take so many forms (Jones 1967, p. 10).

He is clearly aware that a phonological description must state what the speaker knows about his language—it must state what he knows about the citation forms of words. It might be objected that Jones' theory will only account for the internalized competence of a single speaker of the language and will fail to account for the fact that this speaker will be able to apply his competence to the unravelling of the performance of other speakers whose phoneme systems might be held by Jones to be different. He would appear to state that if speaker A's realization of some phonemes are phonetically different from speaker B's, these two individuals have different phoneme systems (Jones 1967, p. 9). In order to account for the fact that these two individuals are able to communicate and speak 'the same language' Jones introduces the concept of 'diaphone':

> It is convenient to have a name for a family of sounds consisting of the sound used by one speaker in a particular set of words (said in isolation) together with corresponding though different sounds used in them by other speakers of the same language (Jones 1967, p. 195).

We may choose to interpret this statement as meaning that *diaphones* constitute the phonological categories shared by members of a speech community whereas *phonemes* constitute the phonological categories of a given individual. I am not sure that this is a correct interpretation and indeed Daniel Jones is not completely consistent in the practical application of his theoretical concepts. In practice (as exemplified, for example, in Jones 1962) he appears to accept the phoneme as the basic phonological category shared by a speech community, the phoneme being established on the basis of the pronunciation of a word in isolation. In practice, too, he does not limit his discussion to words in isolation but considers the possibility of relating reduced forms of words to their citation forms. The reader is referred to Jones' comments on 'strong and weak forms', 'assimilation' and 'elision' (Jones 1962, pp. 126, 217, 230).

The practical approach exemplified in Jones' own writings has characterized the work of other British scholars working in this tradition (see, for example, Gimson 1962). It recognizes the 'ideal' citation form and relates other, reduced, forms back to the citation form in terms of processes like 'assimilation', 'elision' and 'vowel reduction'. The emphasis in works in this tradition has been on the description of the articulation of segments in isolation, and the patterning of stress in words pronounced in isolation. The reason for this emphasis is that the descriptions are meant to provide manuals for teaching the pronunciation of clearly articulated citation forms. Comparatively little attention has been paid to the patterns of simplification which occur in connected speech. In some works the only recognition of connected speech is to be found in the listing of the conventional 'weak forms'. Even in those major works, like Gimson 1962, which discuss connected speech at some length, it is not made clear that the patterns of simplification described there are patterns which one must expect to find in every English sentence spoken reasonably fast and within a discourse, rather than in isolation. There may, rarely, be occasions when native speakers speak to each other with maximum articulatory clarity but these are the exception rather than the rule. This is true of public speakers as well as of participants in a conversation. I have recently made a study of the speech of BBC newsreaders (Brown, forthcoming) which is a form of spoken English widely, and rightly, regarded as being particularly clear and easy to understand. But in almost every sentence some form of phonetic simplification will be heard by someone who listens carefully to how the person is speaking rather than to what he is saying. In many sentences complexes of simplification are to be found. People who listen carefully to the phonetic detail of this sort of material for the first time are often surprised, even shocked. But why should they be shocked? The reading is just as clear as every other reading, which they have found perfectly easy to understand. The fact is that normally we pay no attention to the simplifications of performance. We listen for the clues which will enable us to identify words and the structures in which they appear. In other words, we listen for the message. The phonetic detail escapes our conscious observation, as indeed it should.

For foreign students the chief stumbling block in understanding English as spoken by native speakers to each other, whether in public or in private, is the phonetic details of performance which the native speaker can afford to ignore. Many students are only exposed to the sort of English spoken on records and on taped courses specially prepared for foreigners. Many of these courses exemplify the nearest thing to 'ideal' pronunciation that one may ever hope to hear—slow, carefully articulated sequences of vowels and consonants. This is because such material is intended to serve as a model of pronunciation. But the foreign student who wishes to understand native speakers in their natural habitat must be exposed to the sort of speech he will meet with there. And the teacher must be prepared to teach him, in a properly organized and graded course of aural comprehension, how to abstract the message from the simplified, reduced, signal. This is why the teacher needs the second description of pronunciation—the one which describes performance variables, the patterns of simplification. From this description he can devise exercises which systematically teach the student to relate the reduced forms which he hears to the 'ideal' form which contains some meaning for him.

Which of the theoretical approaches I have described offers most to the language teacher who wants to relate the reduced forms found in performance to the 'ideal' citation forms? I think there is little doubt that the practical phoneme theory evolved within the British school has most to offer in this practical area but that, as it stands, it is inadequate. It is important, then, that the implicit acceptance of a citation form—performance variable distinction which is made in descriptions couched in this framework should be made explicit. It should be clearly stated that the phonemes of a language are based on the notion of an 'ideal' citation form and that forms like [læ̃gwɪdʒ] will be related to the 'ideal' forms by processes of assimilation and elision. This distinction has rarely been made explicit in British works. Indeed it was not until the competence-performance distinction was elaborated by Chomsky (1964, 1965) that its importance was fully realized. (The concept of competence-performance was of course to some extent available in the notion of the *langue-parole* distinction drawn by de Saussure. This Saussurean distinction appears not to have affected the work of the British school.)

I have already suggested that in expressing common rules of morphological inflexion, like the formation of regular plurals in English, an analysis in terms of features will capture the generalizations involved more explicitly and more generally than an analysis in terms of unanalysable phonemes. It seems clear to me that teachers should be aware of the generalizations involved. This suggests that teachers should be provided with descriptions which make these generalizations explicit.

2.2 Suprasegmental phonology

In this section I shall range over any theories that seem to me to have anything to contribute to the discussion. In the previous section the scope of the discussion was fairly clearly defined. In the field of suprasegmentals the scope is much less clear. Everyone agrees that one of the basic phonological categories available to English speakers is the category of *stress*, but not everyone agrees how stress is to be defined. Most theories also agree that *pitch* is a basic linguistic category (or categories) but there are very different analyses of the form of pitch, ranging from the analysis of pitch into segment sized tonemes (the American structuralist approach exemplified by Trager and Smith 1951) to the analysis of pitch into intonation contours which has been favoured by British scholars (see Jones 1962, Gimson 1962, O'Connor and Arnold 1961, Halliday 1967). Similarly there are different approaches to the function of pitch variation, some of which I shall discuss later in this section.

Whether these are the only linguistic categories that need to be included is not clear or generally agreed, partly because the study of suprasegmentals necessarily involves studying how they modify the meaning of the message. This very soon takes the linguist out of the area narrowly defined as linguistics and into the area of communication, and once there, where is he to stop? If I say 'I think it's lovely' with a high falling intonation and a smile, does this 'mean' something different from the same words said with a frown and a high rising intonation? The linguist may accept responsibility for the intonation since this is realized by the voice, and the science of phonetics, which is part of linguistics, is concerned with the study of speech sounds produced by the voice. But what is the linguist to do with the frown and the smile? They may be held to modify the 'meaning' of the message in a very important way. Try swapping them over in the examples I suggested above. Is the 'meaning' not changed again? We may arbitrarily decide that the study of linguistics is limited to what is produced by the articulatory organs. Does this mean that such categories as 'sexy voice', 'harsh voice', 'slow speech', 'rapid speech', all of which may modify the meaning of an utterance, are to be included as basic phonological categories? For the moment we leave them out (but see Crystal 1969, Laver 1968 and Brown forthcoming).

2.2.1 STRESS

There are many accounts of the assignment of English stress within words. Most of those prepared in an English language teaching framework list sets of words which have similar stress patterns (e.g. Kingdon 1958). Chomsky and Halle have gone beyond this and suggested that, given a knowledge of the phonological form of a word together with a knowledge of its syntactic function and its historical provenance, the placing of stress can be predicted by rule (Chomsky and Halle 1968). I have already remarked that I think there is no immediate application to language teaching in this work. It is interesting to note that adolescent native speakers frequently place stress on the wrong syllable of a polysyllabic word when they first begin to use it. If these young people, with all the advantage of the native speaker's intuition, as well as control of an extensive active vocabulary, find it difficult to assign stress correctly, I do not believe that a foreign learner who has painstakingly learnt the rules for stress assignment will be in any better position when he confronts a hitherto unknown word. The prediction of stress assignment by rule is an interesting (even exciting) theoretical area, but the language learner must, I think, be confined to sober stress patterns like those of Kingdon and the information provided by the pronouncing dictionary and manuals like McArthur (1972).

Much less has been written on the assignment of stress within sentences. Again Chomsky and Halle have outlined a basic technique for assigning stress by rule, but they themselves point out that their proposals are at the moment of very limited application (Chomsky and Halle 1968, p. 23). Most books written as textbooks for foreign students content themselves with giving examples of sentences with stressed words in them and leave the student to work out why one word rather than another is stressed. A rare exception to this is found in the work of Albrow (see Albrow 1968). Albrow states that stress functions to mark lexical items (and also certain deictic classes of grammatical words) and discusses relationships between stress and syntax. The discussion is not exhaustive but it is an encouraging sign to find someone concerned with the teaching of English as a foreign language who is prepared to make theoretical and general statements in this area.

The stress-unstress contrast may be the biggest practical bugbear in the teaching of pronunciation. There is certainly no other area in which control is so essential, either in pronouncing or in listening. There is rarely much room for doubt about which words are stressed in a sentence, and no doubt at all about which syllable of any word must be stressed. If the same text is presented to a number of native speakers to read aloud there may be some variation in the placing of stress, but in over 90 per cent of cases there will be agreement. Lexical items and some deictic grammatical items will be stressed and most grammatical items will not. The variation often occurs where stress or unstress does not affect the meaning of the message, where the choice is primarily a stylistic one, as for example in the choice of whether or not to stress 'one' in 'one summer day'. Everyone will agree that there must be stress on 'summer', and on the head word of the group, 'day'. Variation also occurs where there is a string of grammatical words and, in order to preserve the rhythm established in the discourse, one word must be stressed, as in 'That's just what I ask myself'. Everyone will agree on stressing 'ask'—there are no options here. The 'natural' word to be stressed in the grammatical string seems to me to be 'just'. However, some people wish to stress 'that's', either as well as or at the expense of 'just', and some wish to stress 'I'. There are clearly several possible interpretations here. This variety of interpretation is much more constrained where lexical words break up the sequence of grammatical words. In general there is wide agreement on the placing of stress in a sentence.

2.2.2 INTONATION

It is much more difficult to establish a consensus on the 'ideal' intonation pattern of a sentence. Whereas the native speaker may 'know' how a word should be pronounced, how it should be stressed, and how a sentence should be stressed, he appears to be much less capable of stating what the intonation pattern of a sentence should be. Anyone who wants to describe the patterns of intonation has to decide what he will regard as an instance of 'the same' pattern and what he will regard as an instance of a 'different' pattern. There is no objective criterion that one can appeal to here. The fact is that men's voices are deeper than women's. Some men's voices are so deep that they may rarely rise as high in pitch as the lowest pitch of a woman with a high-pitched voice. A further complicating factor is that some people normally use more of their voice range than others in ordinary speech. If A normally uses a narrow pitch span his fall from high may be no wider in span than B's normal pitch span. Furthermore no sentence spoken by an individual will have an intonation contour that is acoustically identical with the contour of any other sentence spoken by the same individual.

There is no simple way of deciding what is 'the same' intonation pattern. The result is that there is a wide diversity in descriptions of intonation with regard to the number of different patterns that are recognized. Since early in the century it has been realized that it is possible to break up the pitch pattern of a sentence and regard it as being composed of different parts. All British descriptions recognize a *tonic* or *nuclear* word which bears the moving tone. This is regarded as the essential element in the tone group—all other elements may or may not be present. All descriptions recognize at least one pattern which can occur before the nuclear or tonic syllable. This may be regarded as a 'secondary accent' or 'prenuclear' tone or 'pretonic'. Some descriptions recognize a further point of contrast before the nuclear or tonic syllable. Many descriptions recognize a post-nuclear or post-tonic contrast. Clearly the more points of contrast that are recognized the more possibilities of combination there must be and the larger the number of over-all contours. It seems clear that, in order to reduce the problem to teachable dimensions, we should prefer an analysis which recognizes as few points of contrast as possible in accounting for the data. Unfortunately we really do not know what 'the data' is. If we knew exactly what the function of intonation was we could decide what we wanted to account for—we could decide how many areas of contrast we must recognize.

Most courses which set out to teach intonation reflect a prevailing uncertainty about the function of intonation. They simply present lists of sentences which are pronounced with carefully controlled intonation patterns by an individual who is taking care to speak in the same pitch range and not to vary how he is speaking in any way—neither by smiling nor by speaking softly or loudly, nor by speaking rapidly or slowly. Each list is then said to illustrate the use of one particular intonation pattern. The particular pattern is then glossed as demonstrating some attitude on the part of the speaker. For example a falling tone, even one falling from high, is said to indicate a 'matter of fact, separative, assertive' attitude. A fall from low is glossed as 'curt, impatient, testy'. Anyone listening to the illustrative tapes which usually accompany intonation workbooks might be forgiven for thinking that the British are very unemotional. The high falls, mid falls and low falls on a typical tape or record sound like nothing so much as a man practising high falls, mid falls and low falls in a carefully controlled academic voice which is deliberately excluding all possible display of emotion. The fact is that intonation by itself does not 'mean' anything in particular, it does not denote any particular attitude. However, when combined with other variables it may certainly denote attitude. Consider again this 'matter of fact, assertive' high falling tone. Add a smile, and a generally delighted facial expression, and a little breathiness in the voice, and you have 'excitement' or 'happiness'. Take away the delight and raise the eyebrows, make the voice louder and more rapid and place it higher in the voice range (though still with the same pattern, a fall from high) and you may gloss this as 'desperation' or 'anxiety'. Consider the 'curt, impatient, testy' fall from low. If it is said by a girl with pouted lips and a breathy voice and slow smiling articulation it will hardly be interpreted as 'curt'. If it occurs between two men in the company of other people and is accompanied by a lower placing of the whole pitch pattern in the voice range and is spoken very quietly it may simply be 'confidential' or even 'conspiratorial'. To be 'curt' an utterance must be also spoken rapidly, with no sign of friendship—no smile or approach of one person's head to the other.

Intonation alone cannot indicate attitude. Attitude can be indicated by some of the intonation variables—especially the amount of pitch span, the placing of the pitch movement in the voice range and the direction of the pitch movement —together with other variables like speed and loudness, harsh or breathy voice, a smile or pursed lips. These variables together can narrow down the sort of attitude being expressed. A really precise characterization of attitude, which distinguishes for example between 'confidentially' and 'conspiratorially' can only be given in the context of knowledge of the relationship between two individuals at the time of speaking. (For further discussion of this area see Crystal 1969, and Brown forthcoming.)

It seems clear that pitch variation or intonation does function as one of the indicators of attitude. Until we know how many different types of attitude we need to characterize and how intonation interacts with the other relevant variables we cannot know how delicate our description of intonation must be. For instance it is open to question whether the only part of the tone group in which pitch functions to indicate attitude is the tonic or nuclear word. Do we also make judgements about the attitude of the speaker from the intonation contour of the part of the tone group that precedes the tonic or nuclear syllable? It has always been tacitly assumed that we do not. Descriptions of intonation always impute the function of attitude marker to the tonic or nuclear word—never, to my knowledge, to the pre-nuclear or pretonic part of the tone group. If this assumption is correct, and it may not be (though one still might regard the tonic or nuclear word as characterizing or focusing the attitude expressed throughout the tone group), all that is required for the description of the function of intonation in expressing attitude would be a range of variables on the tonic or nuclear word. I have already suggested what I think the relevant intonational variables should be—pitch span, placing in voice range and pitch direction.

It is generally agreed that intonation also has some linguistic function, though there is a good deal of uncertainty about just what that function might be. Some attempts have been made to link particular patterns of pitch direction with particular syntactic structures—statements with falls, yes/no questions with rises, and so on. The most ambitious attempt in this direction was by Schubiger (1935, 1958). It can, however, readily be demonstrated that any syntactic pattern can be spoken on any intonation pattern. It might be possible to suggest a tendency for statements to be spoken with falling intonation and yes/no questions with rising intonation. This is the position adopted by many writers on intonation. I suspect that even this may be too strong. In the recorded data that I have studied there are many examples of yes/no questions but they are very rarely asked on a rising intonation. High rising intonation occurs regularly on so-called 'echo questions' and sometimes on yes/no questions when it seems to me the questioner is expressing a conciliatory or markedly courteous attitude to the person he is speaking to, when he is expressing some marked attitude. The only regular specifically syntactic function that I can identify for high rise is to mark 'echo questions' (see Brown forthcoming).

The most obvious syntactic functions of intonation have been, curiously, the least described. These are the function of tone groups to demarcate coherent syntactic structures and the function of the placing of the nuclear or tonic tone to mark the focus of information—the head word—within the syntactic structure. There is no consensus on just what syntactic structure must be regarded as the domain of the tone group. Examination of data will yield examples of two complete sentences being spoken within one tone group, or of one sentence, one clause, even one word within a sentence, being spoken in one tone group—with the tone group clearly marked by pauses on both sides of it. Our difficulty is that once again we are examining examples of performance variation. What we want to describe is competence—in this case we want to know what the 'ideal' intonational structure of a sentence would be. Halliday, on the basis of extensive examination of data, has decided that the 'unmarked' or 'ideal' domain of the tone group is the clause (Halliday 1967). Lieberman, working within the framework of generative phonology, suggests that the speaker 'divides the sentence into the longest breath groups that will still manifest the crucial aspects of the derived constituent structure' (Lieberman 1967, p. 114). Much of his discussion is concerned with the function of intonation in distinguishing between such sentences as:

They decorated + the girl with the flowers
They decorated the girl + with the flowers

Most writers on intonation for foreign students have assumed, tacitly, that the 'ideal' domain of the tone group is the sentence—but the examples they give for students to mimic are not very long sentences. It seems clear that there is some rather ill-defined consensus here—the 'ideal' domain of the tone group is of some coherent syntactic structure, a sentence or a major constituent of a sentence, which may be up to half a dozen words long. The function of the tone group is to delimit the boundaries of this syntactic structure. It is not clear how, at the present time, our notion of the 'ideal' domain of the tone group may be sharpened or just what would constitute evidence that one analysis rather than another is correct. It is clearly impossible to furnish phonetic evidence. We have already discussed the intangible quality of the notion 'same intonation contour'. Exactly the same sort of difficulty is associated with defining the boundaries of tone groups in connected speech. Sometimes they are marked by pause and by a lengthening of the final syllable but quite often there is no pause at all, no lengthening, and no way of deciding on the basis of phonetic evidence whether we are at the end of one tone group or already inside the next. Even if we could establish the boundaries in some principled manner we are still left with the problem that each case we examine is an instance of phonetic performance and we have no readily expressible intuitions about what constitutes competence at this level, that is, about what the 'ideal' relationship between intonation and syntax should be.

The placing of the nuclear or tonic tone within a tone group is a much more accessible area of discussion. This, like the function of tone groups, has for some reason largely been ignored in descriptions of English for language teaching purposes. This is particularly surprising in view of the fact that the patterning of the intonation contours described in textbooks varies strikingly with different dialects, whereas the organization of speech into tone groups and the function of tonic placing are common to all accents of English in all parts of the world. An evident result of this neglect is that many foreign students do not know where to place the tonic in their own speech because they have simply learned whole intonation contours placed, as it must seem to them, at random over various sentences. Neither do they know how to use the information given by placing of the tonic when they attempt to interpret the speech of native speakers. Our present partial understanding of the function of the tonic and of the placing of the tonic in English is due in large part to the work of Halliday (Halliday 1967). The function of the tonic is to mark the focus—the head word—of the syntactic structure contained in the tone group. In an 'ideal' decontextualized tone group the tonic word will be the last lexical word in the tone group. In very many tone groups in the data I have recorded the tonic word is the last lexical word in the tone group. If native speakers are asked to read aloud sentences out of context they will nearly always place the tonic on the last lexical word. It seems, then, that we do have agreed and accessible intuitions about competence in the placing of the tonic.

There are, of course, occasions when the tonic appears on some item other than the last lexical word in the tone group. The notion of 'contrastive stress' is a familiar one in English language textbooks. It is not always appreciated however, that an item bearing contrastive stress also bears the tonic. In the following sentences the tonic is written in capital letters; + indicates a break between tone groups:

(a) When HE jumps + SHE jumps
(b) If there is a certain degree of flexiBIlity + on THEIR side + as well as OURS + there is always HOPE + that a settlement might eMERGE.

In both tone groups in (a) and the second and third tone groups in (b) there are examples of contrastive stress, with grammatical items bearing the tonic.

Contrastive stress, like other examples which involve the placing of the tonic on some item other than the last lexical word in the tone group, only appears when an utterance is spoken in context and refers back either to some previous utterance in the same discourse or to some knowledge of the situation shared by the speaker and his hearer(s). We may regard the shifting of the tonic from the last lexical word in the tone group as a performance variable which is dictated by the discourse structure in which the utterance appears. This implies that the function marked by the placing of the tonic should not be regarded as a function which relates to the syntax of the utterances so much as a function which relates to discourse structure.

I shall now attempt to summarize what I have said about suprasegmentals, and what we understand of their functions.

(a) *stress*

(i) marks the shape of words
(ii) marks the lexical items, the meaningful words, within a tone group.

The native speaker 'knows'

(i) what is the correct stress pattern for a word spoken in isolation
(ii) which words in an utterance should bear stress.

(b) *intonation*

(i) marks, together with other variables, attitude
(ii) marks syntactic boundaries
(iii) marks the focus of information in a tone group
(iv) marks the relation of the focal item to the structure of discourse
(v) marks echo questions (and perhaps other syntactic structures).

The native speaker 'knows' which word should bear the tonic, for a sentence in isolation or within a discourse. The native speaker must clearly also 'know' about the other systems involved since he uses them but he is, so far, unable to state

(i) the function of intonation in expressing attitude
(ii) the 'ideal' domain of the tone group
(iii) the function of direction of pitch movement.

I have tried to explain that there are some areas in the treatment of suprasegmentals that we are beginning to understand but that there remain areas which we have not yet found a way into. I have tried to explain that our inadequacy cannot simply be attributed to failure to observe or describe phonetic data in an adequate way. Phonetic data can only yield information about performance variables whereas what we want to know about is the competence underlying the performance. We want to be able to bring to consciousness our knowledge of how the suprasegmentals work. Obviously in some sense we 'know' how they work since we use them in producing or interpreting every utterance that we experience.

It is important that the language teacher should know in which areas he is treading confidently and in which areas there is no adequate theoretical backing. Too many intonation courses are on the market making claims about areas we do not begin to control. The language teacher must select from those courses which actually do what they claim to do. I have tried in this paper to suggest that teachers should choose wherever practicable a course which makes a clear distinction between competence and performance, between 'ideal' citation forms and the various phonetic forms that will be found to occur in any data that is examined.

3 Further reading

Albrow, K. H. 1968. *The Rhythm and Intonation of Spoken English.* London: Longman. A useful, very basic, introduction to the structure and function of rhythm and intonation in English.

Chomsky, N. and Halle, M. 1968. *The Sound Pattern of English.* New York: Harper & Row. The most ambitious investigation to date of the assignment of lexical stress in English stated in terms of what has become known as the 'standard' theory of generative phonology. The first two chapters present a fairly straightforward introduction to this version of the theory. The penultimate chapter presents a highly technical set of arguments revising much of the theory presented in the earlier part of the book. The final chapter prefigures a yet more basic and drastic innovation which has been received generally with a marked lack of enthusiasm.

Crystal, D. 1969. *Prosodic Systems and Intonation in English.* Cambridge: Cambridge University Press. Contains a detailed discussion of prosodic systems in English, a rather brief discussion of intonation, and a very extensive bibliography.

Halliday, M. A. K. 1967. *Intonation and Grammar in British English.* The

Hague: Mouton. A discussion of the function of the various intonational systems of English: tonality (division into tone groups—information units), tonicity (placing of the tonic within the tone group—information focus) and tone (intonation contours, here illustrated by RP contours).
Halliday, M. A. K. 1970. *A Course in Spoken English: Intonation.* London: Oxford University Press. A very interesting description of the intonation contours of RP, extensively illustrated. (Accompanied by a tape.)
Kingdon, R. 1958. *The Groundwork of English Stress.* London: Longman. A classic description of stress placement in English words.

5 PAUL VAN BUREN
Semantics and Language Teaching

1 Introduction

Let us define a semantic description of a language L as a partial[1] description of the ability of its native speakers to interpret and convey meaningful messages in L. We would expect to find that such a description is relevant to the teaching and learning of L. To illustrate this point let us consider one familiar application of semantic theory, the compilation of dictionaries. It may not be immediately apparent that dictionaries are based on any semantic theories at all but there must clearly be certain guiding principles underlying the making of dictionaries. The difficulty is that these principles are often inconsistent and incomplete, and consequently the end products, that is the entries and their definitions, can be very inadequate. What, for example, is a learner to make of the following definitions (taken from different dictionaries) of the word *naive* as directions for its appropriate use or interpretation:

1 adj. simple, artless, innocent; foolishly frank or credulous; immature.

2 adj. natural and innocent in speech and behaviour (e.g. because young or inexperienced); amusingly simple.

The possibilities of misuse and misunderstanding given these definitions seem endless. For example, given the second definition, can one apply the term to old people without implying that they are 'amusingly simple' or, given the first entry, 'foolishly frank'? Can dogs be naive, or babies? Does 'he acted naturally' imply that the person in question acted naively? Are there such things as naive theories? Can one claim without contradiction that a person may be young and inexperienced but nevertheless not naive?

Clearly a set of directions based on a detailed description of the semantic competence of native speakers of English would be invaluable for teachers

[1] 'Partial' because not every aspect of meaning is subject to systematic investigation. For example the remark 'My uncle is dead' could have different connotations depending on whether it is made by a distant relative who is the sole inheritor of his uncle's vast estate, or by somebody who was very fond of his impecunious kinsman.

and learners. Unfortunately such a description does not exist at the present time. However, some of the main principles underlying various modern theories of semantics may serve as tools for the construction of potentially useful descriptions and it is our aim to discuss these principles in this chapter.

2 The semiotic triangle

Perhaps the most profitable way to discuss recent theories of semantics is to start with some traditional ways of looking at the phenomenon of meaning. Traditionally, but not necessarily universally, the meaning of a word was regarded as a relation between a wordform and the extralinguistic entity it represents, i.e. its referent. This relationship was implicitly regarded as being 'psychologically real' in the sense that it was manifested in the speaker's or hearer's mind as a concept. In other words the concept was regarded as the crucial intermediary between a wordform and its referent and there was consequently no direct link between forms and referents. This absence of a direct link represented the notion that the relation between forms and referents is arbitrary; different languages use different forms (e.g. 'dog' and 'Hund') for the same class of referents (in this case animals of the genus canis) although their meanings are said to be the same. This traditional view is conveniently summarized in the form of what has become known as the 'semiotic triangle':

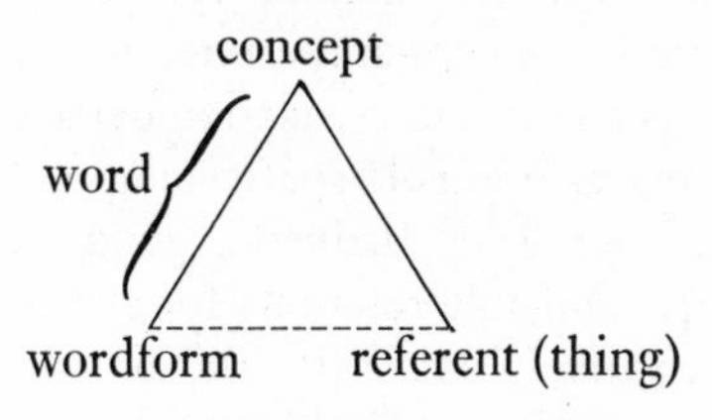

Figure 1

Several points can be made about this theory of meaning to illustrate certain necessary conditions for the construction of adequate semantic theories. First, the linguistic form to be described in this conception of meaning is the word, not the morpheme (that is, the minimal unit of linguistic description that may be said to 'carry meaning'). This fact renders the relationship between forms and concepts obscure for studies based on the morpheme since although it might just be possible to establish a relation between, say, the wordform 'dog' and the concept 'canis' it hardly seems possible to specify a concept corresponding to, for example, the linguistic form 'uncompromisingly' with its four morphological forms *un-*, *compromis(e)*, *-ing*, *-ly*. And if we allow a wordform to correspond to more than one concept we should like to know precisely how these concepts are interrelated. The answer to this question clearly cannot be given on the basis of the semiotic triangle.

Secondly, the word in Figure 1 is not a single entity but a composite one. More precisely, it denotes a pair of entities, namely form and concept, which are different sides of the same coin (i.e. the word) and are therefore inseparable. Behind this duality of representation lies the idea that the form conjures up the concept and vice versa. Now it is not entirely clear what claim is being made about the psychological reality of the word but the notion of 'conjuring up' seems at best unclear. What, for example, is being conjured up when one hears the wordform 'head' as in 'He scratched his head' or 'He is the head of department'? Are different concepts involved here or not? In short, if the triangle represents a partial hypothesis about linguistic performance it seems to fail.

Thirdly, and more importantly, although this scheme implicitly allows on the one hand for total difference in meaning (as exemplified in perhaps its linguistically most telling form, i.e. homonymy, which corresponds here to the same wordform representing two concepts) and on the other hand for total sameness of meaning, or synonymy, it has nothing at all to say about one of the most crucial facts of language, namely, relatedness in meaning. This is a serious gap and indeed it constitutes the crucial difference between traditional and modern semantic theories. We shall see how modern semantics deals with this problem.

The fourth point concerns the obligatoriness of all three terms in the triangle. There must be a form, a concept and a referent for there to be meaning. It follows that there exists an obligatory relation between all linguistic forms and their corresponding extra-linguistic spatio-temporal referents. But what are the referents of words such as 'if', 'naivety', 'good', or 'average'? There do not seem to be any clearly definable referents for any of these. Indeed, it can be argued that only a relatively small (if crucial) part of the vocabulary of a language can be said to bear a definable and by no means direct relation to extra-linguistic entities. This fallacy of the one-one correspondence between form and referent is not to be confused with another common fallacy which equates meaning with reference. The German logician Frege was the first to discuss this fallacy when he pointed out that although the terms 'morning star' and 'evening star' have the same referent (i.e. the planet Venus) they surely do not have the same meaning. (Compare also the forms 'Washington' and 'the capital of the United States'.) Moreover, we must recognize the fact that many forms without referents ('if', for example) are undoubtedly meaningful. Indeed the notion underlying the traditional view of meaning that wordforms in linguistic and/or extra-linguistic isolation are capable of referring at all is almost certainly mistaken even if it is debatable what the minimal syntactic unit of reference should be. An additional difficulty, pointed out by many linguists, is that the referential boundaries of referring expressions need not always be clear for the expression to be understood. What are the precise referential criteria which distinguish, for example, mountains from hills?

The problem of reference, far from being as straightforward as the traditional view implies, constitutes a great challenge to philosophers, linguists and psychologists alike. There is nothing straightforward about a father holding up a pencil to his two-year-old child and saying 'pencil' with the intention of teaching the child the meaning of the word. How does the child know that his father is referring to the object as having a particular function (i.e. 'something to write with') rather than its colour, size, shape or position? Indeed, how does he know why his father is holding it up at all? One thing seems clear: the child must be able to form 'hypotheses' about the significance of pointing and the correct identification of referents. This may be inferred from the fact that children 'make mistakes' in applying the acquired terms but nevertheless approximate to the adult system sooner or later with or without overt corrections. One may postulate the same principle of 'hypothesizing'[1] for the acquisition of referential relations in second language learning, as well as in all other areas of second language acquisition, without losing sight of the fact that the problems for the second language learner appear to be quite different in this respect. Clearly the learner knows in advance the significance of 'pointing' probabilities inherent in ostensive situations. For example, a learner knows that it would be odd for a teacher to hold up a piece of chalk in order to teach the word 'white' without informing him in advance that he is talking about colour. He also knows that it would be perfectly normal for a teacher to hold up a pencil in order to teach the word 'pencil' without prior information that what is being referred to is the function of the object rather than its colour. Finally, textbooks and bilingual dictionaries may create particular problems for the learner in the acquisition of referential relations. An English-speaking learner of German who deduces from a vocabulary list that the German word 'Gemüse' is 'the same as' the English word 'vegetables' is bound sooner or later to commit errors in using the German word.

The semiotic triangle in concentrating exclusively on the word as the central unit of investigation without showing how the meanings of words may be combined to form sentences or utterances does not recognize one of the main problems for any semantic analysis, that is, what falls within the scope of semantics and what does not. It is generally accepted that the study of semantics presupposes a satisfactory solution to the problem of what, if any, the syntactic variables are for any given language and how they determine the nature of the questions to be asked in semantics. For example, if we can show that certain morphemes, words or phrases are fully predictable from certain rules of syntax we can save ourselves the trouble of finding out what the meanings of these elements are. To give a simple example, the first occurrence of the

[1] The inverted commas are meant to indicate that the notion of hypothesis formation used here is not to be taken as identical to its use in scientific contexts but that both are, doubtless, related to the notion of falsifiability.

word 'to' in the sentence 'He wants to go to London' is fully predictable from the rules of English syntax and may therefore be said to have no meaning, whereas the second occurrence of 'to' is not fully predictable. It could be 'through' or 'from' or 'via'. It should be emphasized that the notion of predictability in this connection is entirely a product of one's linguistic theory. An example of this is the question of the meanings of case endings in Latin. If one's theory distinguishes between deep and surface syntax so that the latter does not change the meaning relations in the former but simply 'spells them out', the question of the meanings of case-endings becomes largely a pseudo-question. On a deeper plane, if the theory reduces, say, the difference between 'buy' and 'sell' to the semantic notion of a financial transaction between two parties X and Y such that the movement of goods follows the direction X-Y or Y-X, then depending on the direction of the movement plus the placing of either X or Y in (superficial) subject position both 'sell' and 'buy' are entirely predictable. Consequently the distinction between 'buy' and 'sell' would not be a meaningful distinction since it does not involve any choice over and above the semantic notions mentioned.

At present this problem of the 'division of labour' between syntax and semantics is one of the central issues in linguistics. Its solution should have some relevance to language teaching in that the notion of predictability and the associated concepts of generalization and explanation are fundamental to the writing of textbooks, the presentation and grading of materials and, more directly, the dialogue between teacher and learner.

The final comment on the semiotic triangle concerns the obligatory status of the concept. The question is whether the postulation of concepts is necessary or desirable for the formulation of an adequate semantic theory. Modern theorists are divided on this issue. Some would maintain that everything worth stating about the nature of semantic systems can be said without invoking the notion of 'concept', whereas others take the view that if any progress is to be made towards the formulation of a universally applicable theory of semantics it is difficult to see how theoretical entities corresponding to the traditional notion of concept could be avoided. The following two sections will examine both viewpoints in somewhat greater detail.

3 Collocational theory

All modern approaches to the semantic analysis of natural languages are based on the idea that lexical items are interrelatable. This idea takes three forms depending on whether the relationship is viewed as roughly speaking probabilistic, implicational or conceptual. The probabilistic view of lexical relations was advocated in the work of the British linguist J. R. Firth and has become known as the collocational theory of lexical meaning. Firth maintained that it is part of the meaning of the word 'night' that it is more likely to co-occur (collocate) with the word 'dark' in a discourse than with, say, the word 'hippopotamus'. Or, given the word 'father' that it collocates significantly with 'son', 'shave', 'mother', etc. rather than with 'nail varnish'. These probabilistic lexical relations cut across and are therefore independent of grammatical structure as may be illustrated by the following utterances: 'Father didn't shave this morning', 'Mother couldn't find father's slippers' or 'Like father like son'. Indeed, items may collocate across several sentence boundaries. Moreover, lexical items are not co-extensive with any grammatical unit. 'Put up with' is three words but must be counted as one lexical item if it is found to collocate significantly with a unique cluster of other items. In many cases the criterion of statistically significant collocation will yield overlapping 'definitions' for certain lexical items. For example, 'chair', 'settee', 'stool' and 'seat' might be identified as collocating with the same items, e.g. 'sit', 'comfortable', etc. It must be emphasized that this definition of lexical similarity is independent of referential or conceptual similarity. On the one hand items computed as belonging to the same set on the criterion of collocational overlap may have different 'reference potential' (e.g. 'father' and 'mother') whereas items with the same reference potential may have very different ranges of collocation (e.g. 'kite' and 'aeroplane', where the former is air force slang for the latter).

It is difficult to assess the value of the collocational view of lexical meaning for language teaching. Indirectly, a collocational dictionary based on a collection of samples taken from a number of registers operating in, say, British English would undoubtedly be useful for the construction of teaching materials in spite of the fact that the statistical and computational problems involved in a large-scale study may prove in the end to be unsurmountable.

The difficulty with the collocational theory of lexical meaning lies in several related facts. First, it does not seem to have any clearly definable psycholinguistic implications since nobody, including native speakers of a language, can know in advance of a computational study what the lexical items of his language are, nor how lexical items are related statistically.[1] Moreover, the Firthian view of lexical meaning does not take into account certain facts of 'semantic competence'. The reason is that probabilistically defined lexical relations unlike other approaches are by definition both text-oriented and non-structural. For example, we can demonstrate that native speakers of English know that there is a relation between the words 'father' and 'male' (or 'man') by virtue of the fact that the proposition 'He is a father' implies 'He is male' rather than 'He is female'. But this relation is very unlikely ever to be captured by a probabilistic study of lexis since 'father' and 'male' may never collocate significantly in any sample of English. Speakers of English know the implication in question but they will hardly ever find it necessary to mention the items explicitly in collocation.

[1] It is quite possible that some notion of probability should be included in the concept 'native speaker's competence'. But this notion would not be statistical in nature.

The Firthian view of lexical meaning, then, is unique in that it does not seek to explicate what is generally and intuitively understood by the term 'meaning'. It may be true that the formal criterion of collocation is more objective than other approaches (although this is certainly questionable if one takes a somewhat less restricted view of objectivity) but it may also be true that collocational relations constitute a semantic 'epiphenomenon' in that they may exist as functions of other, more directly relevant factors.

4 Structural semantics

The second approach to lexical relatedness, which we have called 'implicational' for want of a better term, is based on what are known as 'meaning postulates' or 'semantic rules' and derives to a large extent from the eminent logicians and philosophers Tarski and Carnap. The idea of a meaning postulate or semantic rule may be illustrated by the following simple examples:

rule (*a*) father → male
rule (*b*) mother → female

where the arrows are to be understood as expressing a relationship of logical implication (in ordinary language terms *if . . . then*). It should be emphasized that the elements appearing in rules of this type are actual words existing in the language under investigation, and not 'concepts' or 'features'. Stated informally, rule (a) expresses the following proposition: There exists a relationship of implication between the two lexical items 'father' and 'male' in English such that the sentence 'If X is a father then X is a male' is true by virtue of its meaning alone. That is to say, we do not need to prove that as a matter of fact all fathers are male, this is simply a consequence of the meaning of the word 'father'. This criterion of 'true by virtue of meaning' is known in logic as 'analytic truth' and is distinguished from the criterion of 'true as a matter of fact' for which the technical term is 'synthetic truth'. Analogously, a distinction is made between analytic and non-analytic implication. The relation of analytic implication is essential to and holds for all meaning postulates by definition. It is implied by the theory that the meaning of a lexical item is specified by the set of all the meaning postulates in which it appears.

One linguistic semantic theory which develops notions akin to Carnap's meaning postulates is the theory of structural semantics. By 'structural' semantics is meant a theory which specifies the 'sense relations' holding between the lexical items of a language. As a preliminary example consider the following set of lexical items: green, husband, large, offer, learn, nice, flower, dead, red, wife, small, accept, know, tulip, alive. At first sight this seems a random collection of items, but if native speakers were asked to group these items according to similarity or dissimilarity in meaning the following grouping would have an excellent chance of being chosen: green-red, husband-wife, large-small, offer-accept, learn-know, flower-tulip, dead-alive, nice-? The question of why this grouping has a greater-than-chance possibility of occurring can only be answered satisfactorily if we know how to specify the relations between the various items precisely. But what is a precise specification? What, to put it differently, are the basic tools for investigating the relationships between the items in question? The following four concepts are postulated to be fundamental to the definition of lexical sense relations: pragmatic analytic implication, implicit and explicit assertion, implicit and explicit denial, and restricted context.

A hypothetical example illustrates how these terms taken together define the experimental techniques by which data about semantic structure may be obtained. Suppose we want to know what the precise relation is between the English words 'red', 'green' and 'nice'. We could confront native speakers with the following questions: 'In your dialect does the sentence *The book is red* imply the sentence *The book is green*?' Suppose the answer is 'No'. The following question might be: 'Does the sentence *The book is red* imply the sentence *The book is not green*?'—'Yes'. And so on until the following generalized set of data is obtained (the arrow denotes 'implication'): (i) X is red → X is green?—No; (ii) X is red → X is not green?—Yes; (iii) X is green → X is red?—No; (iv) X is green → X is not red?—Yes; (v) X is red → X is nice?—No; (vi) X is red → X is not nice?—No; (vii) X is nice → X is red?—No; (viii) X is nice → X is not red?—No; (ix) X is green → X is nice?—No; (x) X is green → X is not nice?—No; (xi) X is nice → X is green?—No; (xii) X is nice → X is not green?—No.

The following relevant facts emerge from these data: (a) 'red' and 'green' are explicitly asserted to imply each other negatively; (b) no explicitly asserted implication holds between 'red' and 'green' on the one hand and 'nice' on the other. We have, it seems, discovered an explicitly stated relation between 'red' and 'green' which is different from either of these and 'nice'. In fact we may deduce that there is no relation between the colour adjectives in question and 'nice'. Moreover this explicitly asserted relation between 'red' and 'green' may now serve as the basis for postulating an implicit logical relation of negative implication between 'red' and 'green' which might be termed incompatibility. In abbreviated form this relation may be represented as follows: $X \rightarrow \sim Y$ (where '$\sim$' denotes 'not').[1]

Two further points should be made about this example. The first is that the

[1] The relation between 'red' (or 'green') and 'nice' may be represented as $X \rightarrow (Y \wedge \sim Y)$ where '$\wedge$' denotes 'or' and the formula should be read as 'X implies either Y or not Y'. The near vacuousness of this formula indicates that there is no systematic relation between the colour adjectives and 'nice'. Note that the formula is not completely vacuous since it contains at least the (implicit) information that both 'is red' and 'is nice' can be predicated of the same entity (say 'dress'). Compare this with the following proposition which is clearly a non-starter: 'The butter is rancid' implies either 'The butter is deaf' or 'The butter is not deaf'.

diagnostic questions must be capable of being asked without the investigator having to presuppose anything in the context of situation other than that the addressee is a native speaker of English. To use Lyons' terminology the test must be carried out in a restricted context. Secondly, the implication obtained in tests of this sort must be analytic, that is, true by virtue of the meaning of the words in question. In practice this conjunction of the two requirements of restricted context and analyticity may give rise to difficulties in that an informant might construct his own (and therefore non-restricted) context, thereby invalidating the analyticity of his implications. For example, if we had asked our hypothetical informant 'Does the sentence *She is wearing her red dress* imply *She is wearing her nice dress*?' He might have said 'Yes' if he had thought about a particular lady and a particular dress. In other words it is of paramount importance for the investigator to construct the right diagnostic questions, that is, questions which eliminate the risk of undesirable contextualization.[1] This also holds incidentally, for the frequent cases in which the investigator uses himself or a fellow-linguist as informant.

Negative implication (or incompatibility) is one of the logical relations in terms of which a number of important sense relations holding between lexical items may be defined, namely hyponymy, antonymy and converseness.[2]

Hyponymy (or 'inclusion') is a typical relation of incompatibility holding between members of a lexical set or 'lexical field'. It presupposes that the members of such a set have a defining property in common (say the property 'is a flower' or 'is a soldier'). The following data concerning the set of lexical items *tulip*, *rose* and *flower* may serve as an example:

(a) X is a tulip → X is not a rose.
X is a rose → X is not a tulip.
(b) X is a tulip → X is a flower.
X is a rose → X is a flower.
(c) X is a flower → either X is a tulip or X is a rose.

It is clear that 'tulip' and 'rose' are incompatible and that they have something in common (the predicate 'is a flower'). In short, the items 'tulip' and 'rose' are said to be co-hyponyms whereas 'flower' is the superordinate term of the

[1] It might be argued that since there is no cast-iron guarantee against this happening and since consequently we can never be sure of getting consistent results without indoctrinating our informants, which may in itself invalidate the results, the notion of objective informant testing may be at best an act of faith and at worst a vacuous procedure. However, no matter how great the practical and theoretical difficulties may be in this kind of objective testing it seems quite clear that the use of implications in one form or another is a necessary condition for making semantics empirical (however broadly or narrowly we define the term 'empirical').

[2] There are other relations which have been explicitly formulated and undoubtedly many others yet undiscovered, but the ones described here may suffice for illustration. For a full treatment see Lyons 1963.

set. It should be noted that, in general, the lexical field thus defined may denote a continuum (for example colour-terms) or not (for example military ranks). In addition it may be observed that there is no necessity for a lexical field to have a one-item superordinate term. The field of colour terms is a case in point. It would be a mistake to take the adjective 'coloured' as the superordinate term of this set since, to raise but one objection, 'coloured' may be opposed to 'white' in English. (Compare 'He is not coloured, he is white', etc.)

The lexical relation of *antonymy* has traditionally been called 'oppositeness of meaning'. This traditional terminology has the disadvantage that it lumps together a number of relations which should really be kept apart in view of the fact that their underlying logical relations are different. For example, the relationship between the items 'dead' and 'alive' is distinct from the one between 'young' and 'old'. There is a logical relation between 'dead' and 'alive' such that to predicate of X that it is dead implies analytically that it is not alive whereas to predicate that X is not alive can only imply that X is dead. In other words the items are contradictory with respect to each other. However, although 'young' certainly implies 'not old', it is not the case that 'not old' necessarily implies 'young'. It could imply, say, 'middle-aged'. In logical terms we would say that 'young' and 'old' are contraries rather than contradictories. The difference is clearly due to the fact that a set of contradictories always consists of two members whereas a set of contraries contains more than two members.

As a consequence the items in the two-member sets are logically non-gradable (i.e., they cannot logically be placed on a scale of intensity typically expressed by the use of the items 'more' or 'less') whereas the items belonging to a set of contraries are gradable, this manifesting itself in their comparative and superlative forms. There is an apparent complication in the fact that it is certainly not impossible to use what we might term 'pseudo-comparative' expressions involving contradictory terms as exemplified in the sentences *He was more dead than alive* and *I am half-dead*. However, there is no getting away from the fact that the logical implication here undoubtedly is that the subject is alive. This is not to say of course that matters of usage such as these should not be the concern of linguistics. It might even be argued that anomalies of this type epitomize man's linguistic creativity and should therefore be central to the linguist's search for explanations. The notion of grading, which was first studied by the American linguist Edward Sapir (see Sapir 1921) is important for two reasons. It is undoubtedly a universal and it may be either explicit or implicit. Explicit grading manifests itself in the overt comparison of predicates (traditionally known as the comparative and superlative degrees). Implicit grading, as the name suggests, never appears on the surface but is nevertheless there. It applies whenever inherently antonymous adjectives appear in their non-compared forms. For example, to be able to predicate of a house that it is large implies that one knows at least one other house which is in the speaker's opinion or as a matter of fact smaller. This allows us to resolve a paradox of Greek philosophy concerning an entity X which is shorter than Y but longer than Z. The question was how can an entity be long and short at the same time? It is clear that this is only a paradox by virtue of the fact that relative terms (gradable adjective) are being confused with 'absolute' terms (i.e., non-gradable adjectives). There is no contradiction in saying that an entity may be large for an animal but small for an elephant.

One final fact may be noted in connection with antonymy. Given two pairs of antonyms in English (say large and small) it is generally the case that one item is 'marked' whereas the other is 'unmarked'. The notion of 'markedness' as used here has nothing to do with morphological markings nor with degrees of probability of occurrence (as in some theories of generative phonology) but with what is presupposed as knowledge by speakers and hearers when they are engaged in discourse. For example, if a speaker wishes to know the relative size of an object 'without prejudice', he will ask the question (a) 'How large is it?' rather than (b) 'How small is it?' Compare also 'How long is it?' with 'How short is it?' In other words (b) is marked for presupposition whereas (a) is not. This general area of 'presupposition' and 'conversational implicature'[1] has received a great deal of attention recently. It should be pointed out that this important but non-obvious part of linguistic competence has been neglected in language teaching.

The lexical relation of *converseness* has often misleadingly been called 'oppositeness of meaning'. It concerns the relation between pairs of items such as husband—wife, buy—sell, please—like, etc. The logical implications holding between these pairs may be illustrated with the following set of examples:

X is the husband of Y $\supset$ Y is the wife of X
X buys Y from Z $\supset$ Z sells Y to X
X likes Y $\supset$ Y pleases X

In other words converseness is a typical case of a relation which takes syntax into account for its logical specification. We might say that it resembles antonymy under conditions of transformation. All the cases dealt with so far involve pairs of items between which holds a relation of 'strong' converseness, that is, the relation exists between two items rather than three or more. However, there are numerous cases of 'weak' or 'disjunctive' converseness where the relation holds between more than two lexical items. The items *offer*, *accept* and *refuse* may be used to illustrate this notion of weak converseness. The logical relation between these three items is:

$$\text{X offers Y to Z} \supset \begin{Bmatrix} \textit{either} \ \text{Z accepts Y} \\ \textit{or} \ \text{Z refuses Y} \end{Bmatrix}$$

[1] There is not much consistency in the use of these terms in the literature. For a general discussion of presupposition in linguistic theory see Fillmore (1971). The notion of 'conversational implicature' is discussed in Gordon and Lakoff (1971).

That is, the relation between 'offer', 'accept' and 'refuse' is always defined relative to the item 'offer' rather than either of the others. The lexical relation of weak converseness illustrates two important points about the theory of structural semantics. The first point concerns the notion of 'application' (which corresponds to the widest possible interpretation of the term 'reference') and the important fact that sense relations may not hold for all possible contexts. The French triplet *offrir*, *accepter* and *refuser* illustrates this fact. Viewed in the abstract, without regard to their application to particular situations, the French items in question are clearly bound together by the relation of weak converseness as are their English translation equivalents. However, there are situations in French where the relation of weak converseness is suspended in favour of a relation of strong converseness between *offrir* and *accepter*. It is perfectly acceptable in French to say *Je lui ai offert un sac-à-main pour son anniversaire* of which the unacceptable literal English equivalent is 'I offered her a handbag for her birthday'.[1] Note that English comes very close to this situation in the phrases 'to offer a free pardon', or to a lesser degree, 'to offer a reward'. Is the relation of weak converseness suspended in these cases or not?[2]

Examples like these show that the appropriate application of lexical items and the possibility of 'suspension' of sense relations should be considered as much part of a native speaker's competence as his knowledge of the corresponding sense relation in the abstract. It goes without saying that one could hardly overestimate the usefulness to language teachers of a compendium incorporating information about the intricate networks of sense relations in a language as well as detailed rules about the application of lexical items.

The second point about a theory of sense relations illustrated by the items 'offer', 'refuse' and 'accept' concerns the status of a conceptual analysis of the items in question compared with a strictly non-conceptual view. We might ask: Does the lexical item 'offer' have a conceptual status over and above the fact that it stands in a relationship of weak converseness to the items 'accept' and 'refuse'? The short answer must be 'No' if we take existing dictionaries as our guide. They invariably define the verb 'offer' as 'hold out in hand or tender in words or otherwise, for acceptance or refusal', or paraphrases thereof. And indeed it is difficult to see how a 'feature' or 'componential' type of analysis, which we are about to discuss, could improve on this definition, whereas it is easy to see how it might distort the facts. There seems to be no valid *a priori* reason why 'lexical competence' should not be a mixed system,

[1] We must add that the English equivalent is not unacceptable in a situation where John and Mary are having a discussion prior to Mary's birthday about the desirability of Mary being given a handbag. In this case it would be perfectly appropriate to add 'but she refused'; hence 'offer' would be in order.

[2] Consider also, on a different plane, the difference between 'offer prayer' and 'give prayer'. Is the former less 'presumptuous' than the latter?

assuming that there is a non-trivial difference between analyses based on concepts and those based on rules of implication between actual lexical items plus their application. A mixed view would explain the fact that it is possible to use the word 'father' correctly in English if one merely knows the features involved (e.g. male, first ascending generation, etc.), but that it does not seem possible to use the verb 'offer' correctly in English without knowing the precise relationship between it and the lexical items 'accept' and 'refuse'.

5 Componential analysis

So far we have discussed two modern approaches to the semantic analysis of natural languages which are based on the idea that lexical items are interrelatable, namely, a collocational approach and a theory of structural relations in semantics. The third type of analysis, which goes under the name of componential analysis and which shares the assumption that lexical items are interrelatable, differs from the others in two respects. In componential analysis we assume that all lexical items can be 'broken down' into certain component parts, or 'features', and that the relationships between the components which hold across lexical items can be stated and labelled systematically. To illustrate in an informal way that there seems to be some substance in these claims the reader is invited to substitute the correct lexical item for the hyphenated words in the following:

> Listen, true-lineal-male-of-first-ascending-generation-ego-speaking-informally, I need the car tonight.[1]

The fact that many speakers of English can supply the correct item (i.e. 'dad') may be taken to illustrate two general assumptions underlying componential analysis, firstly the assumption that the idea of components or features is inherent in the notion of lexical competence[2] (without prejudging the question of whether these represent the 'correct' components) and secondly the assumption that language at the lexical level is a very economical system for conveying information but that the price we pay for this economy is, to a greater or lesser degree dependent on the type of language, semantic opacity on the surface.[3]

The first task of componential analysis, then, is to discover and state as economically as possible what semantic components or distinctive features there are in a language, and, more significantly, across languages, which

[1] This example is taken from Romney and D'Andrade (1964).

[2] The question arises whether one could actually conceive of a human language which does *not* possess decomposable lexical items. Compare in this respect many animal languages where there exists a one-to-one correspondence between a sign and the thing signified.

[3] Some languages are lexically more transparent on the surface than English, notably 'agglutinating' languages such as Turkish or certain Amerindian languages. Compare also French 'coup-de-pied' and 'coup-de-poing' with English 'kick' and 'punch'.

amounts to a statement about the structural properties of a vocabulary system. This is of course an immense task and in practice the exercise has been limited to an investigation of the structural properties of certain relatively well-defined lexical fields, notably kinship terms. Indeed this type of systematic analysis owes its existence largely to social anthropologists for reasons implied below.

The second task of componential analysis is generally accepted to be that of labelling the semantic components in such a way that they reflect cognitive reality, but it is important to note that this second task by no means forms a necessary condition for carrying out the first task. Indeed the second task may conflict with the first task in certain respects. We may illustrate these points by the familiar example of English kinship terminology using a very restricted set of items, namely *aunt*, *uncle*, *father*, *mother*, *sister* and *brother*.

By a process of factorization involving proportions such as sister : brother : : aunt:uncle, sister:aunt::brother:uncle, we establish the fact that lexical items may share a property along one dimension (sister and aunt, brother and uncle). This technique allows us to construct the following grid for the items in question:

	a	b	c	d	e
aunt	○	+	+	○	+
uncle	○	+	+	+	○
father	+	○	+	+	○
mother	+	○	+	○	+
sister	○	+	○	○	+
brother	○	+	○	+	○

In the above grid the point of reference is Ego (that is, an idealized member of the kinship system) and the columns labelled a, b, c, d, e denote the dimensions along which the items differ (indicated by ○) or agree (indicated by +). With five arbitrarily labelled components (a, b, c, d, e) we have stated the structure of this subsystem, that is, the componential differences and similarities holding between these six items, in the most economical terms. Now we could replace the arbitrary labels a, b, c, d, e by the corresponding semantic features or components: 'lineal' (a), 'collateral' (b), 'first ascending generation' (c), 'male' (d) and 'female' (e). The question is, do these labels 'reflect reality', i.e., are they cognitively valid for native speakers of standard English?

To appreciate some of the problems involved let us consider the following situation. Suppose we label the distinction between *aunt* and *uncle* as a difference in generation instead of a difference in sex such that, say, *aunt* is labelled as two generations above Ego and *uncle* as one generation above Ego. It is fair to speculate that no native speaker would accept this as a valid dimension along which the two terms can be distinguished, although of course the component would distinguish between them. Note also that in order to elevate this speculation to the realm of facts one would have to carry out some rather complicated psycholinguistic experiments involving naive and non-naive subjects alike. In other words the concept of generation is a complex theoretical term, an abstraction from possibly a large number of 'pieces of knowledge' existing in the minds of the members of a kinship system.

Let us suppose, then, that the sex distinction is the relevant one between the items *aunt* and *uncle* (by 'relevant' we mean established as cognitively real). We must now ask, is this the only cognitively valid distinction between the two terms? Suppose for the sake of argument that we discovered, in addition to the sex dimension, a component of 'affection' such that aunts are invariably hated by native speakers and uncles invariably loved. Now if this second component is also cognitively valid the question arises which of the two should be used in a semantic description, and on what grounds. Alternatively we might state both and give up the requirement that components should only minimally distinguish between lexical items, thereby presumably abandoning the principle of maximum economy in semantic description. Moreover, if we did not abandon this principle what claims to cognitive validity would our description possess?

The above example is of an artificial nature but it illustrates the difficulties involved in establishing the cognitive reality of semantic components. Indeed, even in a relatively well-defined field such as kinship terms problems of this sort appear to be virtually insoluble judging by the fact that they have caused serious disagreements among anthropologists for over 25 years.

In addition to the two tasks mentioned above, the third task of componential analysis is regarded by a number of linguists as being the postulation and empirical confirmation of semantic universals, that is, the discovery of all those components whose corresponding cognitive reality resides in the collective mind of the human race. That this is bound to be an extremely long-term task, if indeed it is possible at all, may be inferred from the comments made earlier about the investigation of kinship terminology.

The theories of semantics so far discussed lack one ingredient essential to a full description of linguistic competence: they have nothing to say about what the necessary conditions are for the possible sentences of a language to acquire their meanings from the combination of lexical items and/or morphemes of which they consist. In short, they do not concern themselves explicitly with what has become the central issue in linguistics, the relationship between syntax and semantics.

That there is a problem may be illustrated by the following set of examples:

Visiting aunts can be boring.
It can be boring to visit aunts.
To visit aunts can be boring.
Aunts who visit can be boring.
Aunts can be boring to visit.
Visiting aunts can be boring but I don't mind.
Visiting aunts can be boring but I don't mind them once a month.
Visiting aunts can be boring and I love it.
Visiting aunts can be boring and I love them.
Visiting aunts can be boring but I love it (nevertheless).
Visiting aunts can be boring but I love them (nevertheless).
Visiting aunts can be boring and I hate it (when they do).
Visiting aunts can be boring and I hate them.
Visiting aunts can be boring but I hate it.
Visiting aunts can be boring I suppose but fortunately my aunt never goes out.
Visiting aunts can be boring I suppose but unfortunately my aunt never goes out.
My pretty aunt is a teacher.
I have only one aunt.
I have more than one aunt.
His pretty wife is a teacher.

The reader is invited to identify those sentences which are ambiguous, non-ambiguous, definitely anomalous, relatively anomalous, paraphrases, or presupposed by other sentences in the set. In addition the reader is invited to attempt an explanation of his conclusions with a view to presenting them to an imaginary learner of English.

6 The projection problem

It should be clear from examples like those given above that there is more to semantic competence than knowing the meaning of vocabulary items. That this is so has long been realized by grammarians and others (witness discussions about the difference in meaning between sentences such as *The boy loves the girl* and *The girl loves the boy*) but the American linguists Katz, Fodor and Postal were the first to draw conclusions from these facts about the organization of an adequate linguistic theory (see Katz and Fodor 1963, Katz and Postal 1964). Although their earlier proposals have come in for heavy criticism from linguists (including Fodor and Postal themselves) they are worth summing up because more recent theories relate to them either positively or negatively. The central problem for linguistic description as Katz and Fodor see it is what they call the 'projection problem', that is, the problem of constructing rules which will project or generate an infinite set of sentences in such a way that the rules reflect the speaker's ability to understand and produce a theoretically infinite set of new sentences.[1]

The linguistic representation of this ability on the part of the speaker may be seen as a compositional function, i.e., a specification of the value of the whole in terms of the way in which the components are combined. Syntax solves part of the projection problem and semantics the remainder. According to Katz and Fodor, this follows from the fact that the syntactic component of a grammar can in no way be said to specify the meaning of sentences. For example, the syntactic component may generate equivalent structural descriptions (that is, minus the lexical items) for sentences with different meanings (e.g. *The dog bit the man* and *The cat scratched the woman*) whereas, conversely, it may generate different structural descriptions for synonymous sentences (e.g. *The dog bit the man* and *The man was bitten by the dog*). In other words the distinction between syntax and semantics is a sharp one for Katz and Fodor. This results in their assertion that synchronic linguistic description minus syntax equals semantics (leaving aside phonology).

It should be emphasized that any statements about the way in which utterances are used or understood in situations is ruled out by the above definition. According to Katz and Fodor, semantics should not account in any way for the relation between utterances and situations. This is theoretically impossible by virtue of the fact that the theory would have to account for all the knowledge speakers have about the world. Knowledge of language should not be confused with knowledge of the world. The upper limit of a semantic theory, then, is the way in which speakers interpret sentences regardless of situations. The lower bounds of a semantic theory are such that it should account for at least the following abilities of the native speaker: (a) the ability to detect non-syntactic ambiguities (e.g., *The bill is large*); (b) the ability to eliminate potential ambiguities by determining the exact number of possible interpretations (cf. *The bill is large but needn't be paid*); (c) the ability to detect semantic anomalies or deviation (e.g., *The paint is silent*); (d) the ability to recognize paraphrase (cf. the well-known examples *Two chairs are in the room* and *There are at least two things in the room and each is a chair*).

The other two central assumptions in Katz and Fodor are the following. Firstly, the semantic component in a grammar interprets the syntactic component and therefore presupposes a satisfactory syntactic theory. Secondly, the semantic component interprets only the 'deep' part of the syntactic component. The transformational part of syntax is irrelevant to statements of meaning or, to put it differently, 'transformations don't change meaning'. The reason for this is that surface structure may distort underlying

[1] Or, more correctly, utterances. For the crucial distinction between sentences and utterances see Lyons 1968.

grammatical structure to such an extent that it would be impossible for a semantic component to interpret it. The semantic component consists of a dictionary (i.e., an unordered list of lexical items) and a so-called 'projection rule component'. The dictionary provides representations of the semantic characteristics of lexical items (morphemes) necessary to account for facts about sentences that syntax leaves unexplained (e.g., *The dog bit him* versus *The cat bit him*). However, a syntactic component plus a dictionary alone are not sufficient to determine the correct number and content of interpretations of a sentence. For example, given three senses of the word *seal* how do we select the correct interpretation in *One of the oil seals in my car is leaking*? A combination of syntax and dictionary entries will also fail to account for semantic anomalies. What is needed are rules which will take account of the semantic relations between morphemes plus the interaction between syntactic and semantic information. These are the projection rules which select the appropriate sense of each lexical item in a sentence. As a result they mark semantic ambiguities, anomalies and paraphrases and 'explicate the doctrine that the meaning of a sentence is a function of the meaning of its parts'.

Dictionary entries consist of two parts:

(a) a grammatical section which specifies what grammatical category the lexical items belong to
(b) a semantic section representing the various senses of the lexical item given its grammatical category.

The semantic section is divided into one or more paths (representing the sense or senses of an item); a number of semantic 'markers' or components similar to those used in componential analysis which are represented in round brackets; one or more 'distinguishers' represented in square brackets; and crucially a number of selectional restrictions represented in angled brackets. Semantic markers or components—e.g. (concrete object) (animate) (human) (male) (young) for *boy*—are theoretical constructs and a means for decomposing the sense of a lexical item into its atomic concepts so as to represent semantic structure in a dictionary. An important function of semantic markers is to represent the semantic relations between dictionary entries (e.g. the similarities and differences between the items *boy* and *man*).

Distinguishers by contrast reflect what is idiosyncratic about the meaning of an item. For example, according to the theory, the distinguisher [who has never married] represents what is unique to one of the paths of the item *bachelor* whereas its semantic markers (concrete object) (animate) (human) (male) distinguish it from other items in the language in a systematic way. Only markers will determine which sense of an item will be selected for a lexical item occurring in a sentence. For example, given several senses of the word *honest* the sense-reading 'chaste' will not be selected for the phrase *honest man* as a result of the incompatibility (which is formally expressed for each sense in its attached selectional restriction) between this interpretation and the marker (male) inherent in the item *man*.

Very generally speaking the projection rules must account for the fact that syntactic information can disambiguate the semantic ambiguities which may be inherent in parts of a sentence (e.g., 'The stuff is light' as opposed to 'The stuff is light enough to carry' where *light* is disambiguated). This is effected by proceeding from the bottom to the top of a constituent structure tree so that a series of 'amalgamated' interpretations is created. For example, the item *ball* is at least three-ways ambiguous, as are the phrases *colourful ball* and *the colourful ball*. However, the verb phrase *hit the colourful ball* is only two-ways ambiguous since we can discard the interpretation (social activity), leaving both (physical object) (non-solid) and (physical object) (solid), i.e., in the sense of cannon-ball. Since the subject noun phrase *the boy* does not disambiguate the verb phrase any further, the sentence *The boy hit the colourful ball* has at least two possible interpretations (disregarding the possibility of more than three senses for the item *ball*).

7 Generative and interpretive semantics

Although the theory proposed originally by Katz, Postal and Fodor is somewhat out of favour at present it deserves credit for having initiated the greatest debate to have taken place so far on the integration of semantic phenomena into an over-all theory of language. After eight years of often heated argument the issue has resolved itself into the question of whether a line can be drawn between syntactic and semantic phenomena or not. In other words, the question is whether the notion of an autonomous syntax in generative grammars as originally envisaged by Chomsky can be maintained. As a result two schools of thought have developed within the framework of transformational-generative theory made up of those who believe, on the basis of empirical evidence, that there is essentially no difference between syntax and semantics, and those who believe with Chomsky, and also on the basis of empirical evidence, that there is. The first current of ideas has come to be known as 'generative semantics', the second as 'interpretive semantics'. It should be pointed out that the proposals of the latter school differ in crucial respects from the original assumptions by Katz, Postal and Fodor.

As has already been pointed out, Katz, Postal and Fodor, and Chomsky in 1965, proposed that the semantic component of a grammar should interpret all and only the deep structures of sentences, without transformations contributing in any way to the semantic interpretation of sentences. In other words, the deep structures of sentences fully determine their semantic representations. More recently, however, Chomsky has pointed out that this model of linguistics is too severely constrained and that in order to achieve all-round descriptive adequacy certain semantic phenomena must be accounted for in terms of the surface structures of sentences. Chomsky (1968b) cites the operation of the passive transformation in English as an example. Thus the two sentences

1 Einstein has taught me physics.
2 I have been taught physics by Einstein.

are different in meaning in spite of the identity of their basic grammatical relations, namely those between the agent of the action (*Einstein*) and the verb *taught* on the one hand and the verb *taught* and its semantic object (*I* or *me*) on the other. The difference in meaning lies in the fact that 1 presupposes that the agent (Einstein) is still alive whereas 2 does not carry that presupposition (that is, Einstein may or may not be alive at the time of utterance).

These semantic facts about the perfective aspect in English are clearly part of the competence of a native speaker and must therefore be accounted for in an adequate grammar of English. The question is how? Chomsky maintains that these facts should be regarded as part of the surface structure of the sentences in question and he has consequently modified the theory originally proposed so as to allow in certain cases for transformations which contribute to semantic interpretation. This proposal, however, does not affect the autonomous status of syntax in the theory since the basic syntactic relations are still defined by the base component of a grammar. The generative semanticists, on the other hand, maintain that all semantic aspects of sentences, including the facts about the perfective aspect discussed above, should be treated as being determined uniquely by their deep structures. One important corollary to this proposal, which makes it crucially different from the original theory of Katz and Fodor, is that since the full semantic representations are uniquely determined by deep structures these deep structures should in fact be regarded as identical (or at least equivalent) with semantic representations. In other words, the deep structures of sentences *are* their semantic representations and consequently there is no longer an autonomous level of syntactic description.

It is not possible to describe in detail the controversy between the theory of semantically based grammars and what has become known as the 'extended standard theory'. The adequacy of either type of theory as a device for describing and explaining the phenomenon of human language is far from established. What is certain is that the controversy has yielded a great number of insights into a variety of linguistic phenomena.

The divergence of theoretical viewpoints within the transformational-generative camp was heralded by various publications in the mid-sixties. One of these by G. Lakoff (1968) concerns the nature and status of instrumental adverbs in the base component of a generative grammar. Lakoff considers the following examples:

3 Seymour sliced the salami with a knife.
4 Seymour used a knife to slice the salami.

He argues that both types of construction have identical selectional restrictions. To mention some of these, verbs which are used with either construction must express an activity and therefore 5 and 6 are ungrammatical for the same reason:

5 *Albert knew the answer with a slide rule.
6 *Albert used a slide rule to know the answer.

In addition, the subject noun phrases involved must be animate:

7 *The explosion killed Harry with dynamite.
8 *The explosion used dynamite to kill Harry.

Furthermore, there are no 'instrumentals of instrumentals' possible in either construction:

9 *Harry broke the window with a hammer with a chisel.
10 *Harry used a hammer to use a chisel to break the window.

These are a few examples to illustrate Lakoff's argument that, since it has always been one of the tenets of transformational theory to link sameness of selectional restrictions to identity in deep structure (actives and their corresponding passive being a paradigm case), the *use* and *with* constructions should really be alternative realizations of the same deep structure. It follows, crucially for Lakoff, that the deep structure in question would have to be a great deal more abstract (in the sense of 'more remote from surface structure') than had been envisaged up to 1966.

Chomsky argues against this proposition by citing the following examples and many others:

11 He used the table to lean the ladder (against).
12 *He leant the ladder (against) with the table.

In cases like these the restrictions on the constructions are not identical. Whatever the merits of either argument an explicit semantic connection must be made at some stage in the description of the paired sentences to rule out anomalies such as:

13 *He cut the meat with a knife but he didn't use a knife.

or to predict the synonymy of the following:

14 He cut the meat with this knife all right but he didn't use it properly.
15 He used this knife to cut the meat (with) all right but he didn't use it properly.

Lakoff's solution to the semantic problem of instrumental adverbs in the 'use' constructions led eventually to the theory of generative semantics. Lakoff proposes that the deep component of the grammar is so constrained that it contains no adverbial categories at all and thus no instrumental adverbs. As a consequence the syntactic category 'prepositional phrase' which comprises the functional category 'adverb' has to be transformationally derived.

Two developments in particular may be said to lie at the heart of generative semantics. The first concerns the application of symbolic logic to the formulation of the deep component, and the adaptation of logical categories to suit a wide range of phenomena in natural language as opposed to the rather restricted area of application traditionally associated with philosophic logic. The second development has to do with the operation of lexical insertion in transformational grammars. A simple example of pronominalization in English illustrates how the application of logic may be relevant to the representation of semantic deep structures.

In the 'standard' theory proposed by Chomsky in *Aspects of the Theory of Syntax* the sentence

16 The man saw himself (in the mirror).

is derived transformationally from a deep structure which may conveniently be abbreviated as

17 NP(the man) V(saw) NP(the man)

A pronominalization transformation converts the rightmost NP (*the man*) into the reflexive pronoun *himself* on condition that the two NPs are strictly identical (that is, the lexical item and the referent must be the same in both cases). The point about the deep structure represented in 17 is that it contains no semantic information. The question arises whether this is the correct solution for all cases. McCawley (1968) has argued that it cannot be the correct solution in view of sentences such as

18 Those men saw themselves.

which is ambiguous between the interpretations

19 Each of the men saw himself.

and

20 The entire group of men saw the entire group of men.

In other words, on the interpretation given in 19 there was an event for each man in which he saw himself in the mirror but in the interpretation given in 20 there was a single event in which the whole group of men participated. Clearly, this difference in interpretation is not accounted for in the deep structure given in 17 and therefore, according to McCawley, it constitutes a counter-example to the theory put forward in *Aspects*. McCawley suggests that the deep structures of the two interpretations should contain the relevant semantic information to account for the difference. For example, corresponding to the interpretation represented in 19 we would get a logical (or semantic) formula 21, represented here in non-symbolic terms:

21 For each member x of the set M(= men) there is one corresponding event y(of seeing) such that 'x $\text{saw}_{(y)}$ x'.

That is, 21 represents the fact that there are at least as many events of seeing as there are men, while a different logical formula would represent the interpretation given in 20.

The second central area of development associated with generative semantics relates to lexical insertion in a transformational theory of language. In all versions of transformational theory other than generative semantics the insertion of lexical items into the phrase markers of sentences (which is effected by a general category of transformations called lexical transformations) takes place at a well-defined stage of derivation, namely before any non-lexical transformations apply. Given this state of affairs we may define the deep structure of a sentence as the initial phrase marker produced by the base rules of the grammar and the lexical insertion rules associated with this phrase marker. In contrast, generative semanticists argue that in order not to miss obvious generalizations, both semantic and syntactic, a well-defined stage of lexical insertion cannot be maintained in transformational theories and that some lexical insertion must be allowed to apply after non-lexical transformations have been applied to the initial phrase markers of sentences. Many examples are advanced in the literature involving pairs such as *kill/cause-to-die*, *remind/cause-to-remember* (as one interpretation of 'remind') etc. The generative semanticists hold that for several reasons of generality sub-trees such as *cause-to-die*, *cause-to-remember* should be part of the initial phrase marker of a sentence and after various non-lexical transformations have been applied to the structure in question these sub-trees should ultimately be replaced by the associated lexical items *kill* and *remind*. A single example illustrates one of the reasons why generative semanticists maintain that lexical insertion must take place after certain non-lexical transformations have applied. In 22, it is crucial to the application of the word *latter* that given two preceding human NP's its antecedent should be the one nearest to it in surface structure:

22 It's obvious to John that the president is a great statesman and that's why the latter is admired by him.

The relevant part of the deep structure of 22 is 23:

23 That the president is a great statesman is obvious to John.

In other words, since the antecedent of *latter* precedes the NP *John* in deep structure the lexical item *latter* cannot be inserted at this stage to give the correct result. Two non-lexical transformations (extraposition and it-replacement) must be applied to produce the correct order of constituents for *latter* to apply.

As was stated earlier, one of the characteristics of the theory of generative semantics is that many if not all lexical items of a language are associated with parts of phrase-structure trees which represent the 'essential' part of their meaning. They are replaced by a lexical insertion transformation for these subtrees after the latter have undergone certain transformations such as 'predicate raising'. A schematic example illustrates the operations involved. The sentence *John killed Bill* might be represented in its initial phrase marker as follows (irrelevant details have been omitted):[1]

```
            S0
   ________|________
  |        |        |
  V0       NP       NP
  |        |        |
  do      John      S1
                ____|____
               |         |
               V1        NP
               |         |
             cause       S2
                     ____|____
                    |         |
                    V2        NP
                    |         |
                  become      S3
                          ____|____
                         |         |
                         V3        NP
                         |         |
                        not        S4
                               ____|____
                              |         |
                              V4        NP
                              |         |
                            alive      Bill
```

A cyclic transformation labelled 'predicate raising' applies as follows. On the first application it raises V_4 (*alive*) of S_4 and adjoins it to V_3 (*not*) of S_3. The

[1] The reason why V's appear as initial categories need not concern us here. For a justification the reader is referred to McCawley (1970). The lexical categories relevant to the argument are in italics. Note that the category V marks logical predicates (e.g. *not*) rather than what is traditionally understood by the category 'Verb'. Relevant categories are subscripted 0, 1, 2, etc. for convenience.

resulting composite V_3 (*not-alive*) is in turn raised and adjoined to V_2 (*become*) and so on until V_0 (*do*) is reached. The result is a composite V 'do-cause-become-not-alive'. This is replaced by the phonological dictionary item *kill* which is marked for the appropriate conditions of insertion. It should be noted that the different stages of lexical composition in our example may each be coded by a different lexical item. For example 'not-alive' could be substituted by *dead* and 'become-not-alive' by *die*. There is, in other words, a lexical hierarchy in the dictionary of a generative semantic theory: *alive* is logically prior to *dead*, which in turn is prior to *kill*. To give another example, the semantic characteristics of *remember* are contained in *remind* and therefore the item *remember* may be said to be 'more primitive' than *remind*, or conversely *remind* may be labelled as less primitive than *remember*, or as being 'derived' from it.

The notion of a lexical hierarchy raises the interesting question of what the primitive set of lexical items of a language might be and what criteria are applicable for its establishment. Why, for example should the item *dead* be decomposed as 'not-alive' rather than *alive* as 'not-dead'? There are various possible answers to this particular problem but it is not clear from the literature what, in general, the relevant criteria are for determining the primitive set of items. One might speculate that this set will turn out to be the one closest to perceptual and/or ontogenetic 'reality'. To illustrate this point consider the items *blunt*, *sharp*, *remind* and *remember*. If a child asks us for the meaning of 'blunt' we would probably express our answer in words comprising the items 'not' and 'sharp', but the converse situation would be rather different. An explanation of 'sharp' as 'not blunt' would be absurd. We would prefer to use notions such as 'cutting' or 'wounding' or the like. It seems that most adults whether they are parents or not have a reasonable idea of what is and what is not ontogenetically absurd in vocabulary acquisition. In the case of the pair *remind-remember*, it is difficult to imagine somebody learning the meaning of 'remind' (in one sense only of course) without prior knowedge of the meaning of 'remember'.

The concept of lexical hierarchy points to the fact that generative semantics is based on what we have called an implicational theory of semantics, that is, a theory which specifies the sense relations holding between lexical items rather than conceptual features, plus the added refinement of the hierarchy itself. The implication for a theory of semantic universals seems to be that the primitive set of items has to be discovered for every language and that, hopefully, the individual sets will turn out to be largely equivalent. The differences between the lexical systems of different languages could then turn out to be merely differences of 'encoding', that is, the building blocks of the various systems would be largely identical but the combination of the blocks would be more or less unique to every language. This would not preclude the possibility that the laws underlying the formation of derived items may be universal, depending for example on the nature of the phrase structure configurations available for lexical substitution. In short, the notion of 'possible lexical item' may be subject to universal constraints.

8 Pedagogic considerations

In what ways can we expect a knowledge of semantic theory to be of help to the teacher in the classroom? In attempting to answer this question, we should bear in mind that no language teaching at any level can take place without some reference to linguistic theory, of which semantic theory is a part. Whether or not we make overt reference to linguistic theory in the classroom, depends on essentially pedagogic factors, such as the age of the students, their linguistic sophistication, and the standard that they have reached in the target language. Generally speaking, the value of linguistics to the language teacher can be summed up under the headings of description, explanation and experimentation.

The value of a good description can scarcely be disputed. An ideal theory, or grammar, of a language—using 'grammar' in the widest sense, i.e., including semantics—should capture all the generalizations discoverable for the language. An ideal theory may be said to represent what a native speaker knows implicitly about the underlying language system. This knowledge is not necessarily overt; in fact for most people it is almost entirely unconscious knowledge. Nevertheless a description which represented the grammatical knowledge of a native speaker would provide the language teacher with a most valuable tool, namely a specification of the learner's 'target competence'. Since no existing theory constitutes anything like the ideal assumed here, we shall be obliged to pick and choose among those partial theories which appear to have something to offer from the language teaching point of view.

It goes without saying that no linguistic theory so far available succeeds in covering all the facts. Since different theories concentrate on different areas of semantic description, theories tend to complement one another. A knowledge of more than one theory is necessary in order to maintain a balanced view of semantics, and of the problems that arise in semantic description. These imbalances in existing theories are the main justification for adopting an eclectic approach in the application of linguistics to language teaching.

The requirement that a linguistic theory should provide explanations, in the form of general statements which account for the widest possible range of facts, is fundamental for language teaching. A good example of the explanatory force of transformational theory in the area of syntax and phonology concerns the phenomenon of BE-contraction in English. Consider the following sentences:

24 Tell Joe that the concert is at 2.
25 Tell Joe that the concert's at 2.
26 Tell Joe where the concert is at 2.
27 *Tell Joe where the concert's at 2.

Consider also:

28 John is richer than Bill is.
29 *John is richer than Bill's.

How can we explain the distribution of *is* and *'s* in the above sentences? Why are we able to say *Tell Joe that the concert's at 2* but not **Tell Joe where the concert's at 2*? In order to explain the facts in sentences 24–7 and 28–9 we must refer to the deep structure of these sentences. First, note that in the deep structure of 26 there is a constituent *at some place* (Katz and Postal 1964) which is deleted and replaced by *where* in surface structure. This process can be roughly represented, for the sake of clarity, as follows:

Tell Joe [the concert is *at some place* at 2]
Tell Joe [*where* the concert is at 2]

Similarly, in the deep structure of 28 there is a constituent *rich* (i.e., $rich_1$ in this representation) which is deleted and replaced by *er than* in surface structure:

John is [more than Bill is $rich_1$] $rich_2$
John is rich *er than* [Bill is]

Sentence 24, on the other hand, has no deep structure constituent equivalent to *at some place* in 26.

We are now in a position to formulate the grammatical principle which governs the distribution of *is* and *'s* in 24–7 and 28–9. The principle is as follows: Finite forms of the verb BE cannot be contracted if the constituent immediately following BE in deep structure has undergone deletion. By implication, finite forms of the verb BE can be contracted if there is no deleted constituent following BE in deep structure. Thus, the grammatical principle just formulated correctly predicts the grammaticality of *Tell Joe where the concert's being held at 2*, the derivation of which is roughly:

Tell Joe [the concert is being held *at some place* at 2]
Tell Joe [*where* the concert is being held at 2]

In the above sentence the constituent *at some place* has been deleted, but BE-contraction can take place because the deleted constituent is not adjacent to BE in deep structure.

The question of how the grammatical principle just discussed might best be communicated to the learner is not a matter for the linguist or for the grammar itself, but for the applied linguist or the language teacher to decide. There are some additional linguistic considerations which might be taken into account in applying the grammatical rule concerning BE-contraction to a teaching situation. First, the rule predicts that no finite form of BE can be contracted when it occupies final positions in surface structure (as, for example, in the utterance *Bill is*), since in such a sentence a constituent immediately following BE in underlying structure must have been deleted. The relevant fact here is that there are two kinds of deletion to be taken into account: what we might call somewhat loosely 'sentence deletion', and utterance deletion. The crucial difference between these two forms of deletion is that in the first case (sentence deletion) the deleted constituent is always recoverable from the sentence itself whereas in the case of utterance deletion the deleted constituent(s) can only be recovered from previous discourse. This may be illustrated by the following pair of sentences:

30 Tell him where Bill is.
31 Tell him that Bill is.

The second utterance 31 can only be understood as, say, an answer to an indirect question such as *Harry wants to know who's going*. Given this information the deleted constituent is 'going', recoverable from the preceding question, whereas the deleted constituent in 30—*at-some-place* or the like—is recoverable from the utterance itself. These considerations suggest how the rule concerning BE-contraction might be explained to a learner in simple non-technical terms. For example, the following test might be suggested: Remove everything from the utterance following 'is', so that 'Tell Harry where the concert is tonight' becomes 'Tell Harry where the concert is'. If the utterance makes sense on its own, that is, if the basic proposition of the subclause can be retrieved ('The concert is at some place') 'is' cannot be contracted in the full sentence corresponding to it. It should be noted that the rule does not explain why the conditions for its application are as they are but it is tempting to speculate that BE cannot be contracted in the cases we have noted because it 'carries the weight' of the deleted adjacent constituent. However, this suggestion cannot be taken seriously until linguists have succeeded in clarifying some further, as yet obscure, principles of English grammar.

The third important contribution of linguistics to language teaching lies in the fact that general theories of language and particular grammars resulting from these theories may suggest hypotheses about how the learning process might be assisted and therefore point the way to useful experimentation. For example, an adequate transformational grammar of English should describe an intricate system of relationships holding between active sentences, passive sentences, pseudo-passives, pseudo-intransitives and a number of other sentence types.[1] On the basis of such a grammar we might ask ourselves if there is a 'best' way of teaching the facts described. Should actives be taught, say, before passives, passives before pseudo-passives and pseudo-passives before pseudo-intransitives? Or is order of presentation unimportant with regard to these sentences? Might it even be harmful to impose a rigid system of grading on the learner? A final answer to these questions must depend on carefully tested experimental evidence, of which there is very little available at the present time.

Any argument concerning the potential value of linguistic theories in general will also apply to particular semantic theories. Unfortunately, existing semantic theories are inadequate from both the theoretical and the descriptive point of view. No theory, for example, can adequately explain the important phenomenon of 'transference of meaning' or metaphor. However, in spite of their inadequacy, existing theories can give us considerable insight into what semantic competence a language learner must acquire to become a fluent speaker.[2]

We may expect, as language teachers, that semantic theory will provide us with valuable information about sense relations—for example the relations between *tulip* and *rose*, *dead* and *alive*, *buy* and *sell* (see section 4). We might also hope that semantic theory will throw light on the many problems of description which lie on the borderline between syntax and semantics. As an illustration of semantic theory applied to this notoriously obscure area we may cite the analysis of 'performative verbs' and the notion of illocutionary force. A specific example is found in the analysis of English modal verbs. Let us put ourselves in the position of a teacher who is asked by a learner to explain the difference between the following sentences:

32 Exams begin on Monday.
33 Exams will begin on Monday.

An awareness of what linguists mean by the illocutionary potential or force of utterances may help the teacher to find an explanation, which might be

[1] Examples of these categories are the following: (a) *He broke the window* (active), (b) *The window was broken by him* (passive), (c) *The window broke* (pseudo-intransitive), (d) *He was thrown* (e.g., when riding) (pseudo-passive). Note that (c) can be regarded as an intransitive construction because it has no direct object. However, if we compare (c) with the transitive construction (a) we find that the semantic relationship between the Noun *window* and the Verb *broke* is the same in both cases, hence the expression 'pseudo-intransitive'. In the case of (d) we have what appears to be a passive construction but there is not necessarily an implication of a deleted agent as in the 'true' passives *He was arrested* (by somebody, e.g., the police) or *He was thrown into the river* (by somebody, e.g., John).

[2] Actually, the notion of the 'idealized native speaker' is even more questionable in semantics than it is in syntax. Semantic competence varies enormously both qualitatively and quantitatively from speaker to speaker. The decision as to what constitutes the target competence of a learner should clearly be based on sociolinguistic considerations.

stated along the following lines. The two utterances are quite different in their illocutionary force. Whereas 32 seems to be a 'decree' or a report of a decree, 33 is some sort of a prediction. If this distinction is valid it should be demonstrable by means other than an appeal to introspection or the teacher's authority. If the second utterance has, implicitly, the force of a prediction but not, say, the force of an outright guess or merely an opinion then we would expect 34 to be at least anomalous as opposed to 35:

34 Exams will begin on Monday, I think.
35 Exams begin on Monday, I think.

This seems, indeed, to be the case for a majority of native speakers.

Why then is 34 anomalous? The reason seems to be that the same utterance contains an implicit prediction (expressed by 'will') and an overt guess or opinion ('I think'). On the other hand 35 may be paraphrased as 'I believe somebody has decreed that exams begin on Monday' or the like. The point is that in 35 the speaker implies that he may be wrong about the facts, for example the time of the exams. As for 34, a prediction may turn out to be wrong, but it is odd to qualify the act of predicting in this case because the facts are potentially knowable at the time of utterance. This need not always be the case. For example:

36 You'll win, I think.

is acceptable precisely because the facts cannot be known for certain at the time of utterance and so the speaker can legitimately qualify the act of predicting.

Examples like these illustrate another important fact about the relevance of linguistics to language teaching. Although a full linguistic description of certain phenomena may not be available, the awareness of certain broad linguistic categories may be very useful to the teacher in devising a strategy for dealing with language problems. For example, the awareness that illocutionary force and performative verbs are linguistic categories is a prerequisite to explaining certain facts about modal verbs in English. In the same way, an awareness that linguists distinguish between deep and surface structure in the description of sentences is potentially of great value in all areas of language teaching. In making this point we are again stressing the need for language teachers to keep in touch with recent developments in linguistics. We are not suggesting that the language teacher must become an expert on the finer points of linguistic theory. However, by becoming familiar, in general terms, with the categories which emerge from linguistic research the teacher will find himself in a much better position to advance pedagogically useful hypotheses on those occasions when he is called upon to 'be his own linguist' in the classroom.

One of the areas of language teaching most likely to benefit from psychological experimentation is the acquisition of vocabulary, which is arguably the most important area of second language learning. Traditionally three methods of structuring vocabulary have been widely used:

(a) The 'random' method of presenting lexical items in alphabetical lists, or as the need for them may arise.
(b) The 'thesaurus' method of presenting lexical items according to the field of reference to which they belong, i.e., under such headings as 'the kitchen', 'travelling', 'parts of the body', etc.
(c) The principle of frequency distribution, according to which particular lexical items are assumed to occur more or less frequently as a result of measuring them objectively with reference to a sample of texts, or subjectively according to the compiler's idea about what constitutes a reasonable probability of occurrence.

Linguistic theory suggests a number of ways in which lexical items might be presented to the learner, few of which have been systematically tested. For example, should pairs (or triples) of items be presented syntagmatically (e.g. 'pour water' or 'pour cold water') rather than each item separately or in paradigmatic patterns? Should verbs be taught before nouns because they 'carry more information'?[1] Should items be presented according to the sense relations into which they enter? Should 'offer', for example, be taught in conjunction with 'accept' and 'refuse' rather than all three separately or according to some other principle? Does it make psycholinguistic sense to learn by heart whole sentences containing selected lexical items rather than memorize the items from an alphabetical list? Should sets of items be presented according to the minimum number of distinctive features which differentiate them (e.g., 'punch' and 'kick') or the maximum number (say, 'hippo' and 'astrology')? Should items be grouped according to the register to which they belong (e.g., 'toilet', 'cloakroom', compared with 'lav', 'gents' or 'loo')? The choices are compounded by the important consideration of whether active vocabulary acquisition should precede or, more plausibly, follow passive acquisition.

These are but a few of the many ways in which vocabulary items might be presented to the learner. It is the difficult task of the applied linguist to choose, on a principled basis, one or more of the many possible methods of teaching vocabulary which are implicit in linguistic theories.

[1] For example, coming across the word 'give' in a sentence we can deduce that there must be a giver, something given and a receiver either expressed or presupposed. In some languages, e.g. Russian, the verb carries information not only, as in all languages, about its 'participants' but also about the nouns which are morphologically and historically related to them.

9 Further reading

Introductions for the general reader

Bierwisch, M. 1970. Semantics. In John Lyons (ed.) *New Horizons in Linguistics*. Harmondsworth: Penguin.

Bolinger, D. 1965. The atomization of meaning. *Language*, 41, 555–73. A witty and devastating critique of Katz and Fodor's 'The structure of a semantic theory'.

Katz, J. J. and Fodor, J. 1963. The structure of a semantic theory. *Language*, 39, 170–210. The first controversial attempt to integrate syntax and semantics in a generative grammar.

Leech, G. 1974. *Semantics*. Harmondsworth: Penguin Books.

Lyons, John 1968. *Introduction to Theoretical Linguistics*. Cambridge: Cambridge University Press. See chapters 9, 10.

Ogden, C. K. and Richards, I. A. 1923. *The Meaning of Meaning*. London: Routledge & Kegan Paul. A somewhat philosophical and psychological approach, providing thought-provoking treatment of some semantic phenomena.

Technical discussions accessible to the general reader

Fillmore, C. 1971. Verbs of judging: an exercise in semantic description. In C. Fillmore and D. T. Langendoen (eds.) *Studies in Linguistic Semantics*. New York: Holt, Rinehart, Winston.

Gruber, J. 1967. Look and see. *Language*, 43, 937–47.

Katz, J. J. 1966. *The Philosophy of Language*. New York: Harper & Row. A lucid account of how linguistics can contribute to an understanding of the philosophical problems of language.

Steinberg, D. and Jakobovits, L. (eds.) 1971. *Semantics; An Interdisciplinary Reader in Philosophy, Linguistics and Psychology*. London: Cambridge University Press. A collection of papers representing the present state of the art.

More difficult books and articles

Bach, E. and Harms, R. T. (eds.) 1968. *Universals in Linguistic Theory*. New York: Holt, Rinehart, Winston. Three technical papers on the relationship between syntax and semantics. Presupposes a good knowledge of the field.

Chomsky, Noam 1972. *Studies on Semantics in Generative Grammar*. The Hague: Mouton. Three technical papers on the relationship between syntax and semantics.

Fillmore, C. and Langendoen, D. T. (eds.) 1971. *Studies in Linguistic Semantics*. New York: Holt, Rinehart, Winston.

Fodor, J. and Postal, P. 1964. *An Integrated Theory of Linguistic Descriptions*. Cambridge, Mass.: M.I.T. Press. A book of central importance, but difficult for the beginner.

Jackendoff, R. 1972. *Semantic Interpretation in Generative Grammar*. Cambridge, Mass: M.I.T. Press. A very technical account of interpretive semantics.

Lakoff, G. 1970. On generative semantics. In D. Steinberg and L. Jakobovits (eds.) *Semantics: An Interdisciplinary Reader in Philosophy, Linguistics and Psychology*. London: Cambridge University Press. Difficult in parts but necessary for a full understanding of the principles underlying generative semantics.

Postal, P. 1970. On the surface verb 'remind'. In *Linguistic Enquiry*, 1, 37–120. One of the first analyses of lexical meaning based on the concepts of generative semantics.

Weinreich, U. 1966. Explorations in semantic theory. In T. Sebeok (ed.). *Current Trends in Linguistics*, Vol. 3. Mouton: The Hague. A critique of Katz and Postal's integrated theory and an attempt to provide alternative solutions to semantic problems.

C. CRIPER and H. G. WIDDOWSON

6 Sociolinguistics and Language Teaching

1 Introduction

1.1 Sociolinguistics and linguistics

When we say that someone 'knows' a language, what exactly do we mean? In the first place we mean that he has a knowledge of the rules which control the formation of sentences, and which regulate the way in which units of language combine together. With the knowledge of these rules he can produce an infinite number of sentences. That is to say, given inexhaustible supplies of ink and paper he would be able to go on churning out different but correct sentences for the rest of his life. Similarly, he would be able to recognize whether any particular sentence presented to him was correct or not. The knowledge that we are talking about is not necessarily a conscious knowledge but an intuition which enables him to accept all the well-formed or structurally correct sentences of his language but no others. This capacity is acquired by every human being at an early age, but is it the only kind of knowledge required of someone who wishes to 'learn a language'?

While knowledge of these rules, the rules of grammar, will ensure that each sentence generated is correctly formed, it will not ensure that the forms of any utterances are appropriate. To talk of the rules of the grammar is to talk in a social vacuum. It is an abstraction which is not concerned with the specific situations in which language is used. But the very essence of language is that it serves as a means of communication; it involves people in some kind of social interaction. To know a language, then, means to know something about how it fulfils this communicative function. It is not enough to have a knowledge of the rules of sentence formation, we must also know how to make use of such rules so as to produce appropriate utterances. To know language as a formal system we need to know the rules which generate well-formed sentences but to know language as a means of social interaction we need to know those conven-

We would like to record here how much the organization and content of this chapter has derived from our discussions with colleagues and students in the course of teaching over the years. We are particularly grateful to the following for making specific comments: Gill and Keith Brown, Alan Davies, John Laver, John Lyons, Bernard Lott, and David Wilkins.

tions of use which control the selection of well-formed sentences appropriate to a particular social situation.

We make a distinction, then, between the rules of the language system and the conventions which control their deployment in actual situations. Sociolinguistics is the study of language in operation; its purpose is to investigate how the conventions of language use relate to other aspects of social behaviour.

Many linguists have assumed that it is only the rules of the grammar, the linguistic code itself, that is systematic and worthy of scientific investigation. Such an assumption is implicit in de Saussure's classic distinction between *langue* and *parole*. De Saussure uses the first of these terms to refer to the language system itself, which is somehow independent of either the people who speak it or the way that it is actually realized in speech. This realization in speech is considered to be idiosyncratic and specific to the situation in which it occurs; it is *parole*. De Saussure does not consider that the individual acts of speaking are socially constrained in the way that *langue* is constrained.

A similar kind of distinction is made by Chomsky and his followers. Their concern is almost exclusively with the properties of language as an abstract formal system of rules and not with the actual operation of language in social interaction. In their terms, *competence* is the ideal language user's knowledge of the rules of grammar and is considered to be the object of study for the linguist. *Performance* is the actual realization of this knowledge in utterances and involves other constraints, psychological, physical and social.

Both Chomsky and de Saussure have made these distinctions in order to single out an aspect of language which is of particular interest to them. The choice of *langue* and competence as the prime object of linguistic study has enabled them to define the discipline of linguistics by restricting the kind of information about language which has to be accounted for within their theoretical outline. The procedure of attacking limited problems and solving or partly solving them before increasing the complexity of the data to be accounted for is a necessary step in any enquiry. But the approach is too limited for the language teacher. He is concerned with *langue* and competence in describing or contrasting language systems. At the same time he is concerned with the way that these systems are used. Like the sociolinguist, he is concerned with the middle area between *langue* and *parole*, between competence and performance. It is the study of the systematic part of *parole* or performance that receives the major emphasis in sociolinguistics and that is of particular relevance to language teaching.

'Learning a language' means learning the rules of use as well as the rules of the formal linguistic system. Until a learner knows how to use the resources of a grammar to send meaningful messages in real life situations he cannot be said to know the language. He must know what variety to use in what situation, how to vary the style according to whom he is addressing, when to speak or remain silent, when and what kind of gestures are required to go with what speech. In addition to this the language teacher must consider how his teaching will be affected by the learner's motives in wanting to acquire another language, what functions this language has in the society to which the learner belongs, what variety of the language should be chosen as the model for teaching and why. Questions such as these abound for both first and second language teachers. What they have in common is that they relate to the social factors affecting either the learning process or the use of language in social interaction. In other words they all make appeal to sociolinguistic notions.

1.2 Sociolinguistics and sociology

Sociolinguistic notions must obviously draw upon sociological theory. It is not possible here to go into details about sociological theories or explanations but it is pertinent to ask in what way the problems posed in this chapter differ from those which are the concern of Chapters 7 and 8. Is the sociologist trying to explain the same kinds of data as the psychologist, or the sociolinguist the same as the psycholinguist? A look at one type of behaviour may give us some clues. Durkheim published a study on suicide in 1897 in order to show what the study of sociology really was. He is a crucial figure in the development of sociology and also in linguistics insofar as de Saussure derived his *langue/parole* distinction from Durkheim's sociological writings.

No one will dispute that suicide is the most intimate and individual of all acts. There are no laws or contracts which force an individual to commit suicide. One way of studying the phenomenon is to study the mental states of individuals who have tried to kill themselves. This is a valid way of proceeding and comes within the field of psychology, but is this all we need to account for? How is it that, though suicide is such a personal matter, it is possible to predict how many people will kill themselves in any one year? Different societies have different, yet quite regular, suicide rates. We cannot account for this fact in terms of the individual's mental state. Instead we need to look at the kind of influences which are brought to bear on people as members of a particular society. We need to see the way in which people are grouped and classified, what institutions there are in a particular society and what values are associated with them. As Durkheim puts it: 'Wholly different are the results we obtained when we forgot the individual and sought the causes of the suicidal aptitude of each society in the nature of the societies themselves. The relation of suicide to certain states of social environment are as direct and constant as its relation to facts of a biological and physical character were seen to be uncertain and ambiguous.'

Consequently Durkheim was led to look at the varying rates of suicide in different countries of Europe and within them among different groups or categories of people. He distinguished three kinds of suicide according to the way that society becomes the chief determinant of the act. *Egoistic suicide* occurs when there is a minimum amount of cohesion in the groups to which men belong. The more emphasis that is laid on the freedom of an individual to do as he pleases, the higher the suicide rates becomes. Thus, for example, suicide rates are higher among Protestants and urban dwellers, than among Catholics and rural dwellers, the latter pair being more socially constrained and hence less likely to wilfully dispose of themselves. Poverty as such does not impel people towards suicide but 'wealth, on the other hand, by the power it bestows, deceives us into believing that we depend on ourselves only'. This leads to *anomic suicide*, which is caused by the sudden change in the accepted norms and the breakdown of values by which one may have lived for a long time, or in the conflict between desired ends and abilities to achieve them. Finally, there is the rare *altruistic suicide* where an individual will take his life because of his belief that he has behaved in such a way as to bring disgrace on a particular social relationship, e.g., where there is great emphasis on a system of honour'.

This has been rather an extended discussion of one of Durkheim's works but it is extremely relevant to the way in which we need to look at society and the operation of language. In order to see why suicide rates differed it was necessary to look at the institutions in society which, on the face of things, might seem quite unconnected. Thus religion turned out to be a crucial factor in that Roman Catholics killed themselves much less frequently than Protestants, degree of urbanization also turned out to be important in that suicide rates are higher in towns than in rural areas, and so on. The result is that economic, religious and family institutions all needed to be studied in order to see how, together, they influenced the action of the individual.

In looking at language use, we need to follow the same procedure. We need to examine a society and its institutions to see what languages or varieties of language are associated with what institutions and what values are associated with such languages in order to understand how the individual is influenced by society irrespective of whether he is consciously aware of the fact or not. Our study of the social factors affecting language use can be approached in two ways. Firstly, we can look at the society as a whole and consider how language functions within it, and in what way it is associated with different institutions. This is to survey society from above, as it were, from a bird's eye view. In addition we need to look at society from the point of view of an individual member within it. How does the individual make use of the different choices of language open to him? What are the factors which he needs to take into account in any particular situation? These two ways of looking at society, the 'bird's eye view' and the 'worm's eye view', are not contradictory but complementary. We need to see the over-all pattern, the bird's eye view, before we can really understand the pressures applying to the individual. In this chapter we shall consider both ways of looking. In section 2 we shall be concerned with the over-all view which is becoming known as the 'sociology of language', and is of particular interest to language planners and those concerned in educational administration. In section 3 our focus will be on the individual and the constraints imposed upon him; such a study is a part of sociolinguistics proper and is closely related to linguistic theory itself.

2 Sociology of language

2.1 Definitions of a language

In section 1, we pointed out what is involved in knowing a language. But what exactly do we mean by knowing 'a language'? We commonly talk about teaching a language and we say that English, French, Swahili and so on are languages. But how do we know one language from another? How do we know that English and German, for example, are different languages? It might be suggested that German is German and not English because the sound system, the grammar and the vocabulary of German are different from those of English. Just as we must recognize that there are many variations in beliefs and values held by different groups of people in Great Britain so, also, we have to recognize that the sound system, the grammar and the vocabulary of one dialect or variety are different from those of another dialect of English. Why do we claim both these varieties to be dialects of the same language, English, and not two separate languages? One answer might be that it is possible to write a single grammar for English with the different dialectal variations being accounted for in the one grammar. This is not an adequate definition, however, as we can see from other examples. It can be claimed on linguistic grounds that the variety of German spoken in Bavaria is as different from the variety spoken in Hamburg as is the language spoken in Holland. Yet we call the former varieties German and the latter Dutch. Swedish, Norwegian and Danish are very similar in their sound system, grammar and vocabulary, yet they are called different languages. There is no way, therefore, for the linguist to be able to decide, on linguistic grounds alone, whether or not two varieties belong to 'the same' or 'different' languages. To ask 'How similar do the sound system, grammar or vocabulary of two varieties have to be before they can be defined as the same language?' is to put a question to which there can be no answer.

Some have tried to distinguish between languages and dialects on the basis of mutual intelligibility, that is, whether the speakers of language A can understand the speakers of language B and vice versa. The argument runs that varieties which are mutually intelligible are dialects of the same language and those which are not are different languages. Although this definition may be adequate in some circumstances it can create several difficulties. The varieties spoken on either side of the border between Holland and Germany are mutually intelligible, yet on one side of the border the varieties are called dialects of German, while on the other side they are called dialects of Dutch. A further complication arises in that when we talk of mutual intelligibility between varieties, we are not really referring to any properties of the varieties themselves but rather to those of the people who speak these varieties. In trying to measure the degree of intelligibility, we are in fact measuring an amalgam of the social and linguistic factors which influence the extent to which native speakers of one language can understand speakers of another. For example, one way of dissociating yourself from other people is to claim that you both speak different languages which are unrelated and mutually unintelligible, even though the objective facts are quite different. The reverse situation also occurs: people may claim that their languages are related, in spite of evidence to the contrary, if they are likely to gain some prestige by so doing. As a result, we sometimes find 'one-way intelligibility' whereby one group claims that there is mutual intelligibility while the other group claims there is not.

There is yet another difficulty in using intelligibility to determine language boundaries. Sometimes we find a 'dialect chain'; the adjacent varieties are mutually intelligible but non-adjacent varieties become less and less so as they get further apart. The Dutch/German example, mentioned earlier, illustrates the point. While the varieties near the Dutch coast and those in South Germany are very different and not mutually intelligible, there are a number of intermediate varieties which are linguistically closely related to one another and mutually intelligible. We can see, then, that 'a language' is not capable of any strict definition on linguistic criteria. We need to approach our study in a different way without assuming 'a language' as a given linguistic fact.

2.2 Ethnography of communication

In the previous section we discussed the difficulty of characterizing a particular language as distinct from another. In this section we shall consider how we may characterize language in general. Just as we commonly think of a language as some well-defined entity, so we tend to think of language in general as being purely verbal communication. But people have other means of communicating, and these have to be taken into account if we are to understand the function of language in society. The description of this complex communicative behaviour, of which purely verbal behaviour forms a part, is known as the ethnography of communication.

In order for human beings to survive, they have to co-operate, and the different institutions to be found in a society can be regarded as different systems of co-operation. To co-operate, one needs to communicate. It is obvious that without some way of indicating attitudes, ideas, intentions, desires and so on, there is no possibility of co-operation. Co-operation through communication is not, of course, restricted to the human species. All animals have the means of communicating with the members of their own species. Birds, for example, signal to each other by song; every species has its own range of song patterns, each representing a different message. During the mating season, some birds indulge in the most curious antics but each gesture has a particular significance. Much of what appears to the casual observer to be random behaviour in animals can be analytically reduced to systems of communicative functions.

Human language, of course, is also a form of communication. In what way, then, does it differ from, say, bird-song, or animal antics during the mating season? Briefly, the distinction is that human language is not restricted to a fixed set of messages and is not conditioned solely by the immediate situation. That is to say, human language is infinite in that the human being is capable of generating an infinite number of different messages and these messages can be generated independently of any particular situation. A certain kind of bird-song, for example, which is appropriate to mating, is only produced during the mating season; the situation acts as a stimulus which triggers off the message and without the stimulus there can be no message. Human beings, on the other hand, are not bound to situations in this way. They can speak of things which are temporally and spatially remote; they can invent things which do not exist at all; they can lie. Human language differs from other systems of communication, then, in that it is 'generative' and independent of situation. In a word, it is creative. It has to be to meet the complex communicative needs of human society, as we shall see.

Although human beings use the language of words to communicate, they do not make use of verbal communication alone. We think of communication generally in terms of the use of words and sentences, but this is not the only way in which human beings communicate. They retain, for instance, a good deal of their purely animal nature and send messages to each other by those means most commonly associated with animals of a lower order. In our own society, for example, women are very well acquainted with the use of dress, cosmetics and perfume for the transmission of non-verbal messages. Human beings communicate in a variety of different ways. There are societies in which messages of a somewhat intimate and delicate nature are transmitted solely by means of whistling. Our own wolf-whistle transmits a message of a similarly intimate though less delicate nature. Notices in flower shops urge us to 'Say it with flowers'. A recent television advertisement tells us that a watch can say a number of things: it can say 'Well done', or 'Congratulations'; it can even say 'I love you'. Giving watches is fortunately not the only way of saying 'I love you', and this particular message is far from being the only one which can be transmitted by means of gifts. In some societies, gift giving takes on a much more important communicative function than it does in our own.

Some ways of communicating replace speech; some supplement speech. The most obvious of the latter are gestures of various kinds which we make when speaking. These gestures are so naturally a concomitant of speaking that we make use of them even when it is unnecessary to do so, as when we are speaking on the telephone. Gestures are a limited set of social signals and are as specific to a particular society as is the language which accompanies them. A common gesture in one society may carry a quite different significance in another, and this fact has, on occasions, been the source of a good deal of embarrassment and misunderstanding.

The term 'gesture' generally refers to some significant movement of the arms, hands or head. Other physiological means of supplementing the communicative import of actual speech are the use of facial expressions or positions of the body; yet another is the use of the sound producing mechanism itself in some special way. Thus, it is possible for a certain meaning to be overlaid on the actual words by, for example, constricting the glottis and so producing the kind of voice quality often associated with the pulpit; or by superimposing a nasal quality on speech to produce a manner of speaking which, on occasions, used to be affected by members of the upper class in Britain.

We find in different societies that differing use is made of all these possibilities of communication. In one society, a given communicative function may be fulfilled verbally; in another there may be no verbal means available and the function is fulfilled by gesture; in another it may be fulfilled by the giving of gifts and in yet another by some kind of facial expression. We may allow the useful generalization that every society has the means to express what it needs to express. That is to say, the means of communication employed by a society is suited to the maintenance of its institutions. Difficulties arise when a particular society has to incorporate into its structure values, attitudes or beliefs which do not fit neatly into existing social patterns; in this case, its language is frequently called upon to fulfil communicative tasks for which it is not yet fitted. We then get a situation which may require a deliberate modification or extension of normal communicative functions so as to suit the language to its new roles.

The role which verbal communication is expected, and designed, to play varies, then, in different societies. In order to understand the way in which language functions in social interaction, we have to be clear in each case how the role of verbal communication relates to that of other forms of communication; we must be careful not to assume that because verbal communication plays a particular role in our own society, it must necessarily play the same role in another.

These facts have a good deal of importance for the language teacher. As we have pointed out, different societies make use of non-verbal forms of communication in different ways. If the language teacher wishes to develop in his pupils an ability to use the system of the language appropriately as a means of social interaction with native speakers, he will have to be aware of just how the system is used and how its use relates to other forms of communication. It is obviously not enough that his pupils should know what certain linguistic forms 'mean' by virtue of their cognitive content and what their translation equivalents are in the learner's mother tongue. Every language has alternative ways of saying 'the same thing' but these alternative ways are not in free variation; we cannot choose freely from them in every situation. The existence of different message forms suggests that they have some social correlation. The language teacher must not only be aware of the social constraints on the selection of alternative linguistic forms, but also know how these alternative message forms are supplemented by gesture or other non-verbal means. He must know when it is inappropriate to use language at all; when communication is effected by silence. In short, the teaching of language as social behaviour involves an understanding of just how language is used to communicate in the society whose language is being taught. It is precisely this kind of understanding which sociolinguistics can provide.

2.3 Functional language types

We have been concerned up to this point with the dichotomy verbal/non-verbal communication and the differing functions that each may have in different societies. We have spoken as if societies are homogeneous but, in fact, this is never the case. We talk, for example, of British society, French society and so on, as if all the inhabitants of Britain or France shared identical values and beliefs and customarily behaved in the same way. It is true that there are certain values and beliefs which help to define the British as a community different from the French, the Germans, the Italians and so on, and these may be said to serve as a basis for stereotypes such as appear in cartoons and music hall jokes. But of course not all British people are alike. A Yorkshireman, for instance, is quick to point out that his values have little in common with those of his southern compatriots whose hands have never known the feel of honest toil. The Scots distinguish themselves very definitely from the Sassenachs beyond the Border, but among the Scots too the Highlanders are recognized as different from the Lowlanders and Borderers. The notion of homogeneity, no matter how useful it may be as a generalization, is in fact a myth, as will be borne out later when we come to speak of social differentiation.

The corollary of this heterogeneity of societies is that few states have only one common linguistic system, or verbal code. This fact necessarily creates problems for language teaching, which always has to operate within the context of a state; a choice has to be made as to which verbal code is to be taught for which purposes. It cannot automatically be assumed that the various codes have identical functions. On the contrary, we must make the initial supposition that each of them fulfils a different purpose in the state. It is the sociolinguist's task to discover what these functions are. Welsh, for example, is the mother-tongue of a number of people in Britain, as is English. But unlike English it is at present also being identified as a symbol of Welsh culture and the Welshman's attitudes towards its use are quite different from his attitudes to English. Not only attitudes are involved. English is an official language in that it is recognized by the state as the language to be used for all official purposes, from legislation to the law courts, whereas Welsh has not yet been accorded the same degree of official recognition.

By looking at the functions of the various codes found in a community and people's attitudes to them, we can begin to understand what is meant by many of the terms used to refer to functional *language types*. What we need to remember is that just as we were unable to distinguish languages from dialects on structural grounds, so we cannot rely on structural definitions of these language types either.

Take the notion of a *standard language*, for example. By this, we mean that the users of a language accept some form of it as being the 'correct' form; that is, they acknowledge a set of norms defining what ought to be used even though they may not actually conform to these norms in their own usage. In any small group, this set of norms is often unformalized and uncodified. One particular usage may be recognized as the most prestigious and hence as a standard for all the other members of the group. These kinds of informal pressures to conform can work well if numbers are small. But if there are several hundreds of thousands of speakers of the language or several millions, more formal means are necessary to maintain conformity. In this case standardization is likely to involve some formal codification—this implies literacy and the writing of grammars, which come to be accepted as the correct form of the language. Writing, of course, does not necessarily result in standardization since it is possible to have a number of written forms none of which have complete acceptance among all speakers. We can recognize English or French or Russian, however, as typical standard languages where the 'correct' form of the language is enshrined in written grammars and formally taught in school. Swahili in East Africa is an example of a language in which there has been a great deal of variation over the wide areas in which it is used, but where now the increase in literacy and the spread of radio and television broadcasting have stimulated efforts to impose a single recognized standard.

The only difference between a standard language and a *classical language* is that a classical language is one that is not spoken by any group of people as their own mother tongue. Classical or literary Arabic, for example, is learnt by instruction at school and is the only standardized form of the language, but it differs from English or Russian in being no one's mother tongue. In practice it functions as a lingua franca. That is, it is a language of wider communication used by people with different mother tongues who would otherwise be unable to communicate with each other. Latin used to have a similar function in Europe in that it was a standardized language (based on the classical texts) learned formally at school and used by educated speakers to transcend their own linguistic and cultural boundaries.

It is possible, in principle, to divide languages up into two categories: standard languages, which have a variety universally accepted as the prestige norm and non-standard languages which do not. In practice, however, most languages would fall somewhere between these two categories. This is because standardization is an ongoing process which cannot be described without misrepresentation in terms of a static typology. Our purpose in setting up what we have called 'functional language types' is to indicate the processes by which languages develop functionally and the labels we give to these types refer to the end-points of these processes.

We can now look at varieties of language from this functional point of view to resolve the language/dialect problem. For we can see that in common speech we use the term 'dialect' for a variety which is considerered not to be autonomous in the way that a language is—whether a standard or non-standard one. Dialect in this sense usually refers to what is considered an inferior variety of a language irrespective of the degree of linguistic difference. We should point out, of course, that such popular notions of inferiority are not based on any linguistic grounds and are generally repudiated by linguists, who base their identification of dialect on differences in phonological, grammatical and lexical structure (see section 3). The fact that most varieties of language spoken in Holland are associated by their speakers with standard Dutch and the varieties spoken in Germany with standard German leads to the appearance of a clear-cut boundary between Dutch and its dialects, and German and its dialects even though there is no linguistic reason for such a division.

We need to take into account one other factor in understanding this set of functional language types. All the language types so far are considered by their users to be 'normal' languages in that they have developed over time from some remote past. We all appreciate that English has developed over the centuries influenced from many directions and has not been arbitrarily or suddenly created. However, when we talk of a *creole* or *pidgin* language, we infer that a new language has come into being through some (usually recent) confluence of circumstances such as the meeting of two languages or two cultures. The necessity to communicate may lead to the development of a derived language whose simplified structure provides the means for minimum adequate communication across the two cultures. At the early stage of its development the new language may function only as a lingua franca or language of wider communication and may not be spoken by any community as a first language. Later it may become the mother tongue of a group and hence be called a creole. Examples of these types are the different varieties of Pidgin English in West Africa and Melanesia, Pidgin Sango in West Africa, French Creole in the Caribbean and so on. It is worth pointing out that although such languages are commonly stigmatized as 'mongrel' forms of speech, the same linguistic processes that occur in such obvious cases of pidginization may well also have occurred in the pedigree of what are now considered by their users to be 'pure-bred' languages.

The most important lesson that we can draw from this as language teachers is that many of the terms which are used by linguists (as well as ordinary mortals) in fact distinguish types of language defined in terms of the functions they fulfil in a particular society, the way they developed historically and the attitudes of the speakers towards them. A linguist cannot, for example, define a pidgin or a standard language in terms of its grammatical or lexical structure. Once again it becomes clear that we cannot sensibly dissociate language from the social context in which it operates.

2.4 Social differentiation

So far, we have been discussing the importance of putting language into social perspective. We have pointed out that language as verbal behaviour is one aspect of the total communicative behaviour by which members of a society interact; and we have suggested that different kinds of language—standard, classical, creole, etc.—may be characterized in terms of the social functions they fulfil and the social attitudes which attach to them. In this section, we continue to investigate the way language use relates to social factors by looking more closely at the manner in which society is structured and at the implications this has for the study of language in use.

Within any society, people are organized into *groups* and classified into *categories*. The distinction we are making here is based on whether or not the individuals concerned stand in some kind of regular and relatively permanent relationship towards one another. The essence of a group is that the individuals making it up have both rights and obligations to behave in specified ways. For example, we can call the family a group since its members regularly meet together, expect each other to behave in certain ways (irrespective of whether this actually happens in any particular instance) and are treated by the outside world (e.g. inspectors of taxes) as if they were one group. A church community and a political party are groups insofar as their members accept a common leader and act together to further their own interests, even though they may never meet face to face.

A category is no more than a collection of individuals considered by their fellows to have something in common. It is a classification, or formal labelling, which is socially recognized in a particular society. A distinction between male and female is an elementary classification made everywhere. It does not imply the presence of men's or women's groups as such. In our society, men and women are expected to behave in different ways according to their sex, but this does not imply that they have any of the characteristics of a group as defined earlier. Put in another way, being a woman does not imply necessarily being part of any group; joining the Women's Liberation Movement does. This distinction between a group and a category should be borne in mind throughout the following discussion, since clearly the influences brought to bear on any individual as to how he should act or speak are likely to differ in the two cases.

Language diversity is closely dependent on the kind of groups and categories to be found in particular societies. But traditionally linguists have been mainly interested in looking at one kind of diversity. They have mostly looked at *geographical dialects*. Dialect surveys in Britain, for example, operate by looking for, and plotting on maps, the distribution of particular dialect words or of particular sound systems, village by village or region by region. In a similar way, whole language surveys have been carried out with the basic aim of plotting the distribution of particular languages across a country or larger area. The two kinds of survey are generally carried out in a similar way in that it is primarily rural regions which are the object of study, the aim being to pick out those people who have learned their mother tongue in their particular village and have neither moved outside nor been influenced by other ways of speaking.

Examination of some of the linguistic and dialect maps reveals that dialect boundaries coincide very often with geographical boundaries such as mountains or rivers. The reason for this is that if a single community speaking the same variety of language becomes physically split, then the two halves of the community are likely to develop differently and the forms of the language they speak may gradually become distinct. This does not mean that any conscious effort is made to become more different, but that changes which occur in one community are less likely to be adopted by the community which is split off. Hence lack of communication, for whatever reason, between two communities is likely to lead to a gradual differentiation of the language that the two communities speak. One can understand how it comes about that, in a period in which it was difficult to travel by road and there was no alternative form of transport, local rural communities were more settled and their speech, therefore, was more likely to change in a way which was slightly different from that of neighbouring villages. In the present day, with the vast increase in ease of communication brought about by mass media and the development of modern transport, the stability of local dialects seems to be decreasing. Younger people are less likely to speak their local dialect all the time and are likely to be more influenced by the language spoken in the town and on radio and television. This does not mean that there is less variation in language as a whole, only that the particular kind of geographical variation may well be decreasing. What we find instead is that the groups and categories of persons that we identify in our society may have particular ways of speaking which characterize them. In any study of the whole linguistic repertoire of a nation we need to look at these social dialects and the way in which they function, since they are of immediate relevance both to the theoretical concern of the linguist and the practical concerns of the language teacher.

Just as geographical dialect is associated with separation caused by physical conditions, so *social dialect* has to do with separation brought about by social conditions. Let us consider the question of equality. When we look at any society, it becomes plain that the individuals of which it is composed are not all equal. The general and the private soldier, the headmaster and the assistant teacher, the musically gifted child and the child who is mechanically oriented, the tall thin man and the short fat one, the plumber and the joiner, are all pairs of unequals, but the kinds of inequalities implied by these pairs are very different. On the one hand, we can distinguish inequality due to natural or innate differences of individuals, e.g. tallness and shortness, the musically gifted and non-gifted. On the other hand, we can distinguish differences of social position. Sometimes the social positions are considered to be equal in prestige or status, as is the case with the plumber/joiner pair. In other cases, as with the general and the private soldier, there is a clear differentiation in social rank which is reflected in this instance by a difference in military rank.

There are three kinds of social inequality which have special importance when we come to look at any particular society: that which follows from differences in wealth and income; that which follows from differences in prestige or status; and that which follows from an unequal distribution of power. Since they are clearly reflected in language use, all these are of importance to the sociolinguist. They are equally important to the language teacher, who is concerned with decisions about what language or variety of language is to be taught and the social values associated with each.

Let us consider first of all the inequality that relates to differences in wealth and income which, in Britain, is associated with *class*. A person's class has to do with his position in some economic hierarchy and is something which he shares with others who are similarly placed in the economic process of the production, distribution and exchange of goods. Clearly income is a major factor in determining a person's position, but we must also take into account other things such as security of employment and access to education, either for himself or his children. 'Working-class' children, for example, have less chance of gaining entry to University than do children of 'middle-class' parents. As we will see later, it has been suggested by some that working-class children in Britain learn the kind of English at home which puts them at a disadvantage compared with their middle-class peers who, by the time that they go to school, have acquired uses of language which are better suited to formal education.

How far is language connected with the process of production, distribution and exchange mentioned above, that is, with the economic institutions of the country? In a multilingual country such as Uganda where there are more than thirty separate languages spoken within its borders, language can act as a considerable barrier to the mobility of labour. As long as a man remains at home, he runs into no language difficulties. Once he moves from a rural district into a town, however, and finds himself with compatriots from other parts of the country, it becomes essential for there to be some kind of lingua franca. In Uganda, this tends to be English for all those who have been through primary school, and Swahili for the others. An even more extreme example would be New Guinea where there are at least seven hundred different languages spoken. With this situation it becomes essential for all those who take up paid employment to learn some kind of lingua franca with which they can communicate both with their employer and also with their fellow-workers. In the case of New Guinea the lingua franca which is spreading is a form of pidgin English.

Similarly, a trading or marketing situation requires some form of language which can be understood by all those taking part in such transactions. Particular occupations can also have their own form of specialized language or *jargon* which is learned by all those who take up a particular job. Besides being of technical use, this also acts as a way of marking off insiders from outsiders, which explains why the term is often used pejoratively. For example, coal-miners have a very elaborate vocabulary for kinds of work which go on at the pit face. An equally striking example is the language used by lawyers and doctors; a part of its function is that it can be understood only by lawyers and doctors and not by the lay public.

We must be clear that wealth does not necessarily entail high status. Most bookmakers in Britain make much more money than a curate earns but the curate in the pulpit is a more prestigious figure than the tic-tac man on the bookie's stand. Similarly a worker on the production line at a car factory may earn far more than a junior office worker but, in the eyes of some people at least, his job is lower in prestige. To put it in another way, prestige attaches to white collars and suits rather than blue collars and overalls irrespective of the size of the pay packet. Social esteem and prestige, or *status*, are obviously related to class but are not identical to it. To give another example, we can see that though all primary school teachers may have very similar incomes and positions in the education system, they do not necessarily belong to the same status group. This difference in status may be due to differences in social origin, secondary schooling or in the accent that they use. What seems to determine status is more a style of living or pattern of consumption. A car worker has a different pattern of living and spending from the clerical worker. The 'nouveau riche' may be higher placed in the economic hierarchy than the impoverished aristocrat by whom he may strive to be socially accepted. He is likely to succeed only when his behaviour fully models those he is imitating.

In Britain one of the most common markers of status is *accent*. We have mentioned earlier that the number of dialect speakers in Britain seems to be decreasing. However, this does not mean that everybody is becoming alike in the way they speak. With a compulsory formal education system, most people learn to write some form of standard English; or at any rate, if they do not succeed in the actual performance of writing such a standard form, they nevertheless come to learn and to acknowledge it as a norm. The process that we can see happening now is that many of the grammatical and lexical differences which characterize different dialects are dying out as standard English becomes more pervasive through the influence of radio, television, newspapers and other media. Nevertheless people still retain a distinctive kind of pronunciation; they speak standard English but with a local accent. In other words, a dialect incorporates differences in all three areas, phonology, grammar, lexis, whereas an accent is a form of speech which differs from other forms only in the area of phonetics and phonology.

In England we are all aware of the importance of accent as an indicator of status. Through education, a non-localized form of pronunciation, known as 'Received Pronunciation', or RP, has grown up. This refers to the particular way of pronouncing standard English which is the hallmark of those who have been processed through the kind of private educational institution which the English insist on calling a public school. In the past the possession of this accent has been extremely important in marking someone as having a particular high position in the status hierarchy and has served as a qualification for high prestige employment irrespective of what other abilities the work might demand. Until recently, for example, the prestige of local accents of English has been sufficiently low for it to be unacceptable for high officials in the Civil Service or the Foreign Office to speak anything other than RP. Thus, the possession of a local accent has been a very good indicator of what we have described earlier as a style of living. Regional accents and RP have taken on social implications, becoming in effect social accents. One must point out, however, that this is a very exceptional situation; in most other countries, regional accents do not play an important part in the status hierarchy. They remain, in fact, merely regional accents. This means that it is possible to identify the area in which an individual was brought up, but one cannot tell from the accent alone what place in the status hierarchy he occupies.

The recognition of language as an indicator of social status creates great difficulty for the language teacher. What kind of language and what kind of accent should he teach? Is the main task of the teacher of English that of teaching his pupils to speak with an accent which is used by those people with the higher social status? These questions are relevant to both the first and the second language teaching situation. What accent of English, for example, should be taught to foreigners? Again, do working-class children really wish to use language in a way similar to people of higher social status? The answer is, of course, not necessarily. The accent that we call RP is not always thought of as something that ought to be imitated. It is often associated by working-class people with effeminacy or with 'putting on airs', in other words with the opposite of the admired qualities of manliness or matiness. Again, how acceptable is it that foreigners should learn to speak English with a perfect RP accent? It may well be that on the whole native speakers wish foreigners to speak with a foreign accent thus identifying themselves in public as being foreign and so outside the local status hierarchy.

Finally, we need to distinguish the differences in *power*. These differences are not the same as inequalities of class and status, though obviously they are closely related. Let us suppose, for example, that by some strange chance the man appointed as headmaster of an English public school has been educated at a secondary modern school and subsequently at a red-brick university. Let us further suppose that he speaks with a broad Birmingham accent and dresses in the style of a working-class man. Such a person might well be an object of scorn and derision for his middle-class pupils and his middle-class and ex-public school staff. But it does not follow that he would thereby lose his power over them. In another school, one might be able to recognize a particular teacher as having more power in the school by virtue of his long experience, or by the exercise of his personality, than either the headmaster or any of his colleagues, even though he may not be higher in economic standing or prestige.

As with class and status, power affects and is affected by the use of language. One might point to instances where groups of people maintain their power by the use of a language which is restricted to an elite minority, thereby preventing others from gaining access to positions of privilege. This restriction may be achieved by the deliberate imposition of a national language policy. Individuals may also consciously exploit language to impose their will upon others and exert a power which does not derive automatically from their position in the economic and status hierarchies.

2.5 Language and identity

We have spoken so far of the way in which society is differentiated into groups and categories of various kinds and of how language reflects and promotes this differentiation. Our concern in this section will be to examine the notion that the language associated with such social divisions may affect the way in which people conceive of the world in which they live.

Groups can be characterized, as we have seen, in terms of shared attitudes and beliefs, which are expressed by the accepted behaviour of the members of the group, including, of course, their language behaviour. We may consider the case of a group of 'pop' fans. As a condition for continued membership, the people in the group must conform to certain norms of behaviour; these may have to do with certain hair styles and dress, a somewhat cavalier attitude towards 'conventional' mores, and certain ways of speaking. These ways of behaving may appear to be unconventional in the eyes of society at large, but it is important to realize that they are in conformity with the norms of behaviour of the group itself. Paradoxically, there is often more pressure to conform to these 'non-conventional' group norms than to 'conventional' norms of more widespread acceptance.

Group membership, then, is marked by language behaviour; 'pop' fans have a way of speaking to each other which distinguishes them from other groups. This way of speaking comes about in response to the need to give the group some sense of solidarity. It also arises to meet the need which members feel for a means of expressing the attitudes and beliefs which are the unwritten constitution of the group, and which they feel cannot be adequately expressed by other ways of speaking. In other words, a way of speaking is developed which reflects the group's view of the world. People outside the group may feel that this is merely an unnecessary indulgence in 'jargon' because the values which it expresses are not theirs. But everybody has recourse to different ways of speaking corresponding to the different groups they belong to or the different status they hold, and what appears to be quite 'ordinary language' to one group is 'jargon' to another. One might consider defining jargon as 'other people's use of language' in the same way as Oscar Wilde is said to have defined vulgarity as 'other people's manners'.

This is perhaps not an easy point to understand. We all have the ethnocentric tendency to think of our own way of looking at things as being the 'natural' or 'normal' way, as being the way which most truly represents the world as it is. It takes some effort of orientation to accept that there are other ways of seeing things, other values, other uses of language which are just as 'true', 'valid', and 'correct' as our own, since there cannot be any external and objective means of assessment. If we are not sympathetic to, or do not understand, the behaviour of others, then our first reaction will be to translate it so as to fit it into our own scheme of values. What we must remember is that by so doing we necessarily misrepresent this behaviour; we are no longer 'saying the same thing'.

At this point we make contact with a controversial issue in sociolinguistics, which has important implications for language teaching. We have been arguing that there is necessarily an interdependence between ways of thinking and ways of using language. It would seem to be undeniable that when groups of like-minded people are formed, ways of speaking develop which express common attitudes and ideas. Often a private way of speaking develops between husband and wife as a result of years of common experiences and of familiarity with each other's attitudes and beliefs. An unseen observer at the family breakfast table might well understand very little of the conversation over the coffee and toast. We can see, then, that there is a dependence in the direction, as it were, from ideas to language. Is there an equal dependence in the direction from language to ideas? The way we use language reflects our way of looking at the world, but does it do more than that; does it perhaps determine our world view?

Let us approach this question by making one or two general observations about common attitudes to language. First of all, we might notice that people have the feeling that language has the power to impose an order on external reality, hence bringing it under control. Shakespeare tells us that imagination 'gives to airy nothing a local habitation and a name'. Language, we might say, does the same, and by so doing gives a definite conceptual shape to airy nothing and makes it into something which can be talked about and so controlled. Some grammarians have made the point that it is unreasonable to define nouns as the names of persons, places and things, since many nouns in English are the names of none of these but of abstractions like sadness, fear, and courage. This may be so, but the fact remains that such words are grouped together with those which refer to perceptible phenomena like shoes and ships and sealing wax. This enables the speaker of English to think of abstractions as, in some sense, like perceptible things. One might point to the facility most people have in producing and understanding personification and other figurative devices, which, contrary to what many people appear to believe, are an essential and normal feature of language use. It takes no very great effort on the part of an English speaker to understand an expression like 'a flight of fancy' or 'in the grip of fear' because his language has already disposed him to conceive of abstract notions of this kind as entities.

Language enables us to give names to abstractions and we feel that by so doing we give them definite conceptual shape—we pin them down. One effect of this is that it is difficult to distinguish between the name and the concept to which it refers. It is common for people to recognize certain magical properties of language in the sense that they feel that in uttering words they invoke the presence of the things to which the words refer. The name of god or devil is repeated in ritual to invoke his presence, not to invite him to come. In all societies there are taboo words which are avoided because they are felt to give actual realization to what they refer to. In our society, it is not forbidden to talk about sex and death, for example, but certain words which refer to these notions are proscribed in polite company. So we devise euphemisms to keep the notions themselves at a distance, to enable us to talk about them without directly invoking their presence in the sitting room. Thus 'cancer' becomes 'a growth'; 'to die' become 'to pass away', 'pass over' or 'pass on'; and 'a prostitute' becomes 'a lady of easy virtue', and so on. In the course of time, euphemisms themselves develop invocationary power by use and when they draw too close to the notion to which they refer, new euphemisms are devised to keep reality at bay. The word 'knickers', for example, was introduced to replace the word 'drawers', which had become indelicately close to calling up sexual connotations. Now 'knickers' in its turn has lost something of its euphemistic effect, and the word 'panties' seems to be replacing it, with 'lingerie' waiting, as it were, in the wings.

The point then is that the speakers of a language often behave as if they believed that linguistic forms were in some sense embodiments of ideas. Furthermore, as we have seen, one of the principal ways in which people proclaim membership of a group is to adopt the manner of speaking which is felt to express the group's agreed way of looking at the world. All of this prompts us to ask whether it may be the case that the power of language to express and to invoke ideas is such that the ideas which the speaker of a language has are determined by the language he speaks.

Let us consider first the different colour terms which are used in different languages. To an English speaker, it seems natural to think of red, orange, yellow, green and blue as being separate and distinct colours. But other languages divide up the colour spectrum in quite different ways. Sometimes we find that there is one word covering our red/orange or green/blue; sometimes we find several terms referring to what in English is covered by only one. Now does it mean that the speaker of a language which has only one term for, say, our green/blue cannot in fact perceive a distinction between these colours? And does it mean that a speaker of a language which has more than one term for, say, our blue actually perceives more distinctions in the colour spectrum than does an English speaker? Few linguists would maintain that perceptions are determined by language in this way. The most common view is that the distinctions which are recognized in the colour spectrum simply reflect the importance which different people attach to aspects of the physical environment; if there is a need to distinguish frequently between certain colours, then such a distinction is likely to be adopted in the language. Furthermore, this distinction may not be based on the features of colour which English uses to divide up the colour spectrum: luminosity, hue and saturation.

Hanunoo, a language spoken in the Philippines, makes a much simpler division of the colour spectrum than we do in English, having four terms as opposed to our eleven. These terms might be said to be roughly translatable as white/black/red/green. However, the distinctions are based on criteria other than those associated with the English terms, including an opposition between lightness/darkness and between dryness/freshness. Thus, a term which is used to refer to objects which in English might be called 'light green' is also used to refer to the shiny wet surface of freshly cut bamboo, which in English might be called 'brown'. One may say that for the Hanunoo people it is more important to refer to whether plants are young and succulent or not than whether they are green or brown (in our terms). It does not follow, however, that a speaker of English cannot perceive the qualities of wetness and dryness or associate them with the colours he commonly distinguishes. What it does suggest, however, is that such qualities are not regarded as intrinsic to colour, but simply incidental attributes. A speaker of English can refer to something as 'wet green' or 'dry brown' in the same way as he can make up expressions like 'gay red', 'lively yellow' and so on, but the important point to notice is that we do not have single terms like 'wetgreen' or 'drybrown' or 'gayred'. What in one language is an elemental concept in another is a compound concept. In other words, whereas 'wet green', for example, is conceived of as a kind of green, 'wetgreen' would not be so conceived but would be thought of as an elemental and independent quality.

One can make the same point in relation to other areas of vocabulary. As has often been observed, the Arabs have several words for what we refer to indiscriminately as camels. Similarly it is common in languages of tropical areas to find many different terms used distinctively to refer to what for us are simply bamboos and bananas. Different terms naturally arise when it is of importance to a particular group of people to make particular distinctions, and when constant reference to such distinctions makes it convenient to have separate labels. Groups of English-speaking botanists, for example, also have a range of terms for bamboos and bananas; they too need to distinguish types, though for reasons other than those of the Asian villager. Again, to take an example which is very commonly cited, the Eskimos have a number of different words for what we call 'snow'. This does not mean that we cannot perceive that falling snow, snow on the ground, snow compressed in the form of snow blocks and so on are different phenomena because we do not have separate lexemes to refer to them. What it does mean, however, is that whereas our language leads us to focus on the common features of the phenomena, that of the Eskimos does not. This is not meant to imply, of course, that the Eskimo cannot see the common features; even if he had no general term in his language to include them all, he would still be capable of classifying different kinds of snow as being the same general phenomena. In English, for example, we have the words 'dog', 'cat' and 'horse' (which are elemental in the same sense as the Eskimo's words for snow) rather than expressions like 'canine animal', 'feline animal' and 'equine animal' (which are compound in the same sense as expressions like 'falling snow', 'settling snow', 'melting snow' and so on). But this does not mean that we cannot recognize that dogs and cats and horses are all animals; and even if we had no general term 'animal' we would still be able to set up a general classification.

It is commonly the case that an 'elemental focus' comes to replace a compound one over a period of time. The English word 'steamroller', for example, originally referred to a kind of roller: one which was driven by steam. Nowadays, steamrollers are driven by diesel fuel and are thought of not as kinds of roller but as items of road-building plant and grouped together with bulldozers and concrete mixers. Steam rollers, we might say, have become steamrollers, just as, in the classroom, black boards have become blackboards. It does not of course follow that an elemental notion is marked by a single word, whereas a compound one is marked by a phrase, but there appears to be a general tendency in language to approximate to such a match. When something needs to be referred to frequently or to be emphasized as a thing in itself rather than one of a class of things, the compound phrase is often abbreviated, or a new term coined. Thus an electric light bulb becomes a bulb, a tobacco pipe a pipe, a concrete mixer a mixer, and so on. The same result can be achieved by the introduction of loan words from foreign languages. This takes place at an accelerated rate in technical areas of enquiry, where conscious efforts are made to be precise by the use of elemental terms.

What is being suggested, then, is that the lexical structure of a language not only reflects culturally important features of the environment, but that it predisposes the people who share this language to see the world in a certain way. Although their perceptions are not blinkered, it may need some effort to orientate themselves to a view of the world other than that which is reflected in the lexical structure of their own language.

In this discussion of what is commonly known as 'linguistic relativity' we have restricted ourselves to lexical matters, but it is easy to see that one can make the same points about the grammatical structure of different languages. To take one example, the systems of tense and aspect vary widely between different languages and may be said to reflect different ways of dealing with time, and people will be predisposed to think of time in terms of the way in which the grammar of a language expresses it. Again it must be stressed that this does not mean that people cannot think of time in any other way, but it does mean that they might have to make some effort to do so, as anyone trying to understand the basic principles of Einstein's theory of relativity will very soon discover. One is so accustomed to using the linguistic categories of one's own language that one is constrained by force of habit, rather than any intrinsic inability, from changing one's perceptions of the world. One is reminded of the story by G. K. Chesterton in which a murderer goes into a building under the eyes of a number of witnesses who later claimed that no one had entered. The man was dressed as a postman and people are accustomed to think of postmen as 'postmen' rather than as 'persons'. To all intents and purposes the language habits of a lifetime rendered him invisible.

We have been suggesting that speakers of a language will be predisposed to see reality as it is formalized in the lexical and grammatical structure of their language. Two reservations, however, must be pointed out. Firstly, as we have already seen, it is natural for society to be in a constant state of flux, and natural therefore for language to vary in accordance with the demands which are made upon it at different times. When suggesting that linguistic forms reflect the world view of speakers one must be wary of forms which have been fossilized by the normal process of linguistic and cultural change. Secondly, it follows from the heterogeneity of both society and language, which we have previously discussed, that there can be no unitary world view shared by all speakers of a language. When considering linguistic relativity, therefore, we would be prudent to investigate the speech behaviour of smaller groups within a society. But even at this level of generalization we must be careful to bear in mind that to generalize must always be to misrepresent actual facts to some degree.

Let us now consider what implications linguistic relativity might have for language teaching. As pointed out at the beginning of this paper, learning a language is not merely a matter of learning how to fit linguistic forms together to make correct sentences; learning a language involves learning to use such forms to perform communicative acts of one kind or another. In order to do this, one must, to some degree at least, assimilate the ideas, attitudes and beliefs which the language embodies. If one is to learn language behaviour, one has also to learn cultural behaviour and to see the world in a different light. Problems arise, however, if this learned behaviour relates to values which are in conflict with those of the learner's own language and culture. On the one hand, learning how to use a foreign language can best be promoted by associating it overtly with the culture of which it naturally and inseparably forms a part. On the other hand, this approach may have the effect of dividing the learner from his own cultural environment. Such a dilemma is not very apparent in cases where the foreign language is associated with a culture which is not very different from the learner's own. It becomes serious, however, where the foreign language reflects a way of life which is radically different from that associated with the mother tongue. Such is the case, for example, in many developing countries, where the indigenous languages embody cultural values upon which it is felt that their identity depends, but where a foreign language, like English or French, is needed to further economic development. Such nations have somehow to provide for both cultural integration and economic development since their continued independence may well depend on both in equal measure. Promoting a language which ensures the latter may lead to a devaluation of indigenous languages, upon which the former depends. Considerations like these make policy decisions about which languages should be used for which purpose (i.e., language planning) an extremely delicate operation in many countries.

Although the problem is seen at its most acute form in certain developing countries in relation to a choice between two or more languages, it exists also in other countries in relation to a choice between varieties of the 'same' language. If it is assumed that language predisposes people to a certain world view and is therefore a powerful cultural force, it would follow that education should, wherever possible, be in the mother tongue. This seems reasonable where the mother tongue is a standard language, like Bengali, but how reasonable is it where the mother tongue is either a non-standard language or a dialect variety of a standard one? It is just as proper to speak of a dialect as a mother tongue as it is to speak of a language as a mother tongue since, as has been mentioned earlier, no hard and fast distinction can be made between 'a language' and 'a dialect'. The difference is that dialects are popularly believed (though without foundation) to be inferior forms, degenerate offshoots from the accepted standard. Nevertheless they express a way of life and a sense of cultural identity just as much as do more prestigious language types. By conducting education in the standard version of the language one might change the values of the learners which bind them to their background and thereby cut them off from their cultural heritage. Speakers of non-standard English from underprivileged groups, for example, are generally forced to conform to standard English usage in their education and at the same time are made to feel that their own natural way of speaking is inferior and 'wrong'. The effect of this may either be to make the learner resentful of and resistant to the whole process of education, or to open up a rift between himself and the people of his home background. The result is that the learner may be educationally deprived on the one hand and culturally deprived on the other. In view of this, some people have advocated teaching the standard language to non-standard speakers by casting it in the role of a foreign language on the grounds that this might avoid the problem of the relative 'correctness' of one as opposed to the other and the implied denigration of the way of life associated with non-standard speech.

2.6 Language variation and change

We have referred in the previous section to the fact that society and language are both in a constant state of flux. We normally think of change as having to do with variation over time, which we refer to as diachronic variation, but this temporal change has its seeds in the synchronic variation existing at any one time. In describing the structure of a language or its social functions we normally make the assumption that we need not be concerned with change, either as it has occurred in the past or as it is taking place in the present. By making this simplifying assumption, we can identify different varieties of language directly with whole *domains* of a society. In other words, we may associate one language (or language variety) with the domain of kinship or the family, another with the school, another with local administration and so on.

With this in mind, let us return once more to Wales, and in particular to those parts of the country where Welsh is spoken by a significant number of people. We might make the generalization that Welsh is associated with the private domain of family and kinship whereas English is restricted to the public domains of administration, law, and formal education, with the two languages sharing the religious domain according to the type of worship concerned. In consequence, English can be seen to take on the role of an official public language and this bestows on it a certain prestige value. Welsh, on the other hand, is regarded as the appropriate means for talking about private and intimate affairs and does not enjoy the same public status.

Although such a picture gives us some general idea of the situation in Wales, few Welshmen would subscribe to it. The equation between language variety and domain which we have made, though useful for some purposes, is a misrepresentation of the real state of affairs. In the first place, as was pointed out in section 2.4, no society is homogeneous, and the parts of Wales we are discussing are no exception. We cannot, therefore, expect that all families will be of equal status. Although Welsh may be spoken in many homes, particularly in rural areas and among the working class, English is the language of the home in many middle-class families, who naturally identify themselves with the English middle class and adopt their life style. In the second place, the picture we have drawn in the preceding paragraph presents a static situation which does not allow for the ongoing process of change. Some of the activities of the

Welsh Nationalist Movement are directed towards altering the status quo and making Welsh an official language. In other words, they aim at extending the functions of Welsh, thereby changing the whole pattern of language use within the country. Those in authority have to some extent responded to the pressure of national feeling by allowing Welsh official status in certain courts of law and for certain administrative purposes. All of this suggests that the notion of domain as we have previously used it is too crude to capture what is, in fact, going on. To get a more accurate picture of language use in the domain of the family, for example, one would have to take into consideration what language is used between different members of the family: between parents and children, parent and parent, and the children among themselves. In some Welsh families one may find Welsh being used by the older generation and English by the children or vice versa.

We have shown how change can lead to the blurring of functional distinctions between languages in a multilingual society. It does not necessarily follow, however, that all multilingual situations are inherently unstable. In some countries, two languages or varieties of language may exist side by side with quite distinct functional roles. A striking example of this can be found in Arab countries, where two structurally different forms of Arabic are used. The colloquial form is acquired as a mother tongue and it is used in the home, in other informal situations and in exchanges with people of low social status. The classical form, on the other hand, is only acquired through formal education and is used for official, literary and religious purposes. Where the colloquial form varies considerably from place to place, the classical (as we have pointed out in section 2.3) is a standard form serving as a lingua franca which can be understood by speakers in many different regions. Classical Arabic, as its functions might suggest, is the higher prestige form. The fact that this situation has existed for a very long period of time supports the point that there is nothing intrinsically difficult in an individual being able to operate two languages in functionally distinct domains. We can see the same kind of thing occurring nearer at hand in the way that many speakers continue to control both standard English and a dialect in different areas of use.

Where two languages are associated with quite distinct domains of use, a speaker has little difficulty in keeping the language systems apart. When the domains of use begin to overlap, however, one system is likely to interfere with the other. This is the phenomenon known as *interference*, or the mutual modification of language codes by contact. We can also look at the consequences of having two languages in conflict within the same domain for the individual speaker, and here we can return once more to the Welsh family we referred to earlier. If Welsh and English both become languages of the home, it is likely that there will be heavy interference between the two in the speech of the members of the family. It may even be difficult to allocate a particular stretch of speech to one language or the other. This is clearly an unstable situation and we can predict that one language will gradually predominate, and over time will displace the other. This pattern of displacement is particularly common in the immigrant situation, where the language of the host community, by virtue of the power of its prestige and ubiquity, moves from the domains of work and education into that of the home.

In our discussion we have used the terms bilingualism and multilingualism to refer to two separate, though related, phenomena. On the one hand, we have used them to refer to countries or societies and implied that within their boundaries there are found two or more languages. But this societal multilingualism does not imply that all, or indeed any, of the members of that society speak more than one language. Individual multilingualism (or bilingualism) implies that an individual is able to speak more than one language. As we have seen above, the presence of individual bilinguals in a society means that the society must be classified as a multilingual one, whereas the reverse does not follow. For example, England became a multilingual society after the Norman conquest in 1066 in that French and Anglo-Saxon both operated in functionally distinct domains in the country. However, individual bilingualism was of rare occurrence; few Saxons learned to speak French and few Normans deigned to learn the language of the conquered people in the early Norman period.

2.7 Language teaching aims in perspective

What we have tried to make clear in the preceding discussion is that language permeates society and helps to define and maintain social institutions and social values. We have said that in order to survive, man has to co-operate. To do this he has to organize. His organizing activity is evident in the internal structure of language itself, but this structure is only one realization of man's ability to impose order on his environment and his experience. Others are seen in the patterned nature of social life and behaviour. It may be convenient to study these different modes of organization as if they were quite separate phenomena and thus provide subject matter for the 'different' disciplines of linguistics, psychology and sociology, but it is important to realize that they are integrally related in reality. For the purposes of language teaching, it is of particular importance to recognize the relationship between the language system and patterns of individual behaviour, and between the language system and patterns of social life; hence the relevance of psycholinguistics on the one hand, and of sociolinguistics on the other. The purpose of this concluding section is to bring into relief the relevance to language teaching of our discussion on that part of sociolinguistics which is known as the sociology of language.

Let us first of all place language teaching itself in a social perspective. It may be described as an activity which aims at developing in people certain forms of social behaviour which are different from those which they already practise. The language teacher may sometimes imagine that he is simply teaching a set of abilities which are then added to the store of those which the learner already has, like putting extra books on a shelf. But language is not a separate entity of this kind since it is so intricately bound up with other aspects of human life. If language is taught in such a way as to preserve its essential character, and not as a distortion represented simply as a set of grammatical facts, then it must be taught as a form of social behaviour. But if it is so taught, there is bound to be a strong possibility of conflict with the forms of social behaviour represented by the learner's own language. Obviously it is of crucial importance that the language teacher should be aware of this, and should understand the implications of what he is doing.

Let us consider more closely the teaching activity as we have defined it. Why, we might begin by asking, should one want to teach another form of social behaviour anyway? In general, the answer to this is that it is considered desirable to extend the learner's range of experience beyond that which is expressible in terms of his own language, and which is limited by the activities and attitudes of the society to which he belongs. Thus, for example, the case for teaching English to speakers, say, of Tagalog, or French to speakers of Arabic might be that Tagalog and Arabic speakers are thereby provided with a means of access to scientific and technical knowledge which is not available to them through the medium of their own languages. Here, extending the range of experience amounts to the provision of instruction in subject areas of importance for economic development. The case for teaching, say, Swahili to speakers of tribal languages in Tanzania, or Hindi to speakers of Bengali or Gujarati, or other Indian languages, might be that in so doing one provides them with a common means of communication. Here, extending the range of experience involves giving people a sense of belonging to a larger society rather than just to their own small group, thus developing a sense of common identity and furthering the interest of national integration. These are instances of forms of social behaviour which can be associated with 'separate' languages and cultures, but no hard and fast line can be drawn between a 'language' and a 'dialect'. By the same token, there is no obvious distinction between a 'society' and a 'social group' or between a 'culture' and a 'sub-culture'. Therefore, as another example of the way that language teaching could work towards an extension of experience, or broadening of attitude, we can take the teaching of the standard form of the mother tongue to non-standard speakers in the context of formal education or the teaching of basic literacy through a second language where the first language has no written form.

In each of these cases the teaching of language is directed towards what we might call an institutional purpose (economic, political and educational respectively) although, in practice, these purposes are commonly interrelated. The difficulty is that the new forms of behaviour introduced to achieve this purpose may not be easily reconciled with those which the learner has already acquired. Filipino learners of English and Arab learners of French may find that the new language brings with it attitudes and ideas which call their own cultural values into question, and the economic development which it serves to promote may only be attainable at the expense of the way of life with which they identify themselves, and in which they find their basic security. Similarly, national integration may only be achieved by the disintegration of regional cultures as the imposed language encroaches on the social domain of the indigenous languages. As is well known, what is politically desirable may be culturally disastrous for minority groups of people. Again, the standard language which is taught in the interest of education may, as was pointed out earlier, have the effect of destroying the values associated with non-standard forms of expression while putting no values of comparable worth in their place.

The apparently straightforward business of language teaching is, then, bound up with difficulties of a very complex kind. Language is both an expression of established cultural values and a means of exploration and discovery, so that it may act as a force for either conservation or change. When only one language is involved, these forces normally achieve some kind of balance and the language is modified in the natural process of social change so that there is a maintenance of stability. When change comes not, as it were, from within, as a gradual growth by adaptation, but as something imposed from outside by the action of a different language, then the balance of forces is apt to be disturbed, sometimes quite violently. In such a situation, the forces of conservation and change have to be reconciled, and stability achieved, by deliberate policy decisions. It might, for example, be decided to have the mother tongue used as a medium of instruction in the primary school so as to ensure that the child's educational development is rooted in his own cultural heritage, and then transfer to a foreign language as the medium for secondary education. Or it might be thought more practicable to introduce the foreign language at the beginning of the child's school career, but restrict its use to the teaching of certain subjects. Whatever is decided will depend, ideally, on the consideration of a large number of factors: historical, economic, cultural, linguistic and so on.

Decisions like these, which attempt to reconcile the claims of cultural as opposed to economic, educational and political interests, are matters of government policy and are usually out of the hands of the language teacher himself. But it is clearly of great importance that the teacher should understand the factors which are involved, so that he knows for what purpose he is teaching and can adjust his approach accordingly. Above all the teacher should be aware of the social nature of language, so that when he teaches it he knows just what it is that he is doing.

3 Sociolinguistics

3.1 Sociolinguistic perspectives

In section 2 we concerned ourselves with the bird's eye view of the relationship between language and society. In this section we shift perspective and look at the relationship from, as it were, the worm's point of view. As was mentioned in section 1, the study of language use in large-scale perspective is sometimes referred to as the sociology of language to distinguish it from the small-scale study of verbal interaction which is commonly considered to be the main concern of sociolinguistics proper.

Although it is convenient to make a distinction of this kind, it must be stressed that these two ways of looking at language in use are complementary and not in conflict. Certain phenomena are seen more clearly from one point of view than from the other. To take another analogy, we might say that in the first part of the paper we were attempting to distinguish the broad outlines of the 'wood' without paying attention to the individual 'trees'. This perspective enabled us to observe certain general patterns of interplay between linguistic and social factors and to present an over-all picture in which the social functioning of language was fairly clearly perceived down to the level of the domain. In this part we enter the 'wood' itself and examine the 'trees' that make it up. Now the details come into focus and what was previously the smallest object of scrutiny retires to the unfocused periphery of our concern. What we focus upon in section 3 is the speech event: the act of social interaction itself.

3.2 Levels of idealization

Before we begin our discussion on the speech event, it will perhaps be as well to make clear two basic assumptions, which are implied in what has just been said and which underlie the approach to the study of language which has been adopted throughout this paper. The first assumption is that the truth of a generalization about language and its use (like the truth of generalizations relating to other areas of enquiry) is relative to the degree of idealization that is imposed on the data concerned. Making a general statement involves abstracting a pattern from observed phenomena and disregarding those features which do not fit into it. The more general the statement the less likely it is to account for the whole range of observable facts. Furthermore, which features of reality one chooses to regard as essential and which features one reduces to incidental status will depend on where one draws one's lines of idealization. Naturally one will draw these lines in such a way as to make it easier to concentrate on the kind of phenomena one is interested in. All systematic enquiry must proceed by means of idealization of data, and the validity of the results must be measured against the idealization upon which they are based. It must not be assumed that they are a direct reflection of reality.

The second assumption is a corollary to the first. It is that there is no one approach to the description of linguistic phenomena which has a monopoly on the truth. One approach to linguistic description may provide important insights into the nature of language; but at the same time it may do so only by idealizing out certain features of language which another approach might regard as of paramount importance.

As we have suggested earlier in this paper, we believe that the language teacher would be wise to make similar assumptions when considering what linguists and others have to offer that is relevant to the teaching of languages. The language teacher who looks to linguistics for some enlightenment as to the nature of language is frequently confused by the different approaches which are adopted, and by the conflicting claims that are made about their 'correctness'. It might be useful, therefore, to make it clear at this stage how the sociologically oriented approach to language study is related to that which is generally taken by the grammarian.

In the first place, whereas the grammarian tends to idealize his data by making the supposition that there is a uniform set of phenomena representing a language which he can describe as a well-defined system, the sociolinguist, as is clear from section 2, recognizes the fact of language variation and attempts to account for it. As we have seen, there is no way of defining a language in linguistic terms and we have represented the variability of language as being one of its essential characteristics and necessary for it to fulfil its social role. By assuming the existence of a well-defined language system, the grammarian ignores variation altogether; for him it is not an essential feature. He focuses his attention on the properties of the language system by referring to one language variety (often his own) and thus idealizes the data by imposing his own form of standardization. The standardization that the grammarian practises to define the object of linguistic description is not, however, to be confused with the process whereby a single language variety comes to be acknowledged as a norm throughout a speech community (see section 2.5).

Sociolinguistics proper may be regarded as the study of language with a second degree of idealization relaxed. The grammarian not only imposes a standardization on his data, but he decontextualizes it as well. That is to say, he is concerned with sentences and their formal properties in dissociation from the contexts in which they are actually used. He is not primarily concerned with who uses what sentences in what social circumstances and for what purposes. Whereas the grammarian reduces his data by a process of decontextualization, the sociolinguist focuses on the way in which language is affected by the contexts of its use.

In brief, we may say that in section 2 we attempted to discover a pattern in those features of language use which the grammarian idealizes away by his process of standardization. In the sociolinguistic discussion which follows we attempt to focus on those features of language use which the linguist refines from his data by a process of decontextualization. This is not meant to imply that we are revealing truths which the grammarian has failed to discover, nor that our approach is more 'correct' than his. We are simply taking a different point of view and are looking for different things. To repeat the points made earlier, all approaches to the study of language make simplifying idealizations of one kind or another and there is little point in claiming that an approach based on one idealization is more correct than another. It has commonly been assumed that the grammarian's approach to language is the only one which is relevant for language teachers. It is the purpose of this paper to suggest that an approach which describes language without recourse to the same degree of idealization is of equal relevance to the language teacher.

3.3 The speech event

We take as our starting point the *speech event* which may be defined as a piece of linguistic interaction, a communicative happening consisting of one or more utterances. Thus the kind of exchange which takes place between a traveller and a ticket collector is a speech event, as are lengthier exchanges such as that between a door-to-door salesman and his prospective customer and that between two housewives gossiping over the garden wall. A speech event may be such that one speaker more or less monopolizes the speaking role, as in sermons and politicians' speeches, or the speaking may be very evenly distributed as in the rapid exchanges of two music-hall comedians telling a joke. Although we use the term 'speech', the speech event is neutral as to medium, and its constituent utterances may be written (with an addressee presupposed) as well as spoken (with an addressee physically present). Thus sending a telegram is a speech event. So is putting up a notice reading BEWARE OF THE BULL.

As is perhaps apparent, the notion of speech event is not an easy one to pin down. Here we are in much the same position as the grammarian, who finds that the notion of 'sentence' is similarly elusive. But speech events, like sentences, have intuitive reality, as is evident from the fact that labels are readily attached to them. One talks of sermons, sales patter, 'doing the introductions', bargaining over prices, having consultations, and so on. People, then, recognize speech events, even though it is difficult to give formal definition to what it is that they recognize. We will follow the lead of the grammarian, who allows his grammar to define the sentence, by saying that the speech event will be defined in our analysis in terms of the components which go to make it up.

We will build up a model of the speech event by setting down the different factors that come into play when an act of communication takes place. To begin with, we must have someone sending a message to someone else. We may say, then, that three of the constituent factors in the speech event are the *addresser*, the *addressee*, and the *message*. As we pointed out above, the addressee need not be physically present, but any act of communication presupposes his existence. He may not be known as an individual, of course; we commonly address people we do not know in speaking and writing. We know how to address them because we identify them as members of a group or category and we have learnt how to address them in that capacity. Both addresser and addressee may be plural. We can direct our remarks to more than one person either as individuals, or as a collectivity of faceless people; and collectivities of faceless people like the Inland Revenue may address us. Although the message is usually verbal, it is important to realize that it may only be verbal in part, and indeed may not be verbal at all (see section 3.5). Verbal messages are commonly accompanied by paralinguistic phenomena, such as gestures. And a message may be transmitted without recourse to verbal means at all, as when we wink, or cock a snook, or 'blow a raspberry', or make the well-known vulgar variation on Winston Churchill's victory sign.

The message which is sent from the addresser to the addressee is transmitted through some *channel* or other, and this, therefore, is another constituent factor in the speech event. This channel must be one which will establish contact with our perceiving senses. In speaking, the channel is represented by sound waves passing through the air and perceived by our sense of hearing. In writing, we make use of marks which are directed at the sense of sight. People often speak of writing as being 'language in the visual medium', and speaking as being 'language in the aural medium'. It should be noted, however, that messages that are conveyed by means of gesture also make appeal to the visual sense, but the medium in this instance is quite different from that of writing. It is useful therefore to make a distinction between *medium* and *channel*. Writing and gesture are different media which make use of the same channel. It should also be pointed out that writing is not always apprehended by the sence of sight. Braille, for example, employs a channel which makes appeal to the sense of touch. Furthermore, in many speech events more than one channel is brought into operation at the same time; in conversation one makes use of both the aural channel of speech and the visual channel of gesture.

Again, whichever channel is used, a speech event must occur in a *setting*, whether this be of time or of place. When performing an act of communication in a particular setting one normally makes reference to something, so another factor which we need to take into account is the *topic*, the referential content of the message. Finally, if the message is to be understood it has to be expressed in some linguistic or paralinguistic *code* which is, to some degree at least, known by both addresser and addressee.

We may say, then, that the most obvious factors of the speech event are the following:

Addresser	Setting
Addressee	Topic
Message form	Code
Channel	

Although we have separated them out, these factors interrelate in complex ways in particular speech events. Let us consider a few examples. The setting of a speech event may have a very definite effect on the channel which is used. The effect may have to do with the physical circumstances in which an exchange takes place; thus bookmakers at racecourses convey information about betting odds by the use of signs not only to preserve secrecy but to overcome the noise of the crowd, which would drown out any attempts at speech. People communicate by signs across a crowded room for the same reason. The setting may have an effect on the channel not because of physical conditions, but because of accepted conventions of behaviour. Thus, we feel constrained to pass notes to our neighbour if we wish to communicate with him in the middle of a conference. In the eighteenth century in England, married ladies of fashion devised a set of gestures with their fans to communicate with their admirers at entertainments like the assembly and the opera, where any other form of communication would have been highly indiscreet.

The setting may determine the message form. In some societies certain ceremonies require that communication should be effected by the telling of tales or verse recitation. The ritual of the Christian Church in some of its forms requires that language should be cast in the patterns of incantation. Again, there are kinds of discourse which are reserved for less solemn occasions like the drinking of toasts and the making of after-dinner speeches. Among the Subanan, a Filipino people, each stage in an evening of ceremonial drinking is marked by a different way of speaking, the last being a display of verbal artistry which involves breaking into song. In our society, it is quite easy to recognize at what point in an evening's (perhaps less ceremonial) drinking it is appropriate to give voice to bawdy songs—songs, perhaps, which would have earned a look of cold reproof if they had been sung earlier in the evening.

The setting, code and topic are often interrelated. There are certain topics of conversation which are not regarded as suitable during mealtimes among sections of our own community. There is a time and a place for 'talking shop' and wives tend to object when husbands do it at a dinner party. We can see how setting relates to code in bilingual situations, like that of Wales (see section 2), where one language is associated with the home setting, and the other with places like government offices and the law courts. In the Middle Ages, theological matters were discussed in Latin. The Saramaccaner of Guiana have a language which they use when speaking of their ordinary everyday affairs, and another linguistic code which is the language of religious ceremony. Again, in some areas of Norway, people have a command of two language varieties: Norwegian, known as *bokmål*, and another variety known as *landsmål* or *nynorsk*, but it is generally recognized there that one of these codes is appropriate for talking about certain subjects, and the other for talking about others. Thus, *landsmål* is used to discuss family affairs, to exchange gossip, to talk about matters of local interest and so on. However, when the topic relates to issues which have implications beyond the local scene, as would be the case, for example, with national or international politics, then it is *bokmål* which is thought to be the appropriate code.

Just as one can see relationships between topic and code, so we can see that topic is related to the addresser and addressee. A discussion about babies' clothes and feeding times is unlikely to take place between men, and one about motor-bikes or carpentry is unlikely to take place between women, at least in our culture. The traditional upper and middle class convention among the British of having the ladies retire after dinner to leave the men to their port is based on the notion that men and women have different things to talk about; here different settings are established to enable them to speak freely on their respective topics. Attempts to break down established conventions as about who should talk about what are often met with mockery. Samuel Johnson, for example, once observed to Boswell: 'Sir, a woman's preaching is like a dog's walking on his hinder legs. It is not done well: but you are surprised to find it done at all'.

The relationship between addresser and addressee can also have a determining effect on the code which is used. In Paraguay, for example, a large proportion of the population are bilingual in Spanish and the local language, Guarani, but these languages are not used randomly. Most people use Spanish when addressing the doctor, the school teacher and the government official, and Guarani when talking with their neighbours, friends and members of the family. In this case, there is a clear choice between two languages, but the relationship between addresser and addressee can also be reflected in the choice of a 'sub-code' within what on other grounds would be considered one language. Thus in Javanese one can distinguish a number of sub-codes in terms of formal linguistic properties. The addresser makes a choice from among these in accordance with the relative status of himself and the addressee. One can see the same thing happening on a smaller scale between the 'familiar' and the 'polite' forms of the second person pronoun (tu/vous in French; Du/Ihr/Sie in German, etc.). In Javanese, however, the choice is not only between two pronouns and their corresponding verb forms, but between two sub-codes which are distinctive in terms of their grammatical and lexical features.

3.4 Code variation

It was noted in the previous section that, in Javanese, the speaker is required to make a choice from a number of sub-codes according to the relative status of himself and the person he is addressing. This example, together with the others we mentioned, drawn from a wide range of different cultures, illustrate how the different factors in the speech event may be mutually dependent. However, this interdependency is not only a feature of these societies but also of highly urbanized and industrial ones. In English, too, we need to distinguish a number of language varieties and state how the use of one or other of these is determined in some way by the interplay between addresser, addressee, setting, topic and so on.

We need first of all to examine what kind of variation we ourselves make in our speech according to the particular situation in which we find ourselves and the people to whom we are speaking. An example taken from Labov's detailed studies of the English used in New York City shows the factors involved. He studied the alternative pronunciations which people give to the first sound in words such as *thing*. In New York there are three variants, firstly a fricative [θ], secondly an affricate [tθ] and thirdly a stop [t]. Of these three the fricative is the prestige educated variant and the stop is the form which is considered to be the most stigmatized, being associated with the least educated and the lowest socio-economic classes. According to the outline that we gave in section 2.4 we might expect to be able to identify the users of the prestige variant, the fricative, as being all of one particular socio-economic class and the users of the stigmatized variant, the stop, as being all members of another. This may be an approximation which it is appropriate to make for some purposes, but when we examine language usage in detail, we find that in New York City none of the three variants is exclusive to any one particular group of speakers. Here we can see how the two perspectives taken in this paper lead to different but complementary findings.

It appears that in formal situations, when the speaker is particularly conscious of his speech, people from the higher socio-economic class use the stigmatized variant very rarely indeed. However, they may in fact use the stigmatized variant when they are in formal situations and are paying little attention to their speech, even though they may be quite unaware of this at the time and may vehemently deny the fact afterwards. The middle-class teacher, for example, may well correct a pupil whenever he uses such a stigmatized variant in the classroom and be unaware that he himself uses such forms in his own speech when speaking naturally in informal situations. One can observe a similar kind of behaviour amongst those of lower socio-economic class. Thus an unskilled worker when placed in a formal situation is likely to become conscious of the way he speaks and attempt to produce the most 'correct' forms. In consequence he may use comparatively few [t] forms, though possibly more than the middle-class teacher we have referred to earlier. On the other hand when speaking to his peers at home, in informal situations, his use of the stigmatized variant may be very much more frequent. In comparing the behaviour of these two representatives from different groups, we can see that although the lower class unskilled worker makes greater over-all use of the stigmatized variant, he nevertheless operates in the same way as the middle-class speaker. Both use more examples of the stigmatized variant in informal situations and fewer in formal ones.

What defines a formal situation, as we have used the term, is of course a combination of some of the factors of the speech event that we discussed in the previous section. Clearly, the relative status of addresser/addressee will influence the addresser in his perception of how important it is to behave (and therefore speak) in a 'correct' or formal manner. Similarly, certain topics may elicit one kind of speech rather than another. From a practical point of view, one way of eliciting formal and informal language is by manipulating the topic being talked about between an interviewer and the person whose speech is being studied. It may be possible to get people to talk about some intimate subject, such as experiences involving a risk to their life, their honour or their chastity. When involved in such intimate talk a person's attention is likely to switch from a concentration on expression to an involvement in content and he is therefore likely to use the form of speech most natural to him. We have given only one example of a sociolinguistic variable where the form realized is dependent upon the formality of situation and status of the participants. However, we find this kind of pattern repeated with many other variables.

At this stage we can consider the implications of two different ways of describing language variation. One approach has been to try to identify different *registers* or superposed varieties of language by means of a purely formal comparison. It has been suggested, for example, that we might be able to distinguish 'scientific English' from some kind of notional 'ordinary English' by making a formal linguistic comparison between examples of both kinds of language. The argument runs that if, on comparing two different samples of language, we find formal differences between them, then we should look at the context in which the language is being used and attempt to correlate the differences with some significant factor in the social situation. These factors might relate to the status of participants, the kind of channel being used, the geographical or historical context and so on. The implication of such studies is that we can make exhaustive descriptions of each of the varieties that we identify in such a way that 'scientific English' emerges as being formally distinct from 'legal English', from 'working-class English' and so on.

The effect of such an approach is to represent the varieties as different codes in their own right. In certain limited areas this approach may be profitable. The English language of legal documents is perhaps an example of this. Here, it is clear that once one has started writing a document in this archaic legal form one is constrained to continue the discourse in the same way. In other words, there is a fairly rigid set of co-occurrence restrictions operating, such that once one has started with a certain set of forms subsequent choices are constrained by them. In the example that we gave of the *th* variable in New York City, on the other hand, we saw that it would be impossible to attribute the stop variant [t] or the fricative variant [θ] exclusively to one particular variety. Instead, we were forced to recognize that both variants were found in all situations but that the frequency of occurrence of each varied systematically according to both the formality of the situation and social status of the individuals concerned.

Consequently it would seem to be more profitable to think not in terms of distinct registers, defined by their formal properties, but in terms of a single code consisting of features common to all varieties as well as those sociolinguistic variables like *th*, which serve to define appropriate use. Consequently, in writing a grammar or phonology of the languages used by a whole speech community, we need to take into account both the *invariant rules* which always apply to all speakers in the community in all situations and the *variable rules* which account for the fact that particular linguistic forms are used differentially. Rather than aim, therefore, at the impossible task of making a full description of each of the different registers within English, it would perhaps be preferable to focus our attention upon the study of those particular sociolinguistic variables which are crucial for the appropriateness of linguistic behaviour.

We have been arguing that it is misleading to think of a language as a patchwork of distinct varieties, each restricted to a specific area of use. On the other hand, in section 2.4, we spoke in terms of definable groups and categories of people having a variety in common. There appears to be a paradox. It can be resolved, once again, by referring to the notion of levels of idealization discussed in section 3.2. We have seen how the linguist ignores detail in order to arrive at general statements, enabling him to describe patterns which would otherwise be hidden in confusion. All scientific enquiry must make simplifying assumptions of this kind.

But it is not only the scientist who needs to adopt this strategy. All of us make use of broad generalizations about behaviour. When meeting someone for the first time, we assume that the person will conform to some pattern of behaviour which is currently held to be typical of that kind of person. We do not wait to find out what he is actually like as an individual. Our first reactions have to be based on a stereotype, a conventional picture of how groups of people behave. An Englishman, for example, brings to his first encounter with a Scotsman such stereotyped beliefs as that the Scots are mean, canny and dour. Many music hall jokes and cartoons bear witness to the prevalence of this stereotype among those English who have never explored further than Potters Bar. One can travel far in Scotland before meeting any individual who actually conforms to this stereotype. The point is that such an Englishman 'knows about' the Scots in general but does not know them as individuals. In other words stereotypes act as a general model for predicting the behaviour of others in situations where we have no personal information about them. The model may, of course, be false (and indeed it usually is) but we must have some kind of initial assumptions about how to behave towards other people.

Stereotypes are as relevant to the language teacher as to anyone else. A working-class pupil may have a stereotyped picture of his middle-class teacher as a representative of 'them', the posh and well-groomed agents of authority. It may take the teacher years of effort to change the picture his pupils have of him. Stereotypes are extremely resistant to modification. One of the principal reasons for this is that they actually have an effect on perception. Evidence which would run counter to their truth is often unconsciously suppressed whereas any behaviour appearing to conform to them is seized upon as confirmation.

The foreign language teacher has a special problem with regard to stereotypes. There has been much discussion in the past about which accent of English should be used as a model of pronunciation. A foreigner successfully learning RP must recognize that the stereotype that most people in Britain may have of the RP speaker is not always a very favourable one. Even if he finds himself among RP speakers, he might have problems in that he will not be able to benefit from the stereotype which British people have of the foreigner. No allowance will be made for any 'oddities' of behaviour normally associated with people speaking with a foreign accent.

As we have pointed out in section 2.4 the essence of a group is that the individuals making it up have both rights and obligations to behave in specified ways. In other words members of a group have certain specific *roles* associated with them. One might think of a group or society as being made up of a set of related positions, with each of which is associated a role. From this point of view these positions and roles exist independently of the individuals who fill them. Thus we treat group structure as a kind of theoretical construct made up of a number of positions to each of which we can attribute a particular function or role. The old rhyme 'Tinker, tailor, soldier, sailor. . .' might be said to provide an elementary list of roles recognized at that time. The bishop and the actress are roles which have been given prominence in a more recent catchphrase.

Roles need not only be considered from this rather static point of view. They also have a dynamic effect on the way people behave. As with the notion of stereotypes the notion of role is concerned with norms and expectancies of behaviour. In this case, however, the norms and expectancies are related to particular positions in society rather than to groups of people. A patient entering the consulting room will tend to adopt a submissive demeanour in deference to the doctor, not because of his knowledge of the doctor's ability but because of his awareness that such behaviour is expected of him as a patient. We can see, therefore, that in role playing, two at least must play. It might appear to be feasible to attribute norms and expectancies of behaviour to the role 'doctor'. It must be realized, however, that a doctor is not expected to behave in exactly the same way to a patient, a fellow doctor, a hospital consultant and to the President of the British Medical Association. In other words we need to consider role relationship and the reciprocal expectations involved. Playing a role does not involve a rigid adherence to prescribed rules of conduct. The role of doctor cannot be specified in terms of the precise patterns of behaviour to be followed. What we can do is make statements about the aims he and the patient have in mind and about certain limitations on how these may be achieved.

We are not, of course, stating that roles are always consciously adopted. As with speech behaviour, role behaviour is normally unconscious, something we have learned in growing up. We are not normally aware of the set of norms associated with any particular position. This becomes clear when what we have come to regard as normal circumstances cease to obtain and we have to learn a new role. Anyone who has been promoted in the army from the ranks to become an officer will realize that a whole new set of behavioural patterns has to be learned. During this learning process, one is often painfully aware of what it is that one ought or ought not to be doing. One feels exposed to the critical scrutiny both of those one has risen from and those one has joined. Another example of a situation when one is conscious of role playing is when there is a clash between two different roles. For example a doctor/patient relationship is characterized by confidentiality. However, a doctor has a different role in relationship to an official of the law and he may well be asked to provide information about a patient of his who has been suspected of some felony or other. An individual in this situation is then faced with a clash between the opposing norms of a doctor in relation to a patient and a doctor in relation to an official of the law.

We have talked at some length about roles since they are crucial to an understanding of how to reconcile the notions of group structure, social situation and varieties of language. It is common for conclusions to be drawn about the child's linguistic competence on the evidence of his utterances in the classroom. But of course the child behaves in the classroom in a way which conforms to what he, not the teacher, believes to be appropriate to the role of pupil. When the child is asked to adopt the role of teacher, as, for example, when taking charge of a class of smaller children, he modifies his behaviour to conform to this new role. As a result he produces language forms which one would otherwise not believe him to be capable of. The child's language performance may be limited, therefore, not so much by any linguistic deficiency but by his sense of what is appropriate to the roles he plays.

We have discussed the notions of stereotypes and roles and we have shown how they account for some of the regularities of language behaviour. It is easy to see how pressures are brought to bear upon individuals in face-to-face groups to make them conform to accepted norms of language behaviour. Such pressures may take the form of mockery, gossip, or even ostracism. Clearly these mechanisms of social control cannot operate in the same way with large groups or categories where there is no possibility of interaction. In the absence of social control mechanisms of this kind we may make use of stereotypes as a guide to the way we should behave. We may recognize certain prestige groups and attempt to copy their behaviour, either verbal or otherwise, that is to say we adopt them as *reference groups*.

It is important that language teachers should be aware of reference group behaviour. As we pointed out in section 2.5, language, like dress, is one of the principal ways by which people identify with or show their loyalty to a group. One of the recurring questions in education is why children coming from 'deprived' backgrounds do not learn to operate the standard language, which is generally considered to be the prestige norm in the country concerned. Thus educationists in Britain have been concerned about the differential performance of middle-class and working-class children. Fewer working-class children reach the higher stages of education and as a category tend to perform less well in school. This difference has often been attributed to the inability of individual children to operate the code of the standard language. But perhaps this is too simple an answer. How is it, for example, that after thousands of hours' exposure to the standard form of English over the radio and television, in school and in many other situations, a child has still not acquired this particular code? After all, foreign language learners manage to learn English with much less exposure.

To answer this question we need to refer to the notion of motivation discussed on pages 229–30. There is no reason to suppose that children will always be motivated to imitate the norms of language behaviour subscribed to by their teachers. Very often the kind of language being taught in the classroom is that which approximates to the middle-class norm of correctness. However, for the working-class child this particular variety may be associated with a group or category of person within his society with whom he does not at all identify. On the contrary he may feel that the language that he is being taught to use is imposed upon him by 'them', whose interests run counter to his own. The kind of values that he learns at home may be quite different from those that are being taught in school. Consequently he has no motivation to adopt middle-class speakers as a reference group for his own speech behaviour. It is more likely, therefore, that a child's so-called inability to produce standard English can be attributed to the different kind of values that the child holds and hence to the different kind of identification that he makes.

It is not only that the speaker of non-standard English perversely refuses to identify with the values of the middle class by adopting standard English, but he may also attribute positive values to his own kind of speech as one aspect of his total way of behaving. In spite of its high prestige in some quarters, RP, for example, may be considered affected, effeminate and lah-di-dah by some groups, whereas their own pronunciation may be associated with manliness and honest dealing. As a result of this conflict of values the teacher's lot is not a happy one. In the formal classroom situation the teacher may be attempting to get the children to use a variety of English which they do not use at home. A child's peers, on the other hand, may be exerting a far more powerful influence on him by ridiculing any attempt to modify his speech in the direction of that of the teacher. Furthermore the value of the pupil's non-standard variety as a symbol of identification is reinforced whenever he participates in games or conversations with his peers.

We have talked so far as if the differences associated with different roles and reference groups are entirely variations in code. If, however, we look at the classroom situation, the home background and peer group behaviour of different kinds of children in our own or any other society, we can see that they may produce not only different linguistic forms, phonological or grammatical, but may also use language for different purposes. In other words language differs functionally as well as formally. Thus one group may use language primarily as a means of identification with members of the family or of the peer group. This is likely to lead to the adoption of particular kinds of jargon or in-words which, as we have seen in section 2.4, have the function of defining group membership. Another group may be taught to use language rather differently; to express feelings, personal experiences, and so on. Children from the first group may therefore find themselves at a disadvantage in school, where the most favoured functions tend to be those of the second group. No amount of code teaching will compensate the child disadvantaged in this aspect of language behaviour.

3.5 Speech functions

In the previous section we discussed how variation in language might be considered not only in terms of the way the code itself varies according to speaker and situation but also in terms of the varying functions that language is required to fulfil. We will now attempt to identify the most important of the speech functions. To do this we will return to the constituent factors in the speech event which we discussed in section 3.3.

We may consider the factors as in some sense determining the different functions which the use of language fulfils. It has been pointed out that apart from conveying information from one person to another, language may be used to express emotion and to direct the activities of other people. Thus three functions can be distinguished: the *referential*, the *expressive* (or emotive) and the *directive* (or conative). Now if the factors we have distinguished identify the determining features of the social context within which verbal interaction takes place, it seems reasonable to suppose that these same factors will play a central role in characterizing speech functions. With respect to the three that have been mentioned this is indeed the case; the referential function relates to topic, the expressive to addresser, and the directive to addressee. That is to say, an utterance which focuses on the topic, whose principal purpose is to present a proposition of one kind or another, may be said to have a referential function; one which focuses on the addresser and is principally an expression of his personal attitudes and feelings may be said to have an expressive function; and one whose purpose is principally to direct the addressee to do something may be said to have a directive function. Examples of such utterances might be 'Albert is leaving', 'I wish to God he would go!' and 'Clear off!' respectively.

Although the three functions mentioned in the preceding paragraph are those most commonly recognized, we can distinguish others in relation to the remaining speech factors. Thus, an utterance which focuses on the channel fulfils what has been called the *phatic* (or contact) function. Language is used phatically when its purpose is to open up or maintain a channel of communication. We have spoken of the channel as the physical medium through which the message is conveyed and some instances of phatic use relate to the need to ensure that the channel is still operating effectively. Examples of this would be expressions like 'Are you receiving me?' used by radio-operators, and the repetition of 'Hello' over the telephone. The contact may also, however, be conceived of as a psychological link between addresser and addressee which ensures that messages are not only being received but also being processed. Examples of such 'psychological' phatic use would be expressions like 'Do you follow me?' 'All right?' and so on. 'Can you hear me?' and 'Do you follow?' are both expressions which generally fulfil phatic functions, the first being associated with the physical contact and the second with the psychological. Perhaps the most familiar kind of phatic use is that which is employed when strangers meet for the first time. In our culture we talk about the weather, but it is phatic talk in that we do it only to open up the channel either to go on to talk about something else or to establish rapport for its own sake. In some societies, notably the Apache and other North American Indian tribes, the phatic function is effected by silence.

An utterance which focuses on the setting has a predominantly *contextual* function. Expressions like 'The court is now in session' or 'The meeting is called to order' have the sole purpose of establishing settings. The contextual function often serves to give formal notice of a set of conditions which bestow certain rights and impose certain obligations on the participants in the speech event. The police officer's formal statement to his prospective prisoner that anything he says will be taken down and may be used in evidence creates a situation in which conditions of this kind obtain. The oath of the witness in a court of law is another instance of the same contextual function. Turning to another area of human activity, language in Elizabethan plays is often used to create settings. The Elizabethan stage was relatively bare of properties, so that where the characters were meant to be at any particular time had often to be indicated verbally. Thus when Rosalind and Celia appear on stage in Act II Scene IV of *As You Like It*, Rosalind's remark 'Well, this is the forest of Arden' serves the purpose of creating the appropriate setting for the audience. Again Elizabethan plays were commonly performed in the afternoon, so that any nocturnal scene had to be created verbally by what the characters said. When Macbeth invokes night, what he says not only fulfils an expressive and poetic function but, equally importantly, has the contextual function of providing a space and time reference for the audience.

The two remaining functions we wish to identify have to do with the code on the one hand and the message form on the other. The principal purpose of certain utterances is to ensure that the addressee understands the meaning of the code which the addresser is using. Utterances of this kind, which focus on the code, fulfil a *metalinguistic* function. Examples of these would be expressions of the form 'X means Y' or 'X is defined as Y' or 'X is called Y'. Finally, mention might be made of the function associated with the message form. In most uses of speech the message form is subsidiary in that it merely acts as a vehicle for expressing one of the functions we have discussed, for expressing an emotion, referring to a topic and so on. Sometimes, however, the message form itself is the focus of attention. This is the case with nursery rhymes and 'tongue twisters' like 'Peter Piper picked a peck of pickled pepper', where there is no referential, expressive, directive or any other function involved. The utterance only exists as a play upon words and their sounds. Such uses of language are said to have a *poetic* function.

It might be objected against this term that poetry does not fulfil a poetic function since most people would wish to claim that poetry does something more than just play with words and create sound effects. This brings up an important point. The utterances we have cited as examples are those in which one function predominates, largely to the exclusion of all others. It is important to realize, however, that such utterances represent only a small proportion of speech behaviour. Most acts of speech combine more than one function. For example, the utterance 'Your plane leaves at 6 p.m.' when spoken by an airline official handing you your ticket has primarily a referential function. When spoken by an immigration officer to an 'undesirable alien', however, its predominant function is likely to be directive, though, of course, it fulfils a subsidiary referential function as well. By the same token, poetry does not only fulfil a poetic function. Consider the following lines:

> The fair breeze blew, the white foam flew,
> The furrow followed free. . . . (Coleridge)

Here the poet is concerned to create a unique message form by the use of alliteration and so on, but the result is not just an arbitrary collection of words. The lines are intended to have referential value as well.

Analysis in terms of speech functions, then, must take account of the fact that most utterances are multi-functional. The task is to decide which function predominates in any particular instance by reference to the circumstances in which the utterance is made. Misunderstandings may arise when the addressee does not recognize which function or functions are meant to predominate.

An army recruit, for example, may in his innocence interpret apparently referential statements at their face value but is very soon made to realize how pervasive the directive function is in the army's use of language. The following exchange would not be untypical in these circumstances:

Sergeant: Reveille sounded five minutes ago, Jenkins.
Pte. Jenkins (at his ease): Oh did it?
Sergeant: Get out of that bloody bunk! When I give you an order I expect you to jump to it.

Similarly, a child going to school for the first time, or moving to another school of a different kind, like anybody moving into unfamiliar surroundings, may have some initial difficulty in adjusting to the new pattern of speech functions which predominate there.

The examples we have given of the varying functions of speech have to do with individual utterances. One can also distinguish more general patterns of functional differentiation. Thus stages in growing up may be associated with certain broad ways of using language. In early childhood, for example, the expressive, directive and poetic functions appear to be dominant. The referential function which appears to play such a large part in adult language seems to be acquired much later in a child's development. It is possible to think of the child as having a quite different sense of the nature of language than the adult. The process of socialization is one whereby the child acquires adult models of behaviour including of course adult models of language use. As we pointed out in the previous section, however, it must be remembered that children from different social groups will acquire different adult models. The child from a lower class background may be doubly disadvantaged in that not only has he not acquired an adult model of language but also the one he is required to learn at school may not be that which is associated with his reference group.

Although the notion of 'speech function' can be most conveniently discussed in relation to spoken utterances, it is important to realize that it refers to a wider range of phenomena than is usually covered by the term 'speech'. In fact, the term 'speech function' is something of a misnomer in that it suggests that the functions we have been discussing are uniquely associated with spoken utterances. But as has already been pointed out communication is not carried out exclusively by verbal means. Non-verbal paralinguistic behaviour also contributes to the total communicative effect, either on its own or in combination with speech. The functions we have been discussing, then, relate to non-verbal communicative actions like gestures as well as to verbal ones like utterances.

Let us consider gesture from the 'speech function' point of view. The most common gestures are perhaps directive ones: the index finger pressed against the lips (hush!), the imperious finger-snapping of the impatient diner

(Waiter!) and so on. Certain gestures may serve a predominantly referential function: the angler's indication of the size of the fish that he (almost) caught is one such gesture; so is the movement of the hands that some men use to outline the figure of a desirable female. The latter also has some expressive force and might be related to gestures which have a predominantly expressive function: the shaking of a fist expressing anger, the clapping of the hand to the mouth simultaneous with a sharp intake of breath expressing a kind of panic at having forgotten something. The latter is largely affected by women, the masculine version perhaps being the clapping of the hand to the forehead. The most common phatic gesture is the nodding of the head during a conversation to indicate that the channel is still open; another is the pupil's raising of a hand to open up a channel to the teacher (Please, sir!). Examples of poetic gestures would be the extravagant posturing affected by some people in the acting profession (My dear!).

Gesture is, of course, a feature of face-to-face interaction and is therefore associated with spoken utterances. It has its analogue, however, in written communication. If one considers written material of a technical kind—a social survey, a technical report, a description of experimental work, an instruction manual, a scientific textbook, and so on—one notices that not everything is expressed through passages of prose. Together with the ordinary verbal text we find a number of other communicative devices like graphs, tables, flowcharts, line drawings and diagrams. In order to understand how spoken utterances function as communication we have to understand how they relate to non-verbal features like gesture. By the same token, in order to understand how communication is effected in written texts, one has to understand how the verbal means relate to the non-verbal. The non-verbal features of a text are just as much a part of the total message as the actual verbal material. As with gesture and spoken language, the relationship between the verbal and non-verbal media in written communication can be complex; the latter sometimes supplement verbal statements, sometimes they replace them. Furthermore, tables, diagrams, graphs and so on may, like gesture, fulfil a range of different functions. A table, for example, which relates the names of chemical elements to their respective symbols fulfils a metalinguistic function, as does any diagram which identifies a machine part with its name. Diagrams and graphs are referential when they provide a summary of a description presented verbally. Diagrams often serve as instructions for the operation of machines or appliances, or for the conducting of experiments, and as such serve an essentially directive function.

The important point for the language teacher is that when one wishes to teach the communicative functioning of language, one can no longer consider only the verbal elements of discourse, whether this be spoken or written. A consideration of speech function leads, paradoxically, to a recognition that learning the way language is used must involve an understanding of how other communicative devices operate apart from those generally thought of as linguistic. From the sociolinguistic point of view adopted here, verbal behaviour must be regarded as only one aspect of communicative behaviour as a whole.

3.6 Discourse

We have tried to show in the previous section how sociolinguistic considerations enter into the description of language use. In section 3.4 we discussed the nature of language variation and suggested that this be thought of as an intrinsic feature of a common code rather than as a set of distinct registers. This view of variation emerges naturally when one takes a sociolinguistic standpoint and studies the social factors which control the way linguistic forms function in actual contexts of use. In section 3.5 we then focused our attention on the range of functions which language fulfils. It became clear that in order to explain how language is used in everyday life it is necessary to consider other factors in the speech event as well as the code. In short, a study of language and context shows that the code is flexible and consists of variable rules as well as invariant rules of an algebraic kind. To account for language use we have to go beyond a description of the language code itself to consider the different functions it fulfils when associated with other factors in a speech event.

So far, then, we have looked at variation within the language system and also variation in language use. The purpose of this section is to show how the forms of the language system are related to speech functions in actual context: how what is said is related to what is meant. In other words we are concerned with utterances not as exemplification of the code but as types of message, that is to say as examples of discourse.

The term 'discourse' has been used to refer to quite different aspects of language and we should make it quite clear how we are using it here. Many linguists use the term to denote a sequence of sentences and consequently discourse analysis is taken to be the investigation into the formal devices used to connect sentences together. In this sense, discourse is to be regarded as a product of the language code and discourse analysis as an extension of the scope of grammatical description. What we are interested in, however, is the connection between what is said and what is meant and done, between linguistic form and social meaning and action. We wish to discover the relationship between sentences and such different actions as requesting, ordering, promising, predicting and so on. In order to avoid confusion, we might refer to connected sentences as 'text' and the study of such connections as *text analysis*. The relations between sentences and social meanings and actions we shall call 'discourse' and the study of these *discourse analysis*.

Defined in this way, there are two aspects of the study of discourse. The first is related to the study of utterance types, or communicative acts, in isolation. Thus we might wish to specify the conditions whereby a certain linguistic form counts as a certain type of utterance: the circumstances under which a declarative sentence, for example, fulfils the act of ordering or requesting. The ultimate aim of this aspect of discourse analysis is to provide a characterization of different acts of communication in terms of the conditions which must obtain for such acts to be effectively performed. These conditions have to do with the factors in the speech event of which the code, of course, is only one.

The second aspect of discourse analysis concerns the way in which individual communicative acts are linked together to develop larger units of communication. We might say that whereas the first aspect focuses on the relationship between sentences and utterances in order to establish classes of communicative acts, the second aspect focuses on the communicative coherence of utterances occurring in sequence. As we shall see, this coherence is closely associated with the conditions which operate on individual utterances.

We may therefore begin our discussion of utterance types by first observing that there is no neat correspondence between linguistic forms and communicative functions. It has often been pointed out that the structure of the language code necessarily reflects the functions which it is required to fulfil as an instrument of social interaction. It is natural, therefore, that elements of the code should correspond with the different factors in the speech event. The deictic terms 'this', 'that', 'here', 'there', for example, have to do with the setting in which language is used, thus reflecting the contextual function. In the same way, we can account for the existence of imperative and interrogative sentences in the code by reference to the fact that language has to fulfil the directive functions of ordering and asking questions. But although we can establish a relationship between elements in the code and communicative function in this way, it is not the case that the fulfilling of a certain function requires the use of the linguistic form with which it is associated in the code. For example, the imperative form is associated with the directive function, which includes the giving of instructions. Yet one can give an instruction without using the imperative form. The single word GLASS printed in capital letters on a packing case counts as instruction to handle carefully. The fact that glass is referred to and that the word appears in capitals on a packing case are sufficient indications as to how the simple message GLASS is to be understood. In other words, the factors of topic, setting and message form provide sufficient conditions for the message to be conveyed without recourse to the explicit imperative of the code. Although the imperative form is sometimes used by manufacturers in the form of a label reading HANDLE WITH CARE, the labels GLASS and FRAGILE both serve the same directive function.

How a linguistic form is to be understood as a message depends, then, on factors in the speech event other than the code itself. Of course, there must be mutual understanding between addresser and addressee that these other factors in combination do provide the necessary condition for a certain piece of language to count as a particular communicative act. Such an understanding comes about as the result of both addresser and addressee having learned the rules of use of their language. As we mentioned in the introduction to this paper, acquiring such rules of use is just as much a part of learning a language as acquiring the rules of grammar. A workman who lets a packing case marked GLASS drop from a great height and who defends himself by saying that he thought the label simply referred to the contents—that is, had a referential function not a directive one—must be regarded as being either a fool or a trouble-maker. It is always possible to be perverse in the absence of an explicit formal indicator of communicative function. Thus the workman, on being threatened with dismissal, might claim indignantly 'It didn't *say* handle with care, it only said GLASS'. One is reminded of the story of the man who refused to go down an escalator because there was a notice reading DOGS MUST BE CARRIED—and he had no dog to carry. However, we generally assume that the rules of use will operate and be understood normally.

We have said that it would be perverse to interpret a message like GLASS on a packing case as being anything but a directive to handle with care. This is so when addresser and addressee share the same rules of use. Genuine misunderstandings arise, however, when they do not. This is often the case with foreign learners of a language. In foreign language teaching the tendency is to assume an equation between linguistic form and communicative function and to teach language use purely in terms of the code. Thus learners are commonly misled into thinking that commands are uniquely associated with imperative sentences and questions with interrogative sentences. The danger of such a grammar-orientated approach to language teaching is that the learner can come to believe that rules of use are not distinct from rules of grammar and that messages will always match the code forms which most directly reflect the function which the messages fulfil. When learners encounter language in use outside the classroom and the textbook, they often find to their distress that they cannot interpret it simply by reference to their knowledge of the code. So it is that students entering higher education after five or six years of formal English instruction in the secondary school often have great difficulties in trying to cope with the language used as a medium for the subjects they are to study. There is clearly a case, then, for teaching rules of use in addition to, and in association with, grammatical rules; in other words one should pay as much attention to the operation of language as a means of communication as to the formal properties of language as a system.

In what way can we characterize those rules of use which enable the user of the language to relate what is said to what is meant, to know what the use of a given form counts as in terms of communication? We have talked about rules of use. What kind of rules are they? Since they have to do with the operation of language in a social context, it is clear that they must relate to the kind of social notions which have been discussed previously in this paper. Our task is again the sociolinguistic one of relating language to the social factors which act as constraints upon its use. We can perhaps illustrate the kind of rules of use that we have in mind by looking at the conditions which are necessary for a command or order to be given.

The conditions which must obtain for an utterance to be intended and interpreted as an order have to do with social constructs, like roles, rights and obligations, stereotypes, reference groups, categories and attitudes. The characterization of communication involves specifying how language is related to social structure. We might suggest then that for an addresser A to intend that his utterance should count as an order to an addressee B to carry out the notion X, A must believe that at the time of utterance

1 It is desirable for X to be done.
2 A has the right to ask B to do X.
3 B has the obligation to do X.
4 B has the capacity to do X.

For someone seriously to intend his utterance to count as an order he must believe that these four conditions obtain. For someone to interpret an utterance as an order he must believe that the addresser believes that these conditions obtain. Notice that it is not a matter of whether or not they *do* obtain, but whether the addresser believes that they do or, in the case of interpretation, whether the addressee assumes that the addresser believes that they do.

Let us look at just one of the conditions that we have specified in order to see how this relates to the social structure. When someone gives an order, he makes certain assumptions about the relationship which obtains between himself and the person he is directing his order at. He assumes that, at the moment of utterance at least, his role is one which gives him the right to give an order and that the addressee's role is one which imposes an obligation to obey it. Thus the most unambiguous orders are those that are given by people whose roles are widely acknowledged to carry such a right. For example, a sergeant major has the acknowledged right to order a private soldier around, though not of course an officer; similarly a schoolteacher has the right to give orders to children in the classroom. The roles may not, of course, be as clear-cut as in these two examples and this may lead to misunderstandings. We have stated that a teacher has a right to give orders to pupils in his class. Although this may largely be true when the pupils are young children, the actual rights of a teacher and hence the obligations of his students are not clear-cut when the children are nearing adulthood in, for example, a sixth form class. By the same token it is often true that university teachers are themselves not sure of the extent to which they have a right to give orders to university students. Some teachers may feel that they have every right while others may feel they have no right at all.

The important thing to note at this point is that for the addresser to intend an order he must believe in his right to tell the addressee to do something and in the addressee's obligation to do it. For his part, the addressee will understand the addresser's utterance as an order if he recognizes that this is what the addresser believes.

Let us look at some examples of the kind of utterance that a school-teacher may make when telling a pupil to do an exercise of some kind. He may make use of the imperative form:

> Do this exercise by tomorrow morning.

Alternatively he may focus his utterance on one of the other conditions of an order by saying:

> It would be best if we could have this exercise finished by tomorrow morning. (condition 1)

The form of this utterance is declarative but it would be interpreted by the pupils as an order since both teacher and pupil would recognize that the other conditions, that is conditions 2, 3 and 4, are also fulfilled and go, as it were, without saying. The teacher might give an order by using declarative sentences to focus on each of the other conditions:

> I expect you to do this exercise by tomorrow morning. (condition 2)
> You must have this exercise finished by tomorrow morning. (condition 3)
> You will have no difficulty in finishing this exercise by tomorrow morning. (condition 4)

Here we have four different declarative forms, the utterance of any of which would count as an order so long as both the teacher and pupil recognized that the other conditions went without saying. But we have still not exhausted the number of forms which could be used to convey essentially the same message. Apart from the possibility of other declarative forms focusing on the same conditions, it is also possible to use interrogative forms. The teacher may wish to minimize the status difference between himself and his pupil and invite him to agree on the desirability of the action being suggested. To achieve this he may give his order in mitigated form by using the interrogative in the following manner:

> Would you like to do this exercise by tomorrow morning?

That this utterance is to be interpreted as an order can be very clearly seen from the reactions of the teacher if the pupil replies 'No'. A teacher getting this reply might well interpret it as an act of defiance by a member of his class and hence feel the necessity to assert his right to give orders and consequently to be obeyed. His reply might very well be something like

> I've already told you, you will have this exercise finished by tomorrow morning or else.

What we have shown so far is that many different linguistic forms may be used to fulfil the same basic function by virtue of the fact that the conditions for an order which we have specified are in fact fulfilled. But this is only one side of the coin. The same linguistic form may also fulfil a variety of different functions. Again, we may take the imperative as our starting point.

We have spoken of the imperative as being the form of the code most directly related to the communicative act of ordering. This must not mislead us into thinking that the imperative is reserved for this function, any more than this function is reserved for the imperative. Consider the following utterances:

1 Go away.
2 Pass the salt, please (will you).
3 Bake the pie in a hot oven.
4 Invest in premium bonds.
5 Forgive us our trespasses.
6 Come to dinner tomorrow.

Here we have a number of imperative sentences each functioning as a different type of utterance. In the context in which they would most likely occur the first is clearly an order which fulfils all of the conditions that we have given earlier. The second is a request, by which we mean that the right of A to ask B to do something and the obligation of B to do it is not openly acknowledged. It is the function of words such as 'please' and 'will you' to minimize these two conditions. The third example is most likely to be an instruction. In this case the addressee has no obligation to perform the action referred to nor the writer of the recipe any right to ask him to do so, but the action is necessary if a particular end is to be achieved. The fourth example may be a piece of advice given by a friend or a bank manager. There is no obligation on the part of the addressee to carry it out nor does the person giving the advice have the right to insist on this behaviour but the advice is being given in the interests of the person being addressed. The fifth example is clearly an appeal; it is in the interests of the addresser that the action should be done but there is no obligation on the part of the addressee to do it. Finally the sixth example is likely to be an invitation, where there is no right or obligation involved. This is, of course, a very tentative analysis and is meant only to show the kind of relationship that exists between linguistic forms and communicative acts.

We have shown how one basic communicative act can be fulfilled by a variety of linguistic forms and how one linguistic form can be used to fulfil a variety of communicative acts. There is no simple one-to-one correspondence between messages and the forms in the language code which reflect the functions which messages fulfil. What controls whether a given sentence can convey a particular communicative intent is not a set of grammatical rules but a set of conditions which together constitute a rule of use. For the learner to understand the way language operates as discourse he must somehow be made aware of rules of use of this kind.

The language learner who has been nurtured in the belief that messages correspond to code forms in a neat one-to-one way is confronted by two basic problems. In the first place he has to learn to recognize the similarity of function of different forms given a particular set of conditions. This is essentially a problem of receptive learning. One way he might do so might be for him to learn as many such forms by heart as he can. Such a procedure, however, would meet with serious practical and pedagogic objections. The practical objection is that there would be an endless number of sentences to learn and no way of grouping them into functional sets since, as we have seen, the sentences themselves would be multi-functional. The pedagogic objection is that such a procedure would have no explanatory validity and would provide the learner with no strategy for interpreting any new sentence as having a similar communicative value. An alternative and preferable approach would be to develop teaching materials which would make the learners aware of the attendant conditions of different communicative acts and to show them how different linguistic forms relate to such conditions. In the case of the act of ordering, for example, one would direct their attention to key modals like *can*, *should*, and *ought to*.

The second problem has to do with the productive ability and is more difficult. The learner has to know which form to select in a given set of circumstances. Here there would seem to be a case for selecting forms at one or two different points on a scale of mitigation and politeness. One can only at this stage make very tentative suggestions since a good deal of work has to be done on selection and grading—not to speak of presentation—before a programme for the teaching of language in use can be proposed with any confidence. The important point is that, in principle, there is no reason why such an operation should not be undertaken. The grammatical properties of language as a system have been subjected to pedagogic treatment and there seems to be no reason why a similar treatment should not be given to the kind of communicative properties of language in use which sociolinguists set out to describe.

We will take up the question of pedagogic implications again later. Meanwhile we must consider the second aspect of discourse analysis which was mentioned at the beginning of this section. So far we have been concerned with the characterization of utterance types, or acts of communication, in isolation. What we have now to consider is the manner in which one utterance follows another in sequence to form a piece of continuous discourse.

Let us begin by considering two exchanges:

1 A: Can you write down the answer in your exercise book?
B: No, I can't.

2 A: I want you to write down the answer in your exercise book.
B: My pen is broken.

In the case of the first exchange, there is a syntactic relationship between the two utterances which can be accounted for in terms of textual cohesion between the two sentences underlying them. B's utterance can be seen as an abbreviated form of the sentence: 'No, I can't write down the answer in my exercise book'. There is no such textual cohesion between the sentences underlying the utterances in the second exchange. And yet they are clearly related as utterances in a way that the following, for example, are not:

3 A: Could you direct me to the railway station?
B: Jesus loves me.
A: I beg your pardon?
B: The Church of Scotland.

This third exchange might occur in dreams, or in an encounter with someone deranged by an excess of religious feeling, but it cannot be said to represent a normal development of discourse. Yet there is no more syntactic cohesion between the sentences of the second exchange than there is between the sentences of the third. How then do we account for the fact that the second exchange is coherent as discourse without being cohesive as text?

Our discussion of the communicative act of ordering provides us with the answer. The second exchange is coherent as discourse because both utterances refer to the conditions attendant on the act of ordering. A refers to the first condition in giving his order and B deflects the order by focusing on a different condition, in fact the fourth. His utterance, then, counts as a guarded refusal to obey. Knowing that the link between these two utterances lies in their relation to the communicative act of ordering, we can predict how the discourse is likely to develop. A may either accept the refusal and retire, or he may persist, either by selecting to play on another condition or by putting his cards on the table in the use of an explicit form. If he takes the first course, he would continue with an utterance like 'You must write the answer down in your exercise book' or 'This answer must be written down in your exercise book'. If he takes the second course, he would continue with an utterance like 'I am ordering you to write down the answer in your exercise book' or 'Write down the answer in your exercise book. That's an order'. Alternatively A could counter B's move by restoring the condition which B's remark calls into question by saying something like 'You can borrow mine' or 'You can use a pencil'. In reaction to A's persisting in his order, B could concede defeat by himself restoring the condition he has questioned, in which case the discourse might develop as follows:

4 A: I want you to write down the answer in your exercise book.
B: My pen is broken.
A: You must write down the answer in your exercise book.
B: Well, I can borrow Albert's pen.

There are, then, a number of ways in which the discourse represented in 2 above might develop. But the important point is that this development is within a certain range of predictability, which derives from our understanding of the communicative function of the utterances concerned. Discourse, as opposed to text, appears to develop not through the surface forms of sentences but through the acts of communication which the uses of such sentences perform.

So far we have been ascribing communicative function to single utterances. It is convenient to begin the study of language in use by making this assumption, but there is no reason for thinking of communicative acts solely in terms of single utterances. An explanation, for instance, can be performed by the use of a single sentence like 'He stopped working because he was tired'. But explanations can, of course, be much more extensive, and may have incorporated within them a number of subsidiary acts. One of the defining conditions of an explanation may therefore be the presence of a particular subsidiary act. The same applies to such large scale acts as descriptions and reports. A description in technical discourse, for example, may well require the inclusion of a general statement and an illustration as subsidiary acts. In this case, the conditions which must obtain for a piece of language to count as an explanation would be expressed in the form of subordinate communicative acts within the discourse. Seen in this light, the two aspects of discourse analysis which, for convenience of exposition, we distinguished at the beginning of this section merge into one. The problem of discourse sequence becomes the problem of characterizing acts of communication which are performed by the use of more than one sentence. It should be noted that the way in which discourse develops is not uniform but varies in different areas of language use. It may in fact be preferable to characterize different varieties of English functionally in terms of specific conventions of discourse development rather than formally in terms of different sub-codes. (Compare section 3.4, where we questioned the validity of one such formal approach to the description of sub-codes or registers.)

Our discussion of discourse has centred on the spoken language but what we have said applies also to written discourse. The difference is that the kind of conditions we have discussed as being associated with particular communicative acts must, in some way, be accounted for within the discourse itself. Because there is no possibility of feedback from the addressee (the reader), for example, the writer must ensure that both he and the reader share a common code (an essential condition of any communication taking place). He may achieve this by starting the discourse with such metalinguistic acts as definition. A knowledge of how written discourse develops is clearly of crucial importance to the learning of reading strategies and the writing of coherent essays.

3·7 Teaching language as communication

Our purpose in the second part of this paper has been to discuss certain aspects of language which do not generally come within the scope of grammatical description. Broadly, we have been concerned with the social uses of language and the way language functions in the everyday business of communication. As was noted at the beginning of this paper, knowing a language involves not only a knowledge of the formal properties of the language as a system but also a knowledge of how this system is put to use in the performing of social actions of different kinds. In other words, knowledge of a language is not only a matter of grammatical competence but also of *communicative competence*. It follows that the language teacher ought to be as much concerned with the one as with the other.

In the past, the language teacher has generally relied on the guidance of the grammarian and it has been the grammarian's representation of language as an abstract system which has served as his principal reference. But if communicative competence is to be taught, the description of language at this degree of idealization is not sufficient. The teacher also needs to make reference to the kind of information that only a sociolinguistic approach to language description can provide.

The relevance of sociolinguistics to language teaching, then, might be taken as self-evident. There are, however, two ways in which this relevance might be questioned. Firstly, it might be objected that what has been called communicative competence does not need to be expressly taught. The argument might be that the really essential aspect of a language is its grammatical system and that once this is learned, a knowledge of how to put it to use will develop of itself; that once forms are learnt, the functions will take care of themselves. It is possible to hold such a sanguine view when languages are learned in isolation from an immediate communicative purpose. When one is teaching a foreign language to primary or secondary school pupils whose need to actually use the language, if it exists at all, is comfortably far off in the future, one's belief that one is preparing them to meet such a need is not put to the test. When a language is being taught to serve an immediate practical purpose, however, as when it is taught in the context of scientific and technical education, for example, the fallacy of this belief becomes evident. The difficulties which college students have in coping with scientific material in a foreign language bear witness to the fact that communicative competence does not follow naturally from a knowledge of the language system. A knowledge of sentence structure is not sufficient for an understanding of how the language is used to express the essential communicative acts of science.

The second reason for rejecting the relevance of sociolinguistics is in some ways opposite to the first. It is that language use is already taught, so that teachers do not need to refer to the kind of notions which we have been discussing in this paper. It is, after all, one of the principles of the 'modern' approach to foreign language teaching that sentence patterns and vocabulary should be taught 'contextually' in 'meaningful situations'. In answer to this it must be pointed out that situations are created in the classroom to give meaning to language items as elements of the code, and consequently have a fundamentally metalinguistic purpose. Classroom mock-ups of the railway station, the shop, the office and so on do not reflect the actual uses of language that we have discussed. Usually they are devices for stimulating the learner's interest rather than for teaching an ability to handle language in the real world. This is not by any means to say that 'contextualization' of this kind does not have its uses, but only that it does not constitute the teaching of language as communication. It may provide a stereotyped linguistic routine but this is not the same as providing the learner with a strategy for matching linguistic forms with communicative functions. We may say that contextual language teaching may serve as a valuable basis for the later development of communicative competence. In the early stages of language teaching it has the advantage of demonstrating to pupils that language forms are to be related to real life. Furthermore it may serve to provide them with a store of language items commonly associated with certain stock situations. However, at the more advanced stage the learner must be made aware of the complex relationship between form and function which we have been discussing in this paper.

What techniques can best be used to teach communicative competence must ultimately be a matter for the teacher to work out for himself. Our aim has been to draw attention to those aspects of language use which he must be aware of before such techniques can be devised. A knowledge of the formal features of language which the grammarian provides has served as a basis for the development of approaches to the teaching of language as a system. What we are suggesting is that approaches to the teaching of language as communication may also develop from an awareness of the way language functions in contexts of social use.

4 Further reading

Readers in Sociolinguistics

Fishman, J. A. (ed.). 1968. *Readings in the Sociology of Language*. The Hague: Mouton. [Fishman RSL] Contains many of the classic papers on a range of topics from small group interaction and language in social strata to multilingualism and language planning.

Fishman, J. A. (ed.). 1972. *Advances in the Sociology of Language: Vol. I Basic Concepts, Theories and Problems: Alternative Approaches.* The Hague: Mouton. [Fishman ASL] There are four major articles contained in Volume I which attempt to define main areas of sociolinguistics and the sociology of language. The authors are Fishman, Ervin-Tripp, Grimshaw and Labov.

Giglioli, P. P. (ed.). 1972. *Language and Social Context: Selected Readings.* Harmondsworth: Penguin Books. [Giglioli LSC] This is a book of readings primarily for sociologists and anthropologists so that the technical linguistic extracts are minimized. It deals with the same general areas as the other readers.

Gumperz, J. J. and Hymes, D. H. (eds.). 1972. *Directions in Sociolinguistics: The Ethnography of Communication.* New York: Holt, Rinehart, Winston. The volume contains more recent work in the general areas of ethnography of communication, the structure of conversation, code switching and the mechanism of code change.

Hymes, D. H. (ed.). 1964. *Language in Culture and Society: A Reader in Linguistics and Anthropology.* New York: Harper & Row. [Hymes LCS] A very wide-ranging reader containing an excellent set of bibliographies on almost all sociolinguistic topics, up to 1963. The approach is a cross-cultural one.

Laver, J. D. M. H. and Hutcheson, S. (eds.). 1972. *Communication in Face to Face Interaction.* Harmondsworth: Penguin Books. This is a book of readings concerned with face-to-face interaction and hence concentrates on topics such as strategies of interaction, non-vocal communication and speech and personal characteristics.

Pride, J. B. and Holmes, J. (eds.). 1972. *Sociolinguistics.* Harmondsworth: Penguin Books. [Pride & Holmes S.] A selection of readings intended as an introduction to the main concerns of sociolinguistics. It covers many of the topics dealt with in this chapter.

1 *Sociolinguistics and linguistics*

Saussure, F. de. 1955. *Cours de Linguistique Générale.* 5th edition. Paris: Payot (First edition, 1916). English translation: Wade Baskin, *Course in General Linguistics.* New York: Philosophical Library, 1959. Chapter III aims at defining the subject matter of linguistics in terms of the notions of *langue* and *parole*.

Chomsky, Noam 1965. *Aspects of the Theory of Syntax.* Cambridge, Mass.: M.I.T. Press. The distinction between competence and performance is discussed in the first pages of Chapter I.

Labov, W. 1970. The study of language in its social context. *Studium Generale*, 23, 30–87. Reprinted in Fishman ASL. The first few pages discuss a possible confusion in de Saussure's distinction between *langue* and *parole* and suggest how these notions are related to those of competence and performance.

Fishman, J. A. 1970. *Sociolinguistics: A Brief Introduction.* Rowley, Mass.: Newbury House. This is the most elementary introduction to sociolinguistics at present available. Section I deals with the relationship between linguistics as a study of *langue* and linguistics as a wider study of language in social use.

1.2 *Sociolinguistics and sociology*

Berger, P. L. 1963. *Invitation to Sociology.* Harmondsworth: Penguin Books. A very readable approach to the principles of sociological enquiry.

Durkheim, E. 1897. *Le Suicide: Etude de Sociologogie.* Paris: Felix Alcan. English Translation: J. A. Spaulding and G. Simpson, *Suicide: A Study in Sociology.* New York: The Free Press, 1951. An early classic in the sociological method.

2.1 *Definitions of a language*

Wolff, H. 1959. Intelligibility and inter-ethnic attitudes. *Anthropological Linguistics*, 1, 34–41. Reprinted in Hymes LCS. The article examines a situation in Nigeria where the mutual intelligibility of the languages concerned depends not on structural differences but on the social attitudes of their speakers.

Haugen, E. 1966. Language, dialect and nation. *American Anthropologist*, 68, 922–35. Reprinted in Pride & Holmes S. The first part of this paper deals with the problems of defining a language as distinct from a dialect. Haugen points out that there are two ways of distinguishing the two: one formally in terms of linguistic structure and the other functionally in terms of social use. He shows how these two approaches to classification may conflict.

2.2 *Ethnography of communication*

Laver, J. D. M. H. and Hutcheson, S. (eds.). 1972. *Communication in Face to Face Interaction.* Harmondsworth: Penguin Books. This book contains papers on the role of gesture and other paralinguistic phenomena in communication in section 4.

Cowan, G. 1948. Mazateco whistle speech. *Language*, 24, 280–6. Reprinted in Hymes LCS. An account of one non-verbal system of communication.

2.3 *Functional language types*

Haugen, E. 1966. Language, dialect and nation. *American Anthropologist*, 68, 922–35. Reprinted in Pride & Holmes S. The second half of this paper deals principally with the process of standardization and its connection with factors such as literacy and national identity.

Stewart, W. A. 1968. A sociolinguistic typology for describing national multilingualism. In Fishman RSL. This paper shows how languages might be classified into types by reference to the following attributes: standardization, autonomy, historicity, vitality. These are 'ideal' types which show what processes are involved in such a classification and which may therefore serve as a reference for describing actual languages.

Pride, J. B. and Holmes, J. (eds.) 1972. *Sociolinguistics.* Harmondsworth: Penguin Books. Part two of this book contains a number of papers on functional language types and their social operation.

2.4 *Social differentiation*

Abercrombie, D. 1956. *Problems and Principles.* London: Longman. The chapter on English accents contains a discussion on the distinction between accent and dialect. It also deals with the factors to be considered when choosing an English accent as a model for foreign learners.

Halliday, M. A. K., McIntosh, A. and Stevens, P. 1964. *The Linguistic Sciences and Language Teaching.* London: Longman. In Chapter 4 section 3 the authors discuss the kinds of language variation that are associated with social and geographical factors.

Sprott, W. J. H. 1964. *Human Groups.* Harmondsworth: Penguin Books. An introductory description of social groups in society from a social psychologist's point of view.

Kelvin, P. 1970. *The Bases of Social Behaviour.* London: Holt, Rinehart, Winston. Chapter 8 discusses some of the physical properties of groups.

2.5 *Language and identity*

Whorf, B. L. 1956. *Language, Thought and Reality*, edited by J. B. Carroll. Cambridge, Mass.: M.I.T. Press. This is a collection of papers by the best known proponent of the hypothesis that one's view of the world is largely determined by the language one speaks. The articles range in level from the technical to the popular and in the degree of commitment to the notion of determinism.

Brown, R. 1958. *Words and Things.* Glencoe, Ill.: The Free Press. Chapter 7 discusses linguistic relativity and determinism with a wide range of examples and references to other work in the area. It is part of an elementary and readable account of language from an essentially psychological point of view, which makes appeal to the reader's own experience of language.

Fishman, J. A. 1970. *Sociolinguistics: A Brief Introduction.* Rowley, Mass.: Newbury House. In section 6 Fishman considers the Whorfian view of linguistic relativity and attempts to reduce it to a set of testable hypotheses.

Conklin, H. C. 1955. Hanunoo Color Categories. *Southwestern Journal of Anthropology*, 11, 339–44. Reprinted in Hymes LCS. This paper describes a colour system based on features other than those used in English.

UNESCO. 1953. *The Use of Vernacular Languages in Education*. Monographs on Fundamental Education, VIII. Paris: UNESCO. Part reprinted in Fishman RSL. This is a well-known report which recommends the use of the vernacular in initial education so as to provide the child with the most natural means of self-expression.

Bull, W. E. 1955. Review of 'The use of vernacular languages in education'. *International Journal of American Linguistics*, 21, 288–94. Reprinted in Hymes LCS. This is a critique of the Unesco report and gives reasons for questioning its proposals.

2.6 *Language variation and change*

Weinreich, U. 1953. *Languages in Contact*. New York: Publications of the Linguistic Circle of New York, No. 1. This is a fairly technical work on interference, the way in which language systems are affected by contact with others.

Ferguson, C. A. 1959. Diglossia. *Word*, 15, 325–40. Reprinted in Hymes LCS and Giglioli LSC. This article initiated discussion on the way in which different forms of a language are associated with different domains of use. Ferguson examines cases like classical and colloquial Arabic where the two forms have co-existed for centuries.

Fishman, J. A. 1970. *Sociolinguistics: A Brief Introduction*. Rowley, Mass.: Newbury House. Section 5 deals with the relationship between societal bilingualism and individual bilingualism.

Pride, J. B. and Holmes, J. (eds.). 1972. *Sociolinguistics*. Harmondsworth: Penguin Books. Part 1 of this book has readings on bilingualism and multilingualism and Part 3 on language variation and change.

2.7 *Language teaching aims in perspective*

Dakin, J., Tiffen, B., and Widdowson, H. G. 1968. *Language in Education*. London: Oxford University Press. This book consists of three papers, two of which deal with the use of English in education in Africa and the Indian sub-continent. The third paper suggests one way in which English might be taught in the kind of situations described in the others.

Fishman, J. A., Ferguson, C. A., and Das Gupta, J. (eds.). 1968. *Language Problems of Developing Nations*. New York: John Wiley. This is a collection of papers dealing with the description of multilingual societies and the practical problems which arise in framing language policies.

3.2 *Levels of idealization*

Lyons, J. 1972. Human language. Chapter 3 of R. A. Hinde (ed.) *Non-Verbal Communication* Cambridge: Cambridge University Press. This chapter provides a fuller discussion of standardization, decontextualization and regularization of linguistic data.

3.3 *Speech event*

Jakobson, R. 1960. Concluding statement: linguistics and poetics. In T. A. Sebeok (ed.) *Style in Language*. Cambridge, Mass.: M.I.T. Press. This is the article which initiated recent discussion on the constituent factors of the speech event.

Hymes, D. H. 1962. The ethnography of speaking. In T. C. Gladwin, and W. C. Sturtevant (eds.) *Anthropology and Human Behaviour*. Washington: Anthropological Society of Washington. Reprinted in Fishman RSL. This paper provides further discussion on speech factors. It adds certain refinements and gives further illustrations. The terminology used is different from Jakobson's.

Ervin-Tripp, S. 1964. An analysis of the interaction of language, topic and listener. *American Anthropologist*, 6, 86–102. Reprinted in Fishman RSL. The paper gives copious illustrations of how various factors in the speech event interact.

Laver, J. D. M. H. and Hutcheson, S. (eds.). 1972. *Communication in Face to Face Interaction*. Harmondsworth: Penguin Books. Section 3 includes two important papers showing how the relative status and degree of intimacy between addresser/addressee affect the choice of language items used.

Geertz, C. 1960. *The Religion of Java*. Glencoe, Ill.: The Free Press. pp. 248–60 reprinted in Fishman RSL. Excerpt also in Pride & Holmes S. These pages provide examples of the use of different codes in Javanese.

Frake, C. O. 1964. How to ask for a drink in Subanum. *American Anthropologist*, 66, 6, 127–32. Reprinted in Giglioli LSC and Pride & Holmes S. The paper discusses some different linguistic and social factors involved in drinking.

Gumperz, J. J. 1966. The ethnology of linguistic change. In W. Bright (ed.) *Sociolinguistics*. The Hague: Mouton. The article contains a description of the language situation in a village in Norway.

Rubin, J. 1968. Bilingual usage in Paraguay. In Fishman RSL. This paper further illustrates the factors affecting the choice between Guarani and Spanish in Paraguay.

3.4 *Code variation*

Halliday, M. A. K., McIntosh, A., and Strevens, P., 1964. *The Linguistic Sciences and Language Teaching*. London: Longman. In Chapter 4 section 4 the authors discuss the notion of register and how it is to be defined. They attempt, rather unsatisfactorily, to define it in purely formal terms.

Crystal, D. and Davy, D. 1969. *Investigating English Style*. London: Longman. The authors extend the argument of Halliday et al. (see above) in Chapter 3 and put forward a more detailed classification of the dimensions along which registers may be defined. In the rest of the book they attempt to show how their scheme can be put into practice in describing English.

Labov, W. 1969. *The Study of Non-Standard English.* Champaign, Ill.: National Council of Teachers of English. This is an elementary introduction to Labov's work on language variation. In the first part of the book he shows how it is possible to study crucial sociolinguistic variables.

Labov, W. 1970. The study of language in its social context. *Studium Generale*, 23, 30–87. Excerpts in Giglioli LSC and Pride & Holmes S. This is a more technical study than the one quoted above. In the first half he deals with the various techniques that can be used in the direct study of linguistic data. He gives some detailed examples illustrating the use of variable rules to account for language variation within a community.

Kelvin, P. 1970. *The Bases of Social Behaviour.* London: Holt, Rinehart, Winston. In Chapters 3, 4, 5 there is a good discussion from a social psychologist's viewpoint of norms, stereotypes, reference groups and role playing.

Lawton, D. 1968. *Social Class, Language and Education.* London: Routledge & Kegan Paul. The largest part of the book is concerned with a survey of various language oriented factors which affect children's education, e.g. social class, motivation, language and thought. He then provides a critique of Bernstein's work on language and social class before presenting some experimental evidence of his own.

Bernstein, B. 1971. *Class, Codes and Control*, Vol. I. London: Routledge & Kegan Paul. This book contains a number of reprints of articles published by Bernstein in other books or journals between 1958 and 1971. The discussion is intricate and not easy to follow.

3.5 *Speech functions*

Jakobson, R. 1960. Concluding statement: linguistics and poetics. In T. A. Sebeok (ed.) *Style in Language.* Cambridge, Mass.: M.I.T. Press. Jakobson discusses the speech functions which are associated with the factors of the speech event. He considers that any speech event can be characterized by a particular hierarchy of functions.

Hymes, D. H. 1962. The ethnography of speaking. In T. C. Gladwin, W. C. Sturtevant (eds.) *Anthropology and Human Behaviour.* Washington: Anthropological Society of Washington. Reprinted in Fishman RSL. As in his discussion about the factors in a speech event, Hymes refines Jakobson's discussion changing the terminology in the process. He further states that not all speech events can be unequivocally attributed to one predominant speech function.

Halliday, M. A. K. 1969. The relevant models of language. *Educational Review*, Vol. 22, No. 1. Reprinted in M. A. K. Halliday, *Explorations in the Functions of Language.* London: Edward Arnold, 1973. The paper shows a different approach and terminology from that of Jakobson and Hymes but is likewise basically looking at the different functions to which language is put. Halliday points out that the different speech functions develop at different ages in children and that 'language deprivation' may be due to lack of appropriate functions rather than lack of mastery over the code.

Halliday, M. A. K. 1970. Language structure and language function. In J. Lyons (ed.) *New Horizons in Linguistics.* Harmondsworth: Penguin Books. Unlike the previous reference, Halliday is here concerned with a study of the code and how functions are reflected in it. He is not looking at the functions of a speech event considered as an act of communication.

3.6 *Discourse*

Labov, W. 1969. *The Study of Non-Standard English.* Champaign, Ill.: National Council of Teachers of English. The second part of this elementary introduction to Labov's work deals with some characteristics of discourse and their importance for the language teacher.

Labov, W. 1970. The study of language in its social context. *Studium Generale*, **23**, 30–87. Excerpts in Giglioli LSC and Pride & Holmes S. The last few pages of the article also deal with the analysis of discourse.

Laver, J. D. M. H. and Hutcheson, S. (eds.). 1972. *Communication in Face to Face Interaction.* Harmondsworth: Penguin Books. Section 4 deals with strategies of interaction. This is a slightly different approach to Labov but relates to the same problems of how actual communication takes place.

3.7 *Teaching language as communication*

Hymes, D. 1971. On communicative competence. Philadelphia: University of Philadelphia Press. Reprinted in part in Pride & Holmes S. Hymes examines the kind of knowledge implied by the concept of communicative competence and relates it to Chomsky's notion of competence as well as to *langue* and *parole*.

7 ELISABETH INGRAM
Psychology and Language Learning

1 Introduction

Learning occurs when an individual comes to know something he did not know before, or becomes able to do something he could not do before. The learning may occur informally, or it may take place in a formal learning situation. Informal learning goes on all the time, whenever an individual extends his knowledge or his repertoire of skills, without anybody having set about producing this change in the learner in a systematic way according to a predetermined goal and a prearranged plan.

A formal learning situation exists when in addition to the learner there is also a teacher. The term 'teacher' is here to be understood in a very broad sense, to include educational policy makers, syllabus committees, textbook and programme writers, classroom teachers, instructors, etc. The teacher specifies the goals, selects and arranges the materials, presents them to the learner in various ways, requests the learner to carry out specified activities, and evaluates his performance by comparing it with the predetermined objectives. Formal learning situations, in the sense used here, have nothing to do with the relative degree of authoritarianism or permissiveness which obtains inside the classroom. If the desired terminal behaviour has been specified and the steps of the instruction have been planned, in more or less detail, then we are dealing with a formal learning situation.

Language learning consists in acquiring command of a language to a level which is adequate for the communicative purposes of the individual. This means that the learner must understand and be understood, and that the members of the speech community must find his performance acceptable. The learning of one's first language usually occurs informally, but not always; the teaching of deaf children and the enrichment programmes aimed at disadvantaged pre-school children are instances of formal first language learning situations. The learning of reading and writing overwhelmingly takes place in a formal learning situation.

The learning of any language beyond the first may be informal, or partly informal, as in a multilingual community, or it may be almost entirely formal in a school setting. The distinction between second language learning and foreign language learning, which is sometimes made, rests on this: second language learning occurs in a formal learning situation which supplements the informal learning, whereas foreign language learning takes place exclusively in a formal learning situation. I shall use the term 'second language learning' to refer to the formal learning component in both contexts.

Planning and teaching in formal learning situations are guided by certain more or less explicit assumptions about the capacities of the learners, about what it is that the learner brings to the learning situation. For example, when B. F. Skinner and his group started to write programmes for teaching machines and asked teachers what they wanted the terminal behaviour of the learners to be, they kept on getting answers not about what the teachers wanted the children to learn, but about what they thought the children were capable of learning, given the existing conditions.

The aim of this chapter is to examine what it is that the learner brings to language learning, specifically to a formal second language learning situation. There are two sources of information: (a) the accumulated experience and research of those who work within the field of formal second language learning, and (b) the observation of the processes of first language acquisition. Neither source is capable of providing direct evidence. Formal learning situations are partially structured by the assumptions that teachers make about the capacities of the learner, so we do not know how a given learner might proceed if he were free to adopt his own learning strategies. First language acquisition has often been regarded as the 'natural' language learning situation, in the sense that the strategies are determined by the learner, not imposed by a teacher. But the circumstances in which first language acquisition takes place differ from those of second language learning in several important respects. First language acquisition takes place in an informal context, while second language learning takes place in a formal context. The observations made by students of first language acquisition are often very illuminating, but we obviously cannot transfer them automatically to second language learning, because the contexts of learning are so different. Also, second language learners differ from first language learners in that the former already have a language. Apart from the case of child bilingualism, which is such a complex topic that it would need a chapter to itself, second language learners are older than first language learners, with all that this implies in terms of differences in ability and motivation (see Ingram 1964, Diller 1972).

In attempting to discover what it is that the learner contributes to the learning situation we must therefore examine the accounts of both first and second language learning, bearing in mind that in both cases the evidence is only indirect.

2 First language acquisition

2.1 The study of child language

The study of child language began at the end of the 18th century, with parents keeping diaries of their children's utterances. The culmination of this approach was probably the work of the Sterns, who in 1907 published very detailed observations of the progress of their three children (Stern and Stern 1907).

In the first half of the present century most of the studies of child language were carried out by psychologists, who worked within a framework where it was assumed that the process of the child's approximation to adult language use was the product of the interaction between, on the one hand, his experience of language, and on the other his developing perceptual and motor skills and his increasing cognitive abilities. In other words, they assumed that language learning, though very complex, is not in principle different from other kinds of learning.

Most of the early studies were directed at finding reliable language indices of general intellectual development, rather than at describing language as such, which in any case would have been very difficult before tape recorders were generally available. Two useful indices were established:

1 Mean utterance length. The researchers showed that the average length of children's utterances, whether counted in words or in 'syllables' (by which they meant morphemes, that is, both word stems and word endings), increased regularly with chronological age and even more regularly with mental age.
2 Size of vocabulary. They found that the estimated size of children's vocabulary almost invariably correlated very highly with measured I.Q.

The best account of this developmentally oriented research is found in MacCarthy (1954).

A new approach to the study of language and language behaviour began to develop in the 1950's, stimulated first by renewed interest among psychologists in the process of thinking. The term 'psycholinguistics' was coined around this time; it was used by Carroll in *The Study of Language* as early as 1953. Systematic studies were started of the language development of individual children, from the first utterances to school age. The utterances of a few children were recorded at frequent intervals, and then transcribed. The transcriptions have furnished the data for many analyses over the last ten years, both by the original investigators and by others, and the process is still continuing. The records which have been most extensively quarried are probably those of the three children investigated by Roger Brown and his associates (see for instance Brown and Bellugi 1964, Cazden 1968, Brown and Hanlon 1970).

In the early 1960's another very powerful impetus to the study of child language came from the successful consolidation of the revolution in linguistics initiated by Noam Chomsky. The postulate of a deep syntactic structure underlying the apparent or surface structure, and the hypothesis that all human beings have innate knowledge of the essential underlying grammatical relations has had profound consequences for the interpretation of child language.

2.2 Innate knowledge versus environmental learning

In studying child language—as in studying second language learning—there are many problems, but since we are focusing on the learner we shall discuss only three main questions: Who learns? To what standard? What goes on when learning takes place? There is considerable disagreement about the answers to these questions. In first language acquisition the answers depend largely on where one stands on the issue of *innate knowledge* versus *environmental learning*.

In principle one could adopt one of two extremist positions. The extreme environmentalist position would be that the child comes into the world with no innate predisposition; he is a piece of raw material which is moulded or shaped by the experiences he undergoes into some sort of bundle of reactions, which then constitutes his individuality and skills. This view is often wrongly taken to be a typical behaviourist view; in fact it was held by some people for a brief period at a primitive stage of behaviourism, but it has not been seriously considered by reputable psychologists for the last forty or fifty years.

The extreme innateness position is that the child comes into the world with very specific innate endowment, that is, not only with general tendencies and potentialities, but with knowledge of the nature of the world, and specifically with knowledge of the nature of language (see chapter 8, section 4). According to this view children are born with knowledge of the basic grammatical relations and categories, for example, subject, verb and object, nouns, verbs, determiners and auxiliary elements. This knowledge is universal, that is, these categories and relations exist in all human languages and all human infants are born with knowledge of them. In addition the child has a hypothesizing and testing device, which allows him to determine from very small amounts of experience which language out of all possible languages is the one that he is exposed to. In this view '. . . it seems reasonable to suppose that the child cannot help constructing a particular sort of transformational grammar any more than he can control his perception of solid objects or his attention to line and angle' (Chomsky 1965, p. 69). Although this extreme or 'strong' nativist hypothesis is vigorously argued by many transformational linguists and psycholinguists, people who are acquainted with genetics apparently find it difficult to suggest a mechanism by which such knowledge could be genetically transmitted (see, for example, Kalmus 1966, Waterhouse and Fischer 1972).

Those who disagree with the strong innate hypothesis do not adopt the extreme environmentalist hypothesis. They adopt some form of an interaction hypothesis, sometimes referred to as a 'weak' innate hypothesis; they believe that children are born, not with specific knowledge of grammatical or semantic or phonological categories and rules, but with a potentiality for organizing experiences in certain ways, for detecting certain kinds of relationships and for comprehending and producing symbols and structures of symbols. They take the child's development to be the result of interaction between the innate potentialities, and the quality and variety and amount of experience which the individual encounters.

Interaction hypotheses are usually the ones that commend themselves to non-specialist observers, but extreme hypotheses, however much they may go against common sense, can be very valuable because they lead to very specific claims being made, which can then be examined. Whether the claims turn out to be valid, partly valid, or not valid at all, does not matter much in the long run, because the outcome of the investigations which are carried out to test the claims add to our total knowledge of the subject.

I shall discuss three questions concerning first language acquisition: Who acquires language? Is the process of acquisition uniform? What is the nature of the learning process? The answers that are given to these questions depend on whether the writer is essentially a nativist or essentially an interactionist. In the following sections the two points of view are examined in some detail.

2.3 Who acquires language?

The nativist answer to this question is: all human beings, by virtue of the inborn universals, and no sub-humans, for the same reason. There are two conditions: there must be no organic defect and there must be a small amount of exposure to language.

The interactionist answer is: human beings, provided there is no serious organic defect, and provided there is a rich experience of language communication between the child and others, preferably in a context of emotional security. Interactionists leave the question about sub-human capacities open.

The claim that all human beings develop language given normality and minimal exposure is not testable. The more one believes in the importance of satisfying intercommunication between a child and the people around him, the less conceivable is it that one should deprive any child of this experience for experimental purposes. And when one encounters a child who has signally failed to develop language in a normal way, his background is usually made up of such a welter of suspicious circumstances that nobody can with certainty disentangle the causative factors. There may be a family history which could indicate deviant genetic inheritance, there may be signs of organic defects of greater or lesser importance, there may be a home background which indicates that the child has been deprived emotionally or intellectually or economically or all three. The strands cannot be disentangled.

It is only the claim about animals that is testable. The argument that communication between animals is qualitatively different from the communication that takes place between human beings by means of language is long and complicated (on this subject, see Hockett 1960; Lyons 1972).

There is another approach. From time to time there have been dedicated attempts to teach human language to various developed animals, for instance, dolphins and chimpanzees. All attempts seemed to be fruitless until very recently. As long as chimpanzees were required to signal their language by vocal noises, nothing much happened. But a few years ago two psychologists (Gardner and Gardner 1969) reasoned that what monkeys were good at was using their hands. So they decided to try to teach a young female chimp named Washoe to communicate by using the sign language of deaf people. The indications are that Washoe learned not only to use elements of this sign language appropriately, but that she put them together in a way which is qualitatively indistinguishable from the way young human beings behave in the early stages of language acquisition. There is another young female chimpanzee, Sara, who seems to do something very like reading (Premack 1970).

These reports constitute a strong counter-argument to the theory that there are genetically transmitted language universals which are limited to human beings. The reports do not, however, indicate anything directly about the mechanisms of learning in humans. Though an enormous amount of very detailed training, explicitly based on behaviouristic principles, was necessary to get these chimpanzees to exhibit something like language behaviour, it does not necessarily follow that the same is true for human beings.

2.4 Variability versus uniformity of language development

The nativist position is that every child is programmed to construct a grammar for his native language, containing the universal categories and relations of which he has knowledge. Though in its pure form the claim is about knowledge not about performance it has seemed to many people that the identical and invariant knowledge that all children have should be reflected in their performance—that is, in the way they understand and produce utterances in the course of their development. It is from time to time denied that the claim about innate knowledge has any necessary implication for performance. However, if the knowledge is to have any psychological reality, the performance data—in this case the observations on how children progressively understand and produce utterances—should be in conformity with what can be predicted from the postulated knowledge. Regardless of theoretical models, if the innate component is large, the effect of the child's general cognitive capacities and of his environment should be comparatively small, and there should be a large degree of uniformity for all children both in the way the development takes place, and in the general standard reached. Conversely, if any variation is found it should be predictable from consideration of associated factors, such as the general learning ability of the children and the kind of environment they grow up in. Or it could be a matter of individual variation, children taking different paths for no obvious external reasons.

2.4.1 ASSOCIATED FACTORS

2.4.1.1 General cognitive capacities. Beginning to speak early is popularly taken as a sign of intelligence, and cross-sectional studies have confirmed over and over again the relationship between early language development and general learning ability. The disparity between children can be very large. One child can produce spontaneously at the age of two and a half: 'After you finish your eggs all up, then you can have your coffee, Daddy', while other children at the same age are scarcely beyond the one and two word stage. Graham (1968) showed in an experiment the importance of memory for sentence processing. He found that children who could repeat correctly two unconnected items could also repeat correctly

There is a bird flying in the air.

but they could not repeat

The dog that chased the duck is black.

The children who could repeat five unconnected items could also manage the second sentence.

Demonstrations that language development and general cognitive development are closely related can be interpreted in two ways. Nativists will argue that the Graham experiment shows that it is only the limitation on memory span which prevents a child from applying his knowledge of the structure of sentences. Non-nativists would take the findings to show that children can begin to learn to process structures such as inserted relative clauses only when they have developed the cognitive capacity for dealing with them.

2.4.1.2 The environment. The discussion about the effects of the environment on language development has in recent years centred on the social class issue. The majority of those who fail to learn to read and write are 'disadvantaged'; that is, they come from the lower social classes and often from low-prestige racial or national minorities. In the United States 'disadvantaged' is often a euphemism for 'black' and the battlelines are drawn up in advance. The question is, do disadvantaged children suffer from a language deficit or not? Some sociolinguists believe that there is no qualitative difference in the language development of lower-class and middle-class children. It is not that disadvantaged children have less language; what they have is different language (at least partly different), and also they have different ideas about when and how language is appropriately used. In some studies social class is not a relevant factor. For instance when middle-class and lower-class children are asked to substitute a 'proper word' for one of the nonsense words in a sentence like

The tweener baikels meedily

there is no difference in their ability to provide a noun or a verb appropriately (La Civita et al 1966). In another study children were shown a picture of a man balancing a ball on his nose and were told 'This is a man who knows how to zib. What is he doing? He is . . .'. There was no difference by social class in the children's ability to produce the correct form of the verb (Shriner and Miner 1968).

The majority of studies, however, uncover social class differentials. For instance Church (1971) found social class differences at an early age in the ability of children to answer questions about senses and sense organs: What do you smell/taste/touch with? What are your eyes/ears for? Lower-class four-year-olds did relatively worse than the majority of middle-class three-year-olds. Robinson (1971, 1972) found that in various language communication games lower-class five-year-old and seven-year-old London children gave shorter and more fragmented responses and used simpler sentences with fewer subordinate clauses and less complex noun phrases than middle-class children of the same age.

The studies where no difference is found have to do with very elementary grammatical control. The studies where social class differences are found have to do with complexity and elaboration of grammatical patterns, appropriateness of usage, and vocabulary control. So while there is no doubt that the environment effects the way that children learn to *use* language, a deprived background does not handicap children in the acquisition of the basics of language. Again the issue is not settled. Nativists will argue that this means we are born with the basic knowledge, non-nativists that all the environments studied are adequate for the development of command of the basic grammatical relations and categories.

2.4.2 INDIVIDUAL VARIATION

2.4.2.1 The quest for universals. There is the question of how these basic grammatical relations and categories are acquired. If it could be shown that all children work their way towards adult language through trying out the same hypotheses, and revising them in the same way and in the same chronological order, then the case of the nativists would be greatly strengthened.

Claims have been made for phonological universals as well as for grammatical ones. According to Leopold (1953),

. . . the speed and time of sound acquisitions varies enormously between different children, but the sequence in categories and the relative chronology are always and everywhere the same, at least in great outlines.

One of the phonological universals suggested by Leopold is that children develop their vowel system by increasing differentiation of vowel sounds on the basis of sound quality. His daughter first distinguished between *i* and *a*, then added *u*, then *e*, etc. It does seem that this describes the progress of many children. But Velten's daughter (1943) used the dimension of length when she extended her two-vowel system to a four-vowel system: long and short *a*, long and short *u*.

Some children vary the process by adopting rules which do not exist in the adult system around them. It is apparently not uncommon for children to pronounce whole syllables as either voiced or voiceless (Burling 1959; Joan Maclean, Vaughan James, personal communications). When the consonant is voiced the vowel is also voiced: [nana] (banana) [baba] (bye bye). When the consonant is voiceless the vowel is whispered, i.e. also voiceless: [kʰḁ] (up) [fʰḁ] (fire) [fʰl̥ḁ] (flower).

Most of the proposed universals are of a grammatical nature. I shall discuss three of the best known ones: pivot grammar, the appearance of syntactic structures before morphological structures, and word order.

(i) *Pivot grammar*

It has been claimed that the earliest grammatical constructions are universally made up of words belonging to two mutually exclusive classes: the *pivot* class, which is a primitive and undifferentiated class of grammatical words; and the *open* class, which contains all other words. The class is called 'open' because in comparison with the pivot class, it readily admits new members, i.e., the increase in the child's vocabulary is largely in open-class words. The structure of utterances is either pivot + open, open + pivot or open + open. Katie (personal observation) had a general demand word *I͡want* which functioned as a pivot in various combinations:

I͡want this
I͡want off
I͡want horse
etc.

But not all children have pivot constructions as their earliest and most productive formats. Some children start off with agent-action constructions: *Babi give*, *Mummy sleep;* others produce mainly action-object sequences: *hit ball*, *see sock;* yet others produce noun-noun sequences serving various functions, for example, Kathryn reported by Bloom (1970): *sweater chair* (locative: the sweater is on the chair), *Daddy hat* (possessive: Daddy's hat), *Mommy pigtail* (subject-object: Mommy make me a pigtail).

(ii) *Syntax before morphology*

In the field of grammar, syntax comes before morphology. The student of child language becomes very conscious of the fact that morphological devices are a luxury of fully developed languages. The small child gets along quite well without them for a short or long time. (Leopold 1953, p. 107).

This is a claim that children join words together, to form phrases or sentences, before they add prefixes or suffixes to the stems of words to form complex word constructions. The claim appears to be true of many children, particularly those brought up to speak the major European languages. But exceptions can be found, and it may not be an accident that several of these concern children brought up to speak non-Indo-European languages. For instance, Stephen Burling was brought up among speakers of Garo, a Tibeto-Burmese language. In this language syntax and morphology is clearly demarcated, but many of the functions which in Indo-European languages are expressed syntactically are in Garo carried by suffixes. On the same day that Burling senior was sure that his son was using verb + suffix to distinguish future tense and imperative, the child also produced a subject-verb construction: 'Both morphological and syntactical constructions came at the same time' (Burling 1959).

For a short period claims were made that all children everywhere would show a universal word order, regardless of language environment—specifically, that a construction containing Subject Verb Object would always be produced in that order. This could not be maintained for long, and the current modified claim is that each child adopts an invariant order characteristic of the child to signal grammatical relations. There is no doubt that children do to a large extent rely on sequence. But again the status of universality is in doubt. Velten's daughter, for instance, at the two-morpheme stage indicated possession indiscriminately:

hat dap (Grandpa's hat)
pat zu (Pat's shoe)

This is an example, by no means the only one, of a child disregarding sequence, even though she was brought up to speak English, which relies heavily on sequence to signal grammatical relations.

There are suggestions that children who are brought up to speak highly inflected languages, where word order in adult usage is more variable, are rather more likely to depart from the strategy of signalling by sequence. Bar-Adon's Gila produced both

aba ba (daddy come/came)
ba aba (daddy come/came)

and a number of other utterances showing the same disregard for fixed order

(Bar-Adon 1971). If this turns out to be a general trend, it would be an added indication of the importance of experience in language development.

2.4.2.2 Deviant speakers. Even though children do not, it seems, progress towards adult language in an entirely uniform way, the majority do achieve command of the basic elements by school age. But some children, not suffering from identifiable physiological defects, are unable to shed non-adult forms. This seems not to be a matter of simple retardation. In one investigation a deviant three-year-old used relative clauses and conjunctions, which are beyond the average two-year-old. But though the deviant three-year-old could ask questions, he could not frame them correctly, something that most normal three-year-olds are quite capable of. And a deviant seven-year-old might produce a question in the same way as a deviant three-year-old.

To sum up, the great majority of investigations of the development of language in children indicate that there are differences in language control. Though children may take different paths in their progress towards adult language only a very small proportion fail to develop control of basic grammatical categories, but this failure does not seem to be related to the variables of intelligence or social class. Ability to utilize appropriately the full resources of language varies as one might expect; older children do better than younger children, intelligent children do better than less intelligent children, and as a generalization, middle-class children do better than lower-class children. This parallels other aspects of child development and learning.

2.5 The nature of the learning process

The most important of the three problem areas in child language acquisition is the nature of the learning process.

Even a brief survey of the literature forces us to the conclusion that, while there are striking regularities in the language development of children, there are also frequent and interesting individual variations. If language development had turned out to be almost entirely uniform, there would have been no need to look for other factors than the inborn, pre-programmed language acquisition device inside every baby's head. As it is, the search for the relevant parameters of the learning situation continues to be necessary. I shall discuss these parameters under three headings:

The capacities and the strategies that the learner brings to the situation
The intrinsic nature of the learning job
The contribution of the environment

The discussion of the parameters of language learning which follows rests on the fundamental assumption that language development is not something apart from all other aspects of development. It is a part, and a very important part, of cognitive development in general. There is no 'black box' which accounts totally and exclusively for language development.

2.5.1 THE CAPACITIES AND STRATEGIES OF THE LEARNER

It is essential to distinguish strategies, which are what people use, from formal rules, which are what linguists set up in order to characterize the properties of language. It is unsound to conclude that, because people are capable of producing sentences which are grammatically correct, that is, because the end product of whatever goes on inside people is the same as the end product of the operation of formal grammatical rules (when they work), the processes inside people must somehow mirror these formal rules (plus or minus some distortion). This assumption is not always stated in so many words, but it is fairly prevalent. My concern is to re-establish a vital distinction, not to minimize the role of any of the relevant disciplines. In trying to discover the strategies used by language learners, it is obviously essential to take account both of the linguist's and of the psychologist's descriptions of the nature of language.

2.5.1.1 Motivation. Most observers agree that what drives the infant to utter in the first place, and later to master progressively more complex structures, is the need to communicate. Babies have a tremendous need to relate to other human beings, and this need persists throughout life. Most people receive in early life enough encouragement to keep on trying, but not all.

Traditionally the two main communicative functions of language were taken to be the 'expressive' function, signalling demands, and the 'cognitive' function, the purpose of which is to transmit information. I do not believe that either of these functions have very much to do with the child's progressive mastery of the complexities of adult language. Immediate needs and desires can be signalled by very simple means, even non-linguistic ones, and imparting information is a very complex process, which is only gradually acquired, as the sociolinguists are presently demonstrating. Very few children, and not all adults, are able to convey information successfully to a listener who does not already know what the speaker is trying to describe. There are, I believe, three main sources of child language development, each important during various overlapping stages. One source of development is the pleasure of the intellectual game, described by Jespersen for the early stages as 'the joy of recognizing things and remembering the name for it'. Some imitation contexts show clearly that for the child saying things is an interesting activity in itself:

> Mother (to adults): Shall I put the coffee on?
> Karen (1.11): Coffee on

It is a common observation that when children have mastered a new word or structure, it is used a great deal. The Brown group found that their children's use of question tags far exceeded the normal adult frequency, for a short period after acquisition. It seems very likely that this is due to the children's delight in exercising a new skill.

Another source of development is the child's growing perceptual and cognitive understanding of the world. Awareness of more complex meaningful relations forces the adoption of more complex linguistic structures. The process is clearly demonstrated when the cognitive abilities of the child far outstrip the language resources available. Butterworth (1972), observing a thirteen-year-old Spanish-speaking boy learning English among non-Spanish-speaking Americans, was very struck by the boy's constant search for something that worked, some means by which he could make his advanced messages understood, and by his frustration when he failed:

Maybe me watch she me for you

It eventually became clear that what he meant was something like:

If I see her I'll point her out to you.

The third and perhaps the most important source of development is the need to relate to people, to establish and maintain emotional contact with other human beings. Bullowa (1970, p. 195), investigating the development of babies in the first year of life, put it very simply: 'What babies prefer, above anything else, is people.' This need remains throughout life, and later it is served by the sort of largely ritual language interchange which Bernstein has labelled the 'restricted code'. Some writers are puzzled by the fact that children learn complex structures, when from a strict information-imparting view there is no need for them. For instance, why do children learn question tags in English, when a simple 'huh?' with a rising intonation at the end of a statement serves the same function:

He won't do it, will he?
He won't do it, huh?

This puzzle seems to be easily resolved by considering the child's need to qualify for full membership status of his community, which initially is his family. An integral part of group identification is the adoption of the forms and customs and rituals of the group. The process can be observed directly when a child is sent to school where the prevalent accent is different from his own. Such a child will alter his accent very rapidly to conform with what his schoolmates consider to be normal, and intelligibility or the transmission of information has nothing to do with it.

2.5.1.2 Perceptual and cognitive development. The child's cognitive structures are generally in advance of his linguistic structures. For example, at the one-word stage, an utterance such as 'up' addressed to the mother implies both agent and action, and a two-word utterance such as 'Mummy pigtail' implies agent (mummy) action (make) indirect object (me) and direct object (pigtail). When new forms appear they generally serve to make more explicit functions which have already been conceptualized and expressed by more primitive and more ambiguous structures.

At a later stage it is possible to trace children's understanding of complex sentences, by asking them to imitate. This method is full of dangers, but used sensitively it can be illuminating. The usual result is that children indicate comprehension of complex sentences by reproducing the essential meaningful relations of the model sentence, but in a simplified syntactic form, before they produce faithful imitations which indicate both cognitive and syntactic mastery. (We are here dealing with fairly difficult sentences, and children between 3 and 5 years of age.)

Margaret Letham (1970) asked her three children to imitate various sentences with inserted relative clauses, culminating in

> This is the toy which the girl who is going back to her mummy is holding in her hand.

She got three kinds of response:

(a) Cognitive and syntactic over-simplification, indicating that the task was beyond the child at that stage:

> This is the toys the girl is going back to her mummy (Delia 3.10)

(b) Syntactic simplification, changing inserted relative clauses into co-ordinated clauses, reproducing all the information:

> This is the girl and she is going back to her mummy and she holds her new teddy by the hand (Susie 4.10)

(c) Approximately accurate reproduction of syntax as well as meaning. Two months after Susie produced (b) she gave:

> This is the girl who is going back to her mummy and this is the toy she's holding in her hand (Susie 5.0)

showing that she had now reached the stage where her formal skill was beginning to catch up with her ability to handle the meaning relationships, to the extent of managing one relative clause per main clause.

Though the main finding is that cognitive development precedes linguistic development, exceptions can be found. Cazden (1968) reports that one of the differences between the two girls in the Brown series was that Eve, the early and fast developer, said things she did not have the formal means to express while Sarah, whose development was relatively slow, did not usually attempt to communicate before she had the formal means to do it. Popular anecdotes about cute child sayings usually turn on the child misusing a word or construction which he does not know how to use appropriately. Early examples are distributing plural *-s* all over the place, using 'but' without contrasting implication and 'cause' (because) without any intention of explaining anything. These are instances of children trying out linguistic forms before they properly understand how to use them.

An examination of the sequence of development underlines the central importance of perceptual and cognitive factors. The most striking regularities have to do with meaning, not with form. For instance, it seems that the earliest utterances at each developmental stage relate to concrete here-and-now contexts and referents. This is true for the whole of the holophrase stage, and it shows in the early preference for content words like nouns and verbs and adjectives over function words like articles and auxiliary verbs and so on. It is true of the first syntactic semantic relations expressed by two-word constructions, and it is true of the first morphological affixes.

If there are any universals, they are probably cognitive universals, not formal linguistic ones. Children resemble each other in their language development because they have comparable needs, comparable experiences and, within limits, comparable cognitive capacities.

2.5.1.3 Learning strategies. As a learner of adult language, the child employs a number of strategies which in the majority of cases are remarkably successful. I do not mean to imply any conscious awareness of learning techniques in the child. The formulation of the generalizations are those of adults watching the process. Some of the learning strategies employed by children are as follows.

(i) *Learning in context*

Children acquire language by constant reference to the situational and communicative context. Initially children respond to remarks made by adults as one part of the total interaction situation, for instance by cooperating in being dressed and fed in the second half of the first year of life. Their own first utterances are similarly produced in the closest possible relation to a given and familiar stimulus context. The most obvious examples are the early action words like *peepbo*, but the practice of accompanying actions with words persists. Catherine produced *ba* whenever somebody gave her anything, or she handed anything to others. It is interesting that in this there is already a generalization—Catherine perceived that a number of separate, actually occurring situations had something in common which she isolated, recognized when it was present, and labelled consistently.

The same ability to perceive and extract the relevant meaningful aspects of recurring situations enables the child to employ correctly the various grammatical markers, for instance plural *-s* when referring to more than one of a kind; to put nouns in front of verbs to indicate agent function; and to put nouns after verbs to indicate object functions, and so on.

Investigators who ignore the basic fact that children 'talk about something' can be very misled about the capacities of the children they are investigating. At an early stage of the Child Language Acquisition Project in Edinburgh, we tried to get Karen to transform indirect requests for information. We would say (incredibly ineptly in retrospect): 'Karen, go and ask Mummy what colour this brick is'. And Karen looking at the brick would answer, perfectly reasonably, 'Red'. In our frustration we were inclined to conclude that Karen could not at that stage carry out the necessary grammatical transformations. But then one afternoon Karen's father came home early, and without entering the living area went upstairs to change. Karen's mother said casually: 'Karen, ask Daddy if he wants his tea now or in a while' and Karen went half way up the stairs and yelled 'Daddy, do you want your tea now?'. When Karen was motivated by being in a real communicating situation she was able to encode and to transmit information at a level which the artificial 'experimental' situation missed entirely.

(ii) *Simple and complex learning*

Children learn by associating particular items with particular occasions, and by developing generalizations ultimately leading to the correct principles. Initially, specific utterances appear to be linked to specific recurring contexts. This association between a situation and an utterance is an instance of the kind of connection between a specific stimulus and a specific response which is sometimes referred to as rote learning. In the literature on child language this term has somehow acquired derogatory connotations. There is supposed to be something 'mechanical' about the process. The truth is that even the simplest labelling or commenting utterance requires a capacity to abstract. The child must isolate certain more or less prominent stimulus aspects of the situation and recognize them when they re-occur; that is, he must discriminate between appropriate and inappropriate occasions, and then produce. The process can most easily be seen when it goes wrong, for instance a child exclaiming 'doggie!' on seeing a cat. The same process underlies the beginning of the ability to use grammatical structure.

But the most striking thing about language acquisition is that the child goes further than linking specific utterances to specific situations. He goes on to make generalizations; he sets about discovering the rules of the language. The difference between the two processes has been illustrated by Brown, with reference to Adam's wh-questions (Brown et al 1968). At a very early stage Adam heard both his parents say very frequently to him 'What's that?', 'What's he doing?', etc. and he acquired two question utterances:

What's that?
What doing?

This was long before he had the capacity to deal with the generalized structure of wh-questions, and these two forms were always uttered by Adam in the same stereotyped way, never varied to 'What are those?' or anything else.

Later, when Adam was ready to discover the rules governing the structure of wh-questions, he proceeded quite differently. His first hypothesis was that wh-questions are made by putting the wh-word in front of a statement, and this generalized very quickly to all the wh-words in his vocabulary:

What John will do?
Why she want to?
Where John will read?

For a time the stereotypes coexisted with these rule-based questions. With their lack of inversion these later forms might on the surface appear more infantile than the stereotype 'What's that', but they do of course represent a more advanced stage of learning.

The generalization strategies are frequently attested by overgeneralization: tags like *bettern't I*, verb forms like *goed*, *breaked*. In two experiments with adult subjects Palermo obtained a remarkable simulation of the child's early rote learning of the correct forms of frequent irregular verbs (e.g., *broke*, *went*) and the later rule-based learning, leading for a time to 'erroneous' overgeneralizations (Palermo and Eberhart 1968, Palermo and Howe 1970).

In Palermo's experiments adult students were required to learn sequences consisting of two digits and a letter, e.g. 19 followed by F. The digit sequence is taken to be analogous to a word, the letter to a suffix. There were three regular suffixes F, G and C. F regularly followed 5, 7 and 9 whenever they appeared as the second digit, and similarly for G and C. But there were also irregular suffixes, the four vowels I, A, U and O, and these could follow any digit. The student had to learn which letters followed a series of digit pairs. Digit-letter series with irregular letters were presented from four times to twice as often as digit-letter series with regular letter endings. The result showed that the irregular series were learned considerably faster than the regular ones, and that once the regular sequences began to be learned, overgeneralization occurred, i.e. digits which had previously been correctly coupled to an irregular letter were given the regular letter according to the rule for associating the second digit to its regular consonant letter.

Palermo remarks: 'The results suggest that at least two strategies were being used by the subjects. The irregular forms were learned by rote, and because they were presented frequently . . . they were learned relatively rapidly in contrast to any attempts to learn the regular forms by rote. The fact that few errors of regularization occur to the irregular forms until after performance on the irregular forms is perfect, suggests that the strategy of rote learning is not given up until about the time when the irregular forms are mastered, when the rule taking advantage of the regularities is invoked.' (Palermo and Howe 1970, p. 414.)

(iii) *Cognitive constraints*

Children employ strategies which minimize cognitive and memory strain to whatever extent is required at any particular stage (see chapter 8, section 6). When children first express new functions, they very frequently use old, well-learned forms. The first questions are signalled either by intonation:

Daddy? ('Is that daddy coming?')

or later, by preposing a wh-word in front of a statement:

Why he is hiding?

Similarly, according to Slobin (forthcoming), children who are acquiring an inflected language like Russian initially adopt one suffix to indicate a particular function, even though the adult language may use several suffixes. For instance case suffixization in Russian depends on gender (largely phonologically determined), on extra phonological conditions, and on animate/inanimate reference. In an experimental study comprising 200 children it was found that all the children resorted to 'morpheme imperialism', that is, they all adopted one of the case markers of the adult language to serve all nouns; *-u* for the accusative case, *-om* for the instrumental and so on.

Older children who acquire a second language in an informal situation appear to adopt the same cognitive strain-reducing strategy. The thirteen-year-old Spanish-speaking boy acquiring English (Butterworth 1972) at one stage used *for* as an imperial preposition, and also to mark a number of other functions:

Imperial preposition

He go for California (to)
Is for South Laguna (near)
We everydays go my dictionary for my house (take it home)

Conjunction

You for me (and)

Nominalization

He's for English (a teacher in English)

Direct object

He clean for teeth (brushes his teeth)

Benefactive

Go for peoples for drink (get drinks for people)

The remarkable thing is that children do not fossilize, apart from individuals who are regarded as pathological. As soon as practice and growth of abilities permit, more sophisticated solutions are attempted, nearly always in direct approximation to adult language. Bellugi (1971) has described the stages for wh-questions. As mentioned several times before, the first stage is simply to prepose the wh-word:

Adult: Adam, say what I say: Why can he do it?
Adam: Why he can do it?

Later the child succeeds in inverting positive questions, but not negative ones:

Adult: Ask the old lady what she is doing. ('Old lady' is a puppet)
Adam: Old lady, what are you doing?
Adult: Ask the old lady why she can't sit down.
Adam: Old lady, why you can't sit down?

Negatives, on all sorts of evidence, are cognitively more difficult than positives, so Adam has to hang on longer to the more general sequence rule when sorting out information expressing negatives.

What allows the child to proceed in this economical and efficient way is that nobody cares whether he makes 'errors' or not. Recent observations of mothers of English-speaking children indicate that they show neither disapproval of errors or approval of 'correct' utterances. An utterance is successful if it is understood and responded to, and development comes about under the pressure of selective reinforcement. In other words, devices that work are retained, and those that do not are rejected. This is one of the reasons why fossilization of immature forms does not occur. Another reason has already been mentioned, namely that children will strive to get as near as they can to the models provided by the individuals in the environment, in order to signal group membership.

(iv) *Frequency*

Children respond to the frequency of occurrence of any given linguistic event. This is a controversial area. If the number of times a child has heard a word or structure (and the number of times he uses it) can be shown to have very little influence, then that strengthens the nativist position. However, it is not very difficult to demonstrate that frequency is important in the specific link or rote learning situations. Brown attributes the early learning of the stereotyped 'What's that?' and 'What doing?' to the very high rate of *what* questions produced by the parents. The early learning of past tense forms of some irregular verbs has always been connected with their high frequency of occurrence, and Palermo obtained experimental confirmation of the effect of frequency on the learning of irregular forms in an analogous situation.

When it comes to the relationship between frequency of occurrence and the discovery of rules, the debate gets livelier. One of the difficulties about establishing the relevance or otherwise of frequency is that frequency is nearly always related to simplicity of structure. The simplest sentence form in English is declarative (not interrogative), active (not passive), affirmative (not negative). Compare 'The dog chewed the slipper' with 'Wasn't the slipper chewed by the dog?'. The world seems to be made in such a way that the majority of utterance occasions call for simple declarative active affirmative statements. Brown and Hanlon (1970) made predictions about the order of emergence of various sentence types in young children—declarative as against interrogative, positive as against negative and so on. When they compared 19 predictions made on the basis of complexity they found that 17 of these predictions were identical to those based on the frequency of occurrence in the speech of the mother.[1]

There is also a relationship between frequency and here-and-now referential meaning. Various counts of the use of tenses in actual speech show that the (indicative) simple present and the simple past between them usually account for something like 80–85 per cent of all tense forms. These tenses, apart from having the simplest constructions, also have the most concrete reference: action or existence which is real at the time of speaking, or was real at some time in the past. So it is very difficult to find a situation where frequency can be shown to operate alone, because high frequency is nearly always accompanied by simplicity of construction or concreteness of reference. The Brown group counted the frequency of occurrence of various events in the speech of the mothers of the three children, as well as in that of the children, and found that 'frequencies in child speech, within the limits of the child's competence, tend to match adult frequencies'.

Apart from counting sentence types the Brown group also counted the occurrence of grammatical items like prepositions. In the first six recordings Eve's mother used *in* and *on* three times as often as she used *with*, *for*, *of* and *to*. During the next six recordings, Eve used *in* and *on* correctly on more than 90 per cent of all occasions, whereas her correct use of the other prepositions varied between two-thirds and three-quarters of all occasions. Brown points out that the correct usages did not strikingly occur in the same prepositional phrases that the mother had used; it was the general semantic appropriateness that had been induced. This would seem to indicate that frequency is important when the child is trying to work out and establish the principles for the correct application of grammatical items, in this case prepositions. But locatives, that is, words having to do with orientation in space, could be said to have a more directly concrete meaning than the other prepositions; so

[1] Van der Geest observing the language development of Dutch-speaking children has not found the same relationship between frequency and simplicity in his data (personal communication).

though it is reasonable to believe that frequency is relevant, other factors cannot be excluded. This is one of the drawbacks of observing phenomena in their natural setting; the variables are nearly always inextricably mixed up. The reason why people try to set up experiments is precisely to try to disentangle the possible causative factors.

The experiment set up by Berko (1958) provides one of the few occasions where the effect of frequency can be examined without contamination from a structure or meaning. Berko's purpose was to examine whether children could apply the rules governing the form of various suffixes in English, and in order to rule out the effects of rote learning, she used a number of words specially constructed for the occasion, as well as a few 'real' words. Obviously the real words, which were previously known to the children, had been encountered by them with greater frequency than the new words, which were presented for the first time. The words were given meaning and their status as nouns or verbs was established by presenting the children with drawings of animals (or birds or flowers) or of people engaged in various activities. For example, the plurals of nouns were elicited by showing a card with one animal, then a card with two of them and saying: 'This is a *tass*. Now there is another one. There are two of them. There are two . . .'. Other nouns, including the real word *glass*, were presented similarly. The past tense forms of verbs were elicited by producing a card with a man doing exercises, while the adult said: 'This is a man who knows how to *mot*. He is motting. He did the same thing yesterday. What did he do yesterday? Yesterday he . . .'. Other verbs, including the real word *melt*, were introduced similarly.

The results show that children do apply rules. When the rules are thoroughly learned, the children apply them successfully to nonsense words; for instance 97 per cent of children aged between 5.6 and 7.0 gave the correct voiced form of the plural to new words ending in a voiced consonant: *wugz*. But when the rules are still in the process of being learned, when errors still occur, it is apparently easier to apply them to familiar words—those which have been encountered before—than to the new words. Seventy-three per cent of children managed to give the correct full syllable form of the past tense marker to the real verb *melt: melted*, but only 33 per cent could provide the same correct form for the new word *mot: motted*.

From time to time claims are made that frequency has been proved to be irrelevant. For instance, McNeill's report (1966b) that one Japanese child acquired the grammatical marker *ga* before she acquired the marker *wa*, though the mother used *wa* about twice as often as she used *ga*, has been widely cited as showing that frequency does not matter. Logically, of course, what it shows is that frequency may not be all that matters, and that on this occasion some other factor or factors apparently weighed more heavily. What the other factors might be in this case is obscure, since McNeill's account is long and involved (and I have heard its correctness challenged by two native speakers of Japanese, both possessing a fair degree of linguistic sophistication). But nobody claims that frequency is the sole determiner, only that it is one among many. An easier phenomenon to interpret than the Japanese observation is the habit of Russian children of choosing the suffix -*u* as the 'imperialist' marker for the accusative case, though zero marking is probably more frequent. What happens is clearly that the child's preference for a clear and overt marking of a particular function has overridden any effect that frequency might have had. But frequency can in turn be shown to match the appearance of the various case markers within each gender and case, once gender has been established. For instance the most frequent marker for feminine nouns in the instrumental case is -*oy* and for masculine nouns in the prepositional case it is -*e* and these appeared before other less common markers in each paradigm in the speech of Zhenja (Slobin, forthcoming).

(v) *Practice*

A great deal of the early child-mother interaction consists of the child spontaneously imitating his mother's remarks, or fractions of them. Some children do this more than others, but apparently all children do it to some extent. There is disagreement about how much understanding the child should be credited with on the basis of these imitations, but the point here is that the repetitions provide practice, at least for the phonological skills (see chapter 8, section 6). Joan Maclean found that her daughter, about the age of 1.0–1.3, imitated so much that it was difficult to judge when a new vocabulary item had been learned (i.e., used appropriately and with intention to communicate), and when she was simply echoing.

Another form of practice is recorded by Ruth Weir (1962, 1966). Her first son, Anthony, produced long monologues in bed at night, and she found evidence both of sound play and of grammatical pattern practice. She later confirmed these findings with Anthony's two younger brothers. The age range is between 2 and 5 years of age:

	pattern practice	*pattern practice and sound play*
Anthony	what colour what colour blanket what colour mop what colour glass	Bobo's not throwing Bobo can throw Bobo can throw it Bobo can throw oh oh go go go
David	coat 'tis coat where mommy's coat?	I go dis way way bay baby go dis bib

mommy's home sick	all bib
mommy's home sick	bib
where's mommy home sick	dere
where's Mikey sick?	
Mikey sick	

The child's habit of accompanying action with descriptive remarks provides further occasions for practice. Wigdorsky and Wigdorsky (1961) recorded their four-year-old daughter Veronica, who was bilingual in Spanish and English, at play with another four-year-old girl, a native English speaker. The girls are cutting paper figures:

Veronica: Look, Jennie
Look I cut down
Look I cut down, Jennie
I make it.

Another sequence shows mutual imitation between the girls, as they play mummies and children with their dolls:

Veronica: Well, Dolly, you are the little girl
Jennie: Going to school
Veronica: The little girl going to school
Let's play
Jennie: Let's play big girls to school
Veronica: Bring me my umbrella
Jennie: Let's play ladies
Veronica: In my bag
You're a little girl
I've got a little girl because this is the mummy
Because this is the mummy
I've got a little girl
Because then she is a lady and she is a little girl and so the ladies don't look . . .

2.5.2 THE INTRINSIC NATURE OF THE LEARNING JOB

We are obviously very far from being able to do a proper analysis of the characteristics of the learning job. That would require a full analysis of the nature of language and of language use. But it is possible to identify some characteristics which seem to influence the relative ease of learning.

2.5.2.1 Perceptual prominence. The first sounds and sound contrasts that children learn are those which are relatively easy to perceive and discriminate. The first vowel contrast that children operate is usually the one between the high front *i* and the low mid or back *a*, which is about as far apart as one can get in human vowel distinctions. On the other hand, fricatives are acoustically very difficult to distinguish from one another. In English some children are well into school age before they acquire the voiced and voiceless *th*-sounds and some people, even if they are not Cockneys, tend to say 'fings' for 'things' and something like 'vat's' for 'that's' all their lives, when they are not paying attention to their pronunciation.

During the first year or so after children have begun to speak, they do a great deal of spontaneous imitation of adult remarks. Mostly they repeat only a part of the total remark. Recently it has been suggested (Clark et al 1972) that the part which is imitated is the most perceptually prominent part, i.e., the part which is most heavily stressed and where the intonation contour changes most markedly. This part of the utterance is referred to as the *tonic*. In the examples which follow, the tonic of the adult utterances is in italics (Adam is the Scottish Adam, not the pseudonymous Adam of the Brown group).

Adult: What was she doing? Driving the *car*?
Adam: car
Adult: Should I *draw* a car?
Adam: draw car
Adult: Is it, it looks *yellow* to me.
Adam: yellow
Adult: The *chalk* made that scribble did it?
Adam: chalk

Slobin suggests that if the morphological marker for a semantic function is perceptually prominent a child will mark it overtly earlier than if the marker is not prominent, or if it is absent. Slobin cites an observation on children who are bilingual in Hungarian and Serbo-Croat. In Serbo-Croat the accusative marker is *-u*, in Hungarian it is *-t* and the children produced the accusative marker earlier when they spoke Serbo-Croat than when they spoke Hungarian —final voiceless stops are more difficult to hear than final vowels.

2.5.2.2 Formal complexity. Formal complexity, both in grammar and in phonology, can be estimated in many ways. Here, complexity is taken to depend on the number of exceptions that have to be made from a given general descriptive statement. In Danish the order of grammatical elements in a simple sentence is the usual Subject Verb Object. But when a subordinate clause or an adverbial or a prepositional phrase precedes the Subject we get inversion: Adverbial Verb Subject Object. For a child to learn this is obviously more complicated than to learn one order for all cases. Jespersen's son for a time worked on the assumption that the Verb Subject Object sequence was the correct one in all cases (Jesperson 1922).

As Slobin points out, when the child's generalization is correct, the structure is learned early. When the generalization is not correct for all cases, the phenomenon is called overgeneralization, and the structure is said to be acquired late. If there were no irregular verbs in English, children would be said to have acquired the morphological structure of verbs at an earlier stage than they actually do acquire it. For instance, under the stress of telling a story on tape a very articulate and intelligent girl produced 'growed' several times at the age of seven. The marking of the accusative case in Hungarian, by adding *-t* to the noun, is simpler than the marking in German, where the whole noun phrase is marked according to gender, and it has been suggested that accusative marking is acquired earlier in Hungarian- than in German-speaking children.

It takes Russian children up to the age of 6 or 7 to learn to assign gender correctly, though the general statement appears to be simple: nouns ending in a (non-palatal) consonant are masculine, those ending in *-a* or *-ja* are feminine and nouns ending in *-o* are neuter. According to Slobin, learning is slow in the first place because there is no meaning associated with gender, but even so the learning would be completed before it actually is if it were not for exceptions. When the process of palatalization occurs, various complicated rules apply, and the only workable learning strategy is to learn the gender of each word separately.

2.5.2.3 Semantic complexity. It is impossible to characterize semantic complexity without circularity; those semantic relations and concepts which are easy are learned early, and we know that they are easy because they are learned early. We come back to here-and-now reference, to real and tangible objects and events and relations. Things and actions that are visible or audible or touchable in the present are acquired first, then things that were visible or audible or touchable in the past, then projected events in the future, and lastly hypothetical and conditional eventualities. In Russian conditionals are very simple to construct, but Russian children do not produce them any earlier than children who have to grapple with a complicated subjunctive structure in order to express the same concept.

Piaget and his followers have demonstrated that children take a long time to understand fully the concept of comparison. For instance if ten chocolate drops look as if they occupy more space than eleven chocolate drops, children tend to judge that the ten chocolate drops somehow amount to more than the eleven, until about the age of 5–6 (Mehler 1971). But the same children will have used 'more' as a demand for the recurrence of an event at a very early stage: 'more sweet' meaning 'I had a sweet and now I want another'. The games of competitive boasting which set in around the ages of three or four require command of comparative structures:

My daddy is bigger than your daddy
My daddy is stronger than your daddy, etc.

The same language structure serves a variety of semantic purposes, which vary greatly in sophistication. It follows that the presence of this or that structure or form is not an infallible guide to the child's command of semantic complexities.

In general one has to fall back on noting the early functions that children express, and try to relate them on the one hand to the children's perceptual and cognitive strategies, and on the other to the structural means they use for conveying the functions. Apart from the early preference for referents which are perceptually present, one may note that coordination is apparently easier than subordination, that inserting a relative clause inside a main clause is more difficult than tacking a subordinate clause to either end of a main clause, that inserting two relative clauses is rather more difficult than inserting one relative clause, and so on.

It seems likely that the relationship between meaning and form is important. Where there is a one-to-one relationship between function and form, learning is easier than when there is a many-to-one relationship in either or both directions. There is no clear-cut evidence on this, as far as I am aware, but pointers exist. One is the 'inflexional imperialism' noted by Russian investigators. When children learn highly inflected languages, they tend to settle on one affix for all occasions instancing a particular relation, i.e., one affix per case. The affix chosen may not be the most frequent one; zero marking is most frequent in the accusative case in Russian, but Gvozdev's son chose the positive marking *-u*, the next most frequent. Similarly, to mark the instrumental case he adopted the affix *-om*, though the alternative *-oy* is estimated to be the more frequent in the language. The advantage of *-om* over *-oy* is that it marks fewer functions: *-om* marks only one other function (adjectives of masculine and neuter nouns in the prepositional case) while *-oy* marks a variety of functions. Similarly we may note the use that English speaking children make of sequence; they tend to identify the first noun of a sentence with the agent/actor function and consequently misunderstand passive constructions with some regularity up to about the age of 10. Children seem to hang on to the strategy of postulating one-for-one relationships between function and form as long as it is necessary for them to minimize cognitive and memory strain.

An interesting sidelight on semantic/conceptual complexity has recently been provided by Heider (in press). Usually, semantic categories are not entirely clear-cut. For example, some members of the category *fruit* are 'fruitier' than others, e.g. strawberries and apples are very fruity, figs and olives are not very fruity, according to American observers. Heider established central and peripheral members of various categories by asking young adults to rate various instances for centrality. She then made up sentences with central members and peripheral members, and asked children between 9 and 11, and students, to judge whether sentences were true or false:

A pear is a fruit. (true central)
A pear is a metal. (false central)

A prune is a fruit. (true peripheral)
A prune is a metal. (false peripheral)

Central and peripheral words were chosen that have the same frequency in the language according to the Thorndike count. Adults made very few mistakes in general, but they did have longer reaction times on true sentences with peripheral words. Children also had longer reaction times to true sentences with peripheral words, and in addition they made more mistakes on these sentences. The implications are that it takes longer to learn to identify 'peripheral' members of semantic categories than it does to learn the central members. It would be interesting to try to replicate this finding in different cultures, where central and peripheral members might well be different. The point is that the degree of semantic complexity may be even more difficult to determine than had been suspected, because the particular instance chosen to represent a particular semantic category may also contribute to the relative ease or difficulty in dealing with the category.

A final thought on complexity: the concept of 'sentence' is apparently extremely difficult for the child to acquire. A proportion of children leave school without being able to decide where they should begin and end their sentences in their written work. These children distribute full stops and capital letters in a manner which baffles their teachers, even after they have acquired control over the 'mechanics' of punctuation.

2.5.3 THE CONTRIBUTION OF THE ENVIRONMENT

What drives children to talk is the need to communicate, to relate to the people around them. If they succeed, they are encouraged to go on trying. The main contribution that the people in the child's environment can make towards his language development is to play their part in the communication process, to encourage and reward him by initiating interchanges and responding to his initiatives. Early experience of a reasonable measure of success encourages the child to continue and expand his efforts, while lack of experience of success, for whatever reason, seems in many cases to put a brake on the child's development.

Whatever it is that disadvantaged children lack, there is no doubt that there is a considerable difference in the language skills of children by the time they reach school, and that the difference tends to get more and more pronounced throughout their school careers. Various attempts have been made to try to remedy this at the pre-school stage, i.e., the Head Start Project, the Sesame Street television series, the Bernstein group programmes, and many other more local efforts. Like everything else that has to do with children, language and social class, these projects are controversial.

2.5.3.1 Language acquisition and language education. There appears to be a contrast between what works best in the natural mother/child setting and what works best in a remedial situation.[1] White investigated the homes of one- and two-year-old children, whose older siblings had been found to have either a very high or a very low level of achievement in social and intellectual skills. She describes a favourable setting:

Our most effective mothers do not devote the bulk of their day to rearing their children . . . What they seem to do, often without knowing exactly why, is *to perform excellently the functions of designer and consultant.* By that I mean they design a physical world, mainly in the home, that is beautifully suited to nurturing the burgeoning curiosity of the one- to three-year-old. . . .

In addition to being largely responsible for the type of environment the child has, this mother sets up guides for the child's behaviour that seem to play a very important role in these processes. She is generally *permissive and indulgent.* The child is encouraged in the vast majority of his explorations. When the child confronts an interesting or difficult situation, he often turns to his mother for help. Though usually working on some chore, she is generally within earshot. He then goes to her, and usually, but not always, is responded to by his mother with help or shared enthusiasm plus, occasionally, an interesting, naturally related idea. These 10 to 30 second interchanges are usually oriented around the child's interest of the moment rather than toward some need or interest of the mother. . . .

These mothers very rarely spend 5, 10, or 20 minutes teaching their one- or two-year-olds, but they get an enormous amount of teaching in 'on the fly', and usually at the child's instigation. Though they do volunteer comments opportunistically they mostly act in response to overtures by the child. (White 1971, p. 87.)

This description will be readily recognized as fitting in with our cultural expectations of good child rearing. Good nursery practice is generally taken to replicate and extend the same sort of process by providing a varied and interesting material setting, and then subtly guiding and skilfully responding to the child's initiatives and reactions.

It is only natural to suppose that what disadvantaged children need in order to catch up with more privileged children of the same age is this kind of warm permissive enlightened treatment. Apparently it is not so. Cazden quotes several studies (e.g., Moore 1971, John 1968) which compare the effects of deliberate teaching versus various less direct methods. Moore compared the effects on the child's language of two direct treatments and one non-direct treatment. One of the two direct treatments consisted of constant encouragement for the child to talk, as well as providing models for the child to imitate. The other consisted of responding to the child's spontaneous utterances and expanding them so as to provide models implicitly. The non-direct treatment consisted of adult and child just talking in a given situation. The results showed that the two direct methods produced much greater increase in the length and complexity of the child's utterances than the indirect treatment. Interestingly

[1] This section draws heavily upon a recent paper by Cazden (in press).

enough, the second direct treatment where the teacher was encouraged to produce mature language resulted in a great increase in the length and complexity of the teacher's utterances.

In the John investigation the aim was to increase the child's ability to deal with concepts of same/different, and of growth, liquids and solids. In the direct treatment, the teacher questioned the children directly, demanding verbal labels and category judgement and predictions about what would happen if one did this or that. The non-direct treatment was a sort of simulation of bedtime stories, dealing with the same sort of topics, where any child's response or question would be carefully attended to. The story telling was enormously popular, but produced no significant gains. The direct treatment led to striking gains.

2.5.3.2 The effect of direct language programmes. Most pre-school direct language programmes have been very carefully pre- and post-tested and they regularly show significant gains when the children's skills prior to instruction are compared with their skills after instruction. This is a fact which is sometimes contested, but the counter-evidence usually turns out to be not very impressive.

Other criticisms need more careful consideration.

(a) *The gains do not last.* 6, 12 or 18 months after the programme has ceased, there may no longer be a significant difference or only a small difference between participating and non-participating children. This is apparently true in most cases, but I do not see why it should be taken as an argument for the failure of these programmes. We are dealing with three- and four-year-old children, who develop enormously rapidly in all aspects. That twenty minutes a day, five times a week for 26 weeks should be expected to show up significantly a quarter or a third of a lifetime later, seems rather a lot to expect.

(b) *The learning does not generalize.* This is the most serious criticism. If the children learn only to respond to the particular situations which are taught, and if their ability to handle parallel problems and situations does not increase, a great deal of the intended value of the programmes is lost. Not all of it is lost, however; the Sesame Street investigators found that if a black child enters a desegregated school knowing things like parts of the body and the days of the week and being about to count to 20, this puts him in a much better position to cope with the white children who usually know these things (Bogatz and Ball 1971).

One of the goals of the Sesame Street programme was to teach understanding of relational concepts: *first*, *last*, *big/bigger/biggest*, *some*, *more*, *less*, *near*, *far*, etc. The investigators tested the children's ability to identify these relations by getting them to point at pictures.

The investigators found a general improvement of understanding between pre-testing in November and post-testing in May. In order to have a check on the improvement that could be expected on the grounds that the children were six months older at the post-test stage, the comparison was conducted in two areas where television was not available to the poorer sections of the community. The investigators provided the necessary facilities for viewing in the houses of some families and gave a lot of encouragement for viewing the programme, and for other equivalent families they did nothing except send people round to check on 'viewing habits' from time to time. The results for gain on relational terms were as follows:

number of items	not encouraged group (n = 153)			encouraged group (n = 130)		
	score		gain	score		gain
	pre-test	post-test		pre-test	post-test	
17	9.0	10.2	1.2	8.5	11.5	3.0

Two of the 17 items had to do with weight, which was not directly taught on the programme. Comprehension of *heaviest* and *lightest* increased markedly among those children who had viewed the programme:

item	not encouraged group (n = 153)	encouraged group (n = 130)
	gain	gain
heaviest	2%	9%
lightest	6%	19%

This indicates strongly that the learning of comparisons had generalized from specific items taught to other instances of the same concept which were not specifically taught.

However, much of the criticism seems to be inspired by considerations other than the effectiveness of the programmes. Sesame Street and other programmes of a similar nature which set out to teach directly certain language and cognitive skills arouse powerful opposition in many quarters. These programmes constitute a practical and public acknowledgement of the fact that disadvantaged children suffer from various handicaps, and many people fear—not without justice—that this will be taken to demonstrate the inherent inferiority of these children. There is of course no logical justification for this inference, and it would seem both morally and intellectually doubtful to reject useful remedies on the grounds that facts might be misused or on the grounds that they constitute short-term remedies, rather than fundamental ones.

Another kind of opposition stems from attitudes towards education. This was very clearly articulated by a very honest nursery headmistress, interviewed about her reactions to the Peabody Language Development Kit, which is a direct teaching programme for use in nursery contexts: 'The children enjoyed it and certainly learned a lot, but I feel the idea is against all nursery principles' (Quigley 1971, p. 161). The direct programmes use what might be called behaviourist, even Skinnerian, techniques of instruction. The programme designers provide exact specifications of the behaviour wanted, and set up very specific links between stimulus situations and responses in order to get specific learning, e.g., naming of parts of the body. They also vary the contexts in which a particular skill is being trained, getting learning which involves generalization: counting fingers, counting children, counting comics, counting hoots from cars, etc. The skills are built up in small steps, presented so that the probability of success is high. There is constant feedback and much repetition and encouragement to imitate and practise.

Those who object to 'behaviourism' as a world view tend to dislike evidence of the practical usefulness of methods which are derived from it. Also, what many teachers find difficult to accept is the fact that the source of enjoyment and perseverance comes from outside the nursery context. Nobody denies that children enjoy Sesame Street, wherever it has been shown; in all parts of the United States, to black and white children alike, to Mexicans and Puerto Ricans, to Ghanaians and to new and old Australians. Until these programmes arrived, the source of approval and satisfaction in nursery and infant school education was exclusively the individual teacher—the warm relationship existing between the teacher and her class is what makes the world go round. Apparently the effect of these programmes is to move the skilled teacher away, however slightly, from her traditional position at the centre of the stage.

The resolution of the language acquisition/language education paradox may lie in this: a child who has been rewarded by his mother's interest and participation in his exploration and questions and bids for attention, will be able to produce the same sort of behaviour in a nursery or elementary school situation. He will be rewarded for his behaviour by finding the same sort of interest and approval in the teacher. But a child who has had this sort of behaviour knocked out of him in the home setting, may not be able to produce it in a nursery or infant school setting and so he will not have the chance of being rewarded by the teacher. In any teaching/learning situation, there must be some overlap between teacher and taught as to what is supposed to be going on. Perhaps the direct pre-school teaching programmes provide—apart from the particular skills—some sort of pre-training in coping with educational contexts. In a questionnaire following Sesame Street, teachers who did not know which of the children had participated rated children who had viewed the programme as on the whole settling down better in school than those who had not.

It seems then that the adults in the child's environment make the following contribution towards his language development: they talk to him, which provides him with the models he needs, they give the child opportunities to talk to them, and they respond with interest and attention when he does talk. If for some reason a child has not grown up in an environment of this kind, and has failed to develop language skills which put him on a level with other children of the same age, direct training programmes can to some extent help to improve the child's command of the resources of the language.

3 Second language learning

3.1 Theoretical introduction

There are no nativists when it comes to second language learning. The idea that one could learn a second language from the sort of exposure that would be sufficient to test out hypotheses about the form of grammar appropriate to a particular language, would wither at the first contact with reality. Everybody who has gone through the process of trying to learn a second language so that one can function somewhere near one's level of intelligence in that language knows only too well the amount of effort that is involved.

The problem in the field of second language learning, at the theoretical level, is the choice between different models of learning. The extreme position here is to assert that there is only one kind of learning, whichever model one chooses. Like all extremist positions this is very useful in pushing the limits of the applicability of any model; for instance the Russians have done very interesting work within the framework of classical Pavlovian conditioning.

Whatever the possibility of eventually being able to account for all observations of learning behaviour in terms of one all-embracing model, it seems plain that at a descriptive level more than one kind of learning must be recognized. Much writing on second language learning assumes that there are two kinds: habit learning (rote learning) and rule learning (concept learning). This appears to be an oversimplification, and when some sort of incompatibility between the two types is implied, it becomes positively misleading. Gagné (1965), in an analysis of learning directly related to classroom behaviour, distinguishes eight kinds of learning, ranging from the simplest to the most complex, all except one related hierarchically in such a way that the more complex forms of learning depend intrinsically and necessarily on the simpler kinds. The one form of learning not seen as related to the rest is classical conditioning—Pavlovian dogs salivating to the sound of a bell, after the bell has sounded while they have been given food over a number of occasions.

Of Gagné's eight forms of learning, we shall here deal with five: stimulus-response learning, chaining, multiple discrimination, concept learning and principle learning.

3.1.1 STIMULUS RESPONSE LEARNING

In Gagné's scheme this is not a commitment to a particular theory of learning, it is just a symbolization of the most elementary kind of learning, in which a particular stimulus configuration is linked to a particular identifying or recognizing response. This is the ubiquitous and indispensable basis for all kinds of learning, but it is difficult to find pure instances, because, with one exception, in anybody except very young babies other and more complex forms of learning have already been superimposed.

The exception is in the field of second language learning. For instance the process of learning to distinguish and identify sounds and sequences of sounds is S → R learning in the sense defined by Gagné. When German speakers have learned to distinguish and identify the vowel sounds in English *man* and *men*, or English speakers have learned to distinguish and identify the nasalized vowels of the French words *enfin* and *enfant*, they have achieved basic S → R learning. The response consists of a perceptual act of identification, and it is basically a matter of learning to discriminate the relevant stimuli, so that one can distinguish those occasions when the particular stimulus configuration is present from those occasions when it is not present. Learning comes about by increasingly sharp and precise singling out of the relevant stimulus features.

3.1.2 CHAINING

The process of attaching words as labels to objects or actions is often thought of as simple S → R learning, but to Gagné this is an example of a more complex form of learning, namely the chaining of simple S → R links. A chain consists of two or more S → R links. Take the learning of the word *enfant*. First there are two identifying links:

S: presence of child	→	R: identifying response (human, non-adult, small body, large head, etc.)
S: presence of word (i.e. somebody uttering 'enfant')	→	R: identifying response (not 'enfin' not 'avant' etc.)

The identifying response to the sound of the word uttered by somebody else must be linked to the speakers' own uttering mechanisms, by processes which are presumably reasonably well established in the second language learner. The identifying response becomes the stimulus which sets off the pronunciation response:

S: 'enfant' (the word) → R: identifying 'enfant'
↓
S: identifying 'enfant' → R: pronouncing 'enfant'

The naming chain is then associated with the object-identifying link:

S: 'enfant' (the word) → R: identifying 'enfant'
↓
S: identifying 'enfant'
S: identifying child } → R: pronouncing 'enfant'
↑
S: presence of child → R: identifying child

As learning proceeds the first part of the naming chain drops out and we get:

S: presence of child → R: identifying child
↓
S: { identifying child + recall of identifying 'enfant' } → R: pronouncing 'enfant'

When the chain has become well established, the stimulus part becomes internalized and the only observable event is the utterance 'enfant'.

Note that this does not constitute a theory of meaning, and the chain model does not imply inevitability; the presence of a child does not inevitably lead to the utterance 'child' or 'enfant', nor does the utterance 'enfant' imply the presence of a child. What is asserted is that the process of naming involves more than one link, and that this is what makes it an example of verbal chaining. It is a chain that is at the speaker's command when he cares to activate it. Note also that this is a highly schematic account which ignores all sorts of other complications, for instance the problems of precise phonetic discrimination and the matching of articulations to perceptions, as well as possible mediating effects.

Verbal links can also be established by setting up simple first language–second language pairs (whether this is approved or not in teaching circles is another matter):

S: (the word) 'child' → R: (the word) 'enfant'

In such links there is often a mediating element which may or may not be overt, for instance:

S: 'child' → (mediating link 'infant' →) R: 'enfant'

Such mediating links can be useful as mnemonics but they can also be disastrous if they are taken as indications for usage. In English *infant* is specifically a child before the walking stage; in French young people may address a group of friends as *mes enfants*.

Other examples of verbal chains are collocations and idioms:

square meal (cf. square table)

but not

*round meal (cf. round table)

Also all kinds of concord:

un*e* pomme vert*e*
des pomme*s* vert*es*

3.1.3 MULTIPLE DISCRIMINATION

The next form of learning relevant to this discussion is what Gagné calls multiple discrimination. It consists essentially of keeping links and chains intact, without getting them confused. Most people, however superficial their knowledge of a second language may be, can keep intact the naming chains required to produce the words for some parts of the body, for example French *la main* (hand) *le pied* (foot) *les yeux* (eyes) *le nez* (nose) etc. But speaking for myself, I am not always sure about which, *le coude* or *le genou*, means 'elbow' and which means 'knee', and I cannot recall the word for 'cheek' at all, though I have been taught it. One can easily learn a few chains and keep them intact. The problem is to learn hundreds and thousands of chains, and that is what is required for language learning.

Similarly, multiple discriminations are needed in order to retain sound-symbol links:

The spelling *enfant* goes with the pronunciation [ã f ã]
The spelling *enfin* goes with the pronunciation [ã f ɛ̃]

The same sort of multiple discrimination is required in order to keep morphological marking straight. In German *der* + singular masculine noun indicates the nominative case, while *der*+ singular feminine noun indicates the genitive or dative case. Similarly, *den*+ singular masculine noun indicates accusative, while *den* + any plural noun indicates dative. In the end one may induce—or memorize—the rules, but the rule induction depends on multiple discrimination learning, enabling the learner to keep the chains intact.

In other cases rule induction may not be possible, on the information that the learner possesses. In Norwegian there are, according to the analysis one prefers, from eight to twelve morphological classes of verbs, and the formations can be reduced to rules only if one happens to know Old Norse. The learning job for all children and most foreigners consists in establishing links between particular verbs and particular forms, and then keeping them intact by multiple discrimination. For instance:

	infinitive	*simple past*	*past perfect*
1	å bleke (to whiten)	blek*et*	blek*et*
2	å steke (to fry)	stek*te*	stek*t*
3	å rikke (to move)	rikk*et*	rikk*et*
4	å drikke (to drink)	dr*a*kk	dr*u*kk*et*
5	å lekke (to leak)	l*a*kk	lekk*et*
6	å rekke (to pass (trans))	r*akte*	r*a*k*t*

In modern Norwegian there is nothing to distinguish between the verbs in each pair on the grounds of phonology. They are perfect rhymes and all six take the two-tone intonation contour. Syntactically there is nothing to distinguish them either, except that though they can all take direct objects, 6 can also take an indirect object. Verbs 1 and 2 take two different 'weak' inflexions *-et*, *-et* and *-te*, *-t*. In the second pair, verb 3 takes the same weak inflexion as verb 1 *-et*/*-et*, while 4 is an irregular verb with vowel change and zero suffix in the simple past and vowel change and *-et* in the past perfect form. Verbs 5 and 6 show different combinations of vowel change and selection of suffixes. The point is that no rule will enable the learner to choose the appropriate form—each has to be learned and distinguished from other stem affix chains.

3.1.4 CONCEPT LEARNING

Concept learning is the next form of learning in the learning hierarchy. Many people take the view that there is a sharp distinction between concept learning, and whatever simpler forms of learning there may be. Gagné, on the other hand, insists that each higher step in the hierarchy depends on the intactness of the lower or simpler forms.

Essentially concept learning consists in discovering that a number of experiences are in some sense 'the same'; that is, they have characteristics which make it appropriate to respond to them by a given response. When Catherine aged about 1.2 uttered *ba* on a number of separate occasions, each of which involved her handing something to somebody else, or somebody else handing something to her, she could be said to be conceptualizing; she isolated a particular aspect of each total situation, her identification response concerned the give/take relation and by chaining it up with the *ba* sound, the naming followed. The response was not consistent, and it disappeared in time, but it was stable enough for an observer (the mother) to discover the child's working concept.

It can be difficult to determine whether some particular new acquisition represents 'true' learning or is the result of a simpler form of learning, usually referred to as stimulus generalization. Stimulus generalization occurs when the individual is narrowly attending to a particular dominant stimulus feature without taking in the situation as a whole. Concept formation involves the process of isolating and extracting a particular feature from a configuration of features which characterizes a total situation, according to a particular purpose. In practice it is often difficult to decide whether a particular action is the outcome of one or the other learning process. Catherine might simply have been attending to an isolated perceptual feature, in which case her naming would be the result of a chain, rather than the outcome of selective conceptual activity. This does not appear likely since she had picked out a reciprocal situation which is described by two verbs in the adult language, but since perceptual features were involved, stimulus generalization cannot be entirely ruled out.[1]

In order to demonstrate conclusively that it is concept learning that is going on, one has to look for situations which have some non-perceptual or 'abstract' feature or features in common. An example might be the categorizing of occasions prior-to-the-time-of-utterance plus the additional feature of being relevant to the present, as appropriate occasions for the choice of the present perfect tense form. For example, a person replying to the question

I wonder where John is?

might answer in one or the other way according to how he categorizes the situation:

Last year he was in London (but I don't know about now).
He has been in London for the last year (and he is there now).

The concepts can only be said to have been learned when the appropriate tense forms are applied to actual experiences, which are perceived and correctly identified by the individual as examples of a particular category. Gagné maintains that it is impossible to succeed in classifying occasions as belonging to this or that category, unless first of all the identifying perceptual S → R links are established, and then incorporated into chains, with links and chains securely established as the result of successful multiple discriminations.

The continuity is perhaps better illustrated by reference to space rather than time. Consider the concept of triangularity. By repeated exposure to various shapes of triangles, some animals and young children can be taught to pick out other triangular shapes which they have never seen before. One step further, monkeys and very young children can be taught the concept *odd*, i.e. they will pick the odd one of three objects when two are the same and one is

[1] This may sound rather quibbling, but it has importance for theories of learning.

different. For example, let us suppose that there are three drawers, two surmounted by a cross and one by a circle, and the child discovers that there is always a sweet under the circle. The child is then introduced to a variety of shapes, and he finds that the sweet is always under the figure that is different from the two others. After a while the child will waste no time whatever shapes are put in front of him; he will go straight for the odd one. When this happens the child can be said to have acquired the concept of odd; the concept is independent of any particular visual shape, but still based on correct perceptual identification of the three objects.

In language concepts of space can be expressed by various grammatical means. Eve showed that she could distinguish the concept of one object resting on the surface of another and the concept of one object inside another by using the preposition *on* and *in* with 90 per cent success about the age of 2. And because she did not simply use the prepositions in the same expressions that she had heard her mother use, but also used them appropriately on 'new' occasions, it is clear that she was correctly identifying and classifying these 'new' occasions as members of the class of occasions on which the use of one or the other preposition was appropriate. In other words, she had acquired the concepts of what Catford calls 'exteriority' and 'interiority' (Catford 1968). The same relations can also be expressed by means of systems. Finnish has six locative cases expressing 'exteriority' and 'interiority' (as well as whether the object is static, or moving from or moving to). Before a Finnish child can use the 'adessive' case suffix *-lla* appropriately, he must have acquired the concept exterior (and static), and before he can use the 'inessive' case suffix *-ssa* he must have acquired the concept interior (and static). These are concepts which rest on perceptual distinctions, but they are not given in the perceptions themselves. Exteriority and interiority might or might not be relevant to a particular choice of language forms, just as static and non-static might or might not be relevant. The learning of concepts like these which involves the selection of relevant perceptual features is not far removed from the simpler sorts of learning, and in turn these simpler conceptualizations underly the learning of the more abstract conceptualizations which are only remotely or indirectly dependent on perceptions, for instance concepts of odd/even, time relations, and so on.

Forming a concept consists of classifying a number of occasions as equivalent for the purpose of making a particular response—of treating them as equivalent for a particular purpose. All occasions involving the locative feature 'exterior' and the feature 'static' are equivalent for choosing the suffix *-lla*. Here all appropriate occasions for the choice of the suffix share the two essential characteristics. Concepts of this kind are known as conjunctive. But there are also so-called disjunctive concepts, which include a class of occasions exhibiting a particular feature or set of features, as well as another class of occasions which exhibit another and quite different feature or set of features. Both classes are included in the concept, because the same response is appropriate to both. This is often found in languages. In Russian, for instance, the choice of the dative case is appropriate on the class of occasions which contain the feature 'directed motion towards an individual or object' and also on the class of occasions which specify the syntactic element 'indirect object'.

These concepts are more difficult to learn than the conjunctive concepts, particularly if one has to induce them from examples, because people tend, as a basic concept learning strategy, to look for common features across the whole range of occasions. And as always, even when the concept is understood, the ability to give appropriate responses fluently needs a lot of careful practice to establish the correct chains and to keep them intact.

3.1.5 PRINCIPLE LEARNING

The next step in the learning hierarchy, according to Gagné, is principle learning. Principle learning consists in learning relationships between concepts, and between other principles. Principles can be stated in *if-then* terms:

If it is a liquid, then it will boil.
If a verb is in the present tense and relates to a subject in the third person, then it takes the suffix *-s* (English)
If the subject of a main clause is preceded by an adverbial or by a subordinate clause, then there is inversion of subject and verb (Danish, Norwegian).
If the object referred to is (a) static and (b) exterior to another object, then the noun takes the adessive case (Finnish).

What in linguistic theory are referred to as categories are in this scheme a subclass of concepts, and similarly linguistic rules are a subclass of principles. The advantage of using the terms 'concept' and 'principle' when discussing learning is that they refer to more than one field of knowledge.

There are two parts to concept learning (and therefore to principle learning). The first part consists of learning to respond appropriately to instances of the concept. This means learning to distinguish positive instances from negative instances and then carrying out the appropriate action. In language it consists of correctly identifying the various elements of the utterance situation and then choosing the appropriate linguistic forms. A child shows that he has a concept of 'time past' when he uses past tense forms more or less appropriately, and in contrast with forms expressing non-past references.

The second part of concept learning is the ability to define the concept, to state explicitly what it is that makes an instance a member of the category in question. Though one might like to think that a full understanding of a concept requires both kinds of learning, it is a fact that either part quite frequently exists without the other. We are all able to operate the concepts and principles of our native language but we are none of us able to describe adequately the categories and rules which we so successfully employ. Conversely a linguist engaged in describing a language will know far more about the grammatical categories and relations of that language than a native speakers does, but he will not be able to operate these in actual speech nearly as well as the native speaker.

The learner may understand a concept perfectly well, but not always manage to respond to it appropriately. Examples are failure to use *he* and *she* for third person reference in English if the native language has only one third person pronoun, like Hindi, or failure to use reciprocal verbs like *teach/learn, bring/take* if one's own language makes do with only one verb in each area. This kind of situation is frequent in language learning. It arises from what Gagné calls 'oververbalization'; the result of attending mainly to the second part of concept learning, so that the explicit formulations are not sufficiently connected with practice in the immediate identification of instances and the smooth execution of appropriate responses.

The learner who does not understand the grammatical concepts which are used in definitions and statements of rules is of course even worse off. It is no use to a learner to be able to quote definitions ('Adjectives are words which modify nouns') and rules ('Nouns functioning as subject take the nominative case') if he is not sure what a noun is, has only the vaguest idea of subject and is completely baffled by the concept of case. School-children in many countries are frequently in this position after a year or two of foreign language instruction. In many countries, mother tongue teachers have rejected the idea of teaching 'grammar' with reference to the pupils' own language, while second language teachers sooner or later want to refer explicitly to grammatical concepts like case and tense. And so the children are expected to learn the unknown in relation to the unknown. They do not understand the concepts in terms of which they are expected to organize their second language constructions, and they do not have usage skills against which they could check and verify their understanding of the explicit grammatical concepts.

3.2 Application of the analysis of concept learning to second language teaching methods

The controversies over 'grammar-translation' methods and various versions of 'direct' or 'audiolingual' methods can best be seen in the light of the two-part learning of concepts. The grammar-translation method concentrated on teaching explicit rules, and linked them to a problem-solving situation: Given a written sentence in one language, how do you formulate the content correctly in another language? The grammar-translation method was highly successful in terms of its original aims, but since it was not linked to communicative skills, these skills did not of course develop to any great extent.

When the aims of language teaching began to change, the 'oververbalization' connected with the grammar-translation approach was noted, and any explicit reference to generalizations and concepts and rules of any sort was energetically discouraged. The proponents of the 'direct' or 'audiolingual' method argued that language learning could only be achieved through mastery of the simpler sorts of learning, and so they concentrated on precise perceptual discriminations, accurate pronunciation, the learning of chains in close reference to actual objects and situations, and the establishment of chains and multiple discrimination by pattern practice and substitution tables. Through organized practice the students were supposed to induce the rules implicitly, as a child appears to do with his first language. This method also was and is highly successful—in its own terms. Learners by and large achieve a much better pronunciation than was the case earlier, and they acquire a smaller or larger repertoire of utterances which they can produce with great fluency and precision, but they may not be so skilled in matching these utterances to appropriate occasions, or in composing new sentences for unrehearsed contexts.

Since there is more to language command than either solving contrastive grammatical problems on the one hand, and exchanging fluent language tokens on the other, the search for better methods goes on. In many school systems it has been the practice for some time to organize instruction according to the view that language is 'communication in context', at least for the elementary stages. The result has been a marked emphasis on teaching the spoken language, and in many countries this trend has been backed by the widespread use of language laboratories. A great many teachers have now had experience of teaching by audiolingual methods, and inevitably the very optimistic statements that were made in the beginning about the superiority of this approach have been found to be only partially justified. The stubborn fact remains that learning a language is a massive task and there is no simple formula for success.

Partly as a result of disenchantment with the audiolingual method, and partly no doubt reflecting contemporary trends in theoretical psychology and linguistics, the pendulum now appears to be swinging back towards a 'rule-based' or 'cognitive code' approach to language teaching. According to this view, an understanding of the systems of a language should aid the acquisition of language control. This approach represents a recognition of the fact that, as they leave early childhood, people develop an ability to grasp abstract statements and to relate them to concrete instances. They can go from the particular to the general and from the general to the particular; in other words, they become able to acquire both parts of concept learning. There is no doubt that properly balanced access to the explicit formulation of rules can aid the practical learning of a second language. One might hope that this time the baby is not thrown out with the bathwater, and that recognition of the importance of the more complex kinds of learning does not lead to a neglect of the basic kinds of learning. It is perhaps fortunate for generations of language learners that whatever teaching method happened to be publicly advocated at the time, within their own classrooms many teachers have always tended to adopt an eclectic approach. Most teachers will select useful ideas from a number of different methods and experiments, and try them out in order to find the combination which is best suited to their own particular group of students.

3·3 Conditions of second language learning

The conditions of second language learning will be discussed from the point of view that both simpler and more complex forms of learning are relevant, and that their relevance is readily apparent. S→R learning is necessary for the precise discrimination of sounds and sequences of sounds, and for the accurate control of articulators in order to produce acceptable utterances. Chaining is necessary to provide the link between what the speaker wants to talk about —the referents—and the accompanying linguistic forms. Chaining is also needed to accumulate a repertoire of language sequences which can be called upon when required and which can be produced easily and smoothly as one unit. Multiple discrimination is necessary to keep the repertoire intact—to preserve the chains free from contamination from other chains. Concept and principle learning are required for the appropriate use of a language repertoire. The learner must achieve the proper categorization of utterance occasions, and learn how to match these occasions with the appropriate language forms. Even though chains embrace links between the objects and situations referred to and the appropriate language forms, chains are not sufficient because there is not a one-to-one relationship between utterance occasions and utterances. Chains are necessary, but language utterances do not consist of fixed and invariable units, and it is only by the categorization of communicative purposes and occasions—and in second language learning, recategorization—that the language repertoire can be effectively deployed.

In one formulation or another, most people would probably agree that both simple and complex learning is necessary. The argument tends to be about how the more complex forms of learning are best achieved. There are those who believe that modelling and imitation and contrastive practice directly aimed at the simpler forms of learning will tacitly and inductively lead to the necessary concept formation. Others take the view that overt and explicit attention to the relevant language concepts and principles will lead to better concept learning, and that this in turn will also assist learning at the simpler levels because these concepts will then be available as mediators for the simpler learning processes.

The following discussion presupposes that all forms of learning are hierarchically related and interdependent, and at the same time that there are differences in the nature of the learning job as one progresses from the simpler levels to the more complex, and that therefore the relative importance of the conditions which assist efficient learning will vary to some extent according to the form of learning which is involved. The relative importance of external factors changes most obviously between S → R learning, chaining and multiple discrimination on the one hand, and concept learning and principle learning on the other.

3.3.1 PRACTICE

Practice is central to all learning; in fact the efficiency of any method of instruction is usually assessed by finding how many repetitions are needed in order to reach a given level of achievement—the fewer the number of repetitions, the more efficient the method. The study of a language is like other forms of learning in that it is heavily dependent on practice. It is not difficult to learn a few new words or chains with a minimum of repetition, and if one did not have to learn a few more the next day and a few more the day after that, and so on, these few words and utterances would probably never be forgotten. But in learning a language there are thousands and tens of thousands of chains to be acquired, and that is why practice extending over long periods is essential in order to maintain words and patterns readily available for use.

For S → R learning the effect of practice is to increase accuracy of discrimination. At the chaining stage practice serves to establish chains so that they can be smoothly executed and so that they can be kept distinct from one another and intact over a period of time. For concept learning, what is needed is a number of trials rather than a number of repetitions. The learner needs to test out his preliminary hypothesis about the nature of the concept he is trying to discover. A learner beyond the first few years of life is aided by verbal clues and directions from an instructor; but he still needs to verify over a number of occasions that he is capable of identifying instances of the concept, and he needs to know whether his identifications are correct or not.

In second language learning practice is needed to link up the correct categorization of utterance occasions (concept learning) with the language rules that contain these categories (principle learning) and the actual surface utterance that the rules prescribe (chaining). If any stage of learning is insecure, the utterance will not be appropriate and fluent. For instance, the learner must understand the concepts of noun, verb, third person and present tense, and he must know the rule that in order to form the present tense in a sentence where the subject is third person, the suffix *-s* must be added to the verb; and he must also produce the correct form of the verb on every appropriate occasion.

Occasionally, at the level of concept or principle learning, a discovery can be made in a single experience, and provided it is based securely on lower forms of learning, it may never be forgotten.

3.3.2 REINFORCEMENT

At all stages of learning knowledge of right and wrong is extremely important.

It is no use practising anything without being able to find out whether one is doing the right thing. This is where some language laboratory systems fall down badly. Requiring a learner to imitate a taped model, if the learner has not begun to distinguish the difference between the native speaker's utterance and his own, is a complete waste of time. Conversely, Pimsleur et al. (1961) have shown that students can learn fairly quickly to distinguish between acceptable and non-acceptable pronunciations of the sounds of the second language, if immediate feedback is provided. The experiment was conducted in a language laboratory setting where American learners of French listened to different pronunciations of French words with nasalized vowels and where their judgement of acceptability was immediately confirmed or disconfirmed.

There is ample evidence that in any learning job the rate of learning is improved when learners can notch up a steady rate of success. This implies that the steps of learning must be so arranged that the learner can achieve progress, and that his progress should be manifest. The provision of feedback has two functions. In the first place it is informative, it tells the learner if he is on the right track; for instance, it tells him whether a pronunciation is acceptable or not, or whether a conceptualization is correct or not. In the second place feedback, if it reflects sufficient gains, serves to maintain motivation. The point about motivation is that it keeps people at it. There is a delicate balance to be struck here, depending on the learner's previous experience of success. People who have a history of successful formal learning behind them have the confidence to keep on slogging away even in periods of no visible advance, because they back themselves to succeed sooner or later. With learners who do not have a history of success, either very young children or older people who have experienced earlier failures, it becomes very important indeed to arrange for quick and regular reinforcement. However, if the job is so arranged that there is no possibility of being wrong, as was the case in some early language laboratory drill exercises, there is no challenge at all and the task becomes unutterably boring.

There is no doubt that the fear of unpleasant consequences such as failure in examinations or lack of promotion also has the effect of keeping people at it, provided the learner believes that he has a reasonable chance of avoiding these unpleasant consequences. If the threat is all too likely to be realized, the effect is of course totally detrimental.

3.3.3 MEDIATION

It is now generally accepted that practically all learning is mediated. When we see a red blob or a straight line we recognize it for what it is because we have stored away something from previous experience. What we have stored is not a similar image—this would be much too uneconomical a procedure—but a code by which we reconstruct the perception and, if called upon, the verbal label that goes with it. There are many indications that such coding is itself verbal—i.e., symbolic—rather than involving any kind of image. However that might be, it can easily be demonstrated that words facilitate very simple perceptual learning as well as more complex learning—that is, words act as mediators. Katz (1963) presented children between 7 and 9.6 years of age with four irregular shapes, introduced as 'funny-looking animals from Mars'. During the training period one group of children was presented with the figures so that each was linked to a nonsense word of its own; e.g., the leftmost figure was associated with the label *boz*, the next figure with the label *ric*, etc. Another group of children had two shapes associated with the same label, e.g., the two figures on the left were associated with the label *boz* and the two on the right with *ric*. The third group was presented with the figures for recognition with no verbal labels.

For testing, the children were presented with pairs of shapes chosen from the four, some pairs being identical and some different, and the children were asked to say whether the members of the pairs were the same or different. There were twenty pairs made up of different shapes, and on these the mistake consisted in judging them the same. The distinct label group made an average of 1.94 errors per child, the common label group made 4.31 errors per child and the no label group came in between with 3.06 errors per child. The findings illustrate the influence of word labels on perceptions, for good and for bad. On the other hand, even the provision of distinctive labelling, i.e. one label to one symbol, does not guarantee discrimination learning. Each group of children was shown each figure 150 times, and even then under the most favourable conditions there were still nearly two errors per child on twenty presentations.

It was suggested earlier that concepts also mediate in learning. Kendler and Kendler (1961) trained four-year-olds and seven-year-olds always to choose the larger of two squares, rewarding them with a sweet for correct choices. Then they reversed the task by making the smaller square the correct one. The seven-year-olds required 8 trials on the average to learn the new task, but the four-year-olds required 23 trials. The authors suggest that the reason for this difference is that the seven-year-olds possessed the mediating concept 'opposite' and the four-year-olds did not.

Findings such as these give strong support to those who hold that simpler and more complex forms of learning are interrelated. Mediators may of course hinder as well as help learning. The possible mediator *infant* in the naming chain

S 'child' (→ 'infant') → R 'enfant'

could help the retrieval of the French lexical item, and hinder the proper pronunciation of it.

Very little is known about what produces helpful mediation. For instance we do not know whether and under what circumstances it is helpful to provide overt mediation for the learner, or to let him provide his own internal mediation, of which he is very often unaware. In education the effects of mediation have been studied mainly in the context of concept learning and of transfer. We shall now turn to these two topics.

3.3.3.1 How is concept and principle learning best achieved? Concepts and principles can be attained inductively—the learner discovers them through experience with various kinds of examples and non-examples. They can also be learned deductively; someone formulates the definition and states the rule, and the learners then practise identifying members and non-members of the concept, and the application and execution of the principle. The reaction to the 'oververbalization' of concepts that had been going on in the grammar-translation approach led to a total rejection of any overt formulation at all—the learners were supposed to learn purely by inductive discovery.

In recent years a number of experiments have been carried out to try to throw some light on how concept learning is best achieved. Most of the experiments have used mathematics as the subject, because there the concepts and rules are explicitly stated. The usual procedure is to compare discovery learning (induction from examples), directed learning (statement of principle provided, followed by practice) and an intermediate approach, guided discovery, in which the instructor points out that there is a principle involved and gives some help in the right direction. The results are somewhat contradictory. It is usually found that on immediate testing at the end of the experiment, the directed group does best. This is probably related to the fact that the directed group has had most practice on the correct solution, while the other groups have spent some of their time working along irrelevant lines. On retesting some weeks later, each method in turn has been found to be superior; i.e., in one experiment the discovery group has done best, in another the guided group and in a third the directed group. It has been suggested that these findings are relatable to the degree of difficulty of the task; if the task is very difficult for the particular learners involved, the discovery group never gets there and even the guided group may not get very far. Only the directed group has any chance. At slightly less drastic levels of difficulty the guidance may be just enough for the majority of the guided group to reach the solution, while the majority of the discovery group does not, and in such cases the guided group tends to be superior on retesting. If the problem is such that the discovery group can solve it, then their retention is superior. The moral seems to be that if the children are able to discover the relevant concepts and principles for themselves, this produces more durable learning, and a discovery technique should therefore be preferred to straight directed teaching (Kersh and Wittrock 1967).

In an experiment carried out under Carroll's direction by McKinnon

(Carroll 1969), children were taught a pidgin language from New Guinea called 'Police Motu' under varying conditions of practice, order of presentation and guidance.

In the 'inductive presentation' the children were not given any special instruction, being allowed to figure the grammar out for themselves. In the 'deductive presentation', the teacher pointed out the structural features such as: 'The word that tells what the person is doing comes at the end of the sentence'.

The result showed that the deductive procedure produced better learning. Such a finding taken in isolation could be only too easily interpreted as 'proving' the superiority of a deductive procedure in all circumstances. It is only by comparison with other findings that a more detailed and perhaps truer interpretation becomes possible. In this particular case the deductive procedure produced better learning, presumably because the children in the inductive group were unable to induce the helpful generalizations for themselves.

In the same experiment random versus systematic order of presentation did not produce any difference in learning. This suggests another possible pitfall in interpretation: one might conclude that the order of presentation does not matter in general, whereas in the light of the general failure to make inductions, the interpretation should probably be that in this case the induction was so difficult that the method of presentation was neither here nor there.

In another experiment two groups of adult Swedish learners of English were taught certain points of grammar, *some* and *any*, passives, etc. One group was given explanations, the other group got additional drill. On testing immediately afterwards the directed group did best (von Elek and Oskarson 1972). Two things are worth noting. Firstly there was no retesting, to see which group remembered best after a period of time. Secondly the problems were of the sort that we have good valid rules for. The outcome on an experiment involving the use of articles or tenses might be different.

The need to interpret the results of experiments with caution does not mean that experiments are no use. One has to get the information wherever one can. It should be remembered that the experience of practising teachers, which is the major source of knowledge, is in a sense the outcome of the simplest form of experimentation there is—trying something out in a particular situation, and seeing if it works in that situation. The interpretation of both kinds of results has to be checked against the experiences of other people and the outcome of other experiments.

3.3.3.2 Transfer. Transfer has to do with the effect of past learning on present learning and with the effect of intervening learning on the recall of past learning. Both aspects are important, but since the effects are broadly parallel, I shall discuss only the learning paradigm.

Transfer is either positive or negative. Positive transfer helps new learning. For instance it is easy to learn to pronounce aspirated voiceless stops in a second language, if the first language also has aspirated voiceless stops. Negative transfer hinders new learning. If in one's first language one has learned to change voiceless consonants to voiced ones when they occur immediately before a voiced consonant—as Greeks have—it is difficult to learn to pronounce 'this man' properly as /ðis man/ rather than /ðiz man/.

There are three main difficulties about predicting whether transfer will take place, how strong its influence will be and in what direction it will go. The first difficulty has to do with similarity relations, the second with the fact that language learning proceeds simultaneously on many different levels, and the third has to do with what is taken to be successful language learning.

(i) *Similarity relations*

As a simplification, one can say that when learning consists of producing already acquired responses in new situations, transfer will be positive, and when learning consists of producing new responses in familiar situations, transfer will be negative. This supposes that the situations and the responses are either completely different or virtually identical, but in real life we are mostly concerned with situations and responses that are very similar, or rather similar or nor very similar at all. And here we run into circularity; we do not know to what extent situations strike people as similar, except by seeing how much transfer takes place. This makes prediction rather awkward, as well as creating a great deal of theoretical trouble.

However, in the field of language learning two things enable us to get on with the study of transfer effects, at least for practical purposes. Firstly, the difficulties about estimating degrees of similarity can be ignored, at least in the first instance. People either perceive a set of utterance occasions as equivalent and therefore a set of responses (links, chains, principles, plus their surface realizations) as applicable and appropriate, or they perceive them as not equivalent. Transfer will take place according to these judgements of functional equivalence, and the direction of transfer will depend on whether second language learners make the same judgements as native speakers do. Secondly, hypotheses concerning judgements of equivalence and applicability can initially be derived from contrastive linguistic descriptions. The point is not that the categories and rules of the linguists necessarily correspond to the concepts and principles of language users—though relationships must exist—the point is that detailed comparisons of languages provide an independent metric for estimating the similarity or lack of it between the various systems of the languages in question.

There are theoretical difficulties about contrastive linguistics but whatever the theoretical problems, the information derived from small scale comparisons —what Twaddell refers to as 'durable low level statements of the relevant portions of the two languages'—is extremely useful for various applied purposes. For instance in Norwegian the verb of motion is usually omitted in sentences which in English might be

Are you going to Glasgow tomorrow?

So Norwegians often produce

Shall you to Glasgow tomorrow?

because of transfer from

Skal du til Glasgow imorgen?

Sometimes the usefulness of contrastive description is denied because the errors that might be predicted on the basis of incongruent systems do not always occur, and other errors may be found which cannot be accounted for in contrastive terms. There are two points here. Firstly it is reasonable to assume, and the assumption is supported by innumerable observations, that when two language systems are not parallel the learners will, unless prevented, make predicted errors. But good teaching can prevent some of the likely errors from appearing at all. Robert Stockwell confidently expected Tagalog-speaking children learning English in the Philippines to make mistakes in sentences with the verb *to be* since Tagalog does not possess the copula. He found very few mistakes, and the reason was that the teachers were also aware of the problem and drilled such sentences assiduously.

Secondly, not all transfer has its source in the first language. The learner has all sorts of other previous learning behind him, including study strategies and the more elementary stages of the second language. In addition, not all error is caused by transfer. The type of error which most bothers a second language learner is not the misuse of a word or a structure, but a total blank, not being able to recall the item at all, i.e., plain forgetting. Forgetting is associated with lack of practice, length of time since acquisition, obliteration by intervening learning, and unclear understanding; and it is more likely to occur when there is no transfer from the first language, for bad or for good, because the differences are too great. There are also 'unsystematic' errors to be considered. Such errors are unsystematic in terms of linguistic description, but not in terms of the learning process. It is only very rarely that learning is an all-or-none affair, so that one moment the student is ignorant, and the next moment he is fully in command. Learning in the sense of always producing the right form at the right time accrues slowly, and when several things are in the process of being learned at the same time, and too many variables are involved, confusions easily arise; the concepts are fuzzy, the chains are not secure. This is how the funny errors happen, e.g., 'There was jam in the traffic', 'Heat the water and lay an egg in it'.

(ii) *The multi-level nature of language*

There are three main analytical levels in language, semantics, phonology and syntax, and within these levels there are a great many sublevels and distinctions. If one takes the view that people, like children, always 'talk about something', then the starting point of the process that leads to an actual utterance is the decision to transmit content of one sort or another. This means that the originating stimulus situation must be characterized in cognitive/semantic terms.

Next, the communicative intentions of the speaker must be realized in the appropriate language form. For instance, the form of sentences technically known as sentence mood is in fairly direct relation to what the speaker wants to say. If the speaker wants somebody to do something, he is likely to produce an imperative sentence, if he wants information he is likely to use an interrogative sentence, and if he wants to make a statement he will use an affirmative sentence. The relationship between the speaker's intentions and the consequent realization in sentence form is particularly clearly displayed in the 'systemic network' of Halliday and his associates (see for instance Halliday 1967–8, 1971). In Halliday's mood network for independent clauses the first choice is between imperative and indicative clauses. Indicative clauses can be either declarative or interrogative:

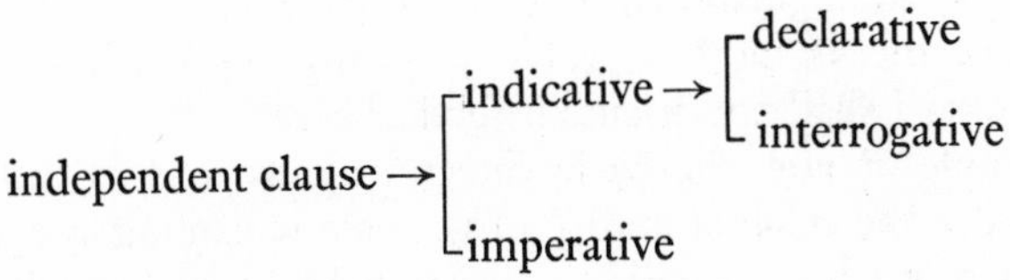

```
                                        ┌ declarative
                       ┌ indicative → [
independent clause → [                  └ interrogative
                       └ imperative
```

One of the reasons for distinguishing as a first step between indicative and imperative clauses is that the choice of the indicative—whether interrogative or declarative—specifies an obligatory subject element; in other words, these sentences must have a subject. But if an imperative sentence form is chosen as appropriate, then nothing yet is determined about the presence or absence of an overt subject. Compare:

The doctor is writing a report. *Is writing a report	declarative
Is the doctor writing a report? *Is writing a report?	interrogative
Doctor, write a report! Write a report!	imperative

If we include specification for overt realization, the network is supplemented:

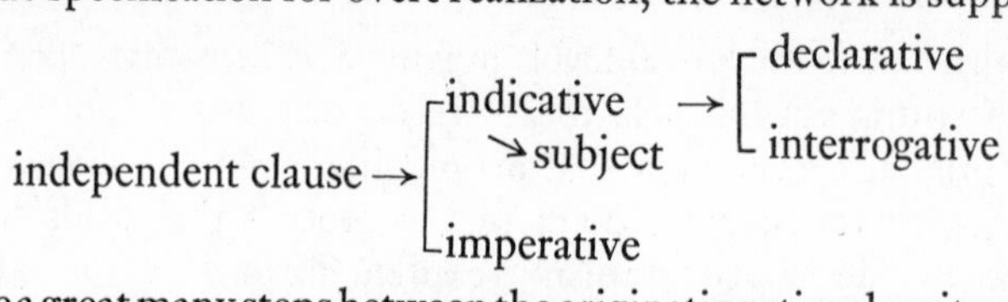

There are a great many steps between the originating stimulus situation which prompts an utterance, and the ultimate overt realization in language form. Whatever the linguistic characterization of these steps may be, in psychological terms they amount to a series of decisions about categorizations, i.e., about relevant concepts and their consequent appropriate responses. Many of these will be mediating responses, that is, they do not have direct overt realizations, rather they may concern increasingly delicate distinctions within more general categories, or they may concern the applicability of combination rules, each decision leading to the next until the actual utterance is produced. Since decisions, even simple ones, take time, and since fluent speakers can produce utterances very quickly, people must in practice have some means of cutting out a number of choice points—presumably by chaining smaller entities so that larger stretches can be triggered off and produced as a unit. How and under what conditions such larger response units become available for language use is something we know very little about. We are concerned here with the psycholinguistic aspect of what Miller calles 'chunking' (Miller 1956) but since this is more a problem of language performance than of language learning I shall not discuss it further here.

As an example of how the basic categorizations lead to different overt choices, consider the celebrated case of the colour naming system operated by the Hanunoo, a tribe in the Philippines (Conklin 1955), which has already been mentioned in chapter 6. In Indo-European languages colour terms are largely arranged according to hue, that is, by the sensations which are correlated with the wavelength of light rays and which are conveniently displayed separated out in the rainbow. The Hanunoo judge colour sensations by the dimensions of lightness and darkness and wetness and dryness, and apply four terms accordingly:

lightness	*darkness*	*wetness*	*dryness*
white	black	light green	maroon
pastels	all dark shades	light brown	red
		yellow	orange

In other words, semantic/cognitive conceptualizations underlie the choice of vocabulary items and distinctions.

The same applies to the choice of grammatical forms. Whatever the underlying categorizations that govern the choice of aspectual form in English and Russian, they are certainly not the same. Very roughly one might say that in

English, the completeness of an action is judged from the standpoint of the time of speaking, whereas in Russian a judgement of completeness requires that the speaker transport himself into the time of the action described, whether past or future. It is notoriously difficult for non-native speakers to learn to use these forms correctly. The point is not that it is impossible for an English speaker to learn to 'think like a Russian' (or vice versa); the point is that he must learn to do so in order to succeed in assigning the verb forms correctly.

At any stage in the processes leading from a decision to say something up to the actual utterance, similarities and dissimilarities between two languages may exist. When a learner is led to make a judgement of equivalence at any level or sublevel, transfer will occur, unless prevented. Unless similarities extend over several levels, the transfer will be positive at one level, and negative at another. For example, consider some of the choices involved in asking questions in English and Norwegian. First there is the decision to produce an interrogative sentence, rather than an imperative or affirmative one. Next the choice has to be made between polar and non-polar forms. Continuing the network we get:

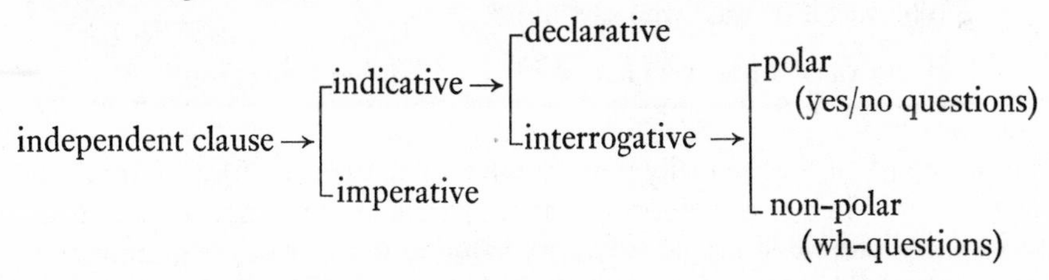

In English the choice of a polar question specifies inversion of the first elements of the verb phrase and the subject:

Have you seen him?

Exactly the same specification obtains for Norwegian:

Har du sett ham?

In English the choice of a non-polar question form specifies a wh- or question element. Norwegian is exactly the same:

English:	what	who	where	when	why	how
Norwegian:	hva	hvem	hvor	når	hvorfor	hvordan

So far the systems are entirely parallel, and transfer must be positive. But the ordering of the sentence elements in English depends on whether we are dealing with a subject question or an object question:

Who saw him?	(subject question)
Who(m) did he see?	(object question)

In Norwegian, in simple sentences the ordering of the sentence elements is already specified by the choice of non-polar, regardless of the locus of question:

Hvem så ham? (subject question, pronoun oblique)
Hvem så han? (object question, pronoun nominative)

Here the systems diverge and it is quite conceivable that a Norwegian might be led by the previous parallel stages to the overt form 'Who saw he?' meaning 'Who did he see?'.

The above example illustrates systems that are partly parallel and partly divergent. But nothing in language use depends on one system alone, and in this case there are two reasons why the transfer that might be expected, considering one system in isolation, does not often occur. In the first place, the do-transformation is assiduously practised in the teaching of English as a second language in Norway. In the second place, Norwegians often produce a rather more complex form of non-polar question both for subject questions and object questions:

Hvem var det (det var) som så ham? (subject question)
Who was it (it was) who saw him?

Hvem var det (det var) han så? (object question)
Who was it (it was) he saw?

The existence of these equally popular alternative question forms diminishes the transfer influence of the forms that are parallel to the English structures.

Another example of partial similarity is found in cases where grammatical forms in two languages are constructed along similar lines but where usage diverges. In both English and French, sentences can be constructed with the two main 'auxiliaries' as the only verb:

English: I *am* happy, I *have* a headache
French: Je *suis* malade, J'*ai* peur

When the collocations are parallel, in addition to the selection of the verb, there is all-over positive transfer:

I am tired → Je suis fatigué

But when the collocations are not parallel, there is positive transfer for the production of the verb, negative transfer for its use in a given context:

I am hungry → *Je suis faim

rather than the correct

I am hungry → J'ai faim

In fact this error does not often occur when English speakers learn French—teachers know by past experience that the error is very likely, and they usually take care to eradicate it at an early stage. However, the effects of mixed transfer situations can be persistent. Even advanced French and German students may be caught out in the use of the simple past in English, since their unmarked tense for referring to the past is constructed in parallel with the English present perfect:

I	have	read
Ich	habe	gelesen
J'	ai	lu

In unguarded moments even very highly able French and German students of English may respond to a question such as 'What did you do last night?' with the answer 'I have read a book'.

In vocabulary learning the same mixed transfer is very frequent. The formal similarities between words in two languages in phonological and morphological structure, as well as in spelling, lead to positive transfer for the recall of the item—one can remember the French word *sympathique* in French because it is very like *sympathetic* in English and forget what the Japanese equivalent is, because it is a totally different kind of word. But the meaning of even cognate words in two languages do not usually coincide entirely, so as far as appropriateness goes, the formal similarities lead to negative transfer effects. Books have been written about these so-called 'false' cognates.

Perceived parallelism at any level is likely to lead to transfer, but if the parallelism does not extend to other levels, the effect on learning tends to be seen as interference. This has implications for the next topic, which has to do with the criteria for judging success in language learning.

(iii) *Criteria of success in language learning*

The question is often asked, 'Is it more difficult to learn a second language which is closely related to one's first language, than it is to learn an unrelated language?'. Some people believe that it is more difficult to learn a closely related language, and recount anecdotes concerning, for example, the Norwegian wives of Swedish husbands who 'never learn to speak Swedish' and similarly for other married couples, e.g., Dutch and German, Serbian and Croat. If this should turn out to be true—if it really is more difficult to learn a closely related language—it would present difficulties for transfer theory. The greater the similarities between languages, the more transfer there should be, and the greater the positive effects should be. However, the idea that a closely related language is more difficult to learn is not confirmed by observation under more closely controlled conditions. In the intensive courses in foreign languages conducted by the American military authorities during and after the Second World War, a number of languages were taught. The methods of teaching were relatively uniform, the motivation of the learners was generally regarded as high, and regular assessments of language learning aptitude were made. On the basis of their experience, the instructors could provide estimates of the time it would take learners of high, average and low aptitude to learn different languages to three levels of proficiency, as shown in the following table. Level I is defined as 'Sufficient proficiency in speaking a

Table 2

Time requirements for foreign language achievement (in months)[1]

Languages	Class hours per day	Levels of proficiency					
		I		II		III	
		High Apt.	Av. Apt.	High Apt.	Av. Apt.	High Apt.	Av. Apt.
Italian, French, Spanish, German, Danish, Portuguese, Dutch, Swedish, Rumanian, Norwegian	1	4	6	No	No	No	No
	2	2	3	4	6	9	12
	3	1½	2	3	5	6	9
Russian, Polish, Persian, Greek, Finnish, Hungarian	1	6	8	No	No	No	No
	2	3	4	9	12	15*	18*
	3	2	3	6	9	12*	15*
Chinese, Korean, Japanese	1	6	9	No	No	No	No
	2	4	6	15	16	24*	30*
	3	3	4	12	15	18	24
Arabic, Vietnamese, Thai	1	6	9	No	No	No	No
	2	4	6	12	15	18*	24*
	3	3	4	9	12	15*	18*

(a) 'No' entries indicate that it is not practical to achieve that level of proficiency on a one-hour-a-day basis.
(b) Entries with an asterisk indicate that one must add three months in part-time training and using the language, preferably in the field.

[1] The table appeared first in Cleveland *et al.* 1960, and is reproduced in Jakobovits 1970.

foreign language to satisfy routine travel requirements'. Level II is defined as 'Basic familiarity with the structures of a language with sufficient proficiency in speaking to conduct routine business within a particular field. Sufficient familiarity with the writing system to read simple material with the aid of a dictionary'. Level III is defined as 'Fluency and accuracy in speaking with sufficient vocabulary for any ordinary requirements which do not involve the speaker in a technical subject outside his own speciality. Ability to read newspapers and documents with limited reference to a dictionary'.

Apart from other interesting information, the table shows clearly that for American speakers of English other Germanic languages and Romance languages are the easiest to learn, and Slavonic and other Indo-European languages are the next easiest, while non-Indo-European languages are the most difficult, i.e., they require a longer time to learn to comparable standards of proficiency.

The belief that closely related languages are more difficult to acquire probably derives from the fact that observers impose different standards. English people settling in Japan, or vice versa, are quite rightly admired if they manage to sustain their part in any conversation so that communication is achieved at the required level. For a 'difficult' language this represents a great deal of learning. But a Norwegian can settle in Sweden and function at a similar level without doing any learning at all, beyond a few concessions on certain vocabulary items and phrases, rather like an Englishman in America learning to say 'aluminum', 'elevator' and 'hi!'. In other words, it is very rare to learn a second language to such a standard that one is indistinguishable from a native speaker, whatever the second language. But it is much easier to learn to function intelligibly in a related second language, since the large amounts of transfer function in a positive direction when the criterion of learning is communicative effectiveness rather than exact formal correctness.

3.4 The characteristics of second language learners

3.4.1 CHILD BILINGUALISM

I shall not discuss child bilingualism (the informal learning of more than one language) beyond a brief consideration of whether or not children who learn more than one language are handicapped with respect to their monolingual equals. It may be, as Dell Hymes (1971) has suggested, that more children are brought up to speak two or more languages than one language only, taking the world population as a whole; but it is still true that for the majority of people in developed countries the learning of second languages occurs mainly in a formal setting. Most investigations in developed countries show a greater or lesser degree of backwardness in bilingual children, for instance studies in Wales (e.g., Jones 1952) and among immigrants and their children in the United States (Arsenian 1945, Darcy 1946). But other studies do not reveal any handicap, for instance a comparison between bilingual and monolingual Jewish children and monolingual children of English extraction in East London (Davies and Hughes 1927) and also studies on bilingual students of German and Scandinavian extraction at Chicago University.

In general, these findings suggest that bilingual children who belong to low prestige language groups and/or lower social classes tend to emerge with a degree of handicap in tasks requiring the use of the culturally dominant language, while children who come from groups who regard themselves as at least the equals of the surrounding groups show no reduction in their ability to perform in the wider community. Bilingual medium schools form an intermediate step between the informal 'natural' bilinguals and the typical formal learning situation. The findings here indicate that high prestige projects with children who are not disadvantaged work well, i.e., children do not lose ground in their vernacular and learn more of the second language (Lambert 1970). But in the majority of cases bilingual schools have been set up for members of culturally and socially disadvantaged communities, and on the whole the results are fairly depressing (Gaarder 1970).

3.4.2 LEARNERS OF SECOND LANGUAGES IN A FORMAL SETTING

In the developed countries, the majority of children who learn foreign languages at school start doing so around 11 to 13 years of age. There are in many countries projects under which language learning starts earlier, from about 8 or 9 years of age, but as far as I know these projects tend to remain at the 'experimental' stage. In particular the continuity of learning once the child changes from primary to secondary school is often lacking. I shall assume that the significant majority of those who learn second languages in formal school situations are between 12 and 22 years of age, give or take a year or two. Though there are obvious differences between a 12-year-old and a 22-year-old, on the whole the similarities that exist across these age groups are greater than any similarity that exists between the youngest second language learner and very young first language learners.

Firstly, second language learners differ from first language learners in already possessing a language. Secondly, in the cases under consideration, second language learners differ from first language learners in that they are learning in a formal setting. Thirdly, from about the age of 12 onwards, children begin to learn to handle explicit abstractions; they can use formulations of concepts and principles, they can go from the general to the particular and from the particular to the general. Of course the skill and sophistication in handling metalanguage increases over the decade, but the beginnings are there at the age of 12. Fourthly, none of the learners in the older age group have the young child's delight in practising. Young children appear to derive pleasure from endless repetition of skills already perfected or nearly perfected. This can be seen in activities as diverse as the child's endless dropping of objects from a pram at about one year of age, and the tireless practising of question tags, why-questions, etc. at 3 to 7 years of age. Finally, second language learners sooner or later become aware of how much more there is to learn, and though by skilful teaching the feeling of progress can be maintained for long stretches of time, eventually realization sets in of how far there is to go before useful command can be acquired, with consequent loss of morale.

There is a popular notion that young children are somehow more talented at learning second languages, even in formal settings, than older children and young adults. Occasionally this is linked to the notion of critical periods; if the learning has not taken place within a given period, it is supposed not to come about at all, or only with great difficulty. As far as I am aware there is no objective support for this supposition; in fact such findings as there are go in the opposite direction. Thorndike (1928) conducted an experiment in which learners of various ages were taught Esperanto, using the grammar-translation methods which prevailed at the time. The extreme groups consisted of young people between the ages of 9 and 18 on the one hand, and adults over 35 on the other. The young group received twice the formal instruction that the adults received, and yet the children learned less than half of what the adult group learned. Cheydleur (1932) ran an experiment in teaching French, comparing High School students aged 12–17 with adults aged 20–60+ who were attending evening classes. All groups had the same method, the same teachers, the same work and the same test. The results showed that 64 per cent of the adults in the evening classes did as well as the best 25 per cent of the High School students. This experiment also was carried out in a grammar-translation learning situation.

Some people believe that the critical period might well be finished before the ages that are here considered. But the air of disillusionment that has crept into reports on the teaching of second languages to children from the age of 6 or 8 indicate that there is no age at which learning is miraculously easy. Even for first language learning, whatever scant evidence there is goes against the notion of critical periods. Kramer et al (in press) tested children between 8 and 12 and young people between 12 and 20 for their understanding of sentences like

> Ask John what book to read.
> John asked Mary what to paint.

No instruction was given, but those who failed were retested two years later. There was no difference between the two age groups in amount of increased understanding.

There remains the notion that what children may be better at is discrimination and pronunciation. This idea is on the whole more reasonable but even here there is no very compelling evidence.

3.5 Individual differences in second language learners

Though broad similarities exist, particularly in comparison with pre-school first language learners, there are undoubted differences between individuals who receive instruction in foreign languages. Many investigations have been carried out to try to predict success in language learning, and in so doing to identify those characteristics of the learners which are associated with success, e.g. Learned and Wood (1938), Carroll and Sapon (1959), von Wittich (1962), Pimsleur (1966), Davies (1971).

3.5.1 GENERAL LEARNING ABILITY

The relationship between success in learning languages and in learning school subjects in general has been investigated in a number of studies. The relationship is expressed by the statistical index of correlation. A correlation value of +1.00 indicates perfect correspondence between two sets of marks, while a value of 0 indicates no correspondence at all.[1] A number of studies have ascertained the correlation between measured IQ (which expresses general learning potential) and marks for second language learning, as well as the correlation between marks for other school subjects and second language marks:

Correlations between IQ and second language marks

Learned & Wood	von Wittich	Pimsleur	Carroll
0.46	0.48	0.46	0.34–0.53

Correlations between averaged marks for other subjects and second language marks

von Wittich	Pimsleur
0.73	0.62

These correlations indicate that success in language learning has a good deal in common with success in learning other subjects. However, since the correlations are only moderate, there must be other relevant factors at work in language learning.

This realization led to the construction of language aptitude tests, the best known being Pimsleur's Language Aptitude Battery (LAB) and Carroll and Sapon's Modern Language Aptitude Test (MLAT) (Pimsleur 1966, Carroll and Sapon 1959). What intelligence tests mainly sample after the age of 12 or 13 is the ability to carry out logical operations involving verbal abstractions. The correlations show this to be relevant to second language learning but since it is already being tapped by intelligence tests, it would be superfluous to tap it all over again in the additional tests. So the test designers looked for

[1] For a further elaboration on the concept of correlation see the section on testing in Volume 4.

other abilities more directly related to language. In both aptitude tests certain sub-tests have shown themselves over and over again to correlate with language learning success. The tests therefore indicate some of the more specific abilities that are characteristic of good language learners. These may be referred to as phonetic coding ability, grammatical sensitivity, inductive learning ability and associative memory.

3.5.2 PHONETIC CODING ABILITY

'Phonetic coding ability' is Carroll's expression; Pimsleur talks about 'auditory ability'. What both authors refer to is the learner's ability to go from heard sound to printed symbol, and from symbol to sound. It is tested by quick learning jobs, e.g., learning new words to refer to digits and then recognizing the number corresponding to the new words spoken on tape, or learning new symbols for known sounds, e.g., learning to associate phonetic symbols with the sounds of nonsense words. As Carroll puts it:

> Apparently, success in this learning task depends on success in remembering the identities of the sounds. It seems obvious that phonetic coding ability is demanded in the learning of a foreign language, because the individual must not only learn the identities of the new phonemes of that language, but must also recognize and remember the phonetic sequences represented by the morphemes, words, and intonation contours of that language. (Carroll 1971, p. 4)

Pimsleur got correlations of 0.53 and 0.56 with success in French and Spanish on his two listening tests tapping this area, indicating a substantial measure of association.

3.5.3 GRAMMATICAL SENSITIVITY

This is tested in MLAT by asking people to identify the grammatical functions in English sentences. A model sentence which has one part underlined, e.g., the subject, is presented and the person has to choose whatever functions as subject in the second sentence. In this way

> Some adolescents and adults (and even some children) can be made to demonstrate an awareness of the syntactical structure of the sentences they speak . . . Even among adults, there are large individual differences in this ability, and these individual differences are related to success in learning foreign languages, apparently because this ability is called upon when the student tries to learn grammatical rules and apply them in constructing or comprehending new sentences in that language. (Carroll 1971, p. 5)

Pimsleur's Language Analysis, a miniature grammar-translation task involving about a dozen Kabardian lexical items and about the same number of categories and rules, probably taps something of the same ability.

3.5.4 INDUCTIVE LEARNING ABILITY

Carroll defines inductive ability in language learning as 'the ability to examine language material (in either auditory or printed form) and from this to notice and identify patterns of correspondence and relationships involving either meaning or grammatical form'. He goes on:

> A typical method of measuring this ability is to present materials in an artificial language in such a way that the individual can induce the grammatical and semantic rules governing that language. Such an ability might well be called upon in the learning of an actual foreign language, because even in a form of teaching that emphasizes the formal presentation of rules, the learner must inevitably work out the application of the rules for himself. (Carroll 1971, p. 6)

The most direct test of inductive learning ability is probably Pimsleur's Language Analysis where the job is to induce some of the rules of Kabardian.

3.5.5 ASSOCIATIVE MEMORY

This is much the same as 'rote' learning. It is tapped in all four of the sound-symbol tests (two in Carroll and two in Pimsleur). In addition, it is tested by Pimsleur's Language Analysis, and by Carroll's Paired Associates, in which students memorize 24 pairs of Kurdish-English translation equivalents and after two minutes are asked to select the right English word for each Kurdish word.

The isolation of these four specific factors characteristic of good language learners is not the result of intuitive guesswork, it is the outcome of repeated statistical comparisons which estimate what various kinds of tests and sub-tests have in common. The labelling of each factor is arrived at by inspection of the contents of those tests which are shown statistically to group together. Of the four factors which have been isolated, two represent simple learning, i.e., learning in the lower half of Gagné's hierarchy (S → R links and chains), and two represent more complex learning, i.e., learning in the top half of Gagné's hierarchy (concepts and principles). Along another dimension, two factors are specific to a particular level of language, phonetic coding to the phonological/graphological levels and grammatical sensitivity to the syntactic level, while the other two factors, associative memory and inductive learning ability, are not level specific, nor are they entirely language specific. The relationships can be presented in diagram form:

	Simpler learning	More complex learning
More language specific	phonetic coding ability	grammatical sensitivity
Less language specific	associative memory	inductive learning ability

To complete the picture, it should be mentioned that both LAB and MLAT include vocabulary subtests because it has been shown that information relating to the students' vocabulary in their native language is relevant to the prediction of language learning success. One is reminded of the observation that children who develop fast in first language acquisition have strikingly larger vocabularies, not only by age but by stages of syntactic development, than children who acquire their first language at a more moderate pace.

Typical correlations between language aptitude scores and marks for second languages are much the same range as those between IQ scores and second language scores:

author	test	criterion	correlation values	number of learners
Pimsleur	LAB	French marks	0.63	1507
Carroll	MLAT	second language marks	range 0.78–0.25 median 0.54	1868 (the sum for all comparisons)
Davies	LAB	French test scores	0.63 0.37 0.41	1062 144 97

When language aptitude test results are combined with average examination marks in other subjects or with IQ test scores, and the sum is then correlated with second language results, the correlations tend to improve.

Pimsleur at one stage compared the correlations between the LAB subtests and second language marks and got 0.62. Then he added 'grade point average' as another sub-test, and in the 1964 validation study got a correlation of 0.72. Since then grade point average has been included in LAB as a standard subtest, but the dramatic improvement in size of correlations has not been entirely maintained. The 1966 report, dealing with over 3,000 students, gives correlations varying from about 0.60 to about 0.70.

Davies combined IQ test results with LAB scores (version including grade point average) and raised all-over correlation from 0.57 to 0.64 ($n = 1303$).

A number of sub-tests which were tried out failed to correlate with language learning success. For instance Pimsleur eliminated at an early stage a sub-test requiring skill in embedding sentences — at the time referred to as 'double based transformations'. The students were presented with pairs of sentences and had to transform them on the lines of the model:

John claims it } ⇒ John claims he is right
John is right }

At a much later stage Pimsleur rejected a rhymes test which demanded that students should list as many words as possible that rhyme with four given words. The fact that tests which by content seem to have direct bearing on linguistic rules or on 'creativity' fail to show relevance in test situations constitutes interesting (though negative) evidence of what may *not* be involved in language learning.

3.5.6 MOTIVATION

3.5.6.1 Self-rating of interest. Pimsleur includes *interest* in his test—students indicate their degree of interest in language study on a five-point scale. In his population of high school students this is a contributory variable. But Carroll has not found it worth while to include self-ratings of interest, and when Davies tried it in Britain he found that inclusion of an interest inventory raised the predictions by one degree only:

all over correlation IQ + LAB + MLAT/scores on French test	0.64
all over correlation IQ + LAB + MLAT + Interest/scores on French test	0.65

3.5.6.2 Type of motivation. Studies by Gardner and Lambert (1959) and Politzer (1953) have indicated that students who possess an integrated type of motivation tend to do better than students whose motivation is instrumental. Integrated motivation is found in students who admire and want to identify with the people whose language they are studying. Instrumental motivation is involved when students want to learn the language for various practical purposes, ranging from 'course requirement' to having to read the technical literature.

The Lambert and Politzer studies were made among college students in Canada and the United States. I do not know of similar comparative studies elsewhere, but the results may not be valid beyond North America, since general experience from other countries would not seem to confirm their observations. In small countries, where a proportion of the population have to learn in order to function in one or more of the major world languages, people learn. In countries where social advancement comes largely through education people learn, if the educational hurdles include a second language.

The point about motivation is that it keeps people at it. It is a massive learning job to acquire the skills which are necessary in order to function adequately in communicative situations using a second language. It does not matter what it is that makes learners persevere, it is the perseverance which is essential. People do not have to like language learning—though this helps—and they do not have to like the nation whose language they are learning, though this helps too; but as long as economic or social circumstances require successful language learning, determined people will learn.

3.6 Teaching practices and experimental evaluations

Currently there are two fairly prevalent general approaches to the teaching of second languages in formal situations, labelled by Carroll the *cognitive code theory* and the *audiolingual theory* respectively. Carroll describes the cognitive code learning theory as 'a modified up-to-date grammar-translation theory' according to which 'foreign language learning is a process of acquiring conscious control of the patterns of a second language largely through the study and analysis of these patterns as a body of knowledge'; while the audiolingual habit theory 'emphasizes the primacy of auditory discrimination and oral production habits over other aspects of language use, the importance of the automatization of habits and the role of repetition in such automatization'. He also stresses that 'neither theory has any really sound basis in psychological theory . . . apart from vague and tenuous affinities with contemporary Gestalt trends on the one hand and a general behaviourist outlook on the other' (Carroll 1966, pp. 35, 36).

This last point would be irrelevant were it not for the fact that people tend to muddle up their life philosophies with their evaluation of practical results. Jakobovits has described the dilemma in an exceptionally lucid way:

> This is a strange situation indeed. Teachers and therapists are practical people by necessity, and they ought not to be castigated for adopting methods which seem to work. The two most notable and successful accomplishments achieved by the Skinnerians are programmed instruction and behavioural modification, yet the theoretical foundations from which they have sprung are simplistic and inadequate in the extreme . . . . This is a curious paradox wherein surely lies the bankruptcy of the modern social scientific enterprise: what seems to work best on practical grounds should not it seems on theoretical grounds, and the theories that appear to be more sophisticated and more powerful do not enable us to develop effective practical approaches. (Jakobovits 1970, p. 34)

In the face of this honest acknowledgement of a painful dilemma, it is perhaps unkind to point out that theories which have been developed with very close reference to controlled observations and experiments would seem more likely to yield more immediately useful and practical recommendations than theories which aspire primarily to satisfy demands of inherent plausibility, logical coherence and descriptive economy.

The main problem about investigating the efficiency of varying methods of second language instruction is that those who are supposed to know how to set up learning experiments tend on the whole to investigate variables which have rather little to do with what goes on in the classroom—nearly the whole of the technical psychological literature provides examples. On the other hand, unfortunately, those who do know what goes on in classrooms do not usually have much sophistication in setting up controlled experiments or in interpreting results. For example, consider the problem of transfer across sense modalities: if initial learning is through the ear alone, is there transfer to visual presentation and if so how much, or if initial learning is by visual presentation how much, if any, transfer is there to auditory skills? Exaggerated claims have been made from time to time about purely auditory presentation not only producing better pronunciation but also producing better reading skills. When Carroll directed his attention to the problem, the position turned out to be far from simple:

The study by Pimsleur *et al.* (1964) suggests that the relative merit of the two sequences [auditory-visual and visual-auditory] depends on at least three important factors: first, the degree to which visual representations of sounds correspond to previously established orthographic habits of the learner; second, the learner's ability or foreign language aptitude; and third, the stage of learning. For high aptitude students, sequence does not matter either in early or later stages of learning; for low aptitude students, the auditory-visual (A-V) sequence is easier than the visual-auditory (V-A) sequence in early stages of learning, but in later stages of learning the V-A sequence becomes slightly easier than the A-V. For all students, regardless of ability, learning is harder in the case of 'high discrepancy' materials, i.e., materials in which one must learn an auditory response that is different from what the student expects on the basis of the orthography. Asher's (1964) quite elaborate and extensive study further illuminates the role of discrepancy between the spoken and the written language. He found that the amount of transfer from vision to audition depended on the language. It was large and positive for materials in Spanish, Japanese (using the Romaji script), Turkish, and Persian (using the conventional Persian script, completely unfamiliar to the subjects), but negative for Russian materials. Transfer from audition to vision was positive for Spanish, Japanese, and Russian, neutral for Turkish, and negative for Persian. The amount of transfer was generally greater in the V-A sequence than in the A-V sequence, but interactions with foreign language aptitude were not investigated. Asher found, as did Pimsleur *et al.*, that the relative superiority of the V-A sequence over the A-V sequence tended to disappear in later stages of learning. Salzman (1964) found a combined A-V and V-A approach superior to either sequence in the programmed teaching of Russian orthography. (Carroll 1966, 23–4)

Carroll concludes that in practice it probably makes little difference which sequence is adopted as far as ease of learning and amount of transfer is concerned. This quotation illustrates again the dangers inherent in taking the results of any one experiment and generalizing to the whole field.

The problem is related to the notion derived from Francis Galton, writing at the end of the 19th century, that people are divided into those who have predominantly 'auditory imagery' and those who have predominantly 'visual imagery'. The whole conception of auditory versus visual imagery presupposes that symbolic representations in some way mirror sensations, which is conceivable, but an idea that is out of favour at present. More seriously, nobody has succeeded in relating methods of presentation with individuals supposed to possess one or the other form of imagery.

Some very large scale projects have been undertaken in the last decade or so with the purpose of comparing teaching methods. One of the earlier investigations, by Scherer and Wertheimer (1964), caused some stir because it seemed to show that people taught by audiolingual methods were better at handling the spoken language, and people taught by the traditional methods were better at handling the written language. This was contrary to the current view at the time, which was that audiolingual methods produced better results all round. Technically, however, the whole experiment is seriously at fault for three main reasons:

(a) Assignment of students to groups was not random. Students were allowed to choose the type of class they wanted to go to.
(b) Tests to measure achievement were not validated and standardized in advance.
(c) In the second year, because of the experimental prestige effect, many students wanted to transfer from the traditional to the audiolingual classes, and this was permitted.

The Pennsylvania experiment (P. D. Smith 1970) is even more controversial. This large-scale comparison involving upwards of a hundred classes and their teachers in the high schools of the Commonwealth of Pennsylvania seemed to show that the traditional (i.e. the cognitive code theory) approach produced not only better results in tests of reading and writing comprehension, but also equal or better results in listening comprehension and speaking. However, as far as one can judge from the published reports the 'speaking test' (an interview) was technically so unreliable that no attention should be paid to the outcome. The classes taught by audiolingual or partly audiolingual approaches were superior to the traditional classes in a test of sound discrimination. Carroll, in examining the results, suggests that the reason why the traditionally taught students did as well or better than those taught with an audiolingual component might be that the particular test of listening comprehension employed (MLA) depended rather heavily on knowledge of vocabulary, and that the traditional classes had encountered more vocabulary through their reading than the audiolingual classes had.

The design of the Pennsylvania experiment was not seriously at fault. The attacks have concentrated on the practical execution: did the teachers adhere to the prescribed methods? Since there was a turn-over of one-third of the teachers, does this invalidate the experiment? Large-scale experiments are very vulnerable to the charge that practical things go wrong, while strictly controlled laboratory-type experiments are vulnerable to the charge that it is precisely the careful control exercised in the lab that makes the results difficult to apply to real-life situations.

In 1965 Carroll came to the 'rather commonplace conclusion that, by and large, students learn (if anything) precisely what they are taught' (Carroll

1965, p. 1069). Nothing that has happened since then seems to constitute a serious challenge to this statement. On the subject of transfer Carroll goes on to say: 'There are no mysterious transfers between language skills. For example, people do not learn to read unless they are taught to read, but once taught, their knowledge of grammar and lexicon acquired in oral-aural practice will aid them in reading.' And vice versa. Once the learners are beyond the elementary stages and the mechanics of all language skills have been taught, there are indications that there is massive transfer across language modes and skills, i.e., what has been learned either via listening or reading is available for use either through speaking or writing, within limits.

Edinburgh University has for some years required of all first year students whose native language is not English that they should take a test of English as a second language; the test used is the English Language Battery (ELBA). This consists of a Listening Part and a Reading Part. The Listening Part has three sub-tests concerned with phonological structure: phoneme discrimination, recognition of stress patterns and intonation patterns, and one sub-test of listening comprehension. The Reading Part has three sub-tests, one concerning choice of grammatical form in a given context, one vocabulary test and one reading comprehension. There were two standardizing samples consisting of 320 and 293 respectively.

The test scores of both groups were subjected to factor analysis, to see whether any specific factor other than all-over command of English would emerge. The results showed that there was one major factor dominating all sub-tests—in other words they had overwhelmingly more in common than there were differences between them. The common factor could only be labelled 'English'. In one sample there was a suggestion of a small degree of communality between all the listening tests on the one hand and all the reading tests on the other. In the second sample there was a suggestion of a small degree of communality between listening and reading comprehension on the one hand, and all the other sub-tests on the other. Since both effects were small, and neither was replicated in the other sample, not much weight can be attached to this finding. One must conclude that, at least at this level of command, the learners have available to them a general knowledge of the second language which they can draw upon in any task involving that language (Ingram 1970).

4 Conclusions

In reviewing the evidence from first language acquisition and second language learning, there is very little that one can be dogmatic about. Any résumé of findings must be subjective to some extent both in selection and emphasis. For me, the conclusions on balance are as follows.

4.1 First language acquisition

Given that a child is equipped with intact physiological systems, especially neurological systems, he will acquire command of the basic elements and patterns of language, provided he is reared in conditions which are reasonably adequate for his physical and personal needs. Similarly under the same conditions he will learn to walk and run, and to draw and throw things. Command of language is acquired under pressure of the child's need to relate to the people around him, and the need to communicate his developing perception and understanding of the world he is growing up in. The child employs strategies which enable him to communicate at a level compatible with his cognitive capacities. Within this limitation he constantly seeks for more sophisticated means of expressing himself, partly to make himself better understood, and partly to approximate to the norms of the community of which he aspires to be a member.

The main contribution of the people in the child's environment is to initiate the whole interaction game long before anything like language occurs in the child, to provide language models, and to be present and responsive, at least for some part of the child's waking day. All that is required for the child to acquire sufficient command of language is that adults and children should see a lot of one another and talk a lot in a mutually satisfying atmosphere, so that the potential language/cognition interaction can develop fully. In this type of setting, deliberate teaching of the forms of the language is unusual, and when it is tried it does not seem to work. On the other hand, formal and direct teaching of the forms of language has been shown to work for children who have been relatively deprived in the sort of experiences that lead to normal language development. These programmes are also effective with children who are not suffering from any language handicap. Direct teaching takes place not in the context of interaction with parents, but in the form of language games directed by some other adult either on television or in child centres outside the home.

Two reasons for this paradoxical situation suggest themselves. Firstly, a child who is reared in an environment which is favourable for language development is already developing as fast as he can, and mastering as many rules and patterns as his memory span and cognitive ability permit. Anything he is not yet ready for, he simply ignores. Secondly, and this may be the more important reason, in the interaction between children and parents it is mutual understanding that matters, and any attempt by parents to withhold or deny understanding until correct forms are produced will just lead to rage reactions. In a direct teaching situation the child will learn by the usual didactic methods if two conditions are met. Firstly, there must be mutual agreement between teacher and taught about the purpose of the activity, which is not mutual here-and-now communication but the acquisition of certain language skills. Secondly, the skills to be acquired must be within the child's general cognitive span. If these conditions are met, then learning will take place provided the usual learning needs are attended to. The teacher must arouse and maintain motivation, provide sufficient practice in a variety of settings, arrange for suitable spacing of the material to ensure a steady rate of success, and so on.

4.2 Second language learning

4.2.1 LEVELS OF ACHIEVEMENT

There is a general feeling that second language learning is rather unsuccessful, in comparison with first language acquisition. Various explanations for the difference have been offered. It is said, for example, that children do not 'learn' their first language in the usual sense of the word, they are born with it; that children are much better at language learning than adolescents or adults; that the methods of second language instruction are poor; that the teachers are inadequate, and so on. Of course, instances of incompetence can always be found, but I do not believe that the lack of success in second language learning, when it exists, has much to do with inadequacy either in teachers or in students. The dedication of most language teachers and their constant search for improved methods is obvious to any observer, and the learning ability of adolescents and young adults is found to be higher than that of young children in practically all comparative studies. All the same, the vast majority of first language learners acquire proper communicative competence and not many second language learners do. In my view, this is due to the different conditions under which first and second language learning takes place. These conditions can be considered under the headings of exposure, drive, context and reinforcement.

(a) *Exposure.* A typical second language learner is exposed to the target language from four to six hours a week during the school term. This cannot begin to approximate to the amount of exposure experienced, all his waking hours, by a child learning his first language.

(b) *Drive.* The child's drive—his need to relate and to be understood—is one of the central factors of his life. The intelligent interest which a student brings to the task of learning a second language is pale by comparison. There is only one way in which an adult can experience something approaching the intensity of drive which he brought to his first language, and that is by being in a comparable situation. An individual may find himself in a place where people speak a language he does not know, and where there is nobody to interpret. Learning in such cases can be incredibly fast.

(c) *Context.* Children learn in direct and immediate situational context. Second language teachers do their best to provide context for language work for much of the time, but nobody in a formal setting can arrange appropriate contextual support for every utterance. It is rarely possible in a classroom situation to relate utterances to a real communicative purpose, to a direct and practical need to be understood.

(d) *Reinforcement.* Children in homes which provide good learning conditions receive immediate feedback most of the time about whether they have been understood or not. This provides the child with information both about the content and the form of what he has said. The child also receives information specifically about form. In their own speech adults provide the models for the forms of the language, and observations suggest that in the period when the child is learning a particular structure the adults round him tend to produce that structure more often than they do at other times. More directly, though adults do not overtly correct the child's errors, they quite often, when the child has produced some 'error', casually incorporate in their next remark the adult form of what the child just said. In second language learning conditions immediate feedback of right and wrong is difficult to arrange. The information can be provided for only a sample of the learners' productions and for written work it is always delayed. The information usually comes in the form of overt correction of errors, and it is difficult to escape the derogatory implications of this.

4.2.2 THE CONTRIBUTION OF THE SECOND LANGUAGE LEARNER

What the second language learner brings to the formal learning situation seems to be:

(a) A declared general interest in learning the language, which in many cases fades after a couple of years.

(b) A set of general learning abilities, both for simpler and more complex forms of learning, and some special language learning aptitudes, including sound-symbol sensitivity and grammatical sensitivity. These abilities will as a rule vary together, in the sense that a learner who possesses a high level of ability of one sort will also possess relatively high levels of ability all round. In a significant minority of cases there will be anomalies: people who are startlingly good at learning languages and not outstanding at anything else and, conversely, people who do well in other subjects but who are bad at languages.

(c) No idea of the magnitude of the task.

(d) No specially preconceived ideas about how the instruction should proceed, except for what he has picked up from the educational grapevine about the 'modern approach'.

The problem facing the teacher is that until the learner has reached a very high stage of proficiency indeed, his cognitive abilities and communicative needs far outstrip his means of expressing himself in the second language. The learner is therefore denied for most of the learning process the satisfaction of being able to talk about what he wants to talk about—while the child acquiring his first language experiences this satisfaction every day.

The teacher can try to deal with the situation in two ways; either he can try to keep the learner from realizing how far he has to go, or he can find some way of bringing the goals nearer; or he can try to do both. The first approach is the one that is generally practised; the students are made to feel pleased with their progress because they proceed through the book and pass their exams. But at some stage disillusionment sets in, when something makes the students realize that for all their hard work and good marks, they still cannot use the language for any realistic communicative purpose.

The other approach, to shorten the time needed to achieve real communicative competence, could be achieved by intensive courses. (By an 'intensive course' I mean one in which students do nothing but practise the language all day and every day for twelve to eighteen months.) This might not be desirable from the point of view of the learner's general education but it should provide mastery of the language. As far as I know the intensive course approach has never been tried within any school system, although intensive courses for businessmen and especially for military personnel and foreign service officials are not uncommon.

4.3 Implications for second language teaching

The relationship between linguistic and psychological theories and what goes on in the classroom, though real, is very indirect, and the implications of a survey such as this for language teaching practice are not very obvious or compelling. My own conclusions derive from the following four considerations:

(a) Second language learning consists of both simple and complex learning, starting with perceptual identifications and ending up with the understanding and application of abstract rules. All forms of learning are necessary and interdependent.

(b) As the learner grows older he is increasingly able to handle abstract concepts explicitly, while he may lose something of his skill in perceptual and articulatory functions.

(c) From the results of experimental learning theory, it appears that special attention to any form of learning will produce success mainly in that form of learning. If we try to arrange optimal conditions for memorizing chains we are likely to produce good results in memorizing chains; if we try to arrange optimal conditions for the discovery of new concepts we may, with luck, produce good results in discovering concepts.

(d) From a broad survey of the results of language teaching experience and experiments, Carroll concludes that in practice learners learn best what the teachers make them concentrate on.

These considerations point to the need for an eclectic approach to second language teaching, one that combines the best features of the audiolingual and the cognitive code approaches. Among the valuable contributions of the audiolingual approach are (a) the emphasis on perceptual and motor skills, (b) the insistence that the units presented for imitation and practice should as far as possible be actual units of utterance rather than isolated sounds or words, and (c) the insistence that grammar should be presented as sequential syntactic patterns rather than as tables, because the chains that become established by practice must be those which are directly relevant for using the language. Among the valuable contributions of the cognitive code approach are (a) the emphasis given to the need for learning language forms in association with meaning, and (b) the fact that it utilizes the capacity and the need of the learners for understanding the underlying abstract systems of the language. However, the translation of such general conclusions into actual classroom practice is a complicated affair, and it sometimes seems that there are as many recipes for success as there are successful teachers.

5 Further reading

Child Language

Anything by Roger Brown, for instance:

Brown, Roger, Cazden, Courtney B. and Bellugi, Ursula 1968. The Child's Grammar from I–III. In John Hill (ed.) *Minnesota Symposia on Child Development*, 2, 28–73. Minneapolis: University of Minnesota Press. Also in A. Bar-Adon and W. F. Leopold (eds.) 1971, pp. 382–412.

Brown, Roger 1970. The first sentences of child and chimpanzee. *Psycholinguistics: Selected Papers*. New York: The Free Press. Chapter 8.

Bar-Adon, A. and Leopold, W. F. (eds.) 1971. *Child Language: A Book of Readings*. New Jersey: Prentice Hall. The principal sourcebook in the field of child language. There are extracts from longer works and books, starting with Tiedemann 1789, and reprints of whole papers. All the well-known names are represented: e.g. Stern, Jespersen, Jacobson, Leopold, from the earlier European tradition and Brown, Braine, Berko, Ervin-Tripp, Bever, McNeill, Slobin etc. representing the more recent period. With very few exceptions the editors have managed to avoid the more esoteric type of theoretical paper, and have given emphasis to papers which have shown themselves to be durable, either because they present data in an organized or insightful manner, or because the theories propounded have proved fruitful over a period of time.

Huxley, R. and Ingram, E. (eds.) 1971. *Language Acquisition: Models and Methods*. London: Academic Press. The edited report of papers and discussions of a conference in 1968 on child language. One of the first attempts to bring together linguistic, psychological, sociological and clinical views. The volume in preparation by Eric and Elisabeth Lenneberg: *Foundations of Language Development: A Multi-Disciplinary Approach.* UNESCO will be doing the same job on a much larger scale.

Young Native Speakers

Anything by William Labov, for instance:

Labov, William 1970. The study of non-standard English. Champaign, Illinois: National Council of Teachers of English.

Labov, William 1971. The logic of non-standard English. In F. Williams (ed.) *Language and Poverty: Perspectives on a theme.* Chicago: Markham Publishing Co.

Williams, F. (ed.) 1970. *Language and Poverty: Perspectives on a theme.* Chicago: Markham Publishing Co. A series of papers dealing with the problems of deprived children and adolescents, seen mainly from the point of view of the American large city population. Most of the authors are deeply engaged, and their frankly partisan and passionate approach makes very good and interesting reading.

Robinson, W. P. and Rackstraw, S. J. 1972. *A Question of Answers.* London: Routledge. The most thorough investigation of aspects of language use by English children. The orientation is basically that of social psychology. The language data are handled within the tradition of British linguistics.

Second Language Learning

Anything by John B. Carroll, for instance:

Carroll, John B. 1965. Research on teaching foreign languages. In N. L. Gage (ed.) *Handbook of Research on Teaching.* Chicago: Rand McNally. 1060–1100.

Carroll, John B. 1966. Research in foreign language testing: the last five years. In R. Mead (ed.) *Language Teaching Broader Contexts.* North East Conference on the teaching of foreign languages. 12–42

Gagné, Robert M. 1965. *The Conditions of Learning.* New York: Holt, Rinehart, Winston. (London Edition 1969). A non-strident attempt to apply what is known about the psychology of learning to classroom conditions. The author does not presuppose any previous knowledge on the part of the learner, his approach is non-sectarian and empirical, and he is concerned with all subjects not just language learning.

Jakobovits, Leon A. 1970. *Foreign Language Learning: A Psycholinguistic Analysis of the Issues.* Rowley, Mass: Newbury House Publishers. A collection of papers and monographs by an author firmly within the psycholinguistic school. Slightly repetitive, but very useful for systematic surveying of the field, and very lucid on the difficulties of relating theory to practice.

8 RUTH CLARK
Adult Theories, Child Strategies and their Implications for the Language Teacher

1 Introduction

Language teachers teach people, and on occasion chimpanzees.[1] Psychologists often study rats, pigeons, cats, dogs and monkeys. However, they are also supposed to be experts on people and how they learn. They ought, therefore, to be able to help the teacher to decide how to teach. In this chapter I shall view the psychology of language learning through the eyes of different observers. Some see language learning as the acquisition of habits, some liken it to concept formation, others compare it to the acquisition of a motor skill, yet others see in it the manifestation of an inherited structuring device. I shall try and synthesize the various approaches, borrowing some key concepts from Piaget's theory of the development of thought processes in the child. I shall go on to describe some experimental work on comprehension with adults before discussing, within the framework of the above synthesis, some questions which are important to the language teacher. These are: Should error be allowed to occur? Should pupils be exposed to language that they cannot produce? Are drills useful? Should grammar be taught explicitly? etc. Throughout, my examples will be drawn from first language learning since this is the learning situation with which I am most familiar. I hope to show that the insights provided by a study of first language learning can be of great help to the teacher of a second language.

2 Language as simple stimulus response connections

One way of approaching the study of complex behaviour is to look first at the most immediately visible aspects of that behaviour. When listening to people speaking we hear them reacting to situations and to the speech of others, and we hear them producing words in sequence. A natural approach, then, is to look for regularities in the relationship of an utterance to the situation in which it is produced and to the utterance to which it is a response. Another natural approach is to look for regularities in the relationship of a word to the words

[1] See Gardner and Gardner 1969 and Premack and Premack 1972.

with which it occurs in an utterance. It is upon these associations between words in utterances, and between utterances and events in the world, that educationists favouring behaviourist views of learning have concentrated their attempts to account for language behaviour. Two main theories of learning have been advanced by the behaviourists, and have had a major influence on language teaching. I shall refer to these as reinforcement learning theory and contiguity learning theory. In this section I shall concentrate on reinforcement learning. Contiguity learning, which has given rise to mediation theory, will be introduced in section 3 below.

2.1 Reinforcement learning

Reinforcement theory as applied to language learning concentrates on the links between utterances and situations, rather than on the internal structure of utterances. According to proponents of this theory, effective language behaviour consists of producing responses to the correct stimuli. These links between stimuli and responses have become habitual as a result of being reinforced. If a child produces an utterance which happens to be an appropriate response to the situation, or to the previous adult utterance, the mother will reward him with some sign of approval. This makes the response more likely to occur in similar circumstances in the future. If the child's utterance is inappropriate, the mother will fail to reinforce it, and so the probability of the response recurring in similar circumstances will not be increased.

This is an explanation of how the child comes to produce speech, but the theory can also be used to explain how he comes to understand it. If a child responds correctly to a spoken stimulus he will be reinforced, if he responds incorrectly he will not be reinforced. In this way adult utterances will become discriminating stimuli for the production of responses. The child will begin to give evidence of understanding the speech he hears, as well as being able to produce speech which is appropriate to the situation.

But how do these rewards from the mother come to have the effect of reinforcing the responses that occasion them? Some psychologists have argued that at first only basic biological rewards, such as food or the cessation of pain, can have this reinforcing effect. Since in infancy the child's mother is usually the source of relief from hunger and discomfort, her warmth and approval, by constant association with these sensations, come to be reinforcing in themselves. (Explanations are not usually attempted of how the basic rewards have the effect of strengthening the responses which precede them.) This process whereby previously neutral stimuli can come to have the same effect as primary reinforcers is known as secondary reinforcement. According to the theory, any stimulus can become a secondary reinforcer in this way, by association with a primary reinforcer. It follows that verbal stimuli can become secondary reinforcers. Words and phrases, such as 'good' and 'well done' and 'that's right', if paired sufficiently often with primary reinforcers, can themselves become secondary reinforcers and can be used by the mother to establish new habits.

Reinforcement theory, then, accounts for verbal behaviour by identifying utterances as responses, discriminating stimuli or secondary reinforcers. However, if each individual speech habit had to be trained independently, learning would be very slow. We rarely meet a stimulus which is perfectly identical to one we have met before. Yet we are responding to new stimuli all the time. Behaviourists account for this fact in terms of stimulus generalization. If a child has been reinforced for producing a particular utterance in one stimulus situation, he will produce that response to other situations which are similar to the first. Also, if he has been reinforced for responding to an adult utterance in a particular way, he will respond in that way to other utterances which are similar.

To summarize, reinforcement theorists put the emphasis on links between observable events. They see the language capacity as composed of a number of discrete units of behaviour, independently trained, rather than as an integrated system. It is worth pointing out that according to this view the production of an utterance and the comprehension of the same utterance are to be explained by reference to quite independent learning experiences. One learns to produce an utterance by producing it in the appropriate circumstances and then being rewarded for doing so. One learns to comprehend an utterance by reacting to it appropriately and being rewarded for doing so. Essentially the reinforcement model identifies learning with learning to produce responses in the appropriate circumstances; it is not concerned with how the responses themselves are formulated or how they come to be produced in the first place so that they can then be linked by selective reinforcement to the right circumstances. If an explanation is given of how responses come to be produced in the first place it is in terms of simple imitation of adult models. The reason why the child imitates, according to this view, is that the behaviour of the mother functions as a secondary reinforcer—because it is usually she who relieves his basic needs—so it is satisfying to the child if he himself can reproduce that behaviour (Miller and Dollard 1941).

At this point I must mention that the description I have just given of reinforcement theory is a kind of composite of a number of points of view. Most proponents of the theory would agree with the main features, but there is disagreement about detail. For instance, some theorists believe that just as reward increases the likelihood of a response recurring, so punishment decreases the likelihood. Perhaps the best known version of the theory of reinforcement, and the one that has been applied the most assiduously to the explanation of language learning, is that of B. F. Skinner (Skinner 1953). Two aspects of Skinner's particular theory should be stressed here, since they will be picked up later on. In the first place, he is very strongly of the opinion that aversive training by punishment of wrong responses is quite ineffective, and that all reinforcement should be in the form of reward for correct responses. Secondly, Skinner has developed a procedure called shaping, which he has used extensively in the training of animals to perform complex actions. According to this procedure, the trainer will at first reinforce an action which is only a gross approximation to the one he is aiming to make the animal produce. After a while, he will cease to reinforce the animal's action until the animal modifies it so that it resembles the desired action more closely. By a series of such successive approximations to the desired action, the trainer gradually shapes the behaviour of the animal.

2.2 Some problems for reinforcement theory

I have indicated that the concepts of reinforcement, imitation and generalization are basic features of reinforcement theory. I shall now look in more detail at these three aspects of the learning process.

2.2.1 REINFORCEMENT

The first question to be asked is whether it is indeed true, as the theory suggests, that learning cannot take place without reinforcement. It has been shown in laboratory experiments with animals that they will learn to perform a variety of actions even if they are given no reward for doing so (Blodgett 1929, Butler 1954). It seems that activity can be its own reward, and that training procedures do not need to be tied exclusively to the principle of reinforcement. Furthermore, studies of children's conversations with their mothers in the early stages of language acquisition show that it is rare for the mother to praise the child explicitly for producing an appropriate utterance (Brown, Cazden and Bellugi 1968, E. Lieven, personal communication). It seems, then, that the child, in common with the rat and the monkey, will learn without requiring constant rewards for doing so.

In cases where the child is commended, it will often be for producing an utterance which is by no means fully acceptable by the standards of adult English. For instance, when Adam in his third year said 'You a girl, Mummy?' it came more easily to commend his understanding than to criticize his syntax and choice of lexical item. How, then, does the child move from his inadequate version? Skinner would suggest that the behaviour is gradually improved by shaping. However, this explanation is open to question, as we shall see by looking at one instance of a mother withholding reinforcement for an unacceptable utterance. David aged two and three quarters said 'I done it', instead of 'I did it'. The mother said 'What?' to which the child replied 'Like same granny say'. Two things seem to be clear from this exchange and the accompanying behaviour. In the first place the child was aware that his utterance did not meet with approval from his mother. Secondly, the child did not know what precisely was wrong with the utterance. In other words, before he can modify his utterance in an appropriate way the child needs to understand the basis of the reinforcement.[1] By focusing on whether or not a response is reinforced the theory neglects a crucial factor, which is the child's understanding of what makes the structure of his response unacceptable, or what aspect of the relationship of the response to the circumstances in which it was produced makes the response inappropriate. Skinner's theory, in common with other versions of reinforcement theory, fails to provide a theoretical apparatus which can deal with such problems.

Evidently it is not enough to know whether one's utterance is acceptable or not, one needs information as to why it is or is not acceptable. Traditional discussions of reinforcement have confused two of its functions, that of providing reward to motivate action and that of providing information as to the adequacy of an action (Annett 1969). Behaviourists have concentrated on the motivating function, assuming that if they explain *why* habits are formed it is unnecessary to explain *how* they are formed. I have mentioned that learning does not always need to be motivated by externally applied rewards. However, it certainly does depend on the feedback of information about the correctness of response. It may be more fruitful, therefore, to concentrate on this function of reinforcement, and consider how information about correctness of response can be communicated.

One kind of feedback that has been observed in interchanges between mother and child is the expansion of the child's utterance by the mother. The child produces a childlike utterance and the mother expands it into the adult form, usually supplying the missing grammatical words. This may seem to be a very helpful form of feedback, but let us look at a further example of a conversation between mother and child, which shows once more that it is a mistake to postulate mechanisms for language change which take no account of the problems a child will have in making use of the feedback provided. Adam, aged two and a half, said 'Put hat'. His mother expanded 'You're putting your hat on'. Adam modified his utterance to 'Put hat on', but henceforth used 'hat on' to mean 'hat'. He had taken it that he was being corrected because the word he had used was wrong, being unable to respond in any other way at that time to the information provided by the expansion. This usage—'hat on' for 'hat'—persisted for some time, and at a later period, when he was

[1] This recalls a puzzling feature of the technique of shaping behaviour. We have seen that at one stage in the training of an animal the trainer stops reinforcing his responses. According to reinforcement theory one would expect that the animal's response would cease altogether when the trainer was no longer reinforcing it. Perhaps a clue to this problem lies in Skinner's admission that this procedure works best with animals which are experienced in its use. It seems that in addition to the concrete, observable events such as reinforcements occurring in the training sessions there are covert events such as the animal's expectations which are influencing the course of learning. It seems that the experienced animal knows how to interpret the sudden cessation of reinforcement and modifies his behaviour pattern rather than abandoning it.

using prepositions more widely, he uttered a number of times 'Hat on off now' meaning 'I'm going to take my hat off now'. Once more, we have to take into account more than simple links between utterances, and links between utterance and situation, to explain what is happening. We need to take account of the child's assumptions about what the adult intends, and about the basis on which he is being corrected.

If we stop viewing reinforcement in terms of reward and punishment and concentrate on the informational properties we can compare the relative effectiveness of reinforcing correct responses positively and reinforcing incorrect responses negatively without getting involved in the controversy as to whether punishment is an aid to teaching. Some learning experiments have shown that the correct pattern of response is acquired more quickly by learners if they are told when they are wrong (negative feedback) than if they are told when they are right (positive feedback). Others have shown that learners adopt different strategies, and that the use they can make of negative information depends on the strategy they are using. Clearly, in order to be able to produce a correct response in novel circumstances one needs to know implicitly, if not consciously, what the defining characteristics of a correct response are, not merely to have a small number of correct responses firmly established. As I have mentioned, the value of various types of feedback has been studied extensively in concept formation experiments. What we need now are detailed studies of the contribution of negative and positive feedback to the establishment of adequate response patterns in specific aspects of language learning.

In this discussion of reinforcement I have urged that the reward and information functions of reinforcement should be considered separately. I have pictured the learning situation as one in which information is communicated, and I have argued that the value of negative information should be recognized and investigated. I have also stressed that communication must involve at least two people, and that the assumptions and strategies of the learner are of prime importance and cannot be ignored. Reinforcement theorists assume that there is only one mechanism involved in learning, namely that the probability of a response recurring will be altered by the effect it brings about. However, it is evident from studies of learning situations which are more complex than those typically investigated by behaviourists that this is a very limited view of the role of feedback in human communication.

2.2.2 IMITATION

I have pointed out that the approach to language as habit stresses the immediately observable aspects of language behaviour, the verbal and situational stimuli and the verbal and behavioural responses. In my discussion of reinforcement, however, I was led to an analysis of the learning situation which took account of invisible and inaudible factors, such as the learner's assumptions and interpretations. These factors in the situation cannot be directly observed, but must be inferred from observable events. In the case of imitation, too, I shall urge that we need to consider underlying processes to get an idea of the complexity of the skill of imitation.

In the first place, if we compare a child's imitation with the adult model we see that the model and the imitation are rarely, if ever, identical in their audible characteristics. The relationship between an imitation and its model is much more abstract than the appeal to 'simple imitation' by learning theorists would imply. The path by which a child proceeds towards faithful imitations of adult utterances is long and complicated, and we have seen that mothers recognize this, and reinforce imperfect copies. If we attempt to analyse the processes involved in imitating, we see that the child must perceive the model, attempt to reproduce the model, perceive his own attempt and evaluate its relation to the model. To add to the complexity of the process, the child is not imitating visible actions. If he were, he could compare his own efforts directly with the model, since his performance needs to be isomorphic with the model performance. Instead he has to relate the kinaesthetic sensations from his own articulators with the auditory feedback from his own speech, without being able to see what his mother is doing inside her mouth to make the noises she produces. Nor can the problem of accounting for learning always be resolved simply even in cases where the actions are visible. Imagine explaining how people learn to play the piano in terms of 'simple imitation'![1]

Let us look more closely at one aspect of the process just described, i.e., the child's perception of the model utterance. In order to hear an utterance in the first place we need to be attending to it, otherwise we only hear very familiar words or words which we are expecting. The problem for the child in the early stages is that no words are familiar, and he does not have the knowledge of the language on which expectations can be based. Furthermore, to imitate an utterance we have to be able to retain it in the first place. Experiments with adults on short term memory for verbal material show that for effective retention items have to be identified with patterns stored in the long term memory, and for longer retention the items have to be rehearsed. It seems, then, that the ability to preserve speech signals in the memory for long enough to study them depends on a considerable amount of prior learning about the structure of the language. We can hardly appeal, therefore, to simple imitation as an explanatory factor in learning, when imitation involves the capacity to store verbal material, which is itself a product of learning.

Leaving aside the question of the child's ability to produce utterances which formally match those of the adult, problems still remain for a theory which regards imitation as 'simple'. If a child is to use appropriately an utterance

[1] It has, however, been claimed that babies as young as three weeks old can imitate single bodily movements and possibly even sounds, though this capacity may disappear and it is not clear at the moment what relation it bears to later language development (Dunkeld 1972).

he has imitated from his mother, he has to interpret that utterance correctly. Imagine Karen aged two lifting the lid of a sewing box and saying 'leave'.[1] We may assume that the child has copied the word, used by her mother in some situation in which the sewing box, or the action of lifting a lid, or some other thing associated with this context was prominent. A plausible interpretation of the incident seems to be that the child has been asked in the past to leave the box alone. It is difficult to say what Karen took the word 'leave' to mean. She may have interpreted it correctly and may have meant by 'leave' in this context 'I ought to be leaving it alone', but we cannot be sure that this is the case. It looks, therefore, as if we cannot think simply in terms of utterances being imitated and used again in similar situations, since the situation doesn't always make it absolutely clear what the utterance means. Assumptions about the way in which utterances relate to situations and the child's way of construing situations must be taken into account. So long as the child's use of a word does not conflict with ours, we learn nothing about his world. If the child had said 'lid' in the above context the utterance would not have attracted our attention, but even then 'lid' may have meant for her the action of lifting. Once again, we are forced to look below the surface of the observable events.

Appeal to imitation as a source of verbal responses neglects a further feature of language learning, which is that direct imitation will not necessarily lead to correct usage. For instance, Adam at roughly two and a half imitated 'Sit my knee', when an adult said to him 'Sit on my knee'. Adam continued to use this structure for some months in similar situations, i.e., whenever he was about to sit on somebody's knee. In order to reach eventual understanding of the meanings of pronouns and the actor-agent relations between nouns and verbs in sentences, and the way these are communicated by means of word order, the child will have to acquire an entirely different perspective from the one afforded by direct imitation of the adult utterance in the same situation. Adam had by no means fully achieved this perspective at the time of writing, which is nearly six months later (Clark 1972).

A reinforcement theorist would argue that it does not matter if an inappropriate response is learned through imitation, since it will drop out for lack of reinforcement. However, this does not explain how the correct response ever comes to be substituted, since imitation will not suffice as an explanation. Furthermore, how can one communicate the inadequacy of the utterance 'Sit my knee' by failing to reinforce it? One could refuse to take the child on one's knee, or simply fail to register approval for the utterance, but the child needs more information than this. If the mother says 'No, "I want to sit on your knee"' this might compound the confusion. It seems that among his other accomplishments the child needs to acquire a language for talking about language to gain the maximum profit from feedback about his utterances. We need to think again about the concept of expansion as a form of feedback, and

[1] I owe this example to Renira Huxley.

consider what sort of utterances lend themselves to a form of expansion which provides unambiguous information about the nature of the error. Such attention to the mechanics of interaction in conversations may give clues about the relative difficulty of different achievements in language learning. For example, if the child said 'Where the man went?' it would be very natural, but not very helpful, to say 'I don't know where the man went'. This would give the child no indication that his syntax was inadequate. Similarly, if a child said 'I see it' referring to a past event, the reaction 'Did you see it?' would not draw his attention to his mistaken verbal inflexion (Cazden 1968).

In this section I have argued that imitation is not a simple function and that, as in the case of reinforcement, it is necessary to take account of the child's interpretation of the situation, as well as the complexity of the linguistic system he has to acquire.

2.2.3 GENERALIZATION

I mentioned above that the proponents of reinforcement theory invoke stimulus generalization to explain why we are capable of making suitable responses to stimuli we have never met before. They claim that we respond to a novel stimulus with the response which has been linked by reinforcement to a similar stimulus in the past. In the laboratory studies on which the concept of generalization was originally based, dogs were presented with stimuli whose physical characteristics could be measured precisely, so that it was clear in what sense, and to what degree, the novel stimulus was similar to the one to which the response was first trained. In the case of verbal stimuli, however, there are a number of levels on which similarity can operate. Two stimuli, such as 'wine' and 'swine', can be very similar in phonetic or graphic form but far from similar in meaning. Conversely, stimuli which are very different at the phonetic level of analysis may be equivalent with respect to some semantic system. An experiment conducted by Volkova with a group of Russian children will serve to illustrate this (Berlyne 1963). The experimenter rewarded the children if they pressed a rubber bulb when she said 'true'. She did not reward them if they pressed the bulb when she said 'false'. After thorough training the children were presented with a wide variety of statements which were either true or false. These statements bore no resemblance in terms of their measurable stimulus properties to the original verbal stimuli. However, stimulus generalization took place in terms of the truth value of the statements. Children responded to statements such as 'The doctor cures sick people' and 'Two plus two equals four' by pressing the bulb. They failed to press the bulb in response to statements like 'The sun shines at night'. This finding illustrates that the transfer of responses to new stimuli can depend on an extensive network of equivalences which cannot simply be summarized by the cover term stimulus generalization. Such labelling, though it pretends to be explanatory, in fact serves to obscure the complexity of the process it is supposed to explain.

3 Language as stimulus response connections with mediation

In the course of criticizing explanations of language learning which are based on reinforcement theory, I have tried to introduce a richer conception of the psychological processes involved in language learning than the theory presupposes. It might strike the reader as fruitless to pursue any further an approach which does so little justice to the complexity of language and the subtleties of the human mind. However, discussing the inadequacies of a theory can be a useful way of delineating the behaviour which the theory fails to explain. In this section, therefore, I shall discuss mediation theory, which has developed out of stimulus response theory as an attempt to compensate for some of its deficiencies.

What deficiencies does mediation theory seek to remedy? First of all, activity, according to stimulus response theories, is governed by stimuli in the immediate situation. One striking aspect of language, on the other hand, is that it is conducive to our behaviour being influenced by events which are distant in space and time—'the not here and not now', as Piaget describes them. Secondly, the mainspring of behaviourist theory is the belief that our behaviour is based on habits, which are formed through experience. The fact that we can produce in unfamiliar situations a 'novel response that is nevertheless appropriate', to use Brown's phrase (Brown 1958), is an embarrassment for this type of theory. Language behaviour provides an abundance of examples of such novel responses. It is likely that no single sentence in this chapter corresponds exactly to one that I have written before, or to one that you have read before, yet I am able to construct the sentences, and you are able to interpret them, though you may not always agree with the opinions expressed. The capacity to produce and interpret novel sentences seems to depend on a system of abstract rules which govern sentence structure. How can a theory based on habits account for behaviour according to rule? Thirdly, complex activities, such as driving a car or playing the piano or talking, which involve a series of actions in temporal sequence, are supposed according to stimulus response theory to consist of strings of stimulus response connections, each stimulus being produced by the preceding response. However, studies of the nervous system show that the time taken for stimuli to be registered by the brain and for instructions to be transmitted to the muscles would preclude integrated performance of skills if this was constantly under the control of current stimulation (Lashley 1951). Central organization has to be assumed if skilled performance is to be accounted for. We shall see what mediation theory supposes this central organization to consist of.

3.1 Mediation theory

I mentioned above that reinforcement learning theory is used to explain the links between utterances and situations. Mediation theory, on the other hand, has been used more often to explain how links are set up between successive segments within the same sentence.

The concept of mediation developed out of contiguity theory. Contiguity theory is Pavlov's theory, which holds that responses which occur naturally to one stimulus can come to be elicited by another, previously neutral stimulus. As we have seen, reinforcement theory rests on the principle that if a response occurs in appropriate circumstances it can be encouraged to recur by reinforcement. Contiguity theory rests on the principle that a response can be attached to a new stimulus simply by presenting this stimulus frequently in conjunction with the stimulus which already elicits the response. The classic example of this kind of learning is Pavlov's experiment with dogs in which he produced in the dogs the habit of salivating in response to the sound of a bell (as shown in Figure 1). Pavlov achieved salivation by presenting the bell frequently just before feeding the dogs. The dogs eventually came to respond to the bell in the way that they had been responding to the food, and this habit persisted even after Pavlov had ceased to follow the bell with food. However, if the bell continued for a long time to be presented without being followed by food, the habit was eventually extinguished.

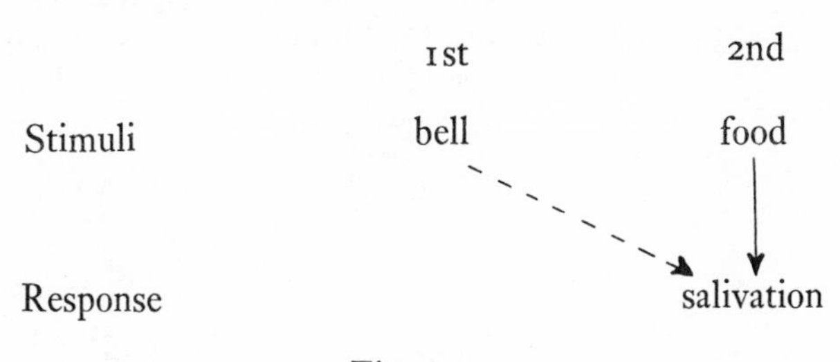

Figure 1

Mediation theorists assume that every response can be analysed into two parts (Osgood 1953). Firstly, there is the external visible response, which can only occur in the presence of the original stimulus (e.g., sniffing, biting, chewing the food). Secondly, there is the detachable part of the response, mainly covert and invisible, which can occur even in the absence of the stimulus (e.g., salivating, marshalling the digestive juices, etc.). The detachable part of the response is called a mediating response (symbolized r_m). Since a mediating response is concrete (though largely invisible to the outside observer), it can function as an internal stimulus. Like the r_m, it is no different from an external stimulus, except that it is stimulating the person from inside, where we cannot see it. This internal stimulus is called a mediating stimulus (s_m) (Figure 2). The introduction of responses and stimuli which can occur in the absence of the relevant concrete objects is claimed to increase the explanatory power of stimulus response theory and to release it from the constraints of a stimulus bound theory. Let us look at some examples of the kind of explanation that meditation theory provides.

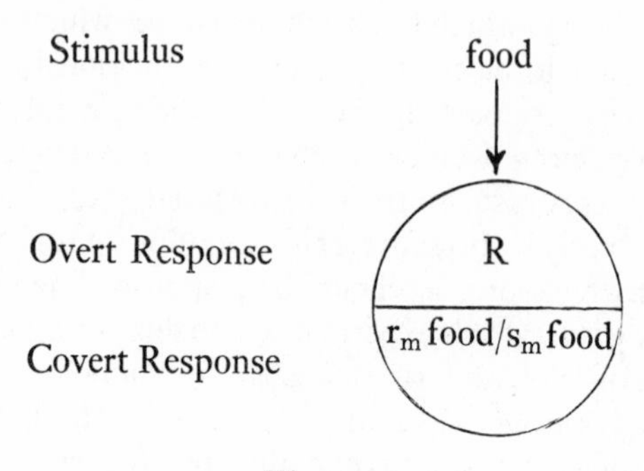

Figure 2

Mediation theorists account for how we learn the meaning of words in terms of contiguity learning. When we frequently hear the word 'food' just before being presented with actual food, we come to respond to the word with the mediating response to food (r_m food). This of course is not the whole response, but the detachable portion of it, since we cannot behave towards a word in precisely the same way as we would towards the object to which it refers:

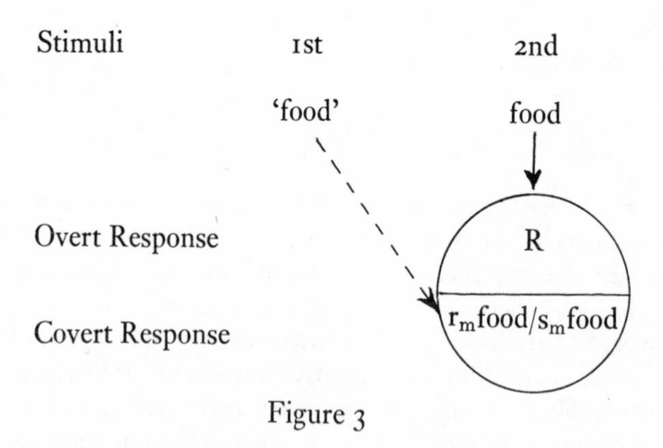

Figure 3

The way is now open for the establishment of all sorts of new associations between objects, through the mediation of words, since some part of the reaction to an object can be made available and transferred to a new stimulus even if the object is not present.

In this way mediation theorists explain the learning of the meaning of words through definitions (Mowrer 1954). For example, assume that the following sentence is spoken: 'An igloo is a round dwelling made of ice'. On hearing the word 'igloo' a learner who already knows the meanings of the words 'round', 'dwelling' and 'ice' will experience the mediating responses r_m round, r_m dwelling, and r_m ice. According to the principle of contiguity, the sensation produced in him by hearing the word 'igloo' will become a stimulus for the production of the r_ms of the other words:

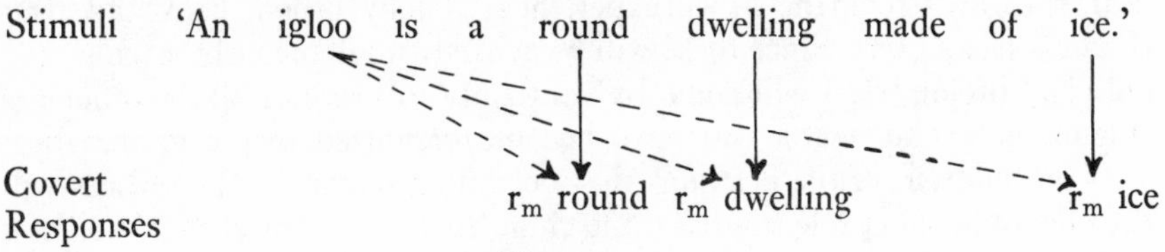

Stimuli 'An igloo is a round dwelling made of ice.'

Covert Responses r_m round r_m dwelling r_m ice

Figure 4

Hence, when the learner next hears the word 'igloo', all the other r_ms will be elicited and these will constitute a meaning for the word 'igloo', though he may never have actually seen one.

The way in which sentences convey information is accounted for in similar terms. Take for instance the sentence 'Tom is a thief'. If we hear this sentence and we know who Tom is, the name 'Tom' will elicit in us r_m Tom. This is, of course, the detachable portion of the response we would normally make to Tom the person. Next time we meet Tom we will react to him with the normal response. This response includes as a subsidiary portion r_m Tom, which is now linked by an internal stimulus response chain to r_m thief (Figure 5a). Thus r_m thief will become part of our habitual reaction to Tom, and we will begin to treat him as we would treat a thief, because of the information contained in the sentence (Figure 5b):

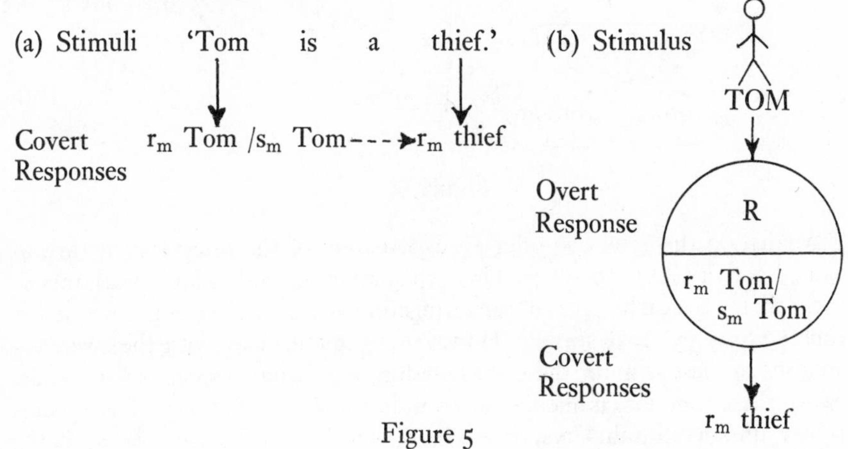

Figure 5

These explanations relate to the not hereness and not nowness of language mentioned above. But what of the human capacity to construct novel sentences which seemed to suggest that sentences have underlying abstract representations? Mediation theorists say that groups of words get organized together into grammatical classes as a result of occurring in identical positions in utterances (Jenkins 1965). For instance, a class of concrete nouns might get set up in the following way. A child might hear these utterances frequently: 'Fetch the dolly', 'Fetch the broom', 'Fetch the book', 'Fetch the sugar'. Whenever he hears the words 'fetch the' he will experience r_ms dolly, broom, book, and sugar (Figures 6a and 6b). Since these will be evoked simultaneously, each s_m (s_m dolly, s_m broom, etc.) will come by contiguity to produce all the other r_ms (Figure 6c). The words will have become organized into a grammatical class on the basis of the positions they occupy in sentences. The words will then be interchangeable, so that if the child has learnt to produce 'dolly' as a response to hearing himself say 'bring', he will also be able to produce the novel utterances 'Bring broom', 'Bring book', 'Bring sugar' (Figure 6d):

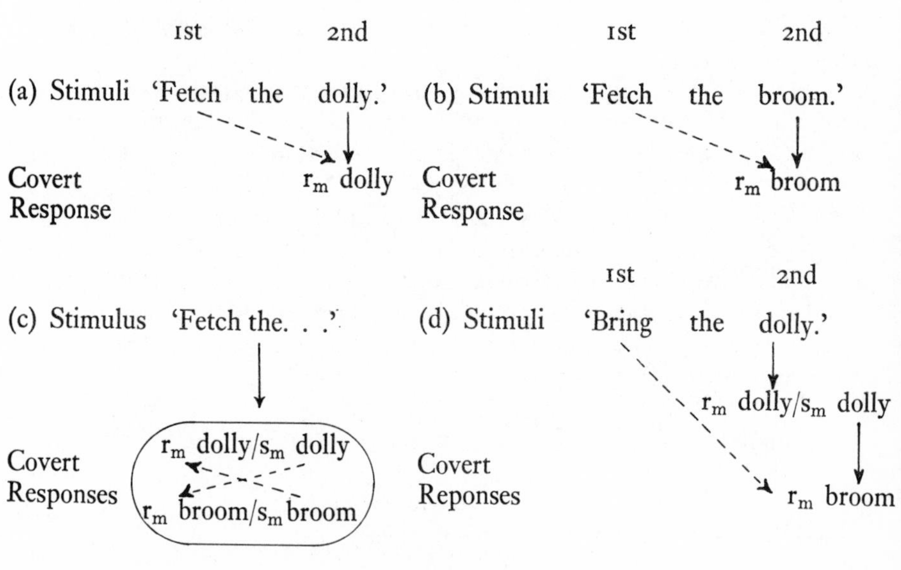

Figure 6

Mediation theorists also offer an explanation of the integrated nature of skilled activity (Osgood 1953). This explanation depends simply on the argument that in the early stages of the acquisition of a skill, activity is governed at each step by external stimuli. However, simultaneously with the overt responses to these stimuli, the corresponding mediating responses will occur. Since these function as mediation stimuli, the s_ms and r_ms will form themselves into a stimulus response chain, which will be capable of being enacted independently of the external stimuli. This chain will enable the behaviour to be speeded up as a result of external stimuli being anticipated before they occur:

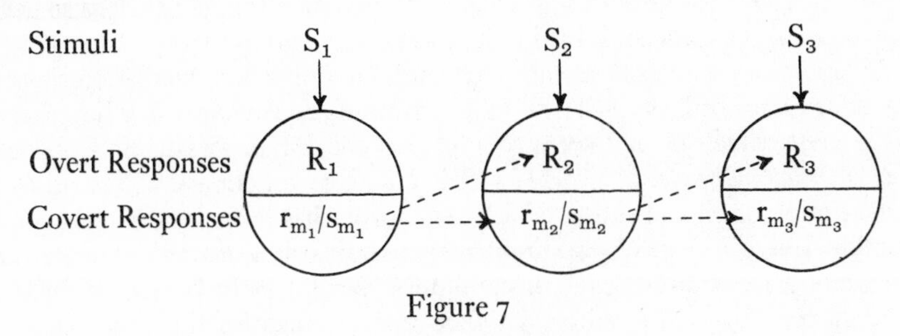

Figure 7

Finally, let us look at how mediation theory might explain stimulus generalization of the type performed by the Russian children in Volkova's experiment described above. Mediation theorists would have to assume that the children had heard in the past utterances like 'That *the doctor cures sick people* is true', and 'That *two plus two equals four* is true'. The r_ms to the phrases in italics will thus have come to elicit the r_ms to the word 'true' (Figure 8a). Therefore, when the children are presented with these statements in the experiment, r_m true will be elicited and this in its turn has been trained during the course of the experiment to bring about bulb pressing (Figure 8b). Hence, bar pressing will occur to true statements (Figure 8c):

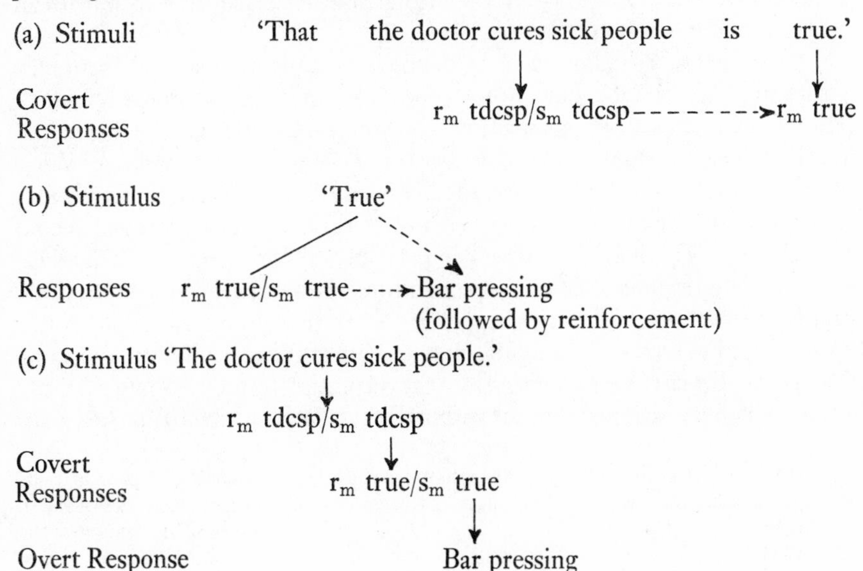

Figure 8

3.2 Mediation theory criticized

The striking feature of mediation theory, then, is that it attempts to account for abstraction without admitting that there is any such thing. I shall raise here just a few of the criticisms one might make of mediation theory.

In laboratory studies of learning by contiguity, on which mediation theory leans for its scientific support, several constraints on such learning have been discovered, which do not seem to apply to the language situation. Pavlov himself was well aware of the fact that language functioned differently to salivation in dogs, and subsequent Russian work has taken this into account, though American work by stimulus response theorists has not. Among the constraints are the following: if contiguity learning is to be successful the stimuli need to be presented together very frequently, the time interval between them has to be very short, the new stimulus must always occur first, and the connection has to be revived periodically or extinction will occur. One would predict on this basis, for instance, that 'An igloo, you know what I mean, I wish I knew how to make one, I usually can't remember what they're called, anyway, it's a round dwelling made of ice' would fail to teach the definition, and so would 'A round dwelling made of ice is called an igloo'. The mediation theorists are asking us to believe in a stimulus response connection theory which is not tied to any of the constraints of traditional contiguity theory, and to accept its validity as an explanatory device. The trouble with mediation theory is that it is so free from constraints that it explains too much. It can explain practically anything after someone else has discovered it, but it can make few clear-cut predictions.

Mediation theory fails to account for any non-sequential aspects of sentence structure. For instance, how do we know that 'an igloo' refers to all igloos? How do we interpret 'is' and 'made of' and how is it that we take an igloo to be a dwelling which is round rather than any round thing and any dwelling? What would we make of 'I don't believe that Tom is a thief'? The idea of a distinct concrete response to most referents is implausible, and many words have no referent, e.g. 'if'. What is the 'ifness' in a stimulus situation that could give rise to a concrete response? 'Ifness' is something to do with the way that minds construe situations.[1] Stimulus response theory has always aimed at causal explanations in terms of observable antecedents of the behaviour in question. Mediation theorists have admitted into the theoretical framework hypothetical events which are assumed to occur within the person. Some mediation theorists

[1] Mindful of this difficulty some theorists treat r_ms and s_ms as abstract representations of objects, rather than as partial responses to objects and the stimulus properties of these. In this way they escape some of the criticisms evoked by the more concrete version of the theory. However, any abstract statement in such terms, if it were sufficiently complex in form to account for the structure of well-formed utterances, would simply be a paraphrase of a grammar, and probably a very clumsy paraphrase at that.

seem to feel that since the hypothetical events are conceived of as being similar in nature to observable events, their theory is scientifically more respectable than theories which use other sorts of conceptual apparatus. This is clearly a false assumption.

We have seen that facts about attention, memory, skilled performance, concept formation and the structure of language force us to adopt a more complex view of language learning than that offered by stimulus response theories. Before passing on to an alternative approach I shall make one or two further points, which should provide a useful basis for comparison with other theories. One important aspect of stimulus response theory, with its emphasis on a simple unit underlying all behaviour, is that it is not a reflexive theory. By this I mean that it would be difficult for a stimulus response theorist to use his theory to explain the behaviour he himself indulges in when he is constructing and evaluating theories. Other psychological theories stress man's activity as an interpreter of his environment or a theory builder in his own right. Such theories can more readily embrace the behaviour of the psychologist himself within their compass.

Stimulus response theory could be compared to an iron. It flattens. It minimizes distinctions between different species of animal and between animals and human beings. It has no theory of stages of development, regarding learning as equivalent in infant, toddler, child, and adult. Of particular interest to us is the fact that it makes no distinction between linguistic behaviour and any other aspect of behaviour. All behaviour is governed by habits.

The stimulus response theorist regards the person as essentially a being rather than an agent. He is passive and moulded by his environment. Stimulus response man has been likened by one critic to 'a bundle of twitches' (Galanter 1966) and by another to 'a ping-pong ball with a memory' (Bannister 1971).

4 Language and innate capacity

If the behaviourist explanation of language learning is inadequate, where can we look for an alternative? One possible alternative is Chomsky's approach to language learning, which is as different as it could possibly be from that of the behaviourists.

4.1 The language acquisition device

Chomsky argues that children are born with a unique kind of knowledge which fits them for language learning. This knowledge is embodied in a mechanism called the Language Acquisition Device, or LAD. Chomsky believes that without postulating such a device it is impossible to understand how children master their native language in such a short time in spite of the highly abstract nature of the rules. This achievement would be particularly difficult without LAD in view of the fact that the everyday speech to which children are exposed is full of irregularities and deficiencies. According to Chomsky, it would be impossible for a child to learn the underlying abstract system of a language from such degenerate data unless he had some prior knowledge about the general character of natural languages. He argues that since children must be equipped to learn any language as a native language, the prior knowledge embodied in LAD must constitute that which is common to all languages, in other words, LAD must contain language universals.

Before discussing LAD further it may be useful to contrast various features of Chomsky's theory with the behaviourist theories we have been considering up to this point. The central difference is that for Chomsky a language is based on a highly integrated system of rules, and it is assumed that a language user must internalize these rules, which form the basis of his performance. The behaviourists, on the other hand, see language behaviour as a collection of habits, not as an internalized system of rules.

Whereas behaviourists see the child as being moulded by regularities and contingencies of reinforcement in the environment, Chomsky believes that the process of language acquisition is mainly determined by forces within the child, who brings to the learning situation the seeds of his own development.

Chomsky differs from the behaviourists also in the distinction he makes between language and other human functions. We have seen that the behaviourists regard language as a jumble of habits, no different in its origin or character from any other set of habits. Chomsky, on the other hand, regards the language acquisition device as a mechanism which is highly specific to language learning, independent of and with no necessary formal resemblance to any other aspect of human functioning. In fact, proponents of LAD often contrast the speed of language learning with the slowness of cognitive development.

For the behaviourists comprehension and production depend on separate sets of habits, separately acquired. Chomsky, on the other hand, believes that the ultimate product of LAD is an internalized system of rules which characterize the structure of a language, and which underlie both comprehension and production.

Finally, the behaviourists regard the experience of linguistic stimuli in situations as crucial to the language learning process. While accepting that the child must be exposed to his native language before he can learn it, Chomsky is inclined to see situations as being a mere precondition for the activation of the language acquisition device. Furthermore, Chomsky believes that the kind of linguistic knowledge the child needs could not be acquired by mere exposure to situations.

4.2 Some difficulties of interpretation

Chomsky's influence on studies of first language acquisition has been profound. However, the literature on the subject is often perplexing. In the first place, it is not very clear what characteristics of the early speech of children would constitute support for Chomsky's hypothesis that the child has innate knowledge of language structure and indeed, in the absence of any precise predictions, investigators have tended to look at what children do and to make this the basis for statements about what LAD contains.[1] In other words, research into language acquisition has not been the testing ground for Chomsky's theory; rather Chomsky's theory has been assumed when accounting for the data. What needs clarification is the kind of knowledge that needs to be incorporated in LAD. Is it prior knowledge of the categories according to which language organizes experience, such as the distinction between nouns and verbs? Or is it prior knowledge of the formal devices that are made use of in languages, such as recursion and transformational rules? Or is it neither of these?

Language acquisition studies within the frame of reference of Chomsky's theory of language have usually sought to establish which are the first grammatical structures and functions to emerge universally during language acquisition. But this approach seems to raise certain problems. Why should a supporter of the LAD hypothesis expect some functions to be expressed earlier than others and some structures to be acquired more readily than others? Perhaps the aspects of language which are learned later are not provided for in LAD? But in that case how can these ever be acquired if, as Chomsky argues, the complexity and abstraction of language makes it inconceivable that it could be learned without the help of LAD? If LAD contains information about the types of structure and function manifested in language, then presumably it contains *all* the necessary information. In that case, if we are to expect a universal order in which the various aspects of linguistic structure are acquired by children, then LAD will have to contain a programme of instructions governing the order of their emergence. Without such an ordering device the theory of LAD does not seem to imply a fixed order of acquisition.

It has been suggested that, rather than direct knowledge about the form and content of linguistic expression, LAD contains a mechanism which enables the child on exposure to an input of utterances to formulate a number of hypotheses regarding the structure of the language, to evaluate these hypotheses, and to select the right one from among them.[2] In other words, LAD may not tell the child directly what languages are like, but only how to find out what they are like. Alternatively, both a hypothesis-forming mechanism and knowledge about linguistic universals might be needed. If this is the case, the function of the hypothesis-forming mechanism will be to help the child discover the actual form which the linguistic universals assume in his particular native language. If we see LAD as a structuring device of this kind, rather than a programme which determines the order of emergence of grammatical

[1] See for example Gruber (1967).

[2] See Matthews (1967) for some comments on this.

features, then perhaps we should expect a different order of acquisition depending on the data to which the child is exposed.

The above discussion has given some idea of the richness and subtlety of Chomsky's theory of language acquisition, but it also shows the difficulty of thinking of LAD in purely abstract terms. In order to discover the manner in which LAD might operate we would need to look at concrete instances of language learning and try to explain them in terms of Chomsky's theory. But, as I have argued, such explanations should not be based, as they usually have been, on the assumption that because all children share the same inherited knowledge of language universals this will necessarily manifest itself in the same order of acquisition of language structures. Rather, the aim should be to show how a common structuring device operates on different inputs to produce different outcomes. We might then expect to find that different languages, and perhaps even different patterns of parental speech in the same language, give rise to different patterns of development.

A further problematical feature of Chomsky's theory is his view of the role of situation in the language learning process. Let us assume, with Chomsky, that the child is born with a predisposition to search for the means his native language has of expressing certain grammatical relations of which he has innate knowledge. It is very difficult to see how the child can come to identify the means without considerable experience of language in situations. But Chomsky's view is that exposure to language in situations is a mere precondition for the activation of the language acquisition device, and is irrelevant to the actual course learning takes. At this point Chomsky appeals to work with animals which demonstrates that certain factors in the situation may be necessary to activate the inherited mechanisms for perception, without determining the character of the mechanisms. But, however complex the stimuli may be which such systems are programmed to recognize, they can at least be specified in terms of their perceptible properties, even if these are relational.[1] Since LAD must be capable of recognizing the appropriate stimuli in any language, it is difficult to imagine how the defining properties of the stimuli to which the mechanism must respond can ever be specified accurately, since the stimuli can have no consistent physical properties at all. In my view, the analogy with the highly specific inherited reaction patterns found in animals is misleading and I further believe that situation has a fuller role to play in language learning than Chomsky implies, though not precisely the role assigned to it by the behaviourists.

4.3 An alternative to inherited structure

We have seen that one function attributed to the language acquisition device

[1] An example of a relational stimulus is supplied by Tinbergen and Kuenen who found that the ratio between size of head and size of body is the criterial feature of the adult bird which stimulates gaping in young thrushes (see Hess 1962).

is that it gives the child prior knowledge about the categories according to which experience is organized by language. But must this knowledge be innate? Could the child not learn the basic categories of which language makes use from his experience of the world during infancy? Chomsky, as we have seen, considers the child's linguistic capacity to be governed by a specific linguistic inheritance, but many psychologists feel that much of the child's early ability for language can be ascribed to his general intellectual development. Some psychologists have used Piaget's theory of cognitive development to account for the forms and functions of children's speech in its early stages (Donaldson 1966, Sinclair 1969). If the structure of children's speech can be accounted for without appealing to LAD perhaps the hypothesis-forming mechanism can be also. Clearly we need to know much more about what children actually do while they are learning to talk and understand before we can formulate an adequate theory of language acquisition. It may be that the strategies involved in the development of linguistic structure are not sufficiently complicated for a complex inherited mechanism to be needed. I shall return to this point in section 6.

It is not immediately obvious why we need to postulate a particular inherited ability for language on the grounds that language is an abstract system. In the course of our lives we master a number of abstract systems. Should we postulate specific inherited structure for each type of abstract learning that we achieve? It would be impossible to specify all these structures, since man is capable of creating new abstract systems which we are not able to foresee.

It is by no means clear that progress towards mastery of the native language is as rapid and effortless as Chomsky presupposes, or that the capacities involved in normal language use are as complex as he implies. Nor has it been demonstrated that all children follow a common pattern of development and even if there are universals of acquisition, these do not necessarily have to be explained in terms of a common inheritance. They may be due to general characteristics of cognitive development or to the internal logic of the system being acquired.

5 Language acquisition and cognitive development

5.1 Piaget's theory of learning

We have seen in the previous section that Piaget's description of the thought processes of the child has been related to the course of early language acquisition. Like Chomsky, and unlike the behaviourists, Piaget is concerned with human behaviour as it reflects underlying organization. Piaget's discussion of organization is especially useful in helping to resolve the conflict between the two traditional views of the infant, i.e., the view of the newborn child as an amorphous lump waiting to be manipulated by his environment, and the view of him as a complex device carrying within himself a full blueprint for his future development.

Piaget distinguishes two types of organization: the organization which determines the general way in which the human being will interact with his environment and learn from it, and the organization which is the product of that interaction. The principles which govern how learning takes place he calls 'functional invariants'. These are inherited characteristics of mental functioning which are common to thinking at all levels, from the infant's discovery of his environment to the scientist's attempt to make sense of the world. The patterns of organization laid down as a result of this learning, on the other hand, are known as 'schemata' or 'cognitive structures', and their ultimate form depends not only on the inherited pattern of functioning, but also on the characteristics of the environment in which the learning takes place. Since we all grow up in environments which are similar in certain crucial respects, the general properties of adult thinking are universal, but this is not because they were fully specified in the infant brain at the outset.

If, as Chomsky claims, special structuring capacities are necessary for acquiring language, Piaget would see them as the product of development during the first year or two of life, rather than as inherited complete. Piaget would regard language learning as sharing the general features characteristic of all learning, as the behaviourists do. Unlike the behaviourists, however, he would not describe learning as consisting of the formation of simple habits.

For Piaget, the central processes of learning, the functional invariants, include assimilation and accommodation. According to this view the child is born with a very limited set of behaviour patterns or schemata, which he seeks to assert on any object he encounters. For instance, he will try to suck blankets and fingers as well as the nipple or a teat. This process, whereby the child seeks to encompass an available object into an activity schema, is called assimilation. While trying to assimilate these objects to his schema, the infant discovers that he has to open his mouth in a different way to suck different objects, so his schema becomes differentiated as a result of interaction with his environment. This process is called accommodation. Combinations of schemata which are often performed as sequences become integrated into more complex schemata. These schemata can form the basis for future purposive activity, since these internalized actions are both representations of past actions and the means whereby the child can anticipate the effects of his future actions.

In Piaget's view, one product of the early period of development is the growth of the symbolic function. Before words are acquired actions are used by the infant to indicate recognition of objects and to represent intended activities in advance of performing them. In early childhood, however, anticipation and representation remain tied to concrete events which the child has experienced. However, as the range and complexity of his mental structures develop through the internalization of action, the child's thought processes will become more flexible and he will gradually become free from his initial absorption with his own activity. Ultimately, through the development of a set of mental operations whose properties Piaget describes in terms of logic, the adolescent will be able to deal with abstractions.

During the course of this development the child's thought processes form systematic, interrelated wholes rather than developing piecemeal. A stable stage will be followed by some development which disrupts the system, and cognitive functioning will be in a state of flux until some higher level of organization is achieved, when there will be relative stability again. Piaget calls these stable stages 'states of equilibrium' and he sees the whole course of development as a 'dynamic equilibrium'. Each successive state of equilibrium is more elaborate than the last, and consequently more capable of assimilating new experience and accommodating to it without disturbing the stability of the whole structure. This whole process is seen as self-motivating. The child enjoys exercising schemata while they are in the process of development. Motivation is intrinsic, there is no reinforcement by an external agent to govern what is learned. The child's own mental structures govern what is attended to and how the new information is construed.

Piaget's work on cognitive development is of monumental stature, and it has been described in the barest outline here. However, in the next section I shall give a number of examples of children's utterances which illustrate how the concepts of schemata and of assimilation and accommodation can be applied to language acquisition.[1] While others applying Piagetian concepts to the study of language acquisition have often been concerned with cognitive structures, the following section will emphasize the role of functional invariants in language acquisition (see Sinclair 1970).

5.2 Language acquisition as cognitive learning

We have seen that for Piaget the child's reaction is not determined simply by the nature of the stimulus presented, but the child's current intrinsic structure governs the degree to which he can encompass the complexity of the stimulus. We can apply this principle to language learning. The child is always construing the novel in terms of the familiar. Thus, if an unfamiliar utterance occurs he will not fail to respond to it entirely, but he will try to make sense of it in terms of patterns which are already familiar to him. This will happen at all levels of language: the lexical, the phonological, the syntactic and the semantic. Here are some examples.

Adam's family was driving away from the house when his mother said 'Look, there's a dandelion on the path'. Adam, then aged two, had recently been to a safari park and had learned the word 'lion', which he pronounced

[1] For another extension of Piagetian concepts to linguistic behaviour see Herriot (1970) Chapter 7. My earliest encounter with the idea developed in this section was through Dakin (see Dakin 1973). See also Slobin and Welsh 1968.

'yaye'. He got quite alarmed, and kept looking round, saying 'yaye, yaye' in an agitated manner. The familiar word had determined the way the child perceived what his mother had said.

Another characteristic of Adam's language development at the same period was that if a word beginning with a vowel was acquired on being heard in an utterance it would be treated as if the final consonant of the previous word belonged to it. For instance, on hearing the phrase 'come off' he acquired the word 'moff', which he used subsequently to mean 'off'. This suggests that Adam had certain phonological patterns available to him which determined the form a word could take, and that having no pattern beginning with a vowel he was unable to perceive the input as structured in that way.

Next a syntactic example. David, aged two and a half, was playing with an empty reel from which the flex of a microphone had just been unwound. He said 'Nothing on it'. One of the adults present said 'What a shame!'. 'A shame on it', replied the child. Apparently, David had fitted to the adult utterance a syntactic pattern which treated the final noun phrase as being substitutable for 'nothing' in his own utterance. Perhaps he was used to being told, 'That's a . . .' when a vocabulary item was being corrected, and he could not distinguish 'What a . . .' from this.

Another interesting example in which syntax affected lexis, arose from Adam's confusion at two years of age over the word 'together'. He first acquired the word as 'dogede' (having no voiceless alveolar stop in his phonetic repertoire at that time). Shortly after learning this word he learned to produce constructions in which 'do' occurred. While learning to fit a toy together one day, he said 'do dogede', and for a day or two he fluctuated between this version and the shorter 'do gede'. 'Together' was thereafter pronounced as 'gede'. Apparently he had analysed the word by applying a newly acquired syntactic structure to it. To make sense of it in these terms he could not treat the initial 'do' as part of the adverb.

A ten-year-old Pakistani girl learning English was presented with a series of passive sentences in which both the agent and the object of the action were animate beings, e.g. 'The sheep was chased by the dog'. The child had to say in each case who or what was performing the action. Throughout the series she assimilated the passive sentences to her schema for active sentences, ignoring the intrusive words *was* and *by*. Then a sentence was presented in which the object of the action was inanimate: 'The door was shut by Tom'. Since the child couldn't make sense of this in terms of her previous strategy she was forced to accommodate to the special characteristics of the passive sentence, and she stated correctly that the boy was the agent. Thereupon she went back through the entire set of sentences, correcting her original interpretations.[1]

Examples of assimilation and accommodation are also easy to come by in the field of semantics. These examples show that the child may not at first

[1] This example is taken from Bradley 1966 and is discussed more fully in Dakin 1973.

grasp the full implications of a word as used by an adult, but may get some broad general idea, which gradually becomes more refined. For instance, Adam aged two learned the word 'heavy' when his mother said he was heavy as she carried him downstairs. He then used it in a number of situations to indicate difficulty or discomfort of some kind, for instance if he could not climb onto a chair or open a door which was stiff. Again, in his early usage the word 'big' seemed to express discrepancy in size between two objects. There was no clear evidence from his utterances that he distinguished which of two objects it was that was 'too big'. He also acquired the idea of vertical motion, either upward or downward, and for some time did not differentiate between the two directions in production or comprehension of the word 'down'.

These examples illustrate that Piaget's conceptual framework may very readily be used to describe language development. New experiences are construed in terms of existing patterns. These may be too limited to encompass the full complexity of the input. Development is a gradual process with the child responding to the environmental stimuli at a more and more adequate level as interaction with the environment promotes his structuring capacity.

5.3 Comparisons with other viewpoints

Clearly, Piaget's emphasis on structure distinguishes him from the behaviourists, who regard behaviour as the effect of a set of unstructured habits. Furthermore, Piaget would not make the concept of 'stimulus' a cornerstone of his theory, since what matters for him is the way the stimulus is construed in terms of the child's own mental structures. However, structure as Piaget sees it is not directly attributable to inheritance in the way it is for Chomsky. Piaget, as we have seen, distinguishes between function, which is inherited, and structure, which develops through the interaction of the child with the environment. Piaget would agree with Chomsky that a complex human faculty cannot merely be engraved by experience on the mind of a passive child. At the same time, he would feel that he could account for the ultimate development of complex processing without having to attribute to the child any precise innate knowledge of the structures of thought. However, Piaget's concept of a number of successive equilibrium states has some affinities with Chomsky's view of language development, if LAD is thought of as giving rise to a number of successive grammars, each more adequate than the last.

In terms of the relationship between language and thought there are striking differences between the viewpoints of Chomsky, Piaget and the behaviourists. The behaviourists see language behaviour as just another set of habits, not qualitatively different from other habits. For the behaviourists there is no problem in accounting for the conceptual basis of language acquisition, because they do not believe there is any such thing. Both Chomsky and Piaget distinguish between language and thought. Chomsky is concerned with the structure of language as a system of rules, and considers that language is based on a specific inheritance separate from other intellectual functions. According to Chomsky, the conceptual categories that are important for language acquisition are themselves linguistic categories. Piaget, on the other hand, considers thought to be a basic function, on which language depends. As we have seen, Piaget regards thought as originating in internalized actions. These internalized actions come to function as representations, and this is how the symbolic function develops. The development of language is dependent on the prior development of the symbolic function, and actions are used as symbols at the same time as words are. However, once language has been acquired it can, because of its flexibility, become a highly valuable tool of thought.[1]

There is a marked difference in emphasis between Piaget and Chomsky in the way they approach language. Chomsky has been criticized by a Piagetian (Sinclair 1971) for concentrating too intensively on the structure of language and neglecting its role as a means of representing experience. Piaget, on the other hand, could be criticized for paying too little direct attention to the acquisition of language as a system of communication. In his experiments Piaget tends to take what the child says as a direct reflection of the level of cognitive development he has achieved, ignoring the fact that the child's linguistic system, as well as his cognitive system, is in process of development.

In the previous section I applied the concepts of assimilation and accommodation directly to the learning of the structure of language. Piaget has not concerned himself directly with the acquisition of linguistic structure and, as we have seen, psychologists discussing language acquisition in a Piagetian framework have often been concerned with the view of the world reflected in the child's early utterances rather than with the problem of how children learn sentence construction. However, psychologists working with Piaget in Geneva are now turning their attention directly to the study of language acquisition (see, for example, Sinclair 1970 for a discussion of the origins and nature of children's early one-word utterances).

Because Piaget sees thought as arising out of internalized action, and because he believes that early symbols represent objects by means of the actions performed on them, he has been likened by some to the behaviourists, who

[1] The idea that linguistic development depends on prior conceptual development is supported by many utterances of children which illustrate that the child may have a conceptual grasp of a situation before he has acquired the linguistic devices for describing it. For example, David, at two and a half, was in his car, sitting at the back with his mother and his baby sister. I asked him where his mother was. He wanted to tell me that she usually sat at the front, but was now sitting at the back (The baby's chair was broken so his mother was there to hold her). David had a very restricted verbal system at the time, and very limited means at his disposal for making such a distinction. However, he achieved it, saying 'Mummy there (pointing at her), mummy do at front' (pointing at the front).

emphasize learning through responding to environmental stimuli rather than learning which consists of merely observing objects and registering connections between them without responding overtly. However, the differences between Piaget and the behaviourists are far more evident than the similarities. While Piaget is trying to explain structure in terms of internalized action, the behaviourists use the concept of a response to explain structure away.

There is one further respect in which Piaget's theory differs from both Chomsky and the behaviourists. Piaget's theory is reflexive; that is to say, his view of mental functioning is sufficiently complex to account for the activity of Piaget himself in investigating behaviour scientifically. I have stressed that the behaviourists put the emphasis on external, observable aspects of behaviour, and by this means they keep their subjects at a safe distance in the interests of objectivity. Chomsky feels the need of a preformed structure to account for complex mental acts. Piaget accepts that the psychologist's task is to provide an explanation for human activity, and that this activity includes his own behaviour as a psychologist.

6 Towards a broader framework

In the course of this discussion I have described a number of processes, each of which has been proposed by one theorist or another as being basic to language acquisition. In the literature the concepts of reinforcement, imitation, hypothesis-formation and evaluation, assimilation and accommodation jostle with one another for central position. It is time to try and formulate a few general principles which will help to make sense of this confused picture and which will be of use in discussing the methods of second language teaching. Much of what I say in this section will be speculative, and the speculations are based, like most current work on language acquisition, on a severely limited amount of data. However, the intention is to sketch a broader framework than is normally provided for the discussion of language acquisition, rather than to present a definitive model. Many of the remarks will not seem immediately relevant to the problems of teaching a second language, but I hope that the connection will become clearer after a reading of section 8.

6.1 Learning by producing

First let us consider how much the child can achieve in the early stages of language acquisition before he has mastered any syntax, merely by using his knowledge of vocabulary and his familiarity with everyday situations. Word order, inflexions and the use of grammatical words are often not necessary for the communication of meaning. For instance, a child might hear the utterance 'Daddy painted the door yesterday'. If he knew the words 'daddy', 'paint', 'door' and 'yesterday' he would not need to take account of the position of the word 'daddy' to infer that daddy was the agent of the action described by the verb, since a door cannot be an agent of such an action, nor would he need to notice the past tense ending on the verb, because the word 'yesterday' indicates that the event is in the past. Similarly, in the utterance 'The book is on the floor' the relationship between 'book' and 'floor' can hardly be other than spatial.

In some cases a little information about the situation would be required to make grammatical cues entirely redundant. For example, if a child heard someone say 'Throw the ball to daddy' it would be clear what was to be thrown, but the child might interpret it as an instruction to daddy to throw the ball, unless he knew that daddy did not have the ball, but someone else did. Some utterances require the child to make use of a different type of knowledge before he can disambiguate them without the help of syntax. For instance, if a child who is incapable of interpreting the syntactic cues for the passive heard the utterance 'Little Tommy was slapped by his mummy' he might need to know something about social norms to avoid misconstruing the subject of the verb. In well-run households little boys do not slap their mothers. Alternatively the information that little Tommy was slapped by his mummy might have been offered in explanation of why little Tommy was crying. In this case the child would need to know what could plausibly account for a child's tears.

It seems, then, that in principle a great deal of progress in the comprehension of language can take place without knowledge of syntax. In fact, we might postulate that the child acquires syntax by interpreting the utterances that he hears by reference to the situation, noting the semantic relationship between the words, then perceiving the syntactic correlates of that relationship.

Such a theory, however, takes for granted the child's ability to exploit redundancies in the language he hears. It seems that this ability itself may be the result of a slow development running parallel to the development of syntactic structure. Adam, aged two, failed to understand the utterance 'Put teddy in the bed', though the words 'teddy' and 'bed' were highly familiar to him, and the relationship between them might readily have been inferred from the situation. However, once he had learned the game of putting teddy to bed, he gave evidence of understanding the utterance the following day, probably because he could relate the two words as a unit to the now familiar situation.

If there are strict limits to the child's capacity to follow what the adult is saying, when his command of the language is still limited, how does this command ever increase? One way for the child to reach an understanding of how words can combine to express grammatical relations is for him merely to string words together haphazardly in the first instance, perhaps producing two words in sequence, both of which are relevant to a particular situation. As a result of producing and practising such sequences he may come to realize that combining words in utterances in a particular order can function as a syntactic device. Only after achieving this understanding could his utterances be said to have internal structure.[1]

If this view of the acquisition of grammatical relations is correct, and there is some evidence, described elsewhere (Clark et al 1972), that Adam's early development may have been of this kind, several points should be made in comparison with the other approaches we have discussed. In the first place, this view accords considerable importance to the idea that the production of language in concrete situations is fundamental to the language learning process. In this respect it conflicts with Chomsky's suggestion that situation may merely be the occasion for LAD to function but has no crucial role in determining how language develops. On the other hand, although in the present view situation is considered important, the role of situation is quite different from that ascribed to it by the behaviourists. It takes an active brain as well as a situation combined with reinforcement to produce development along the lines described.

A distinction is being made in this approach between two manners of uttering words in combination: accidental combination and combination with understanding of the underlying relationships. Such a distinction between two occurrences of the same response would be unacceptable to the behaviourists. But nor is such a distinction commonly found in discussions of early language acquisition by the proponents of Chomsky's view. As I have pointed out, it is the internal structure of utterances that such theorists are mainly concerned with, hence they will often analyse the child's utterances from the point of view of their internal structure, without considering whether, psychologically speaking, the utterances are produced by syntactic rules. I shall have more to say on this point later.

A further point is that according to the view being advocated here the child is gradually acquiring abstract patterns through actively exercising their concrete realizations. This approach is heavily influenced, then, by Piaget's view of cognitive development. The process by which combinations of words can become organized into larger syntactic units can be likened to the process by which schemata become organized into higher-order schemata when they are enacted in combination.

Finally, the present approach assumes that a number of skills will be implicated in language development, and that these skills will interact with one another in complex ways. The child's capacity to attend to more than one word in the input at a time, and to integrate the words together into a meaningful

[1] There is no implication in this view that the rules are not abstract in nature, or any suggestion that the mere production of sequences could lead to the development of rules in an organism unfitted to develop rules. The point is that we need not conceive of the child as learning merely through listening. Sequences may be produced accidentally before the rule governing them has been mastered, and the production of the sequences may facilitate the acquisition of the rule.

whole is just one example of the type of skill involved. Thus the pattern which learning assumes at any age will be dependent on the levels and development of the relevant skills.

6.2 Learning by imitating

I suggested above that in the early stages the utterances the child actually produces himself may be his source of information about certain aspects of the grammar of his language. As the child's perceptual capacities and memory capacity develop he becomes able to copy sequences of words from adult utterances. He will omit certain grammatical words from his imitations (Brown and Bellugi 1964), and it may be that at a certain stage only words with which he is already familiar can be copied in such sequences (C. Smith 1970).

In Adam's case new linguistic patterns seemed often to be acquired as invariable routines and retained intact for some time before the internal structure was modified in any way (Clark 1972). For example, he learned to say 'Wait for it to cool' when hot food was brought to the table, and it was some months before he extended this pattern and said, on seeing a wet garment, 'Wait for it to dry'. Similarly, he acquired the expression 'shall we. . .' at a time when he was not using 'we' in any other context. This is the only yes/no question he has produced so far (at the age of three years and two months). The expression has since dropped out and seems to have been an unanalysed routine (see Brown 1968 and Cazden 1968). The sequence 'Sit my knee' already described and others like it seem to be similar. In these instances the child seems to be concentrating on mastering the form of the utterance without paying full attention to the meaning, except as a global connection between utterance and situation. They are a kind of holophrase consisting of more than one word.[1]

In Adam's speech over a long period there was evidence for the use of such set phrases with strong internal cohesion within many of his utterances, and he seemed to have difficulty in breaking down these well-practised routines into their component parts. For instance, a previous utterance would be retained and incorporated in its entirety into the next utterance where an adult would have reduced it to a shorter form. For example, he might say 'Change trousers', wanting his trousers changed, followed by 'That change trousers' (presumably = 'There are the trousers') when he saw some clean ones. Similarly, whole utterances learned as units functioned as constituents in other utterances and were resistant to correction. For example, Adam said '*All fall down* water' when he saw a tree trunk lying in a stream.

Syntactic development can proceed quite a long way by combining such

[1] 'Holophrase' is the term used to describe the child's early one-word utterances which seem to have a total meaning in the context rather than being mere citations.

imitated routines, or incorporating them as constituents into simple structures.[1] We saw that earlier on Adam juxtaposed pairs of words. At this later stage he would juxtapose two longer speech routines, or incorporate them in simple structures which were common in his repertoire. By this means he achieved a number of extended utterances whose internal structure was quite simple from his own point of view, though the analysis would be quite complex if they were treated as being the product of conventional syntactic rules. Here are some examples, with one of the two units underlined in each case:

> I want *you get a biscuit for me*
> That a bunny *taking a book home*
> I don't know *where's Emma gone*
> Where's *the boy brought the milk* (looking for the milk the boy had brought.)

Notice that in some cases this strategy does not lead to the appropriate structure from the point of view of adult English, though in some cases it does.

Another simple device involving imitation used by Adam was to repeat an interchange between himself and an adult, expanding the structure of his utterance by this means, with the adult reply forming an additional constituent. For example 'Adam turn de light on', said while he was lying down having his nappy changed, would often receive the reply 'Soon'. After a few occurrences of this interchange Adam started to say 'Adam turn de light on soon' as the first instance of an utterance with a time adverbial.

Even more complex structures, which superficially seem to involve the transposition of words, may develop through imitation and simple combination. For instance, during his 38th month Adam started to copy adults' question-tags, e.g. 'aren't they', 'can't you'. After a while he would copy a tag, and repeat it immediately as part of the next utterance:

> Adam: It's cold.
> Adult: Isn't it.
> Adam: Isn't it. Isn't it dark too.

Adam had thus arrived at a negative yes/no question which appeared to be the product of a transformation, but not applying a rule to transpose the words *it* and *is*. These structures coexisted with wh-questions in which there was no transposition, e.g. 'What you are doing?'.[2]

Another point worth noting is that linguistic structures can be acquired by such processes as I have been describing, and can be in active use without their function, any more than their internal structure, being fully understood.

[1] How long these routines have been in use and how much internal structure they have acquired before being combined in this way remains to be investigated.

[2] See Bellugi and Klima 1966, Gruber 1967.

For instance Adam will use tag questions in a way which demonstrates that he has not understood that they presuppose a commitment on the part of the hearer to the point of view expressed, e.g.: 'I want ice cream, don't I', where the hearer does not have access to the relevant information until the utterance is spoken, and 'Baby wants milk, doesn't he' when the hearer has already stated that the baby is not thirsty. Once the child has mastered a linguistic structure he can then observe the circumstances in which it is used by adults and gradually come to a realization of what its function is. He may, thereby, gain access to aspects of the communication situation which he may not have noted otherwise.

The instances of syntactic development described in the last few paragraphs have far-reaching implications for a theory of language acquisition. In the first place, if syntactic development takes place in this sort of fashion one should not expect to be able to treat all the utterances of a given period as products of an integrated system.

In the second place, it may be more appropriate to think of a range of very simple strategies serving as the basis for language acquisition, rather than a complex device for forming and evaluating hypotheses. If the explanations given here are valid then the strategies employed by the child may be fairly simple and it may not be necessary to postulate a sophisticated inheritance of innate verbal equipment to account for them. Only by a careful examination of what the child actually does during the period when he is learning his first language can we discover how large are the steps by which the acquisition of syntax progresses. If the steps turn out to be small, and if we can account for them plausibly in terms of the child's experience and other aspects of his psychological development, we may be able to dispense with the hypothesis of an elaborate innate structuring device. It may turn out to be the case that the different structures which linguists relate transformationally in their grammars may develop independently of one another, and the child may come to a realization that they form a system only after the structures have been fully established for some time.

6.3 The changing role of imitation

I have suggested that learning is qualitatively different at different stages of development. Too often theories of language acquisition posit one uniform principle to account for the entire language learning process. Since I have argued that imitation has a crucial role to play in language learning, it would be appropriate to make some further suggestions about the changes in form and function that this activity may undergo during a child's development.[1]

There seems to be no justification for either of the extreme views regarding imitation, (a) that with reinforcement, it can fully account for language acquisition and (b) that it has no relevance whatever to that process. Nor does

[1] See also Clark 1972.

there seem to be any reason to assume that imitation will have only one function to fulfil in language learning. Early on in the language learning process children will often imitate automatically, without seeming to be attending to the meaning of what they are saying. At this stage it is usually the last word or two in the utterance that is imitated. Later on, they seem to be picking out the words they recognize in the adult utterance without the resulting combination making any sense, and without having any obvious relationship to the established structures in the child's repertoire. It may be that in the first case imitation is a means of practising lower level phonetic skills and that in the second case it is a means of building up the repertoire of patterns which seems to be necessary for the perception of speech.

As we have seen, studies of memory conducted with adults suggest that if material is to be retained for more than a second or two it has to be rehearsed. Imitation could be a form of overt rehearsal for children, who perhaps can only learn to rehearse covertly after considerable practice. Adults, when they are having difficulty in understanding what they are reading, may speak the words out loud to themselves in order to aid concentration. For children, the comprehension of quite simple speech is a task comparable in complexity to that which faces the adult dealing with much more difficult language. If it is true that memory depends on rehearsal then in order to remember for even a short time the utterances he hears it will be necessary for the child to build up a productive repertoire. In this case a great deal of early imitation may serve to consolidate the schemata underlying the child's productive capacities.

6.4 Language learning and the processing load

Before leaving this discussion of first language acquisition I want to look at the process from another psychological perspective, which involves the question of the load that is involved in cognitive processing.[1] I have already suggested that at different stages of development the child may be attending to different aspects of the structure of adult speech. Where phonological skills are not fully established he may concentrate on these to the exclusion of other levels of analysis. At this stage he may imitate the input without attending to its meaning. At a later stage, when syntactic skills are immature, he may make a crude, global interpretation with respect to the situation without attending to the internal structure of the utterance. An example of this is Adam's use of 'Sit my knee' already quoted. Until the participant skills become fully proficient, various other devices have to be used for alleviating the strain of production. One such device, very common in Adam's speech towards the end of his third year, is to incorporate a whole segment of the previous adult utterance into his own to relieve him from the burden of constructing an

[1] See also Clark (1974). Montgomery (1972) has approached reading strategies in learners and native speakers of English from a similar point of view and has influenced my own thinking on first language acquisition.

entire new utterance for himself. For instance, one day he was trying to put his coat on by laying it flat on the ground, putting his arms in the sleeves and pulling it over his head. An adult told him it was upside down and tried to help him on with it. He said 'No, I want to upside down', indicating by gesture that he wanted to put it on himself. At this time he showed evidence of understanding what 'upside down' meant, so this was not a case of misinterpretation, but a case where Adam was opting out of full responsibility for constructing his own utterance.

Yet more evidence of competition for processing space between different levels of linguistic skill comes from instances where the child can modify the structure of an utterance so that it corresponds more closely to the correct adult form, provided the structure is not made more complex by the addition of a constituent. For example, Adam used to reverse the order of nouns in utterances which expressed a relationship of location between two objects. He would say 'My shoes on a polish' instead of 'Polish on my shoes'. On one occasion he was able to correct himself when an adult produced the right version for him. He said 'Polish on my shoes' but then when he tried to add an adjective he reverted to his immature form, i.e. 'My shoes on a brown polish'. An increase in complexity in one area had to be compensated for by compromise in another.

6.5 Summary

I shall now summarize very briefly the arguments of this section. I am claiming that situation and imitation are important aspects of language learning, but not in the way the behaviourists claim. I am also arguing that the mechanisms involved in language learning may not be complex enough to require support from an elaborate innate structuring device. I am advocating that discussions of language acquisition should be extended in scope to include close attention to the actual characteristics of interchange between parent and child. I am advocating that a developmental theory should be formulated which allows for different processes to be operative at different stages. I am advocating that when utterances are analysed attention should be paid to the psychological processes that produced them and that they should not just be treated as raw material for a uniform analysis, regardless of the level of sophistication of the child.

Even a cursory consideration of the complex listening and productive skills the child has to master makes it clear that in future investigations of language acquisition much more attention will have to be given to the development of the psychological processes of perception, memory and attention. Clearly the concept that all these skills are maturing independently of one another and independently of language is untenable in the light of recent developments in psychology.

It is very noticeable that a number of qualitative changes take place during development. In the early stages it may seem that the child is not reacting to speech at all if he is absorbed in play. Much later he may appear not to be taking any notice, but if a familiar word or phrase occurs in the course of conversation he will suddenly repeat it. Later still he progresses from imitation of the last word in an utterance to re-enacting from memory exchanges consisting of several utterances. As the child's world expands and he grows in knowledge and skill he gradually acquires the capacities for selective attention, and for the preliminary processing of material to which he is not fully attending, which are characteristic of adults. These developments cannot be irrelevant to the study of language acquisition. Our object must be the study of the whole child, not just his operant behaviour, not just his thought processes and not just the internal structure of his utterances.

7 Some studies of comprehension by adults

So far I have been discussing the child's acquisition of his native language. I have looked at the process from a psychological point of view and stressed the influence of syntactic and semantic expectations on interpretations. Since I believe that the framework I have developed is of relevance to the adult speaker also, I should like to describe briefly some limited studies I have performed on comprehension by adults which I think bear on the issues raised so far.

A variety of different measures of complexity of structure have been used by psycholinguists. One possible measure is based on accuracy of retention when sentences differing in structure are committed to memory. Another is based on the time taken to evaluate the truth of statements formulated in different ways. A technique which I have found useful is to expose the experimental subject to material which he cannot interpret unambiguously, either because some information is missing, or because it is too difficult. This puts the speaker in a situation analogous to that of the second language learner and leads him to reveal the strategies he relies on and the structures that are most accessible to him. The question whether the syntactic and semantic expectations he works on are equivalent to those of the second language learner is a fruitful area for further research.

The participants in the experiments about to be described were groups of students doing diplomas or summer courses in applied linguistics, or diplomas in speech therapy. The linguistic sophistication of the participants imposes a severe limitation on the extent to which we can generalize the results. So also does the fact that the experiments had to be administered to a whole group at the same time in far from ideal conditions. For these reasons the findings are not intended to be taken as conclusive, though where it seemed meaningful statistical analyses have been done and the findings are given.

Rather, my purpose is to illustrate a number of techniques which may prove to be of value to the teacher.

Experiment A

The participants were asked to provide completions for six sentence openings ending in 'and'. One sentence opening was 'Make sure they plan every detail in advance and . . .' The sentence could be completed in three different ways.

(a) The 'and' could be followed by another sentence having the same implicit subject as the sentence opening, e.g. '(You) make sure they plan every detail in advance and (you) *have them show you their plans before they start working*'. Six out of the 34 completions were of this type.
(b) The 'and' could be followed by a sentence coordinated with 'they plan every detail in advance' as the complement of 'make sure', e.g. 'Make sure they plan every detail in advance and (make sure) *that nothing has been overlooked*'. Only four completions out of 34 were of this type.
(c) The 'and' could be followed by a verb phrase sharing the subject 'they' with 'plan every detail in advance', e.g. 'Make sure they plan every detail in advance and (they) *tell you the cost*'. As many as 17 out of the 34 completions were of this type.[1]

In all six sentences it was the (c) type of completion which predominated; that is, the completion consisted of a second verb phrase to combine with the subject noun phrase overtly expressed in the sentence opening. It may be that the expectation that 'and' will be followed by a completion of this syntactic form influences the ease with which various types of continuation after 'and' are read. On the other hand, such syntactic expectations may not be general, but specific expectations may be evoked by the style and content of a particular passage.

Experiment B

This experiment on syntactic prediction was conducted on four different groups of subjects (approximately 120 in all). Completions were required for the following sentence openings:

(a) He went with John and Mary. . . .
(b) They met. . . .
(c) He caught a cold. . . .

[1] A further seven responses were indeterminate as to whether the subject of the completion was 'they' or an implicit 'you', e.g. 'Make sure they plan every detail in advance and (you/they) *allow for the unexpected*.'

Each of these openings is syntactically ambiguous.

(a) 'Mary' could be coordinated with 'John' in a prepositional phrase or it could be the subject noun phrase of a new sentence, e.g. 'He went with John and Mary to the party' or 'He went with John and Mary went with Susan'.
(b) 'Met' could be a transitive or an intransitive verb, e.g. 'They met the Prime Minister' or 'They met outside the cinema'.
(c) 'Cold' could be a noun or an adjective, e.g. 'He caught a cold from his brother' or 'He caught a cold, wet fish'.

It was predicted that the sentence opening would be interpreted in such a way as to make it syntactically as complete as possible, and that the continuation would be chosen accordingly: i.e. 'Mary' would be treated as part of a prepositional phrase more often than as a subject noun phrase lacking a verb phrase, 'met' would be treated as an intransitive verb more often than as a transitive verb lacking a direct object and 'cold' would be treated as a noun more often than as an adjective lacking a head noun. In other words, it was predicted that the sentence opening would be structured as a complete sentence in each case. The prediction was upheld in all four experiments with all three sentences, with the exception that, in a group of applied linguistics students of mixed nationality, non-native speakers of English reacted to sentence (b) differently from native speakers, producing more completions in which 'met' was treated as a transitive verb, though this difference was not significant. The difference between native and non-native speakers here may be due to different syntactic expectations acquired during the learning of the first language, or it may be due to the way English had been taught to the non-native speakers. If the above generalization about the interpretation of incomplete sentences is valid, then it is of central relevance to the reading process, in which wrong syntactic predictions can delay the accurate interpretation of difficult material. Bever presents evidence that when hearers interpret sentences they search for shorter sequences of words within them that can be interpreted as sentences in their own right (Bever 1970).

Experiment C

The purpose of this experiment was to test whether a sentence could be interpreted if all the words were removed save nouns, verbs and adjectives. This task was intended to be analogous to that faced by a foreign learner or a child learning his first language who is unable to interpret the grammatical information and must therefore fall back on constructing the meaning from the content words. I was interested to see what syntactic preferences the reconstructions revealed. The subjects were presented with the following incomplete sentence:

. . . horse . . . left tethered . . . break loose . . . eaten . . . left . . . skeleton . . . stands.

The subjects were told that they could put up to three function words in each space. The original sentence was 'If a horse be left tethered and cannot break loose it will be eaten and left a skeleton where it stands'. The biggest problem of interpretation was the apparent inconsistency between *left tethered* and *break loose*. This was aggravated by the fact that it was *break loose* and not *broke loose*.

Only half the subjects realized that they could reconcile the inconsistency by adding a negative to *break loose*. Once the negative had been established the rest of the sentence was relatively easy to interpret. Of 12 people who put a negative with *break loose*, 10 realized it was the horse that was eaten. On the other hand, of 13 people who treated *break loose* as an affirmative verb only 3 established that the horse was eaten. There seemed to be general resistance to the idea of a horse being eaten. One subject avoided this by having a horse that was worm-eaten; another introduced an extra content word 'grass' as the subject of 'eaten'.

Here are some examples of responses:

A horse which has been left tethered will break loose when it has eaten what is left over by a skeleton as it stands. (Affirmative/Active)

A horse was left tethered and couldn't break loose so was eaten and they only left behind the skeleton as it stands. (Negative/Passive)

A horse was left tethered but did break loose and was eaten and left as a skeleton that still stands. (Affirmative/Passive)

A horse which he had left tethered not to break loose had eaten well and left nothing for the skeleton on the stands. (Negative/Passive)

Another very striking result was that most people took the sentence to be a description of a specific event rather than a timeless statement about what would happen in certain circumstances. There were 9 conditional sentences (like the first one above) and 32 sentences describing events in the past (like the second, third and fourth sentences above).

Experiments such as this draw attention to structures which are particularly difficult for the reader to interpret. They show which syntactic features it is especially important to attend to in reading, for example the negative in Experiment C. Above all, the experiments show the importance of encouraging flexibility of syntactic interpretation. The reader must be prepared to abandon a wrong interpretation quickly and to look for other possibilities. A series of exercises like those described above using the native language may be one way of developing this type of skill.

All the experiments described so far have the same limitation; they are all concerned with the syntactic and semantic interpretation of single sentences only. Studies of the comprehension of complete texts may have more relevance for the language teacher. Experiment C was concerned with whether the relationships between linguistic units could be inferred without the help of syntactic clues. The following experiment is similar, except that two paragraphs of a text were used as the text material.

Experiment D

The experimental subjects were 60 students at an applied linguistics summer school. The experiment was based on an extract from a talk by a doctor entitled 'Cigarette smoking and cancer of the lung'. The facts in the original text were presented to the students as separate pieces of information in random order, and the students were asked to construct their own argument based on these facts. This enabled me to study the coherence of the material and to find out whether it could be understood without clues arising from order of presentation and the logical links made explicit by the author.

The original text was as follows:

First, though death rates from most kinds of cancer have fallen in the past twenty years or so, deaths from cancer of the lung have apparently increased, and increased quite alarmingly, particularly in men, in the same period. I say apparently because some of the reported increase may be due to better diagnosis – some of it, but in most people's opinion there has been a considerable real increase.

This increase is said to have coincided with and roughly paralleled an increased consumption of cigarettes which, of course, proves nothing in itself. The increase has probably also coincided with an increased use of refrigerators and consumption of ice cream. A further step in the argument is that in Iceland, where there has until recently been little cigarette smoking, the same increase in cancer of the lung has not occurred.

The students were presented with the following list of facts. To control for the influence of order of presentation, three different random orders were used.

In the last twenty years the following things have occurred:

(i) an increase in the use of refrigerators
(ii) increased consumption of ice cream
(iii) an increase in cigarette smoking
(iv) some improvement in the diagnosis of lung cancer
(v) an increase in recorded cases of death from lung cancer
(vi) a greater increase in deaths from lung cancer in men
(vii) no increase in deaths from lung cancer in Iceland
(viii) a decrease in death rates from most kinds of cancer
(ix) little or no cigarette smoking in Iceland till recently

The general finding was that the material did lack coherence, that is to say it was difficult for subjects to reconstruct the argument without structural cues from the passage. I shall discuss problems of understanding with reference to the three main strands of the argument.

1 *Improved diagnosis*

The information that diagnosis of lung cancer had improved was rarely linked to the rest of the argument in the way the author had intended. Many people connected the idea of better diagnosis with reduced risk of death, and consequently had to say that an increase in deaths from lung cancer had occurred in spite of better diagnosis, or they had to link better diagnosis with the reduction in deaths from other forms of cancer, though the statement was specifically related to lung cancer. Others attributed to better diagnosis the surer knowledge about incidence of lung cancer and its relationship to smoking.

2 *Iceland*

30 out of the 37 participants included the statements about Iceland in their texts. Of these, 11 interpreted them differently from the original author. The main tendency was to treat the statements as counter evidence to the main argument, since the recent increase in smoking should have led to a corresponding increase in cancer if there was a connection. These people were working on a different assumption about the time it takes to develop the disease. The other feature of these interpretations was they showed the difficulty which people have in dealing with negative information. This has been amply demonstrated in many psycholinguistic experiments. The students apparently found it difficult to appreciate that the lack of both cigarette smoking and lung cancer could be supportive evidence of the relationship between the two.

3 *Consumption of ice cream and use of refrigerators*

Of the 37 participants, 21 incorporated into their text the information that consumption of ice cream and use of refrigerators had increased. Of these, 13 placed a different interpretation on the statements from the one the author had intended, that is, that statistical relationships do not imply causality. Of these, 4 took the relationship between consumption of ice cream and use of refrigerators to be an example of a relationship of the type postulated between lung cancer and cigarette smoking; 3 suggested that eating cold things may be related to cancer; 3 noted that these facts seem to be unconnected with the main theme; 1 pointed out that since there has been an increase in refrigeration everywhere, the lack of an increase in lung cancer in Iceland cannot be due to the beneficial effects of eating cold things; 1 suggested that smoking and eating cold food might affect our stomachs and not our lungs and that the increase in lung cancer should be attributed to something other than smoking; 1 indicated that women eat ice cream instead of smoking, as is shown by increased consumption of ice cream and increased use of refrigerators.

These findings illustrate the variety of ways in which a body of facts can be interwoven into an argument, and underline the necessity for the links that the author wishes to establish to be very clearly spelt out in the text. Some writers on rapid reading recommend that the reader should concentrate on getting the sense out of the passage without attending too closely to the syntax, but it seems that without benefit of syntax it is very easy to construct the wrong sense. The key factor seems to be familiarity with the subject matter. For instance, a person used to the idea that statistical relationships do not imply causal relationships would probably not misinterpret the relevance of the information about ice cream and refrigerators. The question is complicated to the point of paradox by the fact that a reader with little knowledge of the subject matter can fail to respond to and even misinterpret the syntactic cues as a result.

In a similar experiment a passage about the role of genetic mutation in the causation of cancer was presented. The students were required to reproduce as much of the subject matter as they could remember after studying the passage for five minutes. Although the excessive strain on the memory capacity of the students probably limited the usefulness of the experiment, the results did reveal some specific cases of difficulty. For example, it was striking that the students tended to reproduce the facts as separate items of information, without any logical links between the statements. It seemed as if they could not extract the structure of the argument from the passage with their inadequate knowledge about the topic.

A further difficulty the participants had was in distinguishing information that the author was presenting as a vital link in his argument from information that was incidental, or even assumed to be part of the prior knowledge of the reader. For example, the passage began 'Children with mongolism are known to have an increased risk of developing leukaemia, a type of cancerous proliferation of white blood cells. The general relationship of chromosomal abnormalities and a tendency to develop cancer is also interesting'. A subject would reproduce as part of the content of the passage the statement that 'Children with leukaemia have a proliferation of white cells' as if this was new information that the author was presenting, when in fact it was a definition of leukaemia. Similarly, a subject would state that 'Mongol children show chromosomal abnormality' or that 'Irregularity of chromosomes is linked with congenital diseases'. In fact the author seems to be assuming that the reader knows that mongolism is a congenital condition caused by chromosomal abnormality, and that leukaemia is a form of cancer. It is the information that cancers may be related to genetic abnormalities that he intends to communicate. This is a good illustration of the fact that a knowledge on the part of the reader of the sense relationships between various words in the passage is crucial to an understanding of the passage, and in many cases this knowledge may be assumed by the writer without justification.

I would like to make a further point about Experiment D, in which facts about smoking and lung cancer were organized into a continuous text. The experiment was actually intended to compare the ways in which different subjects structured the argument, and to find out whether there was a generally preferred order of presentation of the facts. I could discover no obvious consistencies in the way the passage as a whole was constructed (though a thorough investigation of the order of presentation of information should take account of the fact that the argument was understood differently by different people). Such consistencies as there were relate only to the positions of isolated pairs of sentences. One of the more interesting findings was that 19 out of the 37 subjects put 'an increase in recorded cases of death from lung cancer' next to 'an increase in cigarette smoking', though in the original text they appeared as sentence two and sentence five. One subject, who had in fact read the passage before, reproduced it with the facts in a totally different order to the original. It read as follows:

In the last twenty years there has been an increase in the use of refrigerators and an increased consumption of ice cream, as well as an increase in cigarette smoking. What then makes us connect smoking with lung cancer? It is true that there has been some improvement in the diagnosis of lung cancer, but that is not sufficient to explain the increase in recorded cases of death from lung cancer, even though there has been a greater increase in deaths from lung cancer in men than in women. Finally, there has been no increase in deaths from lung cancer in Iceland, but there has been little or no cigarette smoking in Iceland till recently.

It may be that the different organization of material here is due to the different intention of the writer. The above version seems to be written in a style designed to persuade the reader of the validity of the argument linking lung cancer to smoking, whereas the original passage is much more tentative in its conclusions.

Is it the case then that order of presentation of facts is unrelated to ease of comprehension of an argument? The above experiment did not test this directly. It tested whether subjects organized the argument differently, but not whether the different ways of organizing it actually affected comprehension. Let us now consider another experiment in which subjects' reactions to two different orders of presentation of material were compared.

Experiment E

The passage used was the introductory paragraph to the final lecture in a series about genetics. The lecturer began by putting the series in the general context of human endeavour, narrowing down to mention scientific endeavour, progress in the field of genetics, the BBC lecture series, and finally the place of his lecture in the series. I rewrote the passage, beginning with the final sentence and working backwards, modifying the syntax where necessary to make the text sound natural. By this means the passage was altered so that instead of progressing from the general to the particular it progressed from the particular to the general. The purpose of the experiment was to test whether the first order of presentation was more natural than the second. Each subject, after reading over one version of the passage for a few minutes, was presented with the nine sentences from that version in jumbled order and was required to rearrange the sentences in the order in which they had occurred in the passage he had read. Here are the two versions:

General to particular

The ancient and continuing effort to improve the quality of human life has taken on new features in modern times. It has become the intense concern of all of mankind, including the young, the less privileged, and minority groups. It has profited immensely by results of the physical and life sciences and technologies. And there is a growing awareness that genetics could make further important contributions. Wide publicity has been given during the last few decades to each of the sensational advances of genetics and to their implications for man. Yet the public has had few opportunities to get a comprehensive view of what genetics has accomplished, what it can be expected to accomplish, and how these accomplishments might be used to improve the quality of human life. It was to supply this deficiency that the BBC produced this series on genetic engineering. Several of the previous contributors have had occasion to mention that genetic engineering raises conflicts with current standards of conduct. In this final contribution to the series, I have been asked to discuss these conflicts and the choices they raise.

Particular to general

In this final contribution to the series, I have been asked to discuss the conflicts of genetic engineering with current standards of conduct and the choices they raise. Several of the previous contributors have had occasion to mention these conflicts. It was to supply a deficiency that the BBC produced this series on genetic engineering. This is that the public has had few opportunities to get a comprehensive view of what genetics has accomplished, what it can be expected to accomplish, and how these accomplishments might be used to improve the quality of human life. This is true despite the fact that wide publicity has been given during the last few decades to each of the sensational advances of genetics and to their implications for man. There is growing awareness that genetics can make important contributions to the quality of human life. This has profited immensely already by results of the physical and life sciences and technologies. The concern of all of mankind, including the young, the less privileged and minority groups, with the quality of life has become intense. The ancient and continuing effort to improve it has taken on new features in modern times.

The subjects who had the passage in the general to particular form definitely found the task of reconstruction much easier. It should be mentioned that the order of the jumbled sentences bore a fixed relationship to the order of sentences in the passage the subjects first read, so that the degree of deviation from the original was the same for both groups, i.e., sentence 1 was always 7th in the list of jumbled sentences, sentence 2 was always 9th, etc.

It seems, then, that just as there are syntactic expectations about the way a sentence will be structured there may be expectations about the way whole passages will be structured, and that this will help the reader to assimilate the information if the presentation conforms to his expectations and hinder him if it does not. Such experiments as the above should be tried with different types of material and different measures of comprehension to test whether this view is correct. It may turn out to be the case that certain types of paragraph are easier to understand because their structure conforms to expectations in the mind of the reader. It will then remain to be discovered how these expectations are established.

Whether they focused on single sentences or on texts, the above experiments were all concerned with discovering what types of structure are projected on incomplete material and what types are most readily dealt with by the reader. In pursuing this approach to comprehension we seem to be faced with the following paradox. If the teacher designs material for his learners which they can understand without reference to the structural cues, they need not attend to the structural cues, and so will not learn them. On the other hand, if the material is not intelligible without reference to the structural cues, there will be no way for the learner to infer the functions of the different structures.

8 Problems in language teaching

8.1 Introduction

I must now justify my initial claim for the relevance of first language learning to the problems of the second language teacher. It is often pointed out that a child learns his native language very easily, while acquiring a second language is a more arduous task which may never be fully accomplished. Depending on the cut of one's theoretical coat, one will attribute this either to the particular circumstances in which the learning takes place, or to a special sensitivity for language learning in the young child. In the first case, we might advocate reproducing the circumstances of first language learning in the classroom. In the second case, we will take the two learning operations to be different in nature, and act accordingly. It seems to me that while we cannot entirely ignore the differences between the learner of a first and the learner of a second language, we should not regard their problems as being entirely unrelated.

I have tried to show in this chapter that the two types of learner are not as different as they might appear. For instance if, as I have argued, the capacity to perceive and remember verbal material depends to a large extent on knowledge of the vocabulary and structures of the language being learned, and not solely on the level of maturation of the nervous system, then the learner of a second language is not in such a very different position from that of the young child with respect to the strange noises with which he is bombarded. As I argued in the last section, under certain conditions even adult native speakers may show some of the characteristics associated with children learning their first language.

The question of the relevance of first language learning can, I think, be considerably clarified by appealing to Piaget's distinction between functional invariants and cognitive structures. A young child learning his native language resembles an older person grappling with a second language insofar as both are human beings, equipped with the same basic learning mechanisms, including assimilation and accommodation. The general characteristics of language learning as I have described them seem to be just as applicable to second as to first language learning.

Where the two types of learner will differ is in the cognitive structures they possess at the time of learning. It is for research in applied linguistics to discover which cognitive structures are common to all language learning and which are specific to the different learning tasks. In the previous section I suggested some experimental techniques for exploring the cognitive structures of adults. If we consider the processes which seem to be involved in Adam's learning of syntax, we may decide that they arise partly out of the general characteristics of verbal communication, and so may have implications for second language learning. On the other hand, we may decide that they are specific to his situation as an uninformed, half speechless child, in which case they can have no such relevance. How far do learners of different ages and different experience come to the same conclusions about what something means? How does the child's understanding of the structure of conversations develop with age, and how does it affect his learning strategies? How far are errors by foreign learners dictated by the specific characteristics of their first language? We do not at present have adequate answers to these questions. Nevertheless, I think we may safely derive some implications for teaching from what has been said in this chapter, and I shall now proceed to do so.

8.2 Should error be allowed?

People often argue that it does not matter what the learner assumes the task to be so long as what he actually does is correct. But I have stressed that the learner may appear to be doing what the teacher regards as the right thing, when in fact he has formed a different generalization from that which the teacher intended.[1]

[1] It is worth pointing out that the word 'generalization' may be a misnomer. It seems to refer to a process whereby concepts become more general, having been specific. In fact what may happen is that concepts begin by being general and only later become more specific. For example, when Adam learned to use the word 'heavy' to mean 'difficult' or 'uncomfortable', his concept was more general than the adult one, and was later to become more specific (see Olson 1970 for a valuable discussion of the acquisition of word meaning, also Eve Clark 1973 and Rosch 1973).

It seems that only by allowing errors to occur can we discover any discrepancies that might exist between what the student actually learned and what we intended him to learn. Some classroom techniques appear to be based on the assumption that there can be perfect communication between teacher and pupil, and that misunderstandings need never arise. However, in a real-life classroom it is practically impossible to ensure that the students are always fully in command of the material being learned. Misunderstandings are likely to arise in any communication situation, and if the teacher restricts his pupils to producing utterances that he knows they can produce perfectly, he may be preventing the fact that misunderstanding has occurred from coming to light. It is clear that a child learns his first language by performing, and that many errors are included in the performance. This being so, it is perhaps unreasonable to require that the second language learner should perform entirely without errors on all occasions.

Since the Second World War a great deal of language teaching material has been designed with the aim of ensuring that as far as possible students will perform without errors. The avoidance of error has gained support from Skinner's view that if an error occurs the probability of its recurrence cannot be permanently reduced by punishment, and that all the teacher's efforts should go into rewarding correct responses. There is no doubt that constant punishment is demoralizing. But we have seen that information about mistakes need not be regarded as punishment, but may be a form of information feedback to the learner. Crowder in his branching programmes manages to let students make mistakes without their being discouraged. Besides, students may be allowed to make errors, thereby providing the teacher with information, without being picked up for them on every occasion.

Concept formation experiments in the psychologist's laboratory have shown that in certain circumstances information about wrong responses can be of more use to the learner than information about right ones (see Annett 1969). However, the results of such experiments should be applied with some caution to the language learning situation, since the learner is exposed to a large number of correct and incorrect examples within a much shorter space of time than is usual in the case of language learning. Furthermore, the concepts studied in such experiments are usually of a more formal nature than is the case in language learning. For example, in an experiment by Bruner, Goodnow and Austin (1956) the stimuli were diagrams in which four characteristics were varied systematically. Each card carried one, two or three circles, crosses or squares, with one, two or three borders in one of three colours. A concept was defined in terms of one or more of the three variables, e.g., the concept might be 'red crosses' or 'figures with two borders'. As I said above, we need research into the acquisition of concepts which is rooted more firmly in the materials of real-life language learning.

8.3 Should pupils be exposed to language that they cannot produce?

This question is related to the previous one, since the motive for withholding language which cannot be fully understood by the learner is presumably to prevent him from getting hold of errors. The child in the natural learning situation is exposed to language he cannot produce during the entire learning period. Can some of the more serious and enduring misinterpretations which result from this be prevented in the case of the second language learner by withholding language richer than he can digest? The answer depends on whether one believes that comprehension is generally in advance of production. If this is the case, then misunderstandings need not necessarily arise very often, even if students are exposed to language which they cannot produce themselves. I have suggested above that a distinction should be made between comprehension in the narrow sense and comprehension in the broad sense. By comprehension in the narrow sense I mean decoding of the linguistic cues rather than interpretation based on extralinguistic information. I have argued that in the case of the child comprehension in this narrow sense is not as far in advance of production as is often claimed, and the same may be true for adult learners. But if learners can rely on sources other than syntax for making interpretations, they might profitably be exposed to language which is beyond their current productive capacity.

This raises the question whether the broader aspects of comprehension function differently at different stages in the learning process. It may be that there are certain strategies common to all learners for interpreting material which cannot be fully processed syntactically. On the other hand, one might expect that the older person's capacity to exploit redundancies in the language, and thereby to achieve comprehension in the broader sense, would have grown with his knowledge of the world. There may also be cultural factors, and factors associated with the structure of the learner's first language which determine the way in which he interprets material. This area would repay investigation by the applied linguist. If we could find out the relative effectiveness of the various strategies used for extracting structural information from uncontrolled input, the most useful strategies could be taught. The student could then learn to monitor his own hypothesis formation and testing, and this process need not be confined to the classroom, where time is always limited.

It is clear that most children eventually achieve proficiency in their native tongue despite constant exposure to language which is beyond them. What is more, many of them seem to find the challenge stimulating. On the basis of this, we might argue that the second language learner might also profit from listening to language which is slightly more difficult than that which he has learned to produce. Unfortunately we have little information about how pupils interpret language which exceeds their productive capacity. If further research of the type described in the previous section could produce such information it would no doubt suggest ways in which such exposure could be exploited.

8.4 Some implications for grading

Language teachers are always seeking a principled basis for grading, both for syntactic and for conceptual complexity. Perhaps psycholinguistic studies can be of more practical help here than in any other area of language teaching. There is a large body of studies in which psychologists have investigated the relative ease with which different types of verbal material can be processed by the native speaker. It is beyond the scope of this chapter to review that research, which is in any case not necessarily of direct relevance to the teacher.[1] However, in section 7 I outlined some experiments of my own which have clear implications for grading. The first two experiments on sentence completion suggest that there is a tendency for people to prefer a certain type of syntactic structure where more than one possibility exists. The third experiment draws attention to aspects of sentence structure which cause particular difficulty when an interpretation has to be placed on a sentence containing only content words. The experiments with texts show that the reader may have specific expectations about how a text as a whole will be structured, and that an argument may be interpreted in a variety of ways depending on the background knowledge of the reader. These experiments indicate that experimental techniques can throw some light on the relative complexity of different materials.

As far as the lessons to be drawn from the study of first language learning are concerned, it cannot be assumed automatically that the scale of complexity derived from these studies will be of direct relevance to second language learners. Nevertheless, such a scale will be of considerable interest to the language teacher. During the course of this chapter I have pointed to a number of factors which may determine the order of acquisition of different structures. One factor is whether the structure can be built up by the mere juxtaposition of simpler structures. Another is whether the child's mistakes in producing the structure can readily be indicated within the natural flow of conversation. I have also suggested that linguistic items whose meaning is transparent from the situations in which they are used will be those which are most easily mastered by the child. This suggestion will, of course, have to be followed up by an analysis of what makes items vary in interpretability before it can be made use of by the teacher.

8.5 The role of drills in language teaching

With the current emphasis on language as a complex intellectual human achievement there is a danger that we might forget that language is also a motor-perceptual skill. Such skills require a great deal of practice, but what

[1] But see Further Reading at the end of this chapter.

form should this practice take? If the analogy between first and second language learning holds, then we should bear in mind that a great deal of the child's output consists of a few well-rehearsed routines, which are exercised frequently over long periods before any part of them is modified by the substitution of other lexical items. It may be of considerable value to the student of a second language also to learn a number of phrases off by heart so that they can form a basis for production, and serve as a reference for various points of syntax.

When a child plays the game of building up and dismantling utterances in monologue, his productions are very reminiscent of language laboratory drills. In Adam's case the procedure of substituting words was often fairly automatic, with little attention given to meaning. For instance, at two and a quarter years, it was suggested to Adam that he go and watch Dougal (a character on children's television) before having his bath. He said 'Dougal first' and then catching sight of his potty said 'Dougal potty'. Many of his verbal exercises seemed to have this mechanical, unthinking quality about them. The discussion of Adam's imitations also suggested that he needed a great deal of practice of lower level linguistic skills and that many of his utterances were not fully processed semantically since the phonological aspects of the performance required his full attention. It should be recognized that the adult learner will probably also need a great deal of practice at these levels to consolidate vocabulary and pronunciation, though he will also need to apply his knowledge of vocabulary and syntax in more spontaneous situations. The advantage of drills will be evident here.

However, the example of the child's substitution game described above reminds us that the rhythm of a drill may lull the performer into a trance-like state in which he may not be attending to meaning in circumstances when he should be. If a particular drill is aimed at teaching a point of syntax for which comprehension is necessary, rather than at practising phonological skills, the teacher should not assume that the mere incantation of utterances by the learner according to the teacher's careful design will ensure that the appropriate point of grammar is assimilated.

The advantage of drills is that they make certain aspects of production automatic, so that other aspects can be attended to, and we have seen that this reduction of the processing load may be very necessary to the learner. However, the aim of a structural drill may be defeated if it becomes entirely mechanical. What Dakin (1973) refers to as 'the tum-te-tum effect' is less likely to be a problem if both teacher and learner are quite sure what the aim of the practice is. A drill is more likely to succeed if the learner grasps the grammatical generalization which lies behind the cues to which he is responding. It may be that in many cases a short preliminary explanation can save time by enabling the students to focus at once on the crucial points of a drill, instead of having to work out for themselves what they are supposed to be learning.

8.6 How should grammar be taught?

There has been a great deal of discussion about how grammar should be taught in the classroom. Should grammatical rules be taught explicitly or should the student be led to infer the rules as a result of practising 'model sentences'? The vital question is how abstract rules are learned from concrete instances and how inadequate rules come to be modified. The wrong generalization can easily be inferred from an inadequate set of examples, and this underlines the need for the teacher to pay attention to the learner's errors in order to discover the course that learning is taking. Some training techniques, particularly those influenced by learning theory, put the emphasis on feedback to the learner, while overlooking the fact that the teacher also needs feedback to know if the learner is doing what was intended.

The question of how rules are acquired has not been solved for cognitive development any more than for linguistic development. Thus we cannot turn to psychologists for help as we search for the conditions which are most favourable for the acquisition of rules. While learning theorists have felt habits to be at the basis of performance, and have studied intensively how habits are acquired, psychologists who believe that behaviour reflects an underlying organization have concentrated on discovering what the rules are according to which such behaviour is organized. They have not so far managed to throw much light on how these rules are acquired.

A lot of psychological work on learning has been done with rats, and rats like burrowing around in the dark. However, I have been putting the view that even the animals in the learning theorists' experiments are being informed as well as rewarded by the reinforcement the experimenter provides. If you want to inform a rat you cannot tell him 'If you press that bar a pellet of food will come out'. To a human being, on the other hand, you can say 'If you put five pence in this machine you can get a cup of coffee', or 'If you use a verb in the passive you don't have to specify the agent'. There seems to be no theoretical reason why you should not communicate with a language learner at any level on which he is capable of understanding. It is a matter for empirical investigation, not dogma, whether and in what circumstances this is helpful.

It seems that interest in how language works can arise at quite an early age. Before the age of two Adam would spontaneously run through lists of words belonging to the same lexical set, such as animal names and types of vehicles. At two and a half he invented the game of calling his mother 'daddy' and his father 'mummy', thus showing awareness of the arbitrary nature of the link between a word and its referent. There is some evidence that a child learning his first language is interested in the underlying principles of language structure. This is even more true of adults learning a second language. Many adult learners find it difficult to practise unless they know the rule, and if the teacher does not provide the rule they invent one for themselves. Such interest should surely be exploited, rather than crushed by rigid adherence to a dogma of pattern practice without explanation. It is here that we see the advantage of a reflexive theory which regards the learner's behaviour as sufficiently complex to be accounted for in the same theoretical framework as that of the teacher or the researcher.

The question of what kind of grammar to teach in the classroom is again an empirical one. It is generally acknowledged that a grammar which best describes a language according to the linguists' criteria is not necessarily the best grammar to teach a language learner. But what kind of grammar should be taught to the pupil? In the absence of any definite guidelines for the construction of a pedagogic grammar, most teachers and textbook writers improvise on the basis of personal experience in the classroom. A sounder knowledge of the range of strategies that learners can adopt, and of those aspects of language that present special psychological difficulties, would be helpful here.

8.7 Should first language and translation be used in the classroom?

The problem here is whether direct use of the first language is a help or a hindrance when the second language is being taught. Let us see whether reference to the various theoretical approaches and to the experience of first language learning can help to clarify this issue.

If we attempt to apply stimulus-response theory to the question of translation we get tangled in a web of conflicting arguments. For instance, we may reason that in learning to produce words in the new language the learner is acquiring an additional set of responses to stimuli which originally only elicited responses in the native language. Two sets of responses to the same stimuli have to be kept quite distinct if they are not to interfere with one another. This seems to be the argument which has influenced people who are opposed to the use of the first language in the classroom. However, one could also reason that when it comes to learning the meaning of words in the new language, the first language can be very helpful, since the learner need not repress his habitual responses, but may simply transfer each of the r_ms he already has to an additional stimulus. The learning of lists of translation equivalents could be one method of achieving this. But this would only work if words had exact translation equivalents in the two languages, for otherwise the r_ms would not be capable of being effectively transferred. This shows that we have to take account of the relationship between the two languages at a deeper level, in terms of whether they wrap up the world into similar stimulus bundles. It is not sufficient to think simply in terms of substituting one response for another or one stimulus for another.

To what extent, then, do different languages organize reality in similar ways? This seems to be a matter for dispute. Chomsky's theory stresses the universal basis of all languages. Whorf, on the other hand, believed that different languages imposed different world views on their users and that learning a new language involved acquiring a new conceptual framework. If languages do differ in the way Whorf has argued, then literal translation is impossible. Even if they are related in the way Chomsky suggests, the equivalence between languages is at the level of deep structure, and so word-for-word translation must be discouraged.

What light can the study of first language acquisition throw on the question of whether to use translation in the second language classroom? Perhaps very little, since there is no possibility of a first language being taught via the medium of any other language. However, the study of first language acquisition does show us that a child will construe novel events in terms of the conceptual systems already available to him. It is unlikely, therefore, that even if we wanted to eliminate the effect of the first language on the learning of a second, the banishment of overt verbal stimuli from the classroom would have the desired effect. There seems, then, to be no theoretical objection to utilizing the student's native language in second language teaching. Indeed, making the learner more aware of things he knows implicitly about his own language may be one of the most useful devices available to the language teacher.

9 Summary and conclusions

In this summary I shall pick out those strands of the argument that contribute to the general picture of language learning which I have been trying to build up.

In criticizing behaviourist approaches to language acquisition, I stressed the active role of the child in learning and the need for the investigation to get beyond the superficial aspects of the situation and to consider the child's interpretations of his mother's speech and of the feedback she provides. On the subject of imitation, I stressed the interdependence of linguistic knowledge and perceptual and memory capacity. I also pointed out that straightforward imitation would not help the child to realize that utterances are not interchangeable irrespective of speaker, but that he must make his own role clear with respect to the action described.

In section 4, I suggested that Chomsky's theory does not necessarily imply that the various linguistic structures and functions are acquired in the same order regardless of the child's linguistic environment. I concluded by stressing that we should try to establish how complex are the tasks involved in learning a language before we decide that we have to appeal to elaborate inherited structures in order to explain them.

I went on to touch briefly on Piaget's view of cognitive development, introducing the concepts of assimilation and accommodation which seem to be of vital significance to any study of learning at any stage. However, I pointed out that, since Piaget was concerned with the development of thought processes, he had paid very little direct attention to the internal structure of children's utterances.

In section 6 I described a number of phenomena which I have observed during intensive study of a single child. These have convinced me that utterances should not be considered merely in terms of their relationship to the situation in which they occur, nor in terms of their internal structure, but in terms of their role in the language learning process. The structure of an utterance so far as the child's speech mechanisms are concerned cannot be assessed solely by reference to the utterance itself, or even by reference to a whole corpus of utterances. In assessing 'psychological' structure, decisions must be made as to the developmental history of the different segments of the utterance and the relationship of the utterance to the speech that has occurred. The same considerations seem to be relevant in considering output from learners of a second language.

I went on to show that experimental techniques can throw some light on people's expectations as to the structure of sentences and of texts, as well as revealing how readily sentences and texts can be understood without structural cues.

In the final section I discussed various aspects of language teaching with reference to the ideas raised in the earlier part of the chapter. I drew the following conclusions: (1) If language learning is not habit formation, but successive approximation by assimilation and accommodation to a more elaborate structure, then making errors is an integral part of the process, and reveals the course which learning is taking. (2) Learners can rely on sources other than syntax for making interpretations, so may profitably be exposed to language beyond their current productive capacity. (3) More information about comprehension should be accumulated and used to guide the preparation of materials. (4) Language skills at all levels require practice, so some sort of drilling procedure may have its place in the classroom, but its purpose must be clear to pupil and teacher. (5) An adequate psychological theory of learning should allow for learning by the application of rules, but current psychological theory cannot make any suggestions as to the characteristics these rules should have. (6) If the learner is construing every novel experience in terms of his prior experience, as Piaget assures us is the case, second language teachers can hardly bypass the first language and so, where possible, they should try to exploit it.

In this chapter I have surveyed a number of approaches to the explanation of language learning. The theorists differ in the models they make use of. Since the language teacher is teaching people, he will be best helped by a model which takes very close account of what happens in actual learning situations.

I hope I have achieved my aim of demonstrating the considerable relevance of research in first language learning to the teaching of a second language. I believe that the teacher can hope for further interesting and useful facts to emerge from such studies, and from studies of comprehension by adults.

Linguists are at work revealing the intricacies and complexities of linguistic structure. Perhaps it will be for psychologists to reveal the ingenuity of human beings in making light of complex learning and their resourcefulness in making the fullest use of limited syntactic means to communicate with one another.

10 Further Reading

Section 2. Language and stimulus response connections

Borger, Robert and Seaborne, A. E. M. 1966. *The Psychology of Learning.* Harmondsworth: Penguin Books. This book gives a good introduction to the basic concepts and principles of learning theory.

Lunzer, E. A. 1968. *Development in Learning*, Vol. 1, *The Regulation of Behaviour.* London: Staples Press. This is a much fuller and more critical treatment of learning theories in psychology, and covers Piaget's theory of cognitive development, as well as behaviourist learning theories. It was written primarily for students at colleges of education.

The following contain discussions of areas of psychology which are of relevance to the language teacher, i.e., perception, attention, memory, skill.

Neisser, U. 1967. *Cognitive Psychology.* New York: Appleton-Century-Crofts.

Fitts, P. M. and Posner, M. I. 1967. *Human Performance.* Belmont, Calif.: Brooks-Cole.

Norman, D. A. 1969. *Memory and Attention: An Introduction to Human Information Processing.* New York: John Wiley.

Annett, John 1969. *Feedback and Human Behaviour.* Harmondsworth: Penguin Books.

Summerfield, A. (ed.) 1971. Cognitive Psychology. *British Medical Bulletin*, 27, No. 3.

Section 3. Language as stimulus response connections with mediation

Mowrer, O. H. 1954. A psychologist looks at language. *American Psychologist*, 9, 660–94. In this paper Mowrer expounds his view of the sentence as a conditioning device and how the meaning of words is learnt through definitions.

Jenkins, James J. 1965. Mediation theory and grammatical behaviour. In S. Rosenberg (ed.) *Directions in Psycholinguistics.* New York: Macmillan. This is a discussion of the application of mediation theory to language learning and includes an explanation of the learning of grammatical class groupings in terms of mediation theory.

Fodor, J. A. 1965. Could meaning be an r_m? In R. C. Oldfield and J. C. Marshall (eds.) *Language*. Harmondsworth: Penguin Books. This is a brilliant and witty attack on the mediation theorists' explanation of language acquisition.

Section 4. Language and innate capacity

For Chomsky's theory of language acquisition:

Allen, J. P. B. and van Buren, Paul (eds.) 1971. *Chomsky: Selected Readings*. London: Oxford University Press.

A number of interesting papers relating to Chomsky's theory, and the role of cognitive development in the acquisition of syntax, are to be found in the following symposia:

Lenneberg, E. H. (ed.) 1964. *New Directions in the Study of Language*. Cambridge, Mass.: M.I.T. Press.

Lyons, J. and Wales, R. J. (eds.) 1966. *Psycholinguistic Papers*. Edinburgh: Edinburgh University Press.

Smith, F. and Miller, G. A. (eds.) 1966. *The Genesis of Language*. Cambridge, Mass.: M.I.T. Press.

Hayes, John R. (ed.) 1970. *Cognition and the Development of Language*. New York: John Wiley.

Morton, J. (ed.) 1972. *Biological and Social Factors in Psycholinguistics*. London: Logos.

Adams, A. (ed.) 1972. *Language in Thinking*. Harmondsworth: Penguin Books.

Section 5. Language acquisition and cognitive development

Ginsburg, H. and Opper, S. 1969. *Piaget's theory of Intellectual Development: An Introduction*. Englewood Cliffs, N.J.: Prentice Hall. A brief but very helpful introduction to Piaget's theory.

Flavell, J. H. 1963. *The Developmental Psychology of Jean Piaget*. Princeton, N.J.: D. Van Nostrand. A much fuller introduction to Piaget's work than the above.

For discussions of semantic development in terms similar to those of section 5.2 see papers by Donaldson and by Wales in Hayes (ed.), Morton (ed.) and Adams (ed.), mentioned above and the following paper by Clark:

Clark, Eve V. 1973. What's in a word? On the child's acquisition of semantics in his first language. In T. E. Moore (ed.) *Cognitive Development and the Acquisition of Language*. New York: Academic Press.

Section 6. Towards a broader framework

For a broadly based, brief review of language acquisition research from a psychological viewpoint see:

Slobin, Dan I. 1972. Seven questions about language development. In P. C. Dodwell (ed.) *New Horizons in Psychology 2*. Harmondsworth: Penguin Books.

For other discussions of the development of syntax, concerned with the role of the mother's speech see papers in Hayes (1970), mentioned above and the following:

Brown, R. 1968. The development of wh-questions in child speech. *Journal of Verbal Learning and Verbal Behaviour*, 7, 279–90.
Brown, R. and Bellugi, U. 1964. Three processes in the child's acquisition of syntax. *Harvard Educational Review*, 34, 133–51. (Also in E. H. Lenneberg (ed.) *New Directions in the Study of Language*, Cambridge, Mass: M.I.T. Press, 1964, and in R. Brown *Psycholinguistics*, New York: The Free Press, 1970.)
Ryan, Joanna F. 1973. Interpretation and imitation in early language development. In R. Hinde and J. S. Hinde (eds.) *Constraints on Learning*. London: Academic Press.

Section 7. Some studies of comprehension by adults

For brief introductions to psycholinguistics see the following:

Slobin, Dan I. 1971. *Psycholinguistics*. Glenview, Illinois: Scott, Foresman & Company.

Greene, Judith. 1972. *Psycholinguistics*. Harmondsworth: Penguin Books.

Also chapters in:

Lyons, J. (ed.) 1970. *New Horizons in Linguistics*. Harmondsworth: Penguin Books.

Less work has been done on the comprehension of continuous texts than on the comprehension of isolated sentences. Some work is reported in Fitts and Posner, mentioned above (section 2). Other work with texts is reported in the following papers, of which the first is particularly illuminating.

Bransford, John D. and Johnson, Marcia K. 1972. Considerations of some problems of comprehension. Paper presented at the Eighth Annual Carnegie Symposium on Cognition, Pittsburgh, May 1972.
Rabbitt, P. M. A. 1968. Channel capacity, intelligibility and short term memory. *Quarterly Journal of Experimental Psychology*, **20**, 241–8.
Sachs, J. S. 1967. Recognition memory for syntactic and semantic aspects of connected discourse. *Perception and Psychophysics*, 2, 439–42.
Augstein, Sheila and Thomas, Laurie 1973. *Developing Your Own Reading*. Reading Development Course, Unit 7. Bletchley, Bucks: The Open University Press.

Some papers on the comprehension of texts appear in:

Carroll, John B. and Freedle, Roy O. (eds.) 1972. *Language Comprehension and the Acquisition of Knowledge*. Washington, D.C.: V. H. Winston & Sons. The following are particularly interesting: Wallace L. Chafe, Discourse structure and human knowledge; Edward J. Crothers, Memory structure and the recall of discourse; Ernst Z. Rothkopf, Structural text features and the control of processes in learning from written materials.

List of special symbols

Grammar, phonology and semantics

A	Agentive
Adj	Adjective
Aux	Auxiliary
D	Dative
Det	Determiner
I	Instrumental
L	Locative
M	Modality
N	Noun
NP	Noun Phrase
O	Objective
P	Proposition
Prep Phrase	Prepositional Phrase
S	Sentence
V	Verb
Vb	Verb
Vb_{cop}	Copula Verb
$Vb_{intrans}$	Intransitive Verb
Vb_{loc}	Locational Verb
Vb_{trans}	Transitive Verb
VP	Verb Phrase
$\Rightarrow$	rewrite as (transformational rules)
$\rightarrow$	(1) rewrite as (phrase structure rules) (2) logical implication
$\sim$	not
$\wedge$	or
$\supset$	implies
:	is to, the ratio of
: :	as, equals: used between ratios
*	ungrammatical, or unacceptable, expression
{ }	extensional definition of a class

( )	semantic marker
[ ]	(1) grammatical feature
	(2) phonetic transcription
	(3) semantic distinguisher
+	(1) concatenation
	(2) positive value of binary variable
—	(1) concatenation
	(2) negative value of binary variable
/ /	phonemic transcription
//	tone group boundary

Psychology

S	stimulus
R	response
→	elicits, gives rise to/is connected, associated with
s_m	mediating stimulus
r_m	mediating response

General

RP	Received Pronunciation

Transcription conventions

English
Vowels

ɪ	bit	oi	boy
e	bet	au	cow
a	bat	ou	hoe
o	pot	u	two
ʊ	put	iə	ear
ʌ	but	eə	air
ə	*a*back	ɑ	car/calm
i	beat	ɔ	court/caught
ei	bait	uə	tour
ai	bite	ɜ	bird

Consonants

p	pin	f	fin
b	bin	v	vine
t	tin	θ	thin
d	din	ð	there
k	kin	s	sin
g	give	z	zinc
tʃ	church	ʃ	sheep
dʒ	judge	ʒ	treasure
m	miss	h	him
n	nip	l	lip
ŋ	sing	r	rip

Semi vowels

j	yes	w	win

*French**

Vowels

i	vive	y	mu
e	thé	ø	eux
ɛ	aise	œ	seul
a	table	ə	p*e*ser
ɑ	âme	ɛ̃	bain
ɔ	homme	ɑ̃	banc
o	tôt	ɔ̃	bon
u	boue	œ̃	brun

(: denotes length)

Consonants

p	paix	l	livre
b	bas	r	rare
t	tout	f	faux
d	dos	v	vive
k	cas	s	si
g	gai	z	zéro
m	mais	ʃ	chanter
n	non	ʒ	jupe
ɲ	ga*gn*er		

Semi-vowels

w	oui	j	envo*y*er
ɥ	huit		

* From L. E. Armstrong *The Phonetics of French*. London: Bell 1932.

References

Abercrombie, D. 1956. *Problems and Principles in Language Study*. London: Longman.

Albrow, K. H. 1968. *The Rhythm and Intonation of Spoken English*. London: Longman.

Allen, J. P. B. 1973. Applied grammatical models in a remedial English syllabus. In S. P. Corder and E. Roulet (eds.) *Theoretical Linguistic Models in Applied Linguistics*. Brussels: AIMAV and Paris: Didier.

Allen, J. P. B. and Widdowson, H. G. 1974. Teaching the communicative use of English. *IRAL*, 12, 1–21.

Annett, John 1969. *Feedback and Human Behaviour*. Harmondsworth: Penguin Books.

Arsenian, S. 1945. Bilingualism in the post war world. *Psychological Bulletin*, 42, 65–86.

Asher, James J. 1964. Vision and audition in language learning. *Perceptual and Motor Skills* **19**. Monograph Supplement (1-V, 19), 255–300.

Austin, J. L. 1962. *How To Do Things With Words*. Oxford: The Clarendon Press and Cambridge, Mass.: Harvard University Press.

Ball, Susan and Bogatz, Gerry A. 1970. *The First Year of Sesame Street: An Evaluation*. Educational Testing Services, Princeton. Available from Teachers College Press, 525 W. 120th Street, New York 10027.

Bannister, D. 1966. A new theory of personality. In B. M. Foss (ed.) *New Horizons in Psychology*. Harmondsworth: Penguin Books.

Bannister, D. and Fransella, Fay 1971. *Inquiring Man: The Theory of Personal Constructs*. Harmondsworth: Penguin Books.

Bar-Adon, A. 1971. Primary syntactic structures in Hebrew child language. In A. Bar-Adon and W. F. Leopold (eds.) *Child Language: A Book of Readings*. New Jersey: Prentice Hall, 434–72.

Bellugi, Ursula 1971. Simplification in children's language. In R. Huxley and E. Ingram (eds.) *Language Acquisition: Models and Methods*. London: Academic Press, 95–117.

Berko, Jean 1958. The child's learning of English morphology. *Word*, 14, 150–77. Also in A. Bar-Adon and W. F. Leopold (eds.) 1971. *Child Language: A Book of Readings*. New Jersey: Prentice Hall, 153–67.

Berlyne, Daniel E. 1963. Soviet research on intellectual processes in children. In J. C. Wright and J. Kagan (eds.) *Basic Cognitive Processes in Children. Monographs of the Society for Research in Child Development*, Vol. 28, No. 2.

Bever, T. G. 1970. The cognitive basis for linguistic structures. In J. R. Hayes (ed.) *Cognition and the Development of Language*. New York: Wiley, 279–362.

Blodgett, H. C. 1929. The effect of the introduction of reward upon the maze performance of rats. *Univ. Calif. Publ. Psychol.* 4, 113–37.

Bloom, Lois M. 1969. Language development: form and function in emerging grammars. Columbia University Ph.D. 1968. University Microfilms Inc. Ann Arbor, Michigan.

Bloom, Lois M. 1970. *Language Development: Form and Function in Emerging Grammars.* Cambridge, Mass.: M.I.T. Press.

Bloom, Lois M. (in press). Why not pivot grammar. *Journal of Speech and Hearing Disorders*, 36, 40–50. Reprinted in C. A. Ferguson and D. I. Slobin (eds.) *Studies of Child Language Development*, 1973. New York: Holt, Rinehart, Winston.

Bloomfield, L. 1933. *Language*. New York: Holt, Rinehart, Winston. London: Allen & Unwin, 1935.

Bolinger, D. 1971. Semantic overloading: a restudy of the verb 'remind'. In *Language*, 47, 522–47.

Bogatz, Gerry A. and Ball, Susan. 1971. *The Second Year of Sesame Street: A Continuing Evaluation.* Vols. I and II. Educational Testing Services, Princeton, New Jersey.

Bowers, Frederick. 1971. Meaning and sentence structure. In *The English Quarterly*. Canadian Council of Teachers of English, Vol. 4 No. 2.

Boyd, J. and Thorne, J. P. 1969. The semantics of modal verbs. In *Journal of Linguistics*, 5, 57–74.

Bradley, D. R. 1966. An investigation of a theory of reading. Dissertation for the Diploma of Applied Linguistics, University of Edinburgh.

Brown, G. (forthcoming). *The Comprehension of Spoken English.*

Brown, Roger. 1958. *Words and Things*. New York: The Free Press.

Brown, Roger. 1968. The development of wh-questions in child speech. *Journal of Verbal Learning and Verbal Behaviour*, 7, 279–90.

Brown, Roger and Bellugi, Ursula. 1964. Three processes in the child's acquisition of syntax. *Harvard Educational Review*, 34, 133–51. Also in A. Bar-Adon and W. F. Leopold (eds.) 1971. *Child Language: A Book of Readings*, 307–18.

Brown, Roger, Cazden, C. B. and Bellugi, U. 1968. The child's grammar from I–III. In John P. Hill (ed.) *The 1967 Minnesota Symposium on Child Psychology*. Minneapolis: University of Minnesota Press, 28–73. Also in A. Bar-Adon and W. F. Leopold (eds.) 1971. *Child Language: A Book of Readings*, 382–412.

Brown, Roger and Hanlon, Camille. 1970. Derivational complexity and the order of acquisition in child speech. In J. R. Hayes (ed.) *Cognition and the Development of Language*. New York: Wiley.

Bruner, J. S., Goodnow, J. J. and Austin, G. A. 1956. *A Study of Thinking*. New York: Wiley.

Bullowa, Margaret. 1970. The start of the language process. *Actes du Congres International des Linguistes*. Bucharest 28 Août-2 Septembre 1967, III, Editiones de l'Académie de la Republique Socialiste de Roumanie, 191–200.

Burling, R. 1959. Language development of a Garo and English speaking child. *Word*, 15, 45–68. Also in A. Bar-Adon and W. F. Leopold (eds.) 1971. *Child Language: A Book of Readings*, 170–85.

Butler, Robert A. 1954. Curiosity in monkeys. *Scientific American*, **190**, 70–5.

Butterworth, G. 1972. Progress report on an adolescent's acquisition of English, U.C.L.A. Reported in E. R. Hatch Studies in second language acquisition. Paper presented at the Third International Congress of Applied Linguistics, Copenhagen, August 1972.

Campbell, R. and Wales, R. 1970. The study of language acquisition. In J. Lyons (ed.) *New Horizons in Linguistics*. Harmondsworth: Penguin.

Carroll, John B. 1953. *The Study of Language: A Survey of Linguistics and other Related Disciplines in America*. Cambridge, Mass.: Harvard University Press and London: Oxford University Press.

Carroll, John B. 1955. The prediction of success in foreign language learning. In R. Glazer (ed.) *Training Research and Education*. New York: Wiley.

Carroll, John B. 1958. A factor analysis of two foreign language aptitude batteries. *The Journal of General Psychology*, **59**, 3–19.

Carroll, John B. 1965. Research on teaching foreign languages. In N. L. Gage (ed.) *Handbook of Research on Teaching*. Chicago: Rand McNally, 1060–1100.

Carroll, John B. 1966. Research in foreign language testing: the last five years. In R. Mead (ed.) *Language Teaching Broader Contexts*. North East Conference on the Teaching of Foreign Languages, 12–42.

Carroll, John B. 1969. Psychological and educational research into second language teaching to young children. In H. H. Stern (ed.) *Languages and the Young School Child*. Language and Language Learning Series. London: Oxford University Press, 56–68.

Carroll, John B. 1971. Implications of aptitude test research and psycholinguistic theory for foreign language teaching. Paper presented at Colloquium 15: Achievements and prospects in the application of psycholinguistics to the teaching of foreign language. XVIIth International Congress, International Association of Applied Psychology, Liege, July 1971. Also Research Memorandum RM 71–14, Educational Testing Service, Princeton, New Jersey.

Carroll, John B. and Sapon, S. M. 1959. The modern language aptitude test. New York: Psychological Corporation.

Catford, J. C. 1959. The teaching of English as a foreign language. In R.

Quirk and A. H. Smith (eds.) *The Teaching of English*. London: Secker & Warburg. Reprinted in Language and Language Learning Series, London: Oxford University Press.

Catford, J. C. 1968. Contrastive analysis and language teaching. Georgetown Monograph Series on Languages and Linguistics, **21**. 19th Annual Round Table Conference, 159–73.

Cazden, Courtney B. 1968. The acquisition of noun and verb inflections. *Child Development*, **39**, 433–48.

Cazden, Courtney B. (in press). Two paradoxes in the acquisition of language structure and functions. In J. S. Bruner and K. J. Connolly (eds.) *The Development of Competence in Early Childhood*. New York: Academic Press.

Cheydleur, F. D. 1932. An experiment in adult learning of French. *Journal of Educational Research*, **26**, 259–75.

Chomsky, N. 1957. *Syntactic Structures*. The Hague: Mouton.

Chomsky, N. 1959. Review of B. F. Skinner, Verbal Behaviour. *Language*, **35**, 26–58. Reprinted in J. A. Fodor and J. J. Katz (eds.) *The Structure of Language*. Englewood Cliffs, N.J.: Prentice Hall, 1964.

Chomsky, N. 1964. Current issues in linguistic theory. In J. A. Fodor and J. J. Katz (eds.), *The Structure of Language*. Englewood Cliffs, N.J.: Prentice Hall, 1964.

Chomsky, N. 1965. *Aspects of the Theory of Syntax*. Cambridge, Mass.: M.I.T. Press.

Chomsky, N. 1968a. *Language and Mind*. New York: Harcourt Brace. New enlarged edition 1972.

Chomsky, N. 1968b. Deep structure, surface structure, and semantic interpretation. In *Studies on Semantics in Generative Grammar*. The Hague: Mouton, 1972.

Chomsky, N. and Halle, M. 1968. *The Sound Pattern of English*. New York: Harper & Row.

Church, J. 1971. Methods for the study of early cognitive functioning. In R. Huxley and E. Ingram (eds.) *Language Acquisition: Models and Methods*. London: Academic Press, 175–93.

Clark, Eve V. 1973. What's in a word? On the child's acquisition of semantics in his first language. In T. E. Moore (ed.) *Cognitive Development and the Acquisition of Language*. New York: Academic Press.

Clark, Ruth 1972. Imitation, production and comprehension and how they are related in children's performance. *Edinburgh Working Papers in Linguistics*, **1**. Dept. of Linguistics, Edinburgh University.

Clark, Ruth, Hutcheson, Sandy and van Buren, Paul 1974. Comprehension and production in language acquisition. *Journal of Linguistics*, **10**, 39–54.

Clark, Ruth 1974. Performing without competence. *Journal of Child Language*, **1**, 1–10.

Cleveland, H., Mangone, G. J., and Adams, J. C. 1960. *The Overseas Americans*.

New York: McGraw Hill.

Conklin, H. C. 1955. Hanunoo Color Categories. *Southwestern Journal of Anthropology*, 11, 339–44. Also in Dell Hymes (ed.) *Language in Culture and Society. A Reader in Linguistics and Anthropology*. New York: Harper & Row, 1964.

Crowder, Norman A. 1960. Automatic tutoring by intrinsic programming. In A. A. Lumsdaine and R. Glaser (eds.) *Teaching Machines and Programmed Learning: A Source Book*. Washington, D.C.: National Education Association of the United States.

Crystal, D. 1969. *Prosodic Systems and Intonation in English*. Cambridge: Cambridge University Press.

Curme, G. O. 1931. *Syntax* (*A Grammar of the English Language*, Vol. 3) Boston: Heath.

Curme, G. O. 1935. *Parts of Speech and Accidence* (*A Grammar of the English Language*, Vol. 2). Boston: Heath.

Dakin, Julian 1973. *The Language Laboratory and Language Learning*. London: Longman.

Darcy, N. T. 1946. The effect of bilingualism on measurement of the IQ of children of pre-school age. *Journal of Educational Psychology*, 37, 21–44.

Davies, Alan 1971. Language aptitudes in the first year of the U.K. secondary school. *Regional English Language Centre Journal* (Singapore), 2, 4–19. London: Oxford University Press.

Davies, Alan 1974. *Language Aptitude and Proficiency*. Final report submitted to the Scottish Education Department. Edinburgh: The Scottish Office.

Davies, M. and Hughes, M. 1927. The comparative intelligence and attainments of Jewish and non-Jewish school children. *British Journal of Psychology*, 18, 134–47.

Diller, K. C. 1972. *Is there an optimum age for foreign language learning?* Paper presented to the Third International Congress of Applied Linguistics. Copenhagen, August 1972.

Donaldson, Margaret 1966. Prepared comments on David McNeill, The creation of language by children. In J. Lyons and R. J. Wales (eds.) *Psycholinguistic Papers: The Proceedings of the 1966 Edinburgh Conference*. Edinburgh: Edinburgh University Press.

Dunkeld, Jane 1972. Unpublished Ph.D. Thesis, Dept. of Psychology, Edinburgh University.

Fillmore, C. J. 1968. The case for case. In E. Bach and R.T. Harms (eds.) *Universals in Linguistic Theory*. New York: Holt, Rinehart, Winston.

Fillmore, C. J. 1971. Verbs of judging: an exercise in semantic description. In C. J. Fillmore and D. T. Langendoen (eds.) *Studies in Linguistic Semantics*. New York: Holt, Rinehart, Winston.

Firth, J. R. 1957a. *Papers in Linguistics, 1934–1951*. London: Oxford University Press.

Firth, J. R. 1957b. Synopsis of linguistic theory, 1930–55. In *Studies in Linguistic Analysis*, a special publication of the Philological Society. Oxford: Blackwell.

Fowler, H. W. 1926. *A Dictionary of Modern English Usage*. Oxford: The Clarendon Press.

Francis, W. Nelson 1958. *The Structure of American English*. New York: Ronald.

Fried, V. (ed.) 1972. *The Prague School of Linguistics and Language Teaching*. London: Oxford University Press.

Fries, C. C. 1945. *Teaching and Learning English as a Foreign Language*. Ann Arbor: University of Michigan Press.

Fries, C. C. 1952. *The Structure of English: An Introduction to the Construction of English Sentences*. New York: Harcourt Brace. Reprinted London: Longman, 1957.

Fries, C. C. 1955. American linguistics and the teaching of English. *Language Learning*, 6, Nos. 1 and 2, 1–22.

Gagné, Robert M. 1965. *The Conditions of Learning*. New York: Holt, Rinehart, Winston. (London edition 1969).

Gahogan, G. A. and Gahogan, D. M. 1968. Paired associate learning as partial validation of a language development programme. *Child Development*, **39**, 119–32.

Gaarder, A. B. 1970. The first seventy-six bilingual education projects. Georgetown Monograph Series on Languages and Linguistics *23*. 21st Annual Round Table Conference, 163–78.

Galanter, Eugene 1966. *Textbook of Elementary Psychology*. San Francisco: Holden-Day, Inc.

Gardner, R. A. and Gardner, B. T. 1969. Teaching sign language to a chimpanzee. *Science*, 165, 664–72.

Gardner, R. C. and Lambert, W. 1959. Motivational variable in second language acquisition. *Canadian Journal of Psychology*, 13, 266–72.

Gimson, A. C. 1962. *An Introduction to the Pronunciation of English*. London: Edward Arnold.

Gordon, D. and Lakoff, G. 1971. Conversational postulates. Paper read at the Seventh Regional Meeting, Chicago Linguistic Society, Chicago.

Graham, N. C. 1968. Memory span and language proficiency. *Journal of Learning Disabilities*, 1, 644–8. Also in E. Stones (ed.) 1970. *Readings in Educational Psychology: Learning and Teaching*. London: Methuen, 408–24.

Gruber, Jeffrey S. 1967. Topicalization in child language. *Foundations of Language*, 3, 37–65.

Halliday, M. A. K. 1961. Categories of the theory of grammar. *Word*, 17, 241–92.

Halliday, M. A. K. 1967. *Intonation and Grammar in British English*. The

Hague: Mouton.

Halliday, M. A. K. 1967–68. Notes on transitivity and theme in English. In *Journal of Linguistics*, 3, 37–81, 199–244 and 4, 179–215.

Halliday, M. A. K. 1970a. Language structure and language function. In J. Lyons (ed.) *New Horizons in Linguistics*. Harmondsworth: Penguin.

Halliday, M. A. K. 1970b. Functional diversity in language as seen from a consideration of modality and mood in English. In *Foundations of Language*, 6, 322–61.

Halliday, M. A. K. 1971. Language in a social perspective. *Educational Review*, 23, 165–88.

Halliday, M. A. K. (forthcoming). Learning how to mean. In Eric and Elizabeth Lenneberg (eds.) *Foundations of Language Development: A Multidisciplinary Approach*. Paris: UNESCO.

Harris, Zellig S. 1946. From morpheme to utterance. *Language*, 22, 161–83. Reprinted in Martin Joos (ed.) *Readings in Linguistics I*. Chicago and London: Chicago University Press, 1966.

Heider, Eleanor R. (in press). On the internal structure of perceptual and semantic categories. In T. E. Moore (ed.) *Cognitive Development and the Acquisition of Language*. London: Academic Press.

Herriot, Peter 1970. *An Introduction to the Psychology of Language*. London: Methuen.

Hess, Eckhard H. 1962. Ethology: An approach toward the complete analysis of behavior. In R. Brown *et al.*, *New Directions in Psychology*. New York: Holt, Rinehart, Winston.

Hockett, C. F. 1942. A system of descriptive phonology. *Language*, 18, 3–21.

Hockett, C. F. 1954. Two models of grammatical description. *Word*, 10, 210–31. Reprinted in Martin Joos (ed.) *Readings in Linguistics I*, Chicago and London: Chicago University Press, 1966.

Hockett, C. F. 1960a. Logical considerations in the study of animal communication. In W. D. Lanyon and W. N. Tavolga (eds.) *Animal Sounds and Communication*. Washington, D.C.: American Inst. Biol. Sciences.

Hockett, C. F. 1960b. The origins of speech. *Scientific American*, 203, 89–96. Offprint 603. San Francisco: Freeman & Co.

Humboldt, Wilhelm von 1836. *Uber die Verschiedenheit des Menschlichen Sprachbaues*. Berlin. Heruitgave, Darmstadt: Claasen & Roether, 1949.

Huxley, R. and Ingram, E. (eds.) 1971. *Language Acquisition: Models and Methods*. London: Academic Press.

Hymes, Dell 1971. Competence and performance in linguistic theory. In R. Huxley and E. Ingram (eds.) *Language Acquisition: Models and Methods*. London: Academic Press, 3–24.

Ingram, David 1971. Transitivity in child language. *Language*, 47, 888–910.

Ingram, Elisabeth 1964. Age and language learning. In P. Libbish (ed.) *Advances in the teaching of modern languages*, *I*. Oxford: Pergamon.

Ingram, Elisabeth 1970. Trial project: the relation between English language proficiency and academic success. Unpublished data Dept. of Linguistics, Edinburgh University.

Ingram, Elisabeth 1971. A further note on the relationship between psychological and linguistic theories. *International Journal of Applied Linguistics*, 4, 335–46.

Ingram, Elisabeth 1972. Review of Philip D. Smith 1970, *A Comparison of the Cognitive and Audiolingual Approaches to Foreign Language Instruction.* (The Pennsylvania Project). Philadelphia: The Centre for Curriculum Development Inc. *International Review of Applied Linguistics*, 10, 384–94.

Jacobson, R. 1966. The role of deep structures in language teaching. In *Language Learning*, 16, 153–60.

Jakobson, Roman 1969. *Child Language: Aphasis and the Phonological Universals.* New York. (Original publication: *Kindersprache, Aphasie und Allegemeine Lautgesetze.* Upsala, 1941).

Jakobovits, Leon A. 1970. *Foreign Language Learning: A Psycholinguistic Analysis of the Issues.* Rowley, Mass.: Newbury House.

Jenkins, James J. 1965. Mediation theory and grammatical behaviour. In S. Rosenberg (ed.) *Directions in Psycholinguistics.* New York: Macmillan.

Jespersen, J. O. H. 1909–49. *A Modern English Grammar on Historical Principles.* København: Ejnar Munksgaard.

Jespersen, Otto 1922. *Language: Its Nature, Development and Origin.* London: Allen & Unwin. New York: Macmillan, 1959.

John, Vera P. 1968. A study of language changes in integrated and homogeneous classrooms. Progress Report 2. Yeshiva University, New York.

Jones, D. 1962. *An Outline of English Phonetics.* 9th edition, reprinted with alterations. Cambridge: Heffer.

Jones, D. 1967. *The Phoneme: Its Nature and Use.* 3rd edition. Cambridge: Heffer.

Jones, W. R. 1952. The language handicap of Welsh-speaking children. *British Journal of Educational Psychology*, 22, 114–23.

Kalmus, H. 1966. Ontogenetic, genetical and phylogenetic parallels between animal communication and pre-linguistic child behavior. In Smith and Miller (eds.) *The Genesis of Language.* Cambridge, Mass.: M.I.T. Press.

Kaplan, Eleanor L. 1970. Intonation and language acquisition. *Papers and reports on child language development, No. 1.* Stanford University, Stanford, California, 1–21.

Katz, P. A. 1963. Effects of labels on children's perception and discrimination learning. *Journal of Experimental Psychology*, 66, 423–8.

Katz, J. J. and Fodor, J. A. 1963. The structure of a semantic theory. *Language*, 39, 170–210.

Katz, J. J. and Postal, Paul 1964. *An Integrated Theory of Linguistic Descriptions.* Cambridge, Mass.: M.I.T. Press.

Kendler, H. H. and Kendler, T. S. 1961. Effect of verbalization on reversal shifts in children. *Science*, **141**, 1619–20.
Kersh, B. Y. and Wittrock, M. C. 1967. Learning by discovery: an interpretation of recent research. In J. P. de Cecco (ed.) *The Psychology of Language: Thought and Instruction*. New York: Holt, Rinehart, Winston, 394–402.
Kingdon, R. 1958. *The Groundwork of English Stress*. London: Longman.
Klima, E. S. and Bellugi, U. 1966. Syntactic regularities in the speech of children. In J. Lyons and R. J. Wales (eds.) *Psycholinguistic Papers: The Proceedings of the 1966 Edinburgh Conference*. Edinburgh: Edinburgh University Press.
Kramer, P., Koff, E. and Luria, Z. (in press). The development of competence in an exceptional structure of English in children and young adults, ages 8–20. *Child Development*.
Kruisinga, E. 1925. *A Handbook of Present-Day English*, 4th edition. Utrecht: Kemink en Zoon.
La Civita, A. F., Kean, J. M. and Yamamoto, K. 1966. Socio-economic status of children and acquisition of grammar. *Journal of Educational Research*, **60**, 71–4.
Lakoff, George 1968. On instrumental adverbs and the concept of deep structure. *Foundations of Language*, **4**, 7–29.
Lambert, W. 1970. Some cognitive consequences of following the curricula of the early school grades in a foreign language. *Georgetown Monograph Series on Languages and Linguistics 23*, 21st Round Table Conference, 229–79.
Lashley, K. S. 1951. The problem of serial order in behavior. In L. A. Jefress (ed.) *Cerebral Mechanisms in behavior*. New York: Wiley. Reprinted in S. Saporta (ed.) 1961, *Psycholinguistics*. New York: Holt, Rinehart, Winston.
Laver, J. D. L. 1968. Voice quality and indexical information. *British Journal of Disorders of Communication*, **3**, 43–54.
Learned, S. and Wood, Ben D. 1938. *The Student and his Knowledge*. New York: Carnegie Foundation.
Leech, G. N. 1971. *Meaning and the English Verb*. London: Longman.
Leopold, W. F. 1949. *Speech Development of a Bilingual Child*, Vol. III. Evanston, Illinois: Northwestern University.
Leopold, W. F. 1953. Patterning in children's language learning. *Language Learning*, **5**, 1–14. Also in A. Bar-Adon and W. F. Leopold (eds.) 1971, *Child Language: A Book of Readings*. New Jersey: Prentice Hall, 135–41.
Letham, Margaret 1970. A case grammar approach to child language. Unpublished M.Litt.Dissertation. Department of Linguistics, University of Edinburgh.
Lieberman, P. 1967. *Intonation, Perception and Language*. Cambridge, Mass.: M.I.T. Press.
Lowth, Robert 1762. *A Short Introduction to English Grammar*.

Lyons, John 1963. *Structural Semantics.* Publications of the Philological Society, 20. Oxford: Blackwell.

Lyons, John 1968. *Introduction to Theoretical Linguistics.* Cambridge: Cambridge University Press.

Lyons, John 1972. Human language. In R. A. Hinde (ed.) *Non-Verbal Communication.* Cambridge: Cambridge University Press.

Malinowski, B. 1930. The problem of meaning in primitive languages. Supplement 1 to C. K. Ogden and I. A. Richards, *Meaning of Meaning* (3rd Edition). London: Kegan Paul.

McArthur, T. 1972. *Building English Words.* London and Glasgow: Collins.

McCarthy, Dorothea 1954. Language development in children. In Carmichael (ed.) *Manual of Child Psychology.* New York: Wiley.

McCawley, James 1968. The role of semantics in grammar. In Emmon Bach and Robert T. Harms (eds.) *Universals in Linguistic Theory.* New York: Holt, Rinehart, Winston.

McCawley, James 1970. English as a VSO language. *Language,* 46, 286–99.

McNeill, David 1966a. Developmental psycholinguistics. In F. Smith and G. A. Miller (eds.) *The Genesis of Language: A Psycholinguistic Approach.* Cambridge, Mass.: M.I.T. Press, 15–84.

McNeill, David 1966b. The creation of language by children. In J. Lyons and R. J. Wales (eds.) *Psycholinguistic Papers.* Edinburgh: Edinburgh University Press, 99–132.

McNeill, David 1970. *The Acquisition of Language: The Study of Developmental Psycholinguistics.* New York: Harper & Row.

McNeill, David 1971. Explaining linguistic universals. In John Morton (ed.) *Biological and Social Factors in Psycholinguistics.* London: Logos Press.

Matthews, Paul H. 1967. Review of N. Chomsky, *Aspects of the Theory of Syntax.* In *Journal of Linguistics,* 3, 119–52.

Mehler, Jacques 1971. Studies in language and thought development. In R. Huxley and E. Ingram (eds.) *Language Acquisition: Models and Methods.* London: Academic Press, 201–25.

Menyuk, Paula 1969. *Sentences Children Use.* Cambridge, Mass.: M.I.T. Press.

Miller, George 1956. The magical number seven, plus or minus two: some limits on our capacity for processing information. *Psychol. Rev.,* 63, 81–97.

Miller, Jim 1973. A note on so-called 'discovery procedures'. *Foundations of Language,* 10, 123—39.

Miller, Neil E. and Dollard, J. 1941. *Social Learning and Imitation.* New Haven: Yale University Press.

Montgomery, M. G. P. 1972. Reading strategies of native and non-native speakers. Unpub. M.Litt., Dept. of Linguistics, Edinburgh University.

Moore, D. 1971. A comparison of two methods of teaching specific language skills to lower-class pre-school children. Unpublished paper, Harvard

Graduate School of Education. Cambridge, Mass.
Moore, T. E. (ed.) 1973. *Cognitive Development and the Acquisition of Language*. New York: Academic Press.
Morton, John (ed.) 1971. *Biological and Social Factors in Psycholinguistics*. London: Logos Press.
Mowrer, O. H. 1954. A psychologist looks at language. *American Psychologist*, 9, 660–94.
Neisser, Ulrich 1966. *Cognitive Psychology*. New York: Appleton-Century-Crofts.
Nesfield, J. C. and Wood, F. T. 1964. *Manual of English Grammar and Composition*. (First edition 1898). London: Macmillan.
Nida, Eugene A. 1966. *A Synopsis of English Syntax*, 2nd revised edition. The Hague: Mouton.
O'Connor, J. D. and Arnold, G. F. 1961. *Intonation in Colloquial English*. London: Longman.
Olson, David R. 1970. Language and thought: Aspects of a cognitive theory of semantics. *Psychological Review*, 77, 257–73.
Osgood, Charles E. 1953. *Method and Theory in Experimental Psychology*. New York: Oxford University Press.
Osser, Harry, Wang, M. and Zaid, F. 1969. The young child's ability to imitate and comprehend speech: a comparison of two subcultural groups. *Child Development*, 40, 1063–75.
Palermo, David S. and Eberhart, V. Lynn 1968. On the learning of morphological rules: an experimental analogy. *Journal of Verbal Learning and Verbal Behaviour*, 7, 337–44.
Palermo, David S. and Howe, H. H. Jr. 1970. An experimental analogy to the learning of past tense inflection rules. *Journal of Verbal Learning and Verbal Behaviour*, 8, 410–16.
Palmer, F. R. 1965. *A Linguistic Study of the English Verb*. London: Longman.
Partridge, Eric 1963. *Usage and Abusage*. Harmondsworth: Penguin Reference Books.
Palmer, F. R. (ed.) 1970. *Prosodic Analysis*. London: Oxford University Press.
Palmer, H. E. 1916. *Colloquial English, Part I: 100 Substitution Tables*. Heffer's Phonetic Series. Cambridge: Heffer.
Palmer, H. E. 1921. *The Oral Method of Teaching Languages*. Cambridge: Heffer.
Pike, Kenneth L. 1967. *Language in Relation to a Unified Theory of Human Behaviour*, 2nd revised edition. The Hague: Mouton.
Pimsleur, Paul 1966. *Manual: Language Aptitude Battery*. New York: Harcourt, Brace.
Pimsleur, Paul, Mace, L., and Keislar, E. 1961. Preliminary discrimination training in the teaching of French pronunciation. University of California,

Los Angeles.

Pimsleur, Paul, Sundland, D. M., Bonkowski, R. J., and Mosberg, L. 1964. Further study of the transfer of verbal materials across sense modalities. *Journal of Educational Psychology*, 55, 96–102.

Politzer, R. 1953. Student motivation and interest in elementary language courses. *Language Learning*, 5, 15–21.

Poutsma, Hendrik 1914–29. *A Grammar of Late Modern English*, 2nd edition. Groningen: P. Noordhoff.

Premack, Ann J. and Premack, David 1972. Teaching language to an ape. *Scientific American*, **227**, 92–9.

Premack, D. 1970. The education of Sarah. *Psychology Today*, 4. See also *New Society*, **422**, 1970, 768–70.

Quigley, Helen 1971. Reactions of eleven nursery teachers and assistants to the Peabody Language Development Kit. *British Journal of Educational Psychology*, 41, 155–62.

Quirk, R. 1959. English language and the structural approach. In R. Quirk and A. H. Smith (eds.) *The Teaching of English*. London: Secker and Warburg. Reprinted in Language and Language Learning Series, London: Oxford University Press.

Quirk, R. and Svartvik, J. 1966. *Investigating Linguistic Acceptability*. The Hague: Mouton.

Robinson, W. P. 1971. Social factors and language development in primary school children. In R. Huxley and E. Ingram *Language Acquisition: Models and Methods*. London: Academic Press. 49–64.

Robinson, W. P. and Rackstraw, S. J. 1972. *A Question of Answers*. London: Routledge.

Romney, A. K. and D'Andrade, R. G. 1964. Transcultural studies in Cognition. *American Anthropologist*, 66, no. 3, part 2 (Special Publication).

Rosch, E. H. 1973. On the internal structure of perceptual and semantic categories. In T. E. Moore (ed.) *Cognitive Development and the Acquisition of Language*. New York: Academic Press.

Ross, J. R. 1970. On declarative sentences. In R. A. Jacobs and P. S. Rosenbaum (eds.) *Readings in English Transformational Grammar*. Waltham, Mass.: Ginn.

Rowe, F. J. and Webb, W. T. 1928. *A Guide to the Study of English*. (First edition 1914). London: Macmillan.

Ryan, J. F. 1973. Interpretation and imitation in early language development. In R. Hinde and J. S. Hinde (eds.) *Constraints on Learning*. New York: Academic Press.

Salzman, I. J. 1964. *The construction and evaluation of a self-instructional program in Russian*. Bloomington, Indiana: Department of Psychology, Indiana University.

Sapir, Edward 1921. *Language*. New York: Harcourt, Brace and World.

Saporta, Sol 1966. Applied linguistics and generative grammar. In A. Valdman (ed.) *Trends in Language Teaching*. New York: McGraw-Hill.

Saussure, Ferdinand de 1955. *Cours de Linguistique Générale*. Paris: Payot, 5th edition. (First edition 1916). English translation by Wade Baskin, *Course in General Linguistics*. New York: Philosophical Library, 1959.

Scherer, George A. C. and Wertheimer, Michael 1964. *A Psycholinguistic Experiment in Foreign Language Teaching*. New York: McGraw-Hill.

Schlesinger, I. M. 1971. The grammar of sign language and the problem of language universals. In John Morton (ed.) *Biological and Social Factors in Psycholinguistics*. London: Logos Press, 98–121.

Schubiger, M. 1935. *The Role of Intonation in Spoken English*. St. Gallen: Fehr'sche Buchhandlung.

Schubiger, M. 1958. *English Intonation: Its Form and Function*. Tubingen: Max Niemeyer.

Searle, J. R. 1969. *Speech Acts*. Cambridge: Cambridge University Press.

Shriner, T. H. and Miner, L. 1968. Morphological structure in the language of disadvantaged and advantaged children. *Journal of Speech and Hearing Research*, 11, 605–10. Also in F. Williams (ed.) *Language and Poverty*.

Shuy, R. W., Wolfram, W. A. and Riley, W. K. 1967. Linguistic correlates of social stratification in Detroit Speech. US Office of Education Co-operative Research Project No. 6–1347.

Siegel, Sidney 1956. *Nonparametric Statistics for the Behavioural Sciences*. New York: McGraw-Hill. International Student Edition.

Sinclair, H. 1969. Developmental psycholinguistics. In D. Elkind, J. H. Flavell (eds.) *Studies in Cognitive Development. Essays in Honor of Jean Piaget*. New York: Oxford University Press. Also excerpts in P. Adams (ed.) *Language in Thinking*. Harmondsworth: Penguin Books. Chapters 15 and 19.

Sinclair, H. 1970. The transition from sensory-motor behaviour to symbolic activity. *Interchange*, 1, No. 3.

Sinclair, H. 1971. Sensorimotor action patterns as a condition for the acquisition of syntax. In R. Huxley and E. Ingram (eds.) *Language Acquisition: Models and Methods*. London and New York: Academic Press.

Skinner, B. F. 1953. *Science and Human Behavior*. New York: The Free Press and London: Collier-Macmillan.

Skinner, B. F. 1957. *Verbal Behaviour*. New York: Appleton-Century-Crofts.

Sledd, James 1959. *A Short Introduction to English Grammar*. Chicago: Scott, Foresman.

Slobin, Dan I. 1966a. Abstracts of Soviet studies of child language. In F. Smith and G. A. Miller (eds.) *The Genesis of Language: a psycholinguistic approach*. Cambridge, Mass.: M.I.T. Press, 363–86.

Slobin, Dan I. 1966b. Grammatical transformations and sentence comprehension in childhood and adulthood. *Journal of Verbal Learning and Verbal*

Behaviour, 7, 876–81.

Slobin, Dan I. 1968. Early grammatical development in several languages, with special attention to Soviet Research. *Working Paper 11*, Language Behavior Research Laboratory, University of California, Berkeley.

Slobin, Dan I. 1970. Universals of grammatical development in children. In Flous D'Arcais and J. M. Levelt (eds.) *Advances in Psycholinguistics*. Amsterdam and London: North Holland Publishing Co., 174–86.

Slobin, Dan I. (forthcoming). Early grammatical development in several languages with special reference to Russian. In T. G. Bever and W. Weksel (eds.) *The Structure and Psychology of Language*, Vol. 2. New York: Holt Rinehart, Winston.

Slobin, Dan I. and Welsh, C. A. 1968. Elicited imitation as a research tool in developmental psycholinguistics. *Working Paper No. 10*. Language Behavior Research Laboratory. University of California, Berkeley. Reprinted in C. A. Ferguson and D. I. Slobin (eds.) 1973, *Studies of Child Language Development*. New York: Holt, Rinehart, Winston.

Smith, C. 1970. An experimental approach to children's linguistic competence. In John R. Hayes (ed.) *Cognition and the Development of Language*. New York: Wiley.

Smith, Philip D. Jr. 1970. *A Comparison of the Cognitive and Audiolingual Approaches to Foreign Language Instruction* (The Pennsylvania Project). Philadelphia: The Centre for Curriculum Development Inc.

Snow, C. E. 1972. Mothers speech to children learning language. *Child Development*, 43.

Stern, C. and Stern, W. 1907. *Die Kindersprache*. Leipzig (4th Edition, 1928).

Sweet, Henry 1891–98. *A New English Grammar, Logical and Historical.* Oxford: Clarendon Press.

Thorndike, E. L. 1928. *Adult Learning*. New York: Macmillan.

Trager, G. L. and Smith, H. L. Jr. 1951. *An Outline of English Structure.* Washington, D.C.: American Council of Learned Societies.

Trubetzkoy, N. S. 1939. *Grundzüge der Phonologie*. Prague: Cercle Linguistique de Prague. French edition, *Principes de Phonologie*, translated by Jean Cantineau. Paris: Klincksieck, 1949.

Twaddell, W. F. 1968. The durability of contrastive studies. *Georgetown Monograph Series on languages and linguistics 21*. 19th Annual Round Table Conference, 195–201.

Uldall, Elisabeth and Kemp, Alan (eds.) 1972. *Work in progress No. 5*. Department of Linguistics, University of Edinburgh.

Vacheck, J. (ed.) 1964. *A Prague School Reader in Linguistics*. Bloomington: Indiana University Press.

Velten, H. V. 1943. The growth of phonemic and lexical patterns in infant language. *Language*, 19, 281–92. Also in A. Bar-Adon and W. F. Leopold (eds.) 1971, *Child Language : A Book of Readings*. New Jersey: Prentice Hall.

von Elek, T. and Oskarsson, M. 1972. An experiment assessing the relative effectiveness of two methods of teaching English grammatical structures to adults. *IRAL*, 10, 60–72.

von Wittich, Barbara 1962. Prediction of success in foreign language study. *Modern Language Journal*, 46, 208–12.

Waterhouse, Lynn and Fischer, Karen 1972. Genetic contribution to individual differences in children's repetition of sentences. Paper to the Linguistic Society of America, University of North Carolina, Chapel Hill.

Weir, Ruth 1962. *Language in the Crib*. The Hague: Mouton.

Weir, Ruth 1966. Some questions on the child's learning of phonology. In F. Smith and G. A. Miller (eds.) *The Genesis of Language: A Psycholinguistic Approach*, 153–68.

White, B. 1971. An analysis of excellent early educational practices: preliminary report. *Interchange 2*. Toronto: Ontario Institute for Studies in Education, 71–88.

Widdowson, H. G. 1972. The teaching of English as communication. In *English Language Teaching*, 27, 15–19.

Wigdorsky, Leopold 1961. Assessment of the progress of a four-year-old child in learning an L2 (grammar). Unpublished dissertation, Dept. of Linguistics, Edinburgh University.

Wilkins, D. A. 1973. The linguistic and situational content of the common core in a unit credit system. In *Systems Development in Adult Language Learning*. Strasbourg: Council of Europe.

Williams, F. and Naremore, R. C. 1969. Social class differences in children's syntactic performance: a quantitative analysis of field data. *Journal of Speech and Hearing Research*, 12, 778–93.

Index of Proper Names

Subject Index